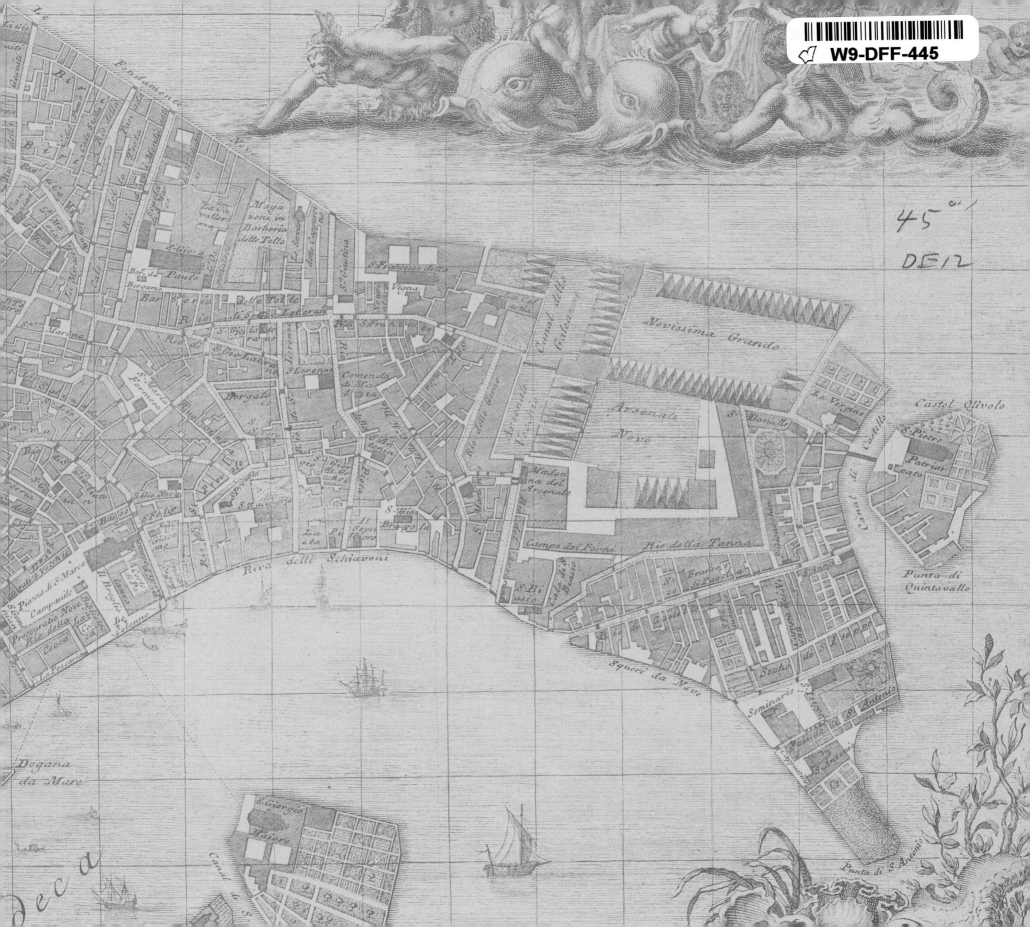

W9-DFF-445

45
DE12

Fondamente
Nove

Magazeni in
Borberia
delle Tutte

S.Francesco della
Vigna

Canal delle Galeze

Novissima Grande

Arsenale
Novo

La Vergine

Castel Olivolo

S. Daniele

S. Pietro

Patriar
cato

Punta di
Quintavalle

Madon
na del
Arsenale

Campo del Povri

Rio della Tanna

S. Biasio

Riva delli Schiavoni

Squeri da Nave

S. Antonio

Seminario

Piazza di S.Marco
Campanile
Il Broglio
Le Colonne
Procuratie Nove
Rio della Zecca
Zecca

Dogana
da Mare

S.Giorgio
Majore

Canal di S

Punta di S. Antonio

Deca

CANALETTO

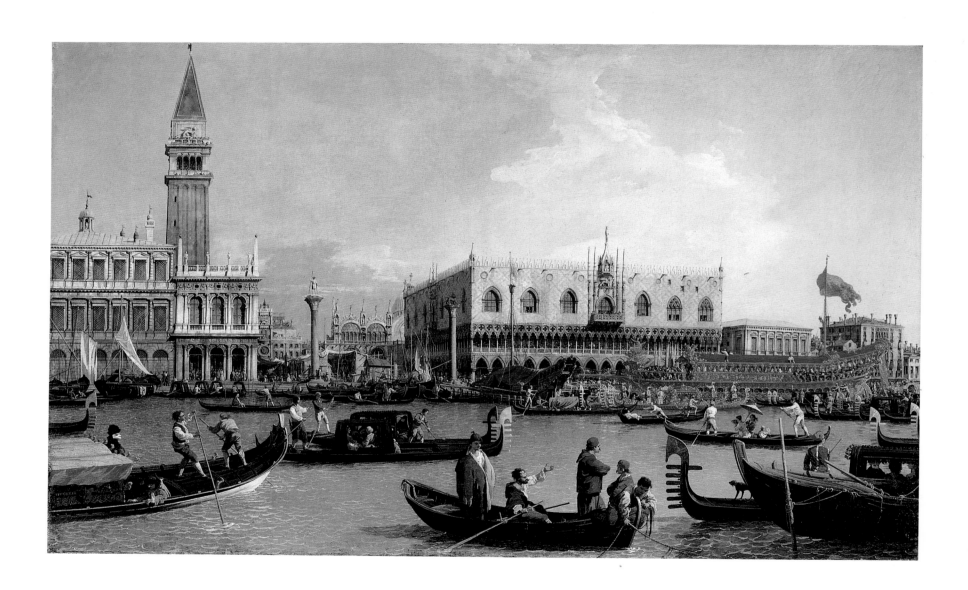

CANALETTO

BY KATHARINE BAETJER AND J.G. LINKS

*Essays by J. G. Links, Michael Levey, Francis Haskell,
Alessandro Bettagno, and Viola Pemberton-Pigott*

The Metropolitan Museum of Art, New York
Distributed by Harry N. Abrams, Inc., New York
1989

The exhibition is made possible by Louis Vuitton.

Additional support has been provided by the National Endowment for the Arts and by an indemnity from the Federal Council on the Arts and the Humanities.

The catalogue is published in conjunction with the exhibition held at The Metropolitan Museum of Art, New York, 30 October 1989–21 January 1990.

Published by The Metropolitan Museum of Art, New York
John P. O'Neill, Editor in Chief
Margaret Aspinwall, Editor
Bruce Campbell, Designer
Gwen Roginsky, Production

Copyright © 1989 by The Metropolitan Museum of Art

Concurrently with *Canaletto*, an exhibition of the artist's etchings, together with prints and a few paintings and drawings by his contemporaries, is being exhibited in the Robert Lehman Wing.

Jacket/cover: Detail of cat. no. 27, *Piazza S. Marco: looking East along the Central Line*
Frontispiece: Cat. no. 44, *The Bucintoro Returning to the Molo on Ascension Day*

Type set by U. S. Lithograph, typographers, New York
Printed and bound in Verona, Italy, by Arnoldo Mondadori Editore S. p. A.

LIBRARY OF CONGRESS CATALOGING-IN-PUBLICATION DATA
Baetjer, Katharine.
     Canaletto / Katharine Baetjer and J.G. Links; with essays by J.G.
Links . . . [et al.].
          p.   cm.
     Catalog of an exhibition to be held at the Metropolitan Museum of
Art, New York from Oct. 30, 1989 to Jan. 21, 1990.
     Includes bibliographical references.
     ISBN 0-87099-559-6. — ISBN 0-87099-561-8 (pbk.). — ISBN
0-8109-3155-9 (Abrams)
     1. Canaletto, 1697–1768—Exhibitions.   I. Links, J.G.
II. Metropolitan Museum of Art (New York, N.Y.)   III. Title.
N6923.C627A4   1989
759.5—dc20   89-36404
                                                                       CIP

Contents

Louis Vuitton is extremely honored to have the opportunity of sponsoring the Canaletto exhibition at The Metropolitan Museum of Art and is delighted at being associated with this great institution and its staff.

The generosity of the lenders of treasured examples of the artist's work has enabled the Metropolitan Museum to assemble an extraordinary number and range of paintings and drawings and will be deeply appreciated by all visitors to the exhibition.

We are happy to join The Metropolitan Museum of Art in celebrating the genius of Canaletto in what I think will be a memorable journey through imagination, time, and art.

Henry Racamier
President and Chief Executive Officer
Louis Vuitton

Foreword

In 1762 King George III of England bought the collection of Joseph Smith, His Britannic Majesty's Consul in Venice. Smith's holdings comprised Old Master paintings, modern Venetian paintings, drawings, prints and printed books, and an otherwise extensive library. Canaletto had long been associated with Joseph Smith, who purveyed his work to English patrons, but Smith had also retained for himself many of the artist's finest works: 49 paintings, 143 drawings, and 46 etchings. The Royal Collection thus became, and still remains, the primary repository of his art. We are most deeply indebted to Her Majesty Queen Elizabeth II, who has sanctioned the loan of thirteen paintings and sixteen drawings by Canaletto that belonged to George III and Consul Smith. This splendid loan is the seed from which the present exhibition has sprung.

Direct descendants of Canaletto's patrons have afforded us the opportunity to show fourteen paintings, a number of which have not been seen in the context of Canaletto's work since leaving the artist's studio: Viscount Coke, and the Trustees of the Holkham Estate; the Duke of Devonshire, and the Trustees of the Chatsworth Settlement; the Duke of Richmond, the Earl of March, and the Trustees of the Goodwood Collections; the Duke of Northumberland; the Marquess of Tavistock, and the Trustees of the Bedford Estates, Woburn Abbey. The Dean and Chapter of Westminster have consented to the loan of a painting of the Abbey which has always hung in the Deanery.

Works from thirty-one museums in the United States, Canada, and Europe are included in the exhibition. I should like to take note of major loans from the Staatliche Museen Preussischer Kulturbesitz, Berlin; the Museum of Fine Arts, Boston; the Staatliche Kunstsammlungen Dresden; and the National Gallery, Washington. We are privileged to have Canaletto's most widely acclaimed canvas, "*The Stonemason's Yard*," by kind permission of the Trustees of the National Gallery, London.

The series of four canvases formerly belonging to the Princes of Liechtenstein, and now to the Thyssen-Bornemisza Foundation, Lugano, and the Ca' Rezzonico, Venice, are exhibited for the first time with the four paintings commissioned by Stefano Conti, now in a private collection, and it is our hope that the study of these works, and the paintings from Dresden, will shed new light on the artist's early years.

This exhibition could not have taken place without the enthusiastic acquiesence of Sir Oliver Millar, now Surveyor Emeritus of the Royal Collection, and of Christopher Lloyd, Surveyor of the Queen's Pictures. The advice of Sir Michael Levey, in his capacity as Director of the National Gallery, London, was most valuable. He and his successor, Neil MacGregor, have made possible the single most important loan. The generosity of public and private lenders has afforded us the opportunity to do justice to Canaletto, and we are appreciative of their understanding of the potential importance of this exhibition from its inception.

From his encyclopedic knowledge of, and passion for, his subject, J. G. Links conceived this exhibition, guided us in our work, and contributed to and shaped this catalogue. Without his authority, prestige, and ties of personal friendship, *Canaletto* would never have achieved its present form. Thanks are also due to the other distinguished contributors to the catalogue: Sir Michael Levey, Francis Haskell, Viola Pemberton-Pigott, and particularly Alessandro Bettagno.

Owing to Henry Racamier's interest in the arts, *Canaletto* has benefited from the most generous and enlightened corporate sponsorship: the exhibition is made possible, appropriately, by Louis Vuitton. We are also indebted, for additional support, to the National Endowment for the Arts and to the Federal Council on the Arts and the Humanities.

Finally, an exhibition is only as good as the guiding intelligence that shapes it into a coherent whole, and Katharine Baetjer, Curator in the Department of European Paintings, deserves our thanks for her exemplary work on this exhibition and catalogue.

Philippe de Montebello
Director

Acknowledgments

Her Majesty Queen Elizabeth II has graciously consented to the loans that have made this exhibition possible, and those with delegated responsibility for the Royal Collection—Sir Oliver Millar, Christopher Lloyd, and the Hon. Mrs. Roberts—have afforded us the benefit of their knowledge and their fullest cooperation. We are indebted to many colleagues, particularly those who have put us in touch with private collectors, or acted as agents for those wishing to remain anonymous. Among others, thanks are due to: Jack Baer, Reinhold Baumstark, Marcus Bishop, Richard Day, Melissa De Medeiros, Silvano De Tuoni, Peter Dreyer, Richard L. Feigen, Sydney J. Freedberg, Derek Johns, Catherine Johnston, F. C. Jolly, Ian G. Kennedy, Alastair Laing, Elizabeth Llewellyn, T. D. Llewellyn, Richard Lockett, David McTavish, Rodney Merrington, Charlotte Miller, John Morton Morris, Teresa-Mary Morton, Gabriel M. Naughton, Michael Pantazzi, Ann Percy, Duncan Robinson, Pierre Rosenberg, Gyde Shepherd, Emma St. John-Smith, John Somerville, E. V. Thaw, Alex Wengraf, and Clovis Whitfield.

I am appreciative of the help of many members of the staff of the Metropolitan Museum: Everett Fahy, John Brealey, Emily Rafferty, Colta Ives, Mary Myers, John Buchanan, Linda Sylling, Gwen Roginsky, Ellen Shultz, Chad Coerver, Andrea Bayer, Marisa Kayyem, Perrin Stein, Jill Hoffer, and Annabel Schneider. Laurence Kanter's interest and the cooperation of the trustees of the Robert Lehman Collection have greatly enriched the exhibition. Jacob Bean has looked kindly on our efforts to do justice to Canaletto's drawings—still for me, to some degree, terra incognita; his knowledge and advice are always invaluable.

The Director has given the *Canaletto* exhibition his unqualified support. The catalogue, designed by Bruce Campbell, owes much to the oversight and enthusiasm of John O'Neill, and to the intelligence and care of Margaret Aspinwall. Alessandro Bettagno's essay was translated by Christ Heffer. The installation of the exhibition has been designed by Dan Kershaw.

This exhibition has been conceived by J. G. Links, through whose good offices, and on account of whose enthusiasm, we have been able to borrow over seventy works from private owners. Many of the paintings in question went directly from Canaletto's studio to the great English homes in which they hang to this day, and some have rarely, if ever, been publicly exhibited. Surely no one has benefited so greatly as I from Mr. Links's legendary generosity to others interested in his subject. Alessandro Bettagno's participation has been essential, and Viola Pemberton-Pigott has restored not only the Canalettos in the Royal Collection, but also a number of other loans to the exhibition. To the contributors to the catalogue may I simply add that I am mindful of the privilege of this association.

My work on *Canaletto* is intended especially for those with whom I have shared life in Venice and London—J.G.L. and M.L.L.; A.B.; T.D.L. and E.H.L.—and is dedicated to my husband and children, and to the memory of Elizabeth E. Gardner, through whose generosity we are occasional residents of the Serenissima.

Katharine Baetjer

Lenders to the Exhibition

Her Majesty Queen Elizabeth II

Viscount Coke and the Trustees of the Holkham Estate
Dr. Carlo M. Croce
The Duke of Devonshire and the Trustees of the Chatsworth Settlement
The Trustees of the Goodwood Collections
The Duke of Northumberland
The Lord O'Neill
Mr. and Mrs. John J. Pomerantz

Mr. and Mrs. A. Alfred Taubman
The Marquess of Tavistock and the Trustees of the Bedford Estates, Woburn Abbey
Thyssen-Bornemisza Foundation
The Dean and Chapter of Westminster
Viscount Windsor
Private collectors wishing to remain anonymous

BERLIN
Staatliche Museen Preussischer Kulturbesitz, Gemäldegalerie (loan of the Streit Foundation, Berlin)
Staatliche Museen Preussischer Kulturbesitz, Kupferstichkabinett

BIRMINGHAM (England)
Birmingham Museums and Art Gallery

BOSTON
Museum of Fine Arts, Boston

CAMBRIDGE (Massachusetts)
Fogg Art Museum, Harvard University

DALLAS
Dallas Museum of Art

DRESDEN
Staatliche Kunstsammlungen Dresden, Gemäldegalerie Alte Meister

FORT WORTH
Kimbell Art Museum

HAMBURG
Hamburger Kunsthalle

HOUSTON
The Museum of Fine Arts, Houston

HULL
Ferens Art Gallery, Hull City Museums and Art Galleries

KANSAS CITY
The Nelson-Atkins Museum of Art

LONDON
The Governors of Dulwich Picture Gallery
The Trustees of the National Gallery
National Maritime Museum

LOS ANGELES
Los Angeles County Museum of Art

MALIBU
The J. Paul Getty Museum

MINNEAPOLIS
The Minneapolis Institute of Arts

MONTREAL
The Montreal Museum of Fine Arts

NEW HAVEN
Yale Center for British Art

NEW YORK
The Metropolitan Museum of Art
Robert Lehman Collection, The Metropolitan Museum of Art
The Pierpont Morgan Library

OTTAWA
National Gallery of Canada

OXFORD
The Ashmolean Museum

PHILADELPHIA
Philadelphia Museum of Art

SAINT LOUIS
The Saint Louis Art Museum

STRASBOURG
Musées de la Ville de Strasbourg, Musée des Beaux-Arts

STUTTGART
Staatsgalerie Stuttgart (loan of Daimler-Benz AG)

TATTON PARK
The National Trust, Tatton Park, Egerton Collection

TOLEDO
The Toledo Museum of Art

VENICE
Gallerie dell'Accademia
Ca' Rezzonico

WASHINGTON, D.C.
National Gallery of Art

Notes to the Reader

Throughout the essays and the catalogue entries, bibliographic citations are abbreviated when the works are listed in the Selected Bibliography. Otherwise citations are given in full at their first reference in each essay or catalogue entry.

C/L refers to the second edition (1976) of W. G. Constable's catalogue raisonné of Canaletto's work, revised by J. G. Links. References to the first (1962) and the third (1989) editions are so indicated. Numerals following C/L denote catalogue numbers in that publication unless specified as page or plate numbers.

Titles follow C/L except in two cases (cat. nos. 102, 109).

Dimensions are supplied by the lender for most works; otherwise they are taken from C/L.

Inscriptions thought not to be in Canaletto's hand have, for the most part, been omitted.

Included in the entries for the paintings and drawings is information headed Exhibited which refers to the work's inclusion in the following three exhibitions, to date the only monographic exhibitions devoted to this artist:

Canada   *Canaletto*. Catalogue by W. G. Constable. Art Gallery of Toronto, National Gallery of Canada, Ottawa, and Montreal Museum of Fine Arts, 1964–65.

London   *Canaletto*. Catalogue by Oliver Millar (paintings) and Charlotte Miller (drawings). The Queen's Gallery, Buckingham Palace, London, 1980–81.

Venice   *Canaletto: Disegni, dipinti, incisioni*. Catalogue by Alessandro Bettagno et al. Fondazione Giorgio Cini, Venice, 1982.

CANALETTO

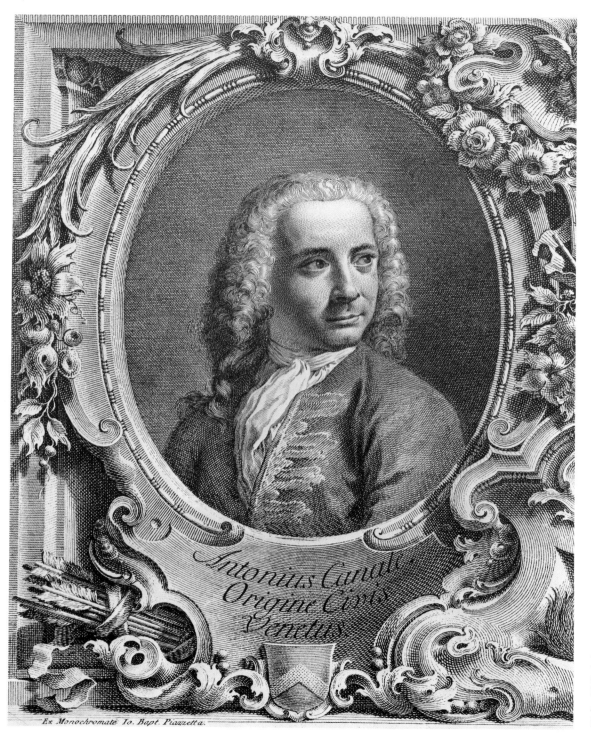

Fig. 1. Detail of the frontispiece from the second edition of *Prospectus*, 1742, showing a portrait of Canaletto, engraved by Antonio Visentini after a drawing by Giovanni Battista Piazzetta.

CANALETTO: A BIOGRAPHICAL SKETCH

by J. G. Links

Canaletto's career as an artist lasted more than forty-five years, most of them successful. His patrons included some of the greatest European connoisseurs as well as men of affairs, English aristocrats, modest collectors, and cosmopolitan print publishers. Many of these varied representatives of the eighteenth-century world must have met him, but if one of them recorded his impressions of the man the record has not survived. He remains, as Francis Haskell observes elsewhere in this catalogue, as inscrutable as he ever was. The few who did know him and write about him were agents who had their own reasons for wanting their clients to believe what they were told about a vain, greedy, and over-successful artist who must on no account be approached except through the writer. Canaletto may have been a difficult man to deal with, but those who so described him cannot be regarded as reliable sources. We must therefore form our own conclusions about the man as best we may. The work, on the other hand, is there to be judged on its merits, and there has never been such an opportunity as the present exhibition affords to judge it. The visitor should be warned, though, that this too presents its problems. For an artist whose work is straightforward and accessible, and whose principal aim was apparently to give pleasure, it is surprising how much there is that is still not understood about Canaletto.

Giovanni Antonio Canal was born at S. Lio, not far from the Rialto Bridge, in Venice on 17 or 18 October 1697.[1] His father, Bernardo Canal, was a painter of theatrical scenery, an important figure in the world of baroque opera, with his name often mentioned in the libretto to the exclusion of the composer's. He was of a well-defined class of Venetian society, entitled to bear arms and to describe himself as Origine Civis Venetus. Canaletto is so described in the only authentic portrait of him (fig. 1), which prefaces the series of engravings after his work by Antonio Visentini (who is himself described merely as Venetus). It is not known how early in his life he became known as Canaletto, the little Canal; the name was certainly in use in the mid-1720s.[2]

In 1719, according to his first biographers, Canaletto went to Rome as his father's assistant, but in 1720 he was back in Venice, as he appears in the register (*fraglia*) of painters under that year. There is good reason to suppose that he had made a series of drawings of Roman views (see C/L 713). There is no evidence that he did or did not meet other artists such as Vanvitelli or Pannini in Rome. Nor is there documentary evidence that Canaletto met Luca Carlevaris who had published 103 etchings of Venetian scenes in 1703 and went on to painting, for the most part in or near the Piazza S. Marco and the Piazzetta. Carlevaris was the true founder of the Venetian school of *vedute*, or view painting, and the two men must have met, although improbably as master and pupil as was rumored at the time.

It is as a view painter that Canaletto's early work must be judged. He almost certainly painted capriccios in the style of Marco and Sebastiano Ricci, and a number of canvases have been attributed to him at this period.[3] In no case is the attribution firm, however, and so little opportunity has existed to study these pictures, which are all privately owned, that they are not included in the exhibition. Against this, very few of the early view paintings are known to exist, but it has been possible to show almost all of them so that the paintings with which Canaletto began his true career can be studied together for the first time.

The first to be painted are no doubt among the four which belonged to the Princes of Liechtenstein (cat. nos. 1–4) and the three from the collection of the Electors of Saxony in Dresden (cat. nos. 5–7). There is no evidence that any were bought directly from the artist since they are first recorded in the collections at a considerably later date; the original owners are therefore a matter of speculation. There is topographical evi-

3

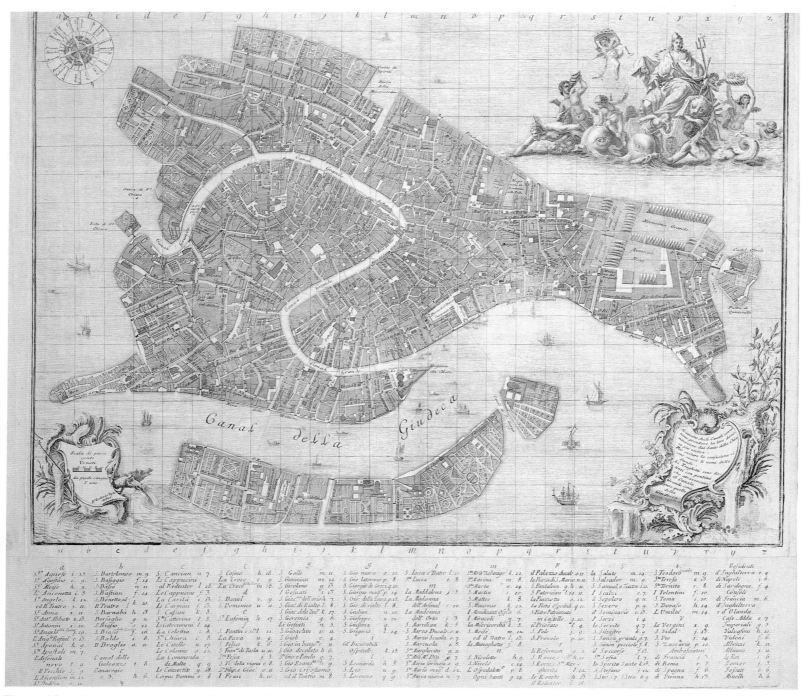

Fig. 2. Plan of Venice, a reduction of Lodovico Ughi's map of 1729, which was published prior to 1779. Map and Geography Division, Library of Congress, Washington.

dence that the Liechtenstein *Piazza S. Marco* (cat. no. 1) was painted about 1723 and (less firm) evidence that another (cat. no. 2) might date from as early as 1719. These seven paintings, and two others at Dresden which are first recorded in that collection in 1741 (C/L 168, 183), enable us to form an impression of Canaletto's method of working before 1725. The drama that pervades most of these pictures has generally been linked to Canaletto's long association with the theater, but Sir Michael Levey's observations on this subject in the present catalogue will be read with interest.

In 1725 Canaletto was twenty-eight years old, yet nothing can be said about his career with absolute certainty. In that year a textile merchant in Lucca, Stefano Conti, decided to add to his small collection of work by living artists and asked Alessandro Marchesini, an artist from Verona who was then living in Venice, to add to the Carlevaris views he had bought many years earlier. In a series of letters Marchesini advised Conti, in effect, that although Carlevaris was still active there was a new man whose work caused everyone who saw it to marvel.[4] Unlike Carlevaris, "Sig.r Ant. Canale" was able to make the sun shine in his pictures (but did he at this stage? The visitor to this exhibition must decide for himself). The Imperial ambassador had bought a view of SS. Giovanni e Paolo at the annual exhibition held outside the Scuola di S. Rocco (the exhibition later portrayed so vividly in Canaletto's picture now in the National Gallery, London; see fig. 3), according to Marchesini, and later in this correspondence the great connoisseur Zaccaria Sagredo was also mentioned as a patron. Conti could not fail to be impressed and, after some argument over the price, ordered two paintings. Before they had been started (although Conti did not know this) he ordered two more. The story of the four paintings, first published by Francis Haskell, has been told in full several times and reveals something of Canaletto's working methods. Not all of it is necessarily to be trusted: Marchesini was an agent and there were certain things he wanted Conti to believe, among them the idea that Canaletto was a difficult man who had to be humored. In the end the pictures were delivered, together with certificates from Canaletto describing them in detail and acknowledging the money paid for them, all of which can be seen in the present exhibition (cat. nos. 8–11 and Appendix).

Before the Conti pictures were completed a new shaft of light was thrown on Canaletto's activities. On 8 March 1726,[5] Owen McSwiney, an Irishman who was living in Italy as best he could after financial disasters in London, wrote to the Duke of Richmond about a scheme McSwiney had initiated for a series of allegorical paintings to commemorate great men of recent English history. Three painters were to collaborate on each picture. Fifteen had been started and six finished, among them the "tombs" of Lord Somers (cat. no. 13) and Archbishop Tillotson (cat. no. 12) for both of which Canaletto had painted the "perspective and landscape" with Cimaroli, the figures being left to Piazzetta and Pittoni, respectively.

McSwiney was to play a key role in Canaletto's career; it was he, not Joseph Smith, who first introduced Canaletto to an English client and who first encouraged the artist to paint small, sunny pictures attractive to the tourist with a less than passionate concern for art, rather than the large, dramatic, and somewhat disorderly masterpieces which had appealed to those who knew the reality of Venice.

In November 1727 McSwiney wrote another long letter to the Duke of Richmond revealing that Canaletto had been painting views for him. He had sold two of the finest to a Mr. Southwell, and he had managed to get two more, done on copperplate, for the duke himself (cat. nos. 14 and 15). But Canaletto, he complained, had more work than he could do properly and demanded higher prices. He was also working for a friend of McSwiney's through whose goodwill he was able to get a few pictures for his own clients. Two weeks later he was able to say that the duke's pair had been sent and were "very fine."

McSwiney's "friend" was Joseph Smith, long resident in Venice, a successful businessman and a great collector of pictures, books, and much else, although, from all accounts, lacking the Irish charm of the highly unsuccessful McSwiney. Smith, it seems probable, had by this time recognized the commercial potential of the kind of picture McSwiney was commissioning but, before considering how to exploit it, he was concerned with acquiring pictures of a very different kind for his own collection. These were the six magnificent paintings of the Piazza and Piazzetta area, two of which are numbers 28 and 29 in the present exhibition (see also cat. nos. 88 and 89 for related drawings).

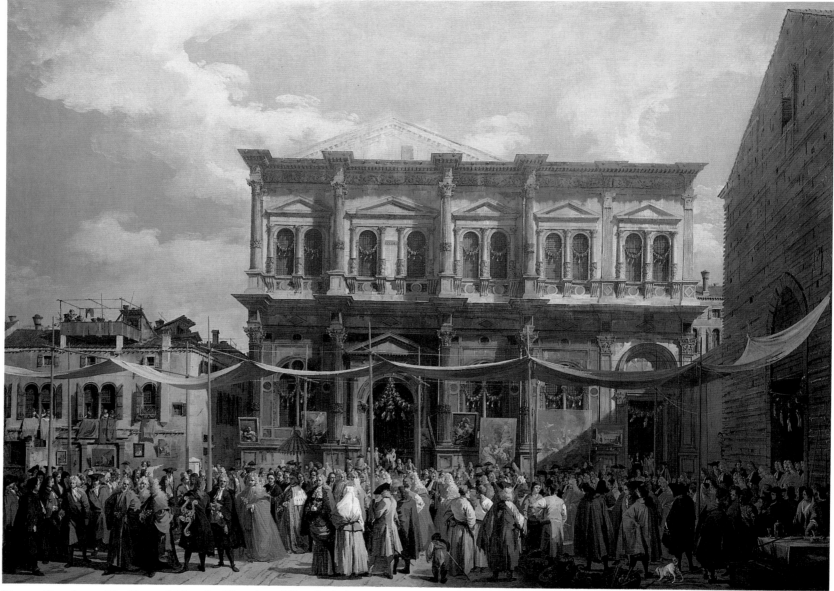

Fig. 3. Canaletto, *The Doge visiting the Church and Scuola di S. Rocco.* National Gallery, London.

Except for two sketches for views dated 1729 (see cat. no. 92 for a discussion of one of them), there is no more documentary evidence concerning Canaletto until 1730. In that year Smith emerged in the role he was to play for many years, the chief purveyor of Canaletto's work to the English visitor to Venice and, by means of engravings of view paintings he held in stock, to those unable to see the originals for themselves. Among the first of these buyers was Samuel Hill of Staffordshire, England, whose nephew, Samuel Egerton, had been apprenticed to Smith for the past year. Smith had been shipping various works of art to Hill and in 1730 was able to assure him that Canaletto had promised to finish the two works ordered by Hill "within a twelvemonth." Smith now joins the chorus of agents complaining of the difficulty of extracting work from the artist who was "so much follow'd and all are so ready to pay him his own price," but Hill is promised that Smith is, as always, willing "to submitt to a painter's impertinence" to serve himself, Smith, and his friends. He ends with a reference to "the prints of the views and pictures of Venice [which] will now soon be finish'd" and warns that if Hill or his friends want any they must "speak in time." In the event Hill did not have to wait a year for his paintings: his nephew, Samuel Egerton, was able to inform him five months later that they would be shipped within fifteen days, and today they hang in the house Egerton himself inherited (cat. nos. 33 and 34).

As if to confirm that by 1730 Smith was dealing in Canalettos, there appeared some years ago in the papers of the Wicklow family a copy of a note detailing the purchase of "two pictures of Canaletti from Venice." It shows that "Mr Smith Mercht" was paid thirty-five Venetian *zecchini*, which converted into sterling at £18 7s 11d, to which the cost of freight, customs duty, frames, and sundry charges were added bringing the total to just over twenty-three pounds. The buyer was almost certainly Hugh Howard whose younger relative became Earl of Wicklow, in whose family numbers 35 and 36 remained until the 1950s. It is a curious fact, which emphasizes the difficulties referred to in the opening words of these notes, that, although dozens of such bills or memoranda of purchases from Smith must have existed in English family archives, only three other documents referring to Canalettos painted during the 1730s have come to light (see cat. nos. 48, 49).

Smith's reference to the prints for which Samuel Hill must "speak in time" is momentous. He can only have been referring to Antonio Visentini's engravings after twelve views of the Grand Canal which Smith had commissioned from Canaletto but which were not in the event published until five years later. How many of the paintings were finished by 1730 can be judged only on stylistic grounds: Smith would naturally want Hill to have the impression that all were done and publication imminent so that Hill would order as many copies as possible. A number, perhaps most, of the paintings were completed by this time and probably some of Visentini's engravings, and it may well have been Smith's intention to publish them quite soon, perhaps individually. However, the final decision was to wait until two of Canaletto's masterpieces in his "new" style were finished (cat. nos. 43 and 44) and to add these to the twelve Grand Canal pictures (of which cat. nos. 39–42 are examples) and publish them all together with a title page dated 1735. This bore the words *Prospectus/Magni Canalis Venetiarum/addito Certamine Nautico et Nundinis Venetis*, making it clear that the "Nautical Contest and Venetian Market" were additions (a market on the Piazzetta was a part of the Ascension Day celebrations, as can be seen from the picture). Another important line of the title page, from Smith's point of view, made it clear that the originals were in the house of Joseph Smith, Englishman, with the implication that there they could be seen and orders placed by those so inclined. The originals were never in fact sold until George III bought Smith's collection, but in 1742, seven years after the first edition of *Prospectus*, Smith published a new edition containing twenty-four more engravings.[6] Of these, the originals of all except one (cat. no. 45) had almost certainly been sold before the engravings were published. This, in summary, is the way in which Smith launched himself as the principal purveyor of Canaletto's work to the English.

In 1730, the year in which Smith is first revealed as Canaletto's patron and agent, McSwiney wrote a letter to a friend, John Conduitt, which raises as many problems as it solves.[7] He is pleased, he writes, that his friend has ordered some Canalettos from Smith and hopes he will like them. But...

> I am, it may be [he continued], a little too delicate in my choice, for of Twenty pieces I see of him, I don't like eighteen & I have seen several, sent to London y' I wou'd not give house room too. . . . He's a covetous, greedy fellow & because he's in reputation people are glad to get anything at his own price.
>
> Tis above Three years y' he has Two copper plates in his hands, for y' D of Richmond & I thought it wrong to sett him at work on new work

till he had delivered w^t he has been obliged to do so long since.

The Two Copper plates of the D of Richm^d Two of Mr Southwell & Two of Sir Wm Morice are in his buon gusto—nay compare these with any other you know & you'l soon discern ye difference.

Sir William Morice's pair can be identified without difficulty: they are numbers 16 and 17. It looks as if the Duke of Richmond may have refused his second pair when, after long delay, they were at last done; perhaps they went to the Earl of Leicester instead (one is a view of the Rialto Bridge as promised) and are numbers 20 and 21. "Mr Southwell" could have been Edward Southwell, father or son, both of whom were in Italy in the 1720s: his pair may have gone eventually to the Duke of Devonshire (cat. nos. 18 and 19). Canaletto's only other known painting on copper is number 22 which may have been one of another pair. Together for the first time since they were painted, the nine copper panels form a remarkable illustration of one man's opinion of Canaletto's "buon gusto."

For the rest, we must retrace our steps and consider the pictures McSwiney would "not give house room" to. Clearly he is writing in pique, as well he might. It was he who had first introduced Canaletto to the English with his "tomb" paintings (cat. nos. 12 and 13). It was he who had first seen the commercial possibilities of small, topographically interesting pictures recalling the beauties of Venice to the tourist. But for him, Canaletto might have continued indefinitely painting in the manner of the first seven paintings in the present exhibition. Despite this, Canaletto had allowed himself to be taken over by McSwiney's friend, the more powerful and aggressive Joseph Smith, without whose help McSwiney could no longer get a picture for his own clients.

Pique, though, cannot excuse the ill judgment of McSwiney's outburst. The years of which he is writing, 1726–30, were those in which Canaletto produced some of his finest works, by no means all with the unsophisticated tourist in mind. There were Smith's great Piazza and Piazzetta paintings, which McSwiney must surely have seen, as he must have seen the first of the Grand Canal series being prepared for *Prospectus*. There were the highly personal pictures in which Canaletto seems to be blending his old style with the style he was adopting for the foreign market (cat. nos. 30 and 31 for example). There was also a group of paintings which, although copied by Joseph Baudin[8] for en-

gravings published as late as 1736 and 1739, seem to have been part of a collection formed many years earlier, possibly (although there is no evidence of this) by Elizaeus Burges, English Secretary-Resident in Venice until his death in 1736 (see C/L 269). One of these was a lost version of the very early *Piazza S. Marco* in the Liechtenstein collection (see cat. no. 1). Three of them (cat. nos. 20–22) were almost certainly among McSwiney's "copper plates." Another was the superb *Piazza S. Marco: looking North* (cat. no. 26) and the splendid Grand Canal pictures, numbers 23 and 24, the latter having as its pendant the *Riva degli Schiavoni*, number 25, which was not engraved. The bringing together in this exhibition of six of the surviving eight paintings of this group may provide clues to its origin, at present entirely speculative.

Above all, among the pre-1730 work as it must surely be, is *"The Stonemason's Yard"* (cat. no. 32). Sir Michael Levey's sensitive words on this supremely beautiful picture, later in this catalogue, make further comment unnecessary. In fairness to McSwiney it may be noted that nothing whatever is known of its early history, and it may be assumed that he never saw it.

Horace Walpole wrote that Smith (whom he called "the merchant of Venice," not intending to be flattering) engaged Canaletto "to work for him for many years at a very low price, & sold his works to the English at much higher rates." We know this to be untrue: Stefano Conti had paid 90 sequins for his four pictures in 1726; the following year McSwiney was paying between 22½ and 35 sequins each for much smaller pictures, yet Smith charged Hugh Howard only 17½ sequins each in 1730 (a sequin was worth about ten shillings, two sequins a pound sterling). In 1736 the Swedish Count Tessin, after a visit to Venice, wrote that Canaletto was engaged to work exclusively for "un marchand Anglais, nommé Smitt" and would sell a "Tableau de Cabinet" for 120 sequins. The price quoted is palpably untrue, as is the suggestion of exclusivity. It is only necessary to quote the case of the fourth Earl of Carlisle who, whatever may have been his reasons, chose some channel other than Smith for his Venice paintings. Inexplicably, he found himself with *The Bacino di S. Marco: looking East* (cat. no. 51), Canaletto's masterpiece of one kind of painting as *"The Stonemason's Yard"* is of another, as well as two good-quality, signed works now in the National Gallery in Washington (C/L 50 and 154), and half a dozen inferior school or studio works.

Had he gone to Smith he might well have missed the masterpiece: Smith preferred to treat all customers alike. Against this, he would certainly not have been sold inferior or school pictures. As a good businessman, Smith valued his reputation. Smith, moreover, would ensure that pictures were delivered in reasonable time, properly framed and packed, and he would advance money to pay the artist until reimbursed, naturally charging interest. All these services were part of his normal business and they served the artist as well as the buyer. Unless the buyer was a true connoisseur, which few of the English upper classes were except perhaps of horse pictures, he was well advised to turn to Smith for Venetian view paintings—if Smith had not already turned to him and persuaded him of the merits of the goods he had to offer. Whether Smith charged a buying commission or made a profit is unknown; no such charge appears on Hugh Howard's bill and any charges made would certainly have been reasonable. It is quite possible that Smith's only reward, apart from the profit on the ancillary services, was a finished drawing of the same subject as pictures which had been sold, and/or a reduced price for works for his own collection.

As a result, between the years 1730 and 1740, a large number of Canaletto's paintings entered English collections under Smith's auspices, as attested by engravings in *Prospectus*. Twenty-four paintings were bought by the Duke of Bedford (see cat. nos. 48 and 49), a further twenty-one were sold to an unknown client and were later owned by Sir Robert Grenville Harvey (see cat. nos. 46, 47, and figs. 6, 9, 10), and others were owned by the second Earl of Normanton (cat. nos. 50 and 53), all these in addition to the pictures already mentioned. Other owners, not represented in the present exhibition, are known to have bought from Smith and there must have been still others who are not known. Although Walpole and Tessin exaggerated, these were indeed the Smith years and, apart from one or two festival paintings taken home by distinguished foreign visitors (C/L 356), it is hard to point to a single Canaletto painting sold to any but an Englishman. Those of other nationalities may have taken the same view as Charles de Brosses, president of the Burgundian

Parlement who, in 1739, wrote of Canaletto that as a view painter "he surpasses everyone there has ever been," adding that it was impossible to do business with him (i.e., the price of his pictures was high).

In the early 1740s a complete change came over Canaletto's career. The demand for his work on the part of the English fell away, no doubt owing in part to the outbreak of the War of the Austrian Succession in 1741 and the consequent difficulties of travel. There is some evidence, though, that the English had enough Venice views on their walls anyway. A rival appeared, the first since the death of Carlevaris in 1730, in the form of Michele Marieschi who published an album of twenty-one Venetian views in 1741. It is hard to tell how much each of these factors contributed to Canaletto's situation, but the fact remains that he was left with virtually only one patron, Joseph Smith. Proving a friend in need, Smith encouraged the artist to take up etching and to devote more time to drawing. Preparation of the etchings must have covered a considerable span of time since one of them, clearly not the earliest, is dated 1741 and yet the album finally published is dedicated to "Giuseppe" Smith, His Britannic Majesty's Consul, a long-awaited appointment that Smith did not attain until 1744. The etchings are a tribute to the mastery Canaletto achieved in portraying sunlight without the use of color. As for the drawings, there was never a period when he was not an accomplished draftsman, but the four drawings of the outskirts of Venice in the Royal Collection (two of them cat. nos. 101 and 102) show an imagination fired by a new subject.

Bernardo Bellotto, the son of Canaletto's sister Fiorenza, had been in his uncle's studio, probably since about 1735, when he was fifteen, and must have played an increasing part in the studio output. The two artists now left Venice for a tour of the Brenta and the mainland during which Bellotto advanced his etching and drawing technique and Canaletto produced a number of captivating drawings (cat. no. 107 for example). There were paintings, too, but these may have had to wait until the artists returned to the studio (see cat. nos. 56–58).

Dates, which up to this point could only be estimated, now become more definite. In 1742 Canaletto signed and dated five great views of Roman subjects for Smith's collection (see cat.

nos. 59, 60). There is no evidence that Canaletto went back to Rome, and it is generally regarded as more probable that he made use of the drawings dating from his 1719–20 visit and perhaps drawings which Bellotto brought back from a tour he certainly made in 1741–42.

Smith, however, had by no means abandoned confidence in the Venetian view. In 1742 he published a new edition of *Prospectus*. This contained engravings of the twelve Grand Canal views and two festival paintings, all still in his collection, to which were added twenty-four views, including ten of churches and *campi*. Was this in reply to the publication in 1741 of Marieschi's etchings? Smith need not have worried: Marieschi was dead by 1743. Nevertheless Smith commissioned from Canaletto four large views of the Piazza and Molo area from which Visentini produced larger engravings than any previously published. All the originals except one (cat. no. 45) of the second and third series of views in *Prospectus* had been sold, but there was of course no reason why Canaletto should not paint other versions, as he had in the case of the first Grand Canal series, if Smith could get him the commissions. The scheme does not seem to have been very successful, judging from the number of variants that have survived, and the four Piazza and Molo paintings remained on Smith's hands (although he *might* not have wished to sell them).

Determined apparently not to let his old friend remain idle, Smith now commissioned a series of thirteen "pieces over doors," as he described them, no doubt for his house at Mogliano. Several of these which remain in the Royal Collection are dated 1743 and 1744. Particular interest attaches to the *Palladian Design for the Rialto Bridge* (cat. no. 61) which is in some, as yet undefined, way associated with Francesco Algarotti.[9] He was an influential, but not universally respected, collector and a buying agent for the Elector of Saxony and he was in Venice in 1744. If, as seems probable, he ignored Canaletto at a time when a new patron was badly needed, it must have proved a severe disappointment.

Smith's generosity could not be unlimited. The war would have caused difficulties in his own business and his new responsibilities as consul must have made demands on his time. Nor was Canaletto the only artist in whom he was interested. No record exists of the discussions which must have taken place as to Canaletto's future. All that is known is that Canaletto signed and dated a drawing of the Campanile after it had been damaged by lightning on 23 April 1745. The next that is heard of him is his arrival in London in May 1746.

The first few years of Canaletto's nine- or ten-year stay in England are by far the best documented of his life. Despite this, no one who met him has left any record of the meeting. George Vertue, an antiquary who kept notes on the events of the art world and who mentions Canaletto five times over five years, describes him as "a sober man turnd of 50" and, later, as "remarkable for reservedness & shyness in being seen at work, at any Time, or anywhere." The description is secondhand but it is all we have on which to judge Canaletto's character; we know nothing of his companions or of how much English he spoke, even at the end of his stay.

He arrived, according to Vertue, "latter end of May" 1746, with a "great reputation." He was expected to do well—but Vertue added an ominous warning: "tho' many persons already have so many of his paintings."

The event of the year was the completion of London's long-awaited second bridge at Westminster which naturally provided the subject for much of Canaletto's first English work, and the commissioners of the bridge included many of the leading figures of the time, valuable introductions for the artist. Probably the first commission, though, came from a visitor, Prince Lobkowitz of Bohemia, for whom Canaletto painted the bridge in its final stages of building, together with a view of the River Thames at St. Paul's Cathedral. These were taken back by the prince to Prague, where they remain (C/L 425, 426). Another painting of the bridge was engraved and published early in 1747; for this Canaletto, no doubt on instructions, showed statues which, in the event, were never incorporated (cat. no. 63).

Consul Smith (as he now was) had written to Owen McSwiney, who had by this time returned to London, asking him to introduce Canaletto to the Duke of Richmond, never one of Smith's clients. This McSwiney did, but through the duke's old tutor, Thomas Hill, who wrote to the duke: "I told him the best service I thought you could do him w^d be to let him draw a view of

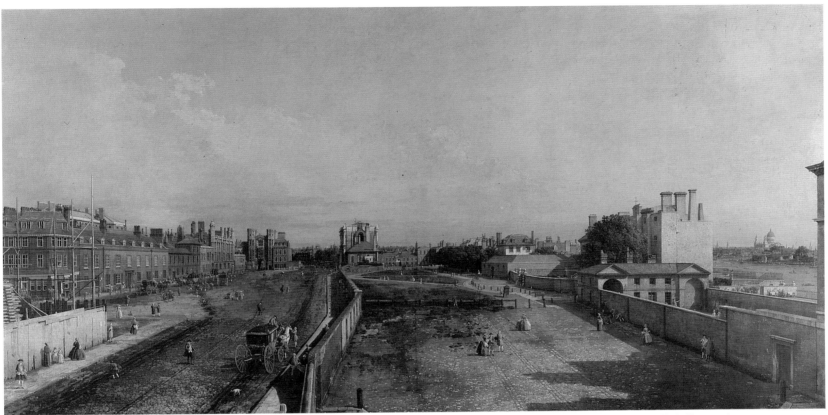

Fig. 4. Canaletto, *London: Whitehall and the Privy Garden looking North.* His Grace the Duke of Buccleuch (The Bowhill Collection).

the river from y^r dining-room, which in my opinion would give him as much reputation as any of his Venetian prospects." The duke was away and took time to respond. Before he did so Canaletto met Sir Hugh Smithson, a commissioner of the bridge, who was to become one of his best English patrons. For him Canaletto painted a view of London through an arch of the bridge (C/L 412), and this was followed by a commission to paint Windsor Castle. The canvas (cat. no. 64) belonged to Sir Hugh's father-in-law, the Earl of Hertford, later Duke of Somerset. This was perhaps the first occasion on which Canaletto had painted (as opposed to drawing) the scene before his eyes, and the opportunity to see something of England outside London may well account for the freshness and vividness of the painting despite the well-worn subject.

In the late summer of 1747 Canaletto was at last allowed to make a drawing from the Duke of Richmond's house close to Westminster Bridge, and a few weeks later he began *The Thames and the City of London* and *Whitehall and the Privy Garden* from Richmond House, the masterpieces of his stay in England (cat. nos. 66, 65). To the English, the *Whitehall* has become perhaps the best loved of all his work, surpassing even *"The Stonemason's Yard,"* and for many their introduction to Canaletto. Some time later, it is hard to say when, he combined the two subjects in a single, wide painting (fig. 4) of which more will be heard.

A pair of pictures of Badminton House for the Duke of Beaufort followed (see fig. 27), duly noted by Vertue, and then a commission to paint Warwick Castle for Lord Brooke. A record exists in

Hoare's Bank[10] that "Sigr. Canall" was paid £58 on 19 July 1748 and on 3 March 1749 "Sigr. G. Anto Canale" received a further £31 10s (30 guineas); one of these sums almost certainly included payment for the *South Front* now in the Thyssen-Bornemisza collection (cat. no. 68).

In July 1749 Canaletto took the strange course of advertising an invitation to see a "View of S^t. James's Park" at his lodgings, perhaps to allay rumors referred to by Vertue that he was not the genuine Canaletto at all (possibly put about by dealers who had been attaching his name to the works of others). A few commissions followed but evidently not enough: Vertue's next note, in August 1751, records that Canaletto had been to Venice for eight months and, now returned, had again advertised his presence. Whether he had intended his return home to be permanent or temporary can only be guessed; he did make an investment in property in Venice, the only investment he had at his death seventeen years later.

At first he had some encouragement, once back in England. Sir Hugh Smithson was now Earl of Northumberland and on his way to becoming Duke. Through his wife he had inherited six seats of the Percy family and he had Canaletto paint three of them, including the much-copied picture of Northumberland House (cat. no. 70). Lord Brooke recalled the artist to Warwick, probably to paint two pictures of the east front of the Castle (cat. no. 69) and two drawings (cat. nos. 112, 113); two payments, of 32 guineas and £50, were made to him in 1752.

Otherwise the documentation for the second half of Canaletto's stay in England is sparse and relies mostly on the dates of published engravings after his work. These sometimes raise difficulties as in the cases of the two pleasure-garden paintings in the exhibition (cat. nos. 71 and 72), which may have been painted after engravings which had themselves been copied from drawings. Various dates have been suggested for the two versions of *Greenwich Hospital from the North Bank of the Thames*, one of which, number 74, now belongs to the National Maritime Museum whose building appears in the picture.

Six of the capriccios shown, numbers 75–80 from the Lovelace family, can be safely ascribed to this period as one of the group is dated 1754. However, Canaletto painted capriccios throughout his career and many of them were copied by other artists, some perhaps directly under Canaletto's influence. The uncertainties surrounding them are such that no attempt has been made in this exhibition to show a representative selection of these often beautiful, but very problematical works.

A usually reliable Venetian diarist, Pietro Gradenigo, recorded in July 1753 that Canaletto had returned from England to his native city, but there is no other evidence of the visit and it seems likely that some misunderstanding occurred. Canaletto's presence in England in 1753–55 is well established, not only by the date on the Lovelace capriccio. In 1754 he also signed and dated five out of six pictures for Thomas Hollis (although they may have been painted earlier). Outstanding among them was *Old Walton Bridge* (cat. no. 73) in which the very northern cloud and the fairy-like bridge compete for enchantment. In the following year Samuel Dicker, who had paid for the bridge, commissioned a painting of it for himself, which Canaletto inscribed in Italian on the back (hardly truthfully) that it was painted in 1755 for the first and last time for "Cavaliere Dickers." A drawing, later published as an engraving, was also inscribed, in Italian, "after my picture painted in London 1755…" (cat. no. 115). This is the last we know of Canaletto in England.[11]

Almost a hundred years after the occurrence, the Reverend Edward Hinchliffe described how, in 1760, his grandfather was traveling as tutor to John Crewe and saw "a little man" drawing in the Piazza in Venice. It proved to be Canaletto who took the couple back to his studio, sold Crewe the painting combining the two views from Richmond House (which he told them he had taken back to Venice because he could not bear to sell it; see fig. 4), and gave him a finished drawing of the Piazza (cat. no. 116). There is no reason to doubt that the meeting took place (although Canaletto's story does not quite ring true) and it provides the first evidence of Canaletto's movements since he left England.

Far more work is now attributed to Canaletto's final years in Venice than used to be the case (see C/L 339), but very little of it can be given specific dates with any confidence. The most important commission he had during these years must have been for four paintings from Sigismund Streit (see cat. nos. 82 and 83, and fig. 8) who catalogued his pictures with loving detail; he

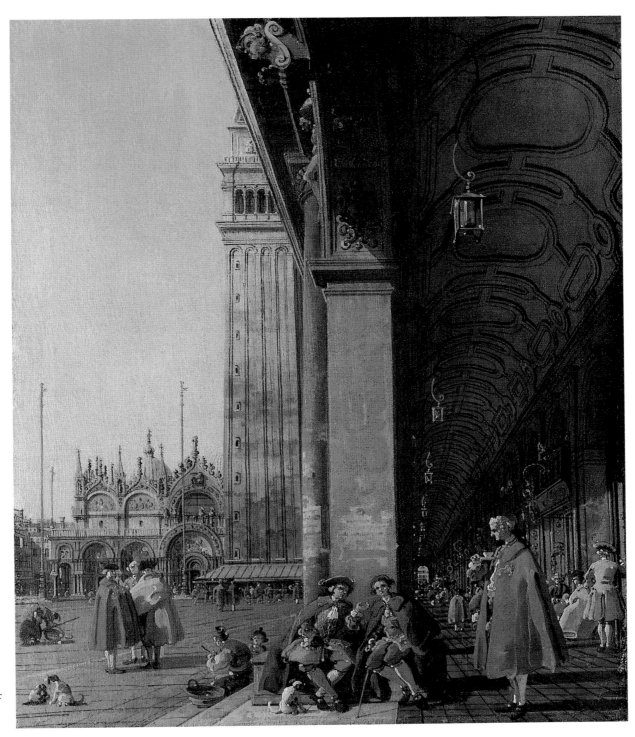

Fig. 5. Canaletto, *Piazza S. Marco: looking East from the Southwest Corner.* National Gallery, London.

recorded no dates, though, and only through a topographical detail can a period be assigned to them. Nor can it be said with certainty when the National Gallery, London, *Piazza S. Marco: looking East* (fig. 5) was painted except that it must have been after the return from England. Joseph Smith bought only one painting from Canaletto during this period, and before 1762 when he sold his collection to George III: this was *S. Marco: the Interior* (C/L 78) of which there is another version in Montreal (cat. no. 81). With the exception of these paintings and the two 1763 and 1765 paintings mentioned below, it must be admitted that in his post-1756 paintings Canaletto's imagination and technical skill are seldom displayed; he too often fell back on earlier work for his subjects, sometimes work done in a different medium.

No such criticism can be leveled against his drawings. The *Capriccio: Terrace and Loggia of a Palace on the Lagoon* (cat. no. 118), which must have been among the last of Canaletto's works to enter Smith's collection, is as fine as anything the great draftsman produced earlier, and at the very end of his life Canaletto undertook a commission to draw twelve Ducal Ceremonies and Festivals for engraving (cat. nos. 122, 123) which must have extended him to the limit of his abilities. And it was on a drawing—an exquisite drawing, for which he made many studies—that, for the first and last time, he made a personal statement to posterity: "Aged 68 Without Spectacles, The year 1766" (cat. no. 127).

Three years earlier, in 1763, Canaletto had been elected to the Venetian Academy, having been passed over earlier in the same year in favor of two nonentities—doubtless on the grounds that he was a view painter and therefore inferior to the history or figure painters. The *Piazza S. Marco: looking South and West* (cat. no. 84) is signed and dated 1763, and it is tempting to suggest that this panoramic view, summing up a lifetime of working in the area, was intended as his reception piece. If, as is possible, the academicians discouraged their new member from offering a view painting, they were kept waiting nearly two years for the *Capriccio* they finally received (cat. no. 85). Canaletto last attended a meeting of the Academy on 23 August 1767.

He died of fever on 10 April 1768 and was buried at S. Lio, where he had been baptized. He left twenty-eight "medium and small" pictures, of which nothing is known, some old clothes, and the most modest household goods. He had the equivalent of some £80 sterling in cash and still owned the property he had bought for 2150 ducats (about £600) during his 1751 visit to Venice from London. For a prudent bachelor it was not a lot after forty-five years of successful painting at prices so many complained were too high.

Two subjects which are frequently raised by writers on Canaletto's career are his use of the camera obscura (or *ottica*) and his employment of studio assistants.

"He paints with such accuracy and cunning," wrote Pietro Guarienti in 1753, "that the eye is deceived and truly believes that it is the real thing it sees, not a painting."[12] Canaletto's contemporaries were convinced that such realism could be attained only by the use of optical instruments,[13] but none was able to suggest how an artist with such technical skill as Canaletto's could be helped by their use. Antonio Conti, who lived in Venice at the same time as Canaletto, was the most confused of all but came, by chance, nearest to the truth. He believed the camera obscura enabled the artist to paint on one canvas "vistas taken from more than one viewpoint."[14] This, as any observer who has stood at Canaletto's viewpoints has learned, was one of his most frequent practices but no instrument was needed for him to follow it.

The use of a camera obscura cannot of course be proved, neither can it be disproved—except in the case of pictures purporting to adopt an unattainable viewpoint such as numbers 17, 34, and 63. It is not impossible that Canaletto found such an instrument useful when deciding on the composition of a picture. It is however very difficult to imagine what further use it could have been to him, particularly bearing in mind the primitive lenses available in the eighteenth century.

Less than two years after Canaletto's death, his colleagues at the Academy were offered some pictures said to be by him. They could not decide whether they were and called on four other artists, including Francesco Guardi, to advise them. (The final attribution was "school of Marieschi.")[15] This was but an early instance of a problem which has persisted until the present day. Given that many paintings and drawings are obviously by Canaletto and that others are equally obviously untouched by him, there remain a considerable number which raise doubts. Did he employ a team of assistants as did other artists?

It must be remembered that Bernardo Canal, his father, was not only a scene painter: view paintings, signed by him, of mediocre quality, exist.[16] He lived until 1744 and seems to have had no significant practice in Venice. Bernardo Bellotto, Canaletto's nephew, was about fifteen when the studio was at its busiest (the mid-1730s) and by the time he was twenty he was an accomplished artist, painting Canaletto's subjects in Canaletto's style; only later, when he left Venice, did he develop his own. It seems quite implausible that increasing use should not have been made of the young artist's talents, nor would one

expect to detect in all cases where he left off and the head of the studio took over. Canaletto's father was far less skilled but he must have been available at an earlier period; even in the 1720s we know that Canaletto had "more work than he can doe...." Given the known output of the studio until the 1740s, there seems no need to look further for assistants.

Writing in 1949 of the repetition, collaboration, copying, and forgery in the field of *veduta* painting, Sir Francis Watson, a pioneer in the study of Canaletto, warned of the need to be "very cautious in our pronouncements."[17] Forty years subsequent experience has not lessened the need for such caution when studying, and enjoying, the work of this endlessly fascinating artist.

Notes

1. Alessandro Bettagno, in *Canaletto*, 1982, p. 19.
2. Constable, *Canaletto*, 1962, 2d ed. revised by J. G. Links, 1976, pp. 8–9. Much of this sketch is abridged from chapter 1, "Biography," pp. 1–50, of that catalogue raisonné, which is hereafter referred to as C/L.
3. C/L, 1989 ed., p. xxii.
4. Haskell, *Burlington Magazine*, 1956, pp. 296–300.
5. For amended date (from 1722), see C/L, 1989 ed., pp. xxiv–v.
6. Reprinted, with introduction and descriptive texts by J. G. Links, *Views of Venice*, 1971.
7. C/L, Addenda, p. 685; and C/L, 1989 ed., pp. xxxi–v.
8. C/L, pp. 675–78.
9. Haskell, *Patrons and Painters*, 1980, pp. 357–58.

10. Buttery, *Burlington Magazine*, 1987, pp. 437–45.
11. "Le Sieur Canalety, Peintre Venetien" is stated on a handbill of about 1755 to be in Paris, but the evidence is too thin to be taken seriously without confirmation. See C/L, 1989 ed., pp. lxxx–i.
12. Guarienti, ed., in Orlandi, *Abecedario pittorico*, 1753, p. 75.
13. Links, *Canaletto*, 1982, p. 104.
14. Haskell, *Patrons and Painters*, 1980, p. 319 n. 3, quoted from Antonio Conti, *Prose, poesie*, 1756, p. 250.
15. Fogolari, "L'Accademia Veneziana di Pittura e Scoltura del Settecento," 1913, p. 383, and Watson, *Canaletto*, 1949, p. 12.
16. C/L, 1989 ed., p. xv.
17. Watson, *Canaletto*, 1949, p. 12.

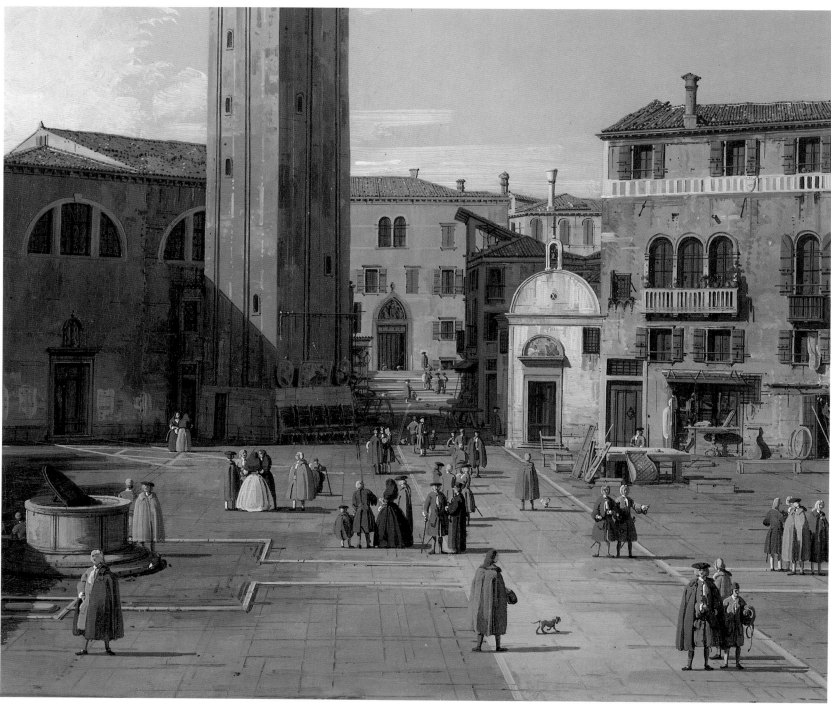

Fig. 6. Detail of fig. 9, *Campo S. Angelo.*

CANALETTO AS ARTIST OF THE URBAN SCENE

by Michael Levey

Towered cities please us then,
And the busy hum of men.
Milton, "L'Allegro"

Anyone strolling through a big modern city—like Paris, New York, or London—will sooner or later come upon some aspect of the scene that brings vividly to mind Canaletto's pictures.

Such associations are not prompted by any momentary, accidental resemblance to Venice or other places that he depicted. They are triggered by a far stronger and deeper affinity, whereby often apparently commonplace phenomena of the man-made environment are seen approximating his vision, lifted out of the local, topical, and everyday to take on a permanent and timeless quality. It may be a ray of sunlight trapped like liquid at the far end of a shadowy tunnel formed by tall facades; the sheer angle and looming presence of a weathered cliff of wall; or the uncannily precise embossing, on a vellum-like sheet of lilac sky, of a distant dome, a slim chimney, or a skeletal cage of scaffolding.

By the very intensity of his vision of phenomena of this kind, Canaletto seems to have taken possession of them, to have "captured" them. However alien the modern city to any city he knew, it can start to compose itself to resemble one of his compositions—an effect of nature imitating art that happens not infrequently in painting, but only when there is a dominant, almost obsessive character to the vision of the artist concerned.

In this dominance of his material lies Canaletto's claim to be considered not simply as a competent topographical painter but as an artist—a very great one and arguably the greatest of all artists of the urban scene. There is a broad sense, as this essay will seek to suggest, whereby Canaletto's Venice—to take the central subject of his work and inspiration—quite fails to reproduce the Venice of reality, for all its powerfully factual air. The very firmness and patternmaking precision he rapidly established as hallmarks of his style (and never lost) are not in themselves particularly suited to depiction of a city built somewhat haphaz-ardly on the water and more than normally exposed to the elements. Nor is that just a post-Romantic way of looking at Venice. The near-contemporaneous work of Guardi shows that another eighteenth-century "view" of Venice could exist, very different from Canaletto's in style, as in mood: one to some extent making a virtue of imprecision and non-firmness, and thereby conveying the unstable, watery atmosphere of the city. By contrast, Canaletto's vision, at its most typical, is of a Venice closer to the celestial city of Revelation: "... pure gold, like unto clear glass."

Canaletto's is, *au fond*, an ideal city, constructed very consciously. The first indications of that are shown by his assured handling of physical facts, disposition of buildings, and so on; keen observer though he was of every aspect of Venice (as his drawings confirm), he unobtrusively asserted his artistic right to modify, move, and rearrange those facts in the interests of creating a picture. Not the least artful result of this process is retention, even perhaps enhancement, of the general air of verisimilitude in the finished work.

Another and more significant indication of Canaletto's exercise of pure art is in his treatment of detail, especially in the diminishing perspectives of his mature paintings, where the spectator's eye is treated to an enchanting, yet literally impossible feast of seemingly unending physical minutiae that in reality would require a telescope to be visible. Always, Canaletto appears to promise, beyond what is visible lie further rooftops, further doorways half wrapped in shadow, and further windows, each with its glazing bars. Only rarely does he totally close a composition. More often there is another corner to be turned at the end of the view, made enticing perhaps by a streak of sunlight, and the spectator will identify with the furthest, pygmy-sized inhabitant of the picture, who pauses forever there: on the point of disappearing into the fresh perspective adumbrated.

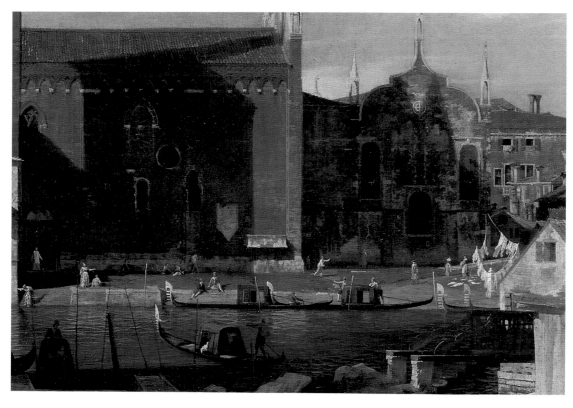

Fig. 7. Detail of cat. no. 32, *"The Stonemason's Yard."*

Such a vision has more in common with Quattrocento aims in painting than with the semi-scientific truth to visual perception associated with, for example, the achievements of Impressionism. Canaletto paints what he knows to be there, unable to blur objects in a concern for atmospheric illusionism. He does so in a thoroughly rational, but far from prosaic, spirit. Hence, incidentally, the superb scope his pictures offer for photographs of details, often capable of passing as pictures in their own right. What Canaletto also manages to do, in yet another demonstration of artfulness, is organize, control, and, when need be, invent the mass of detail incorporated within a picture, taking care to subordinate all to the major concern of coherent composition.

Through that form of bifocalism, he exerts an extraordinary and forceful grasp on every item, small as well as large, that eventually packs the picture area. Yet there are other forms of bifocalism in his vision which are even more impressive. He sees "the city"—Venice primarily, London secondly, and Rome a poor third—in its twin aspects, as a collection of buildings and as a community of people, with a passionate response divided almost equally between bricks and mortar, and flesh and blood. It is hard to think of another townscape painter who has combined such intense feeling for the shape and texture of even the simplest man-made structure with equivalent feeling for the structure's inhabitants. Only in Chardin is something similar combined—in, however, a very different blend, with people taking on all the gravity and dignity of austere still life, while a stove or a few pots and pans exude intimations of humanity. That he and Canaletto should be such close contemporaries is perhaps more than chance: in *"The Stonemason's Yard"* (cat. no. 32 and fig. 7) the fusion of people—humble people, preoccupied with their daily chores—and environment may in its impassive, profound sobriety be called Chardinesque, although this picture is in some ways a far more ambitious one than Chardin ever attempted.

Everywhere in Canaletto's ideal city rises "the busy hum of men," animating it and giving it purpose. His observation of people as people—lively and individual, not serving as mere puppets or just providing a garnish to the solid meat of architecture—has not been much studied, possibly not sufficiently appreciated. Yet his pictures are rich in variety of costume, and even more in variety of action and characters—from boatmen to beggars, via Turks, Jews and priests, servant girls, noblemen, workmen, ladies and children, in a gamut of the Venetian open-air, social scene which runs from the Doge himself (shown in *The Doge visiting the Church and Scuola di S. Rocco*; see fig. 3) down to ubiquitous pet dogs.

Like the boatmen, the boats are remarkably varied, and it is their structure that Canaletto seizes on, rarely with more patently virtuoso joy in complexity, as well as variety, than in the panoramic *Bacino di S. Marco* (cat. no. 51). There is almost a touch of impudence and dignity in the foreground juxtaposition of tiny rowing boat (a crouched figure, vividly observed from the rear, balancing on its prow) and bulky, thickly rigged barge, the interwoven tackle and masts of which are traced with all the innate respect that another painter might have given to the geometric shape of a stringed musical instrument. Beyond this juxtaposition, the expanse of the *bacino* is alive with craft of every description, in a positive, surely contrived anthology of ships and shipping in eighteenth-century Venice—although the effect, like the mid-water viewpoint, is made to appear perfectly natural.

Buildings and boats, and those who have devised them for shelter and livelihood, fit suitably within the microcosm that Canaletto strives to depict. Yet his vision suggests he would penetrate further. Under all the myriad surface observation, and all the patent pride focused on Venice as his native city, still queen of the sea, still "the most serene" of republics, he seems to perceive a serene, ordered structure of universal significance. The concept of building and constructing—of man imposing his artistic will on fluid, formless nature—seems to be the essence of his creed. Thus the city—any city—easily symbolizes the order that man alone can bring to the environment, making sense of previous chaos. To build and build solidly, lastingly, and splendidly, is to defeat nature, and Canaletto is essentially rational in apparently having no doubts or regrets about the defeat. As it

happens, Venice could scarcely be rivaled as a symbol of what art, in the fullest meaning of the word, can achieve—conquering the most hopeless of natural conditions, to create out of a swamp a city which rapidly established so many claims on the world's wonder.

One begins to see why Canaletto chose to be a painter of the urban scene, of "views"—not of landscape or genre (despite an eye far more acute than, say, Pietro Longhi's), and still less of history pictures. Had he ever attempted the latter category, the results would probably have been much closer to Piazzetta than to Tiepolo.

Interestingly, Canaletto is one of the few Venetian painters of the period (Francesco Guardi is another, although a distinct, less dramatic example) who is recorded as switching from the speciality in which he was trained to adopt a totally different type of art. It is easy to understand why, as Zanetti so forcefully put it, he "excommunicated" the theater. The Bibiena-inspired stage scenery of his day was at its typical best when openly fantastic: architecture devoid of people, dream-like in its vast proportions and ingenuity and excess. Canaletto's imagination tended to grow awkward when required to take off into the empyrean: some of the painted capriccios reveal a stolid, almost stubborn attitude to the demand. Not unlike Cézanne, he needed to focus upon a motif in nature and let that stimulate his imagination. In Venice he found the perfect motif, one that never failed him—nor he it—in an active career of over forty years. He was still pursuing, redefining, and putting in order the physical reality of Venice in 1766 when, as he noted proudly on the sheet, he drew "without spectacles" the interior of the Basilica of S. Marco, showing the crossing and the north transept (cat. no. 127).

As a testament to all Canaletto's aims, as well as a triumphant affirmation of art unaffected by old age, there is nothing finer than this drawing. That it is no casual sketch is obvious; in fact, several preparatory drawings were executed, or utilized, in its creation. The ultimate, highly finished effect is of luxurious, proliferating detail rejoiced in but superbly controlled, subordinated in its complexity to the overall sense of design and pattern. Elaborate as the architectural and ornamental framework is, Canaletto enhanced it by peopling the scene with figures in various attitudes of prayer (standing, kneeling, and positively prostrate in oriental fashion), in addition to a seated beggar, a respectful visitor gazing up into the dome and—liveliest of all—a group of singers in the pulpit whose facial contortions are caught by a vivid, near-caricature draftsmanship that brings to mind Rowlandson.

While doing characteristic justice to the statues, the hanging lamps suspended on long chains, the tessellated pavement, the vaults and windows, and the ubiquitous mosaics, Canaletto no less characteristically presents an interior devoid of penumbra or mystery. The building may have been built to the glory of God, but what is depicted, and what the spectator is invited to admire, is the handiwork of man. All is clarity, and never—it seems—has S. Marco looked so evenly and well lit. The lighting is not so much natural as the product of Canaletto's mind. The ancient basilica is mapped in line and outline, with the support of only mild washes to convey depth and shadow; an economy of means and unobtrusive wit give just so much shape as is necessary to convey a sainted pope in a pendentive, or the row of saints along the choir screen, for example, with their skull-like heads. Everywhere a mental crispness is apparent, and the interior of S. Marco is perceived through Canaletto's temperament.

To suppose that any of this indicates a lack of imagination on the part of the artist would be wrong. Certainly, his vision developed into an un-"Romantic" one, with imagination tightly under control and directed toward literally clear purposes, more intellectual perhaps than sensuous, yet always alert. In passing it should be noted that Canaletto's "ideal" etchings reveal his ability to muse as romantically as anyone, although he muses most personally with and among architectural motifs. Imagination of an almost Piranesian grandeur and strangeness is at work in the haunting final state of the frontispiece to the etchings—a composition which in itself would sufficiently rebut any charge of prosaicness in the mind of its creator.

If Canaletto is conceived of as an artist whose fundamental urge is toward order, and who seeks in turn to impose it on visual experience—rather than to be merely a passive recorder of topography—then the evolution of his style, for instance, begins to make sense. The tightening of his grip, which has often

been deplored and taken as a sign of deterioration (not least by the present writer), can be interpreted as part of the artist's determined mastery of his material. The late paintings, of which the *Grand Canal: looking Southeast to the Rialto* (fig. 8) is typical, become triumphs of conscious exactness, down to the precise placing of each paving stone and ripple, with an effect more of mosaic than of paint used in any obviously "free," painterly way. Canaletto has compelled the untidy reality of the assembled bobbing gondolas and other boats at the right here, as well as the bustling activity of rolling barrels or bales along the adjoining quay, to be frozen into deliberate, intricate patterns, with no loss of artistic vitality—only of "naturalism."

Since some convention is always involved in painting the visible world, it cannot be said that Canaletto has grown more conventional in such late pictures as this one—simply that he is more confidently artful in displaying his style, expressed by highly personal calligraphy. He manages to do it, too, with no failure of grasp on the three-dimensional. A passion for clarity and a delight in the solid geometry of buildings meant that he never neglected to observe the properties of light, chiefly as a means of molding form, as it does most subtly in shaping—as it were, slowly and softly—the tall blocks of houses at the right of the *Grand Canal* view. But also—in a different tempo—it provides glittering points of radiance that may be scattered across a roof or dance down a row of faces, like so much sparkling, metallic confetti (yet scattered always with purpose).

In his concern for greater vivacity, he certainly was not afraid of improving on nature—as this *Grand Canal* picture shows—creating a rapid, shorthand symbol of the human figure: angular, almost jerky, with textures of flesh and costume left undifferentiated. Such figures are, however, the ideal inhabitants for the world of Canaletto's late compositions—a far cooler world in atmosphere and mood than that of his early view pictures, more patently artificial and constructed, and for the artist himself possibly more satisfying. In Canaletto's opinion, the *Grand Canal: looking Southeast to the Rialto*, which is indeed a masterpiece of its kind, might well have ranked higher than *"The Stonemason's Yard."*

There is one natural element which Canaletto as a painter of Venice could scarcely avoid confronting and which offered a

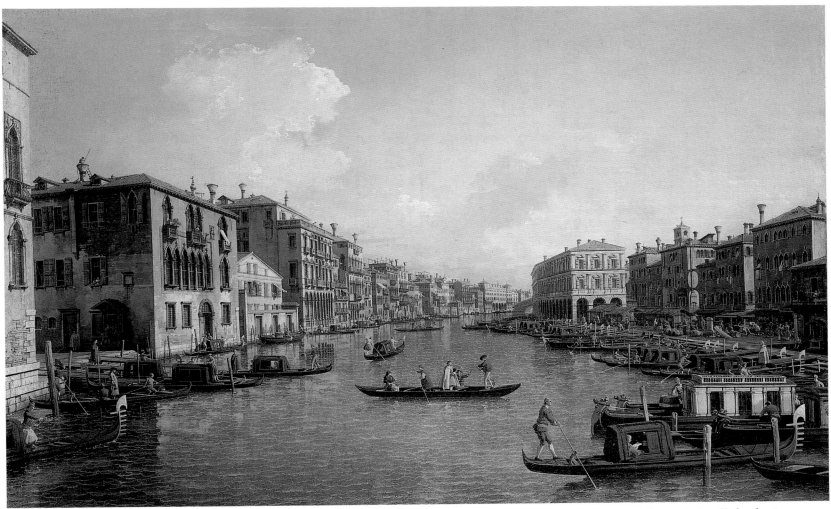

Fig. 8. Canaletto, *Grand Canal: looking Southeast from the Campo Sta. Sofia to the Rialto Bridge.* Staatliche Museen Preussischer Kulturbesitz, Gemäldegalerie Berlin (loan of the Streit Foundation, Berlin).

challenge to his inherent sense of form: water. Whereas the sky and clouds are distant, intangible phenomena, experienced only through the eye and translated into something solid looking, however luminous, for which paint easily finds a formula, water presents a more complex problem. The sky, being the source of light, was something Canaletto had no difficulty in understanding, perhaps instinctively; that he had introduced the sun into view painting was quickly recognized by contemporaries. In his

early pictures the sky is often the location of exciting aerial dramas, and although his later work is more restrained in this way, as in others, with unclouded, sunny skies the preference, he could on occasion create such an effectively thunderous atmosphere as that which gives tension to the view of *Old Walton Bridge* (Dulwich version; cat. no. 73) and captures all the uncertainty of English summer weather. Most of even Canaletto's fervent admirers have probably felt at times that there is something "mechanical" about the way he treats the protean substance of water: tangible yet elusive, colorless yet constantly taking on color, with volume if not density, insubstantial-seeming yet weighty and capable of bearing great weight.

For someone as thoroughly imbued with nineteenth-century ideals of truth to nature as Ruskin, Canaletto's failure—as it appeared—to paint water with any real response to its qualities was the final outrage in the work of a painter stigmatized in *Modern Painters* as "little and . . . bad . . . adding apathy to error." Ruskin was at once angry and pleased that by the standards of Turner Canaletto could be found utterly, despicably wanting, and his rage carried him beyond the question of water as such into a strange, Baron Corvo-style rhetorical outburst about the seamen at the Rialto, with "naked, bronzed, burning limbs . . . who yet keep the right Giorgione colour on their brows and bosoms." To Canaletto, those glorious Venetians would have been almost as ludicrously improbable as Turner's visions of Venice itself.

Yet, as nearly always with Ruskin, a grain of real perception lurks amid wordy spume. Canaletto appears nothing like as attentive to the properties of water as he is to the properties of brick and stone. He is totally without any sense of wonder at this natural element which was to excite Turner no less than Ruskin. To Canaletto, its constant, shifting surface and movement, so much part of its fascination, was probably distracting, if not positively disquieting.

If the "ideal" compositions among his etchings are taken as evidence of Canaletto at his most uninhibited, free from pressure to produce "views" of any precise location and without requirement to satisfy anyone but himself, it is significant how relatively unimportant a part water plays in them. And in the big, splendid set of six early pictures for Joseph Smith (now in the Royal Collection; see cat. nos. 28, 29) water is scarcely present at all. That might be explained by the nature of the subjects, but it is also true of *"The Stonemason's Yard."* From the other end of his career, in the very late architectural capriccio (Accademia, Venice; cat. no. 85) conceived as his presentation piece to the Academy, water is almost entirely banished. Altogether, it would not be excessive to conclude that Canaletto found little in water as such to fit in with his essential vision or to accord with the appeal of hard, usually man-made materials. In dealing with water, he seems at first unresponsive—indeed almost apathetic—but gradually he learned that it was susceptible to being "fixed" (almost in a slang sense), slotted into his personal universe, transmuted in the process into something effective and fascinating, although scarcely natural.

Where water is present in the earliest pictures (as, for example, in cat. no. 2, *Grand Canal: looking East, from the Campo S. Vio*), it tends to be the grayish green of a badly tarnished mirror, although more opaque—a somewhat summary blur of pigment without much suggestion of depth. Here and there, a few further strokes of the brush convey ripples. One can hardly counter Ruskin's assertion that none of this is "true" to the character of water. What the canals seem to be filled with—long before modern pollution—is a heavy, viscous oil.

Canaletto must soon have realized that such slack treatment did little justice to his artistic standards. He was anyway engaged in the process of burnishing and solidifying the forms in his pictures, themselves becoming much more patently constructed. It was as though he now polished up the mirror of the water in them and discovered that it could have a function in the overall lucidity at which he aimed. The water congealed into a glassy, quartz-like substance, taking on a rare quality with its own excitement and awe—a shining expanse of mineral-hard ice, in tone aquamarine, mauve-blue, or opalescent green, serving now as the Bacino di S. Marco, now as the Thames in London. Its surface was composed of a fine mesh of countless flicks of paint, most resembling chain mail laid over marble, while reflections of an often quite arbitrary kind gave it additional sheen.

Between skies of brilliant blue and white—skies whipped to a fresco-like, plaster-like texture and vivacity—and crystalline waves that glint yet never move, Canaletto builds block by block his city. With nature conquered, he had leisure for the real exercise of his art; in a very different mood from that of early nineteenth-century English poets rhapsodizing over Venice, he nonetheless set about making structures rise, "As from the stroke of the enchanter's wand"—that is, from his brush.

Canaletto seldom—or perhaps never—created a fully convincing tonal relationship between sky and water. Sometimes he shows the Grand Canal an inert grass green under a vivid cobalt sky; the exquisitely radiant atmospheric envelope in which Cuyp, for instance, bathes a complete scene was not to his purpose. His eye—so sharply sensitive to everything he needed for his art—was elsewhere: fastened perhaps on a striped awning, on the serrated steel prow of a gondola, or on the folds of the gondolier's shirt, all minute phenomena which light turned to jewels that he would eventually embed in the intricate mechanism of his composition.

Never before had the architecture of Venice been scrutinized with as voracious an appetite as that of Canaletto, whose annotated drawings on the spot seize and penetrate to the bones of the city without being indifferent to its skin. He cannot cease marveling as he studies a wavering line of juxtaposed facades and records the varied styles of their windows—Gothic, Renaissance, or contemporary—and such "human" touches as shutters added at every angle, a friendly lamp suspended at an alleyway corner or, set along a balcony whose precise method of iron support, too, he scrupulously observes, wooden troughs to hold ranks of terra-cotta flowerpots.

It was not for patrons but for himself that Canaletto thus built his view of Venice. Half the detail he amassed must have been meaningless to most foreigners, and the average visitor seeking a pictorial souvenir of the city would have settled for a neatly colored, straightforward view of the Piazza S. Marco or the Rialto.

It was as artist that Canaletto took his dry-seeming pen sketches and terse notations—forming as it were the private notebook of a surveyor or even an engineer—and poured over them all the magic liquid power of light. The bones assumed a sensuous life. A figure or a facade that had previously been mapped in schematic outline alone now became palpable as it took on color and solidity and bloomed in paint.

Of course, Canaletto was not literally dependent on previous drawings for the appearances of either buildings or figures in his pictures: in them a fresh creative process is at work. Canaletto goes back to the inspiration of the urban scene in all its actuality—probably recovering it, in point of fact, by an act of the imagination in the studio rather than by renewed study on the spot. Nonetheless, freshness is apparent in the succulent, often juicy, handling of paint itself, as it constructs solid patterns of glowing light and luminous shadow, and peoples the composition with an ever-fresh observation of humanity—all testifying to the continuing masterly pursuit of art.

The first person to stress that Canaletto was no mere craftsman but an artist was the painter himself.

Typically enough for a Venetian painter of the period, Canaletto's personality, private circumstances, and opinions generally are hard to gauge. He seems to have been a somewhat isolated figure, more famous than esteemed, without friends among other painters, as well as without a wife or children. Yet it is clear that from his earliest years of activity as a view painter—and perhaps just because that activity lacked prestige—he insisted on his status as an artist. He would have reacted violently to being referred to as "cet ouvrier," the term applied to him in the *Lettres d'Italie* of the Président Charles de Brosses—who in fact admired Canaletto's achievement.[1] It is inconceivable that painters like Sebastiano Ricci, Amigoni, or Pellegrini—and, still less Pittoni or Tiepolo—would have been so described.

Despite de Brosses's admiration, he stigmatized Canaletto as impossible to make a deal with, because the English had spoiled him by offering him far more money for his pictures than he asked. There is some irony in this comment, dating from 1739, since more than a decade earlier Owen McSwiney—one of the first non-Italians to commission pictures from Canaletto—had complained that "the fellow is whimsical and vary's his prices every day," going on to say, significantly, "and he that has a mind to have any of his work, must not seem to be too fond of it, for he'l be ye worse treated for it, both in the price and the painting too."[2] Even taking into account a possible tendency for McSwiney, in the time-honored way of agents and middlemen, to exaggerate his own ability to handle an awkward personality, it is apparent that Canaletto already knew his own worth, artistically and financially, and was, rightly, determined to see it recognized. As he was not in the modern retail trade, he was fully entitled to vary his prices, and some of McSwiney's annoyance obviously arose from encountering an artist who proved no soft touch. Canaletto's opinion of McSwiney is unfortunately not recorded, but the wisest judgment comes from a modern scholar, who sums up the situation with the reminder that "Canaletto evidently had some tight-fisted people to deal with and the greed was not all on one side."[3]

"Greed" is actually rather a harsh word to apply to the painter when he had no other income than what he could earn from his art (and his circumstances at his death scarcely suggest vast wealth gained, but instead sad, virtually pauper-style austerity). Nor could Canaletto, given the category of picture he chose to produce, expect to be highly honored in academic-artistic circles. He was very much on his own. He had to establish himself as the supreme exponent of the view picture in a Venice where Carlevaris lived on, although no longer active at the end, until 1730—and, unlike Carlevaris, Canaletto had no learned, intellectual standing and no patrician support. It may even be that the overwhelmingly truthful-seeming impact of his pictures, for all its novelty, was liable to be interpreted by some sophisticated aesthetic tastes as merely a clever but limited proto-photographic (i.e., unimaginative) skill. His very popularity with foreigners and tourists may not have commended itself to everyone in Venice. The dreary question of Canaletto and the *camera ottica* has its relevance, too, insofar as the rumored use of such a device would have encouraged the idea of an artist who was merely an "ouvrier." Indeed, as late as 1849 Bryan's *Dictionary of Painters and Engravers* went out of its way to stigmatize Canaletto for his "mechanical execution" and, less conventionally for the time (in its entry for Francesco Guardi), contrasted him unfavorably with Guardi, a true artist, as opposed to an "artisan" working with the aid of the "Camera lucida."[4]

From such contemporary evidence as exists, Canaletto emerges as almost aggressively resolved not to be taken for granted. His reputed temperamental character was again noted, in 1736, by the Swedish Count Tessin as "fantasque, bourru, Baptistisé,"[5] which amounts to whimsical, surly, and clownish (probably). At the same time, the evidence of his work is of great, steady, sober industry. The paradox is surely a simple one: Canaletto found it convenient—as did Degas, in a very different way—to adopt a brusque, difficult persona, all the more necessary for an artist in an age only too inclined to refer, as the future Consul Joseph Smith did, to "a painter's impertinence" when the customer was not served swiftly and cheaply, as by a shopkeeper in his

shop. It is Smith, suitably enough, who reveals in the same letter (written in 1730) the heart of the matter, speaking of the current success of Canaletto's work, "... which he vallues himself as much as anybody."[6]

Like any artist, Canaletto had to learn about the nature of his own gifts. Although profoundly Venetian and patently proud of being Origine Civis Venetus (see fig. 1), he does not seem to have grown up particularly affected by the visual potentialities of the city. There could be no Constable-like claim by him, at least consciously, that "these scenes made me a painter." Yet, it must have been on his return to Venice from Rome, presumably in 1720, having renounced the stage, that he became aware of the very different "theater" of actuality all around him. The art of Carlevaris may well have sharpened that awareness, and it is hard to resist a feeling that the youthful Canaletto intended to challenge and outdo the older man, whose neat, slightly bland view pictures have every quality except artistic engagement.

Engagement is preferred to neatness in Canaletto's earliest known views of Venice (such as the *Grand Canal: looking Northeast to the Rialto*, cat. no. 3), which have about them an excitement that announces a quite new way of making view pictures. Not only is there frequently playing about the scene a stormy atmospheric drama in which the fabric of the buildings seems almost under threat, but the compositions themselves are full of novelty: novel are the viewpoints from mid-canal, for example (as in the *Grand Canal: looking North from near the Rialto*, cat. no. 9), as well as the selection of sites away from the familiar ones around S. Marco. The people in these pictures, populating the scene far less densely than Carlevaris's, loiter far less; they seem, in every sense, more "engaged," and are certainly less inclined to stare out at the spectator. Something is felt to be happening in these pictures—if only a gondola darting across the water or a woman throwing open some shutters—which quickens their air of immediacy.

It is as though their creator aimed to be the Tintoretto of view painters. A more than natural—indeed, artificially heightened—effect is achieved by bold manipulation of the reality of angles, the proportion of buildings, and the extreme contrasts of light and shade. As if agitated by the hint of a rising storm, sails and awnings flap raggedly, and there is often something ragged about the ant-like figures who add animation to the scene—busy, occupied inhabitants included not as decoration but as of right. The precision of Canaletto's observation of those inhabitants can scarcely fail to be felt, but it is confirmed by his written declaration regarding the *Grand Canal: from Sta. Maria della Carità* (cat. no. 11) to Stefano Conti, who commissioned the work. As carefully as he painted them, he describes the trio of figures standing in the center of the *campo* in strong sunlight: "...two fathers of the same religious order [that of the Rocchetini: Lateran canons] talking to a Savio in violet robe."

The group identified forms a minute knot in a thoroughly—purely—Venetian chain of existence: the state is represented by one of the "Sages," a senior body of councillors in the hierarchy of government, dressed in the distinctive long robe of appropriate color; and the Church by two "Rocchetini," so-called because they wear the *rocchetto* (a variation of the surplice worn only by canons, abbots, and bishops) of the Lateran canons covering their white or cream-colored habits, their costumes topped—as Canaletto shows—by a black biretta. Their presence in the *campo*—and in the painting—is entirely natural since their monastery adjoined Sta. Maria della Carità, and Canaletto obviously found their pale robes pictorially effective. A "Rocchetino," like a tiny scrap of white paper, can be detected in the deep shadow at the base of the campanile of the Carità in *"The Stonemason's Yard"* (cat. no. 32).

Canaletto's early views are big, untidy, and intensely dramatic. It is not surprising that an element of "theater" has often been remarked in them, but it would be a mistake to relate that to the artist's previous experience in scenography. The operatic theater of his day was elevated, stylized, and far removed from later concepts of opera or drama. The sets so ingeniously devised by such scenographers as the Bibiena were nearly always made up of buildings of abstract grandeur in which nobody could possibly be supposed to live. There is no place there for the untidiness ordinary people bring to their environment—any more than there is for a character to pick his nose in a play by Racine.

Canaletto was far closer in artistic affinity to such vulgarity (not afraid, after all, to paint a child urinating in *"The Stonemason's Yard"* and men presumably likewise engaged on the quay-

sides in other pictures). It was all part of the urban scene, and in the wish to embrace its every aspect—to embrace it and recreate it in his art—he was bound to see further than the bold yet visually limited, sketchy, somewhat impressionistic view of Venice presented by those early pictures whose style today is found to be so sympathetic. The Tintorettesque vision was gradually to be exchanged for that of perhaps a gifted watchmaker, but the shift should not be deplored; Canaletto had his reasons —good artistic ones—for developing a style that would allow him to look longer and more penetratingly and to fix his sensations more precisely; to organize, in brief, a more complex mass of visual phenomena. Freed from any hectic striving by his rapid defeat of Carlevaris, soon followed by the latter's illness and death, he must have realized that the real challenge lay not outside but in himself.

His style evolved to meet his own urge toward a more thorough grasp on Venice—Venice as he experienced it through renewed scrutiny and deepening knowledge. The importance of *"The Stonemason's Yard"* in his evolution is that it combines a summation of his early manner with anticipations of the later one, with extraordinary, calm assurance. The grid of horizontals and verticals in the composition—firm and strong, without any wavering or exaggeration—makes for calmness. The atmospheric drama becomes unforced and subtle, and within it the buildings rise as tremendous physical presences, each virtually breathing under its worn surface of brick and plaster.

There is calmness too in the handling of paint, even in the foreground where the early style is most manifest, although restrained and refined with no loss of vigor. It may be less obviously exciting—and it is certainly less hasty-seeming—than Canaletto's Piazza and Piazzetta series for Joseph Smith, but there is much more concentrated, patient observation, which helps to give the foreground workmen, for example, their Chardinesque quality.

So skillfully is the eye led across the canal, to the area around and at the base of the church of the Carità, that probably no break in style is felt. Yet in that distance lies the germ of Canaletto's future development. A complete world of life and activity is created there with quite new precision—a separate picture, which could be detached from the main composition.

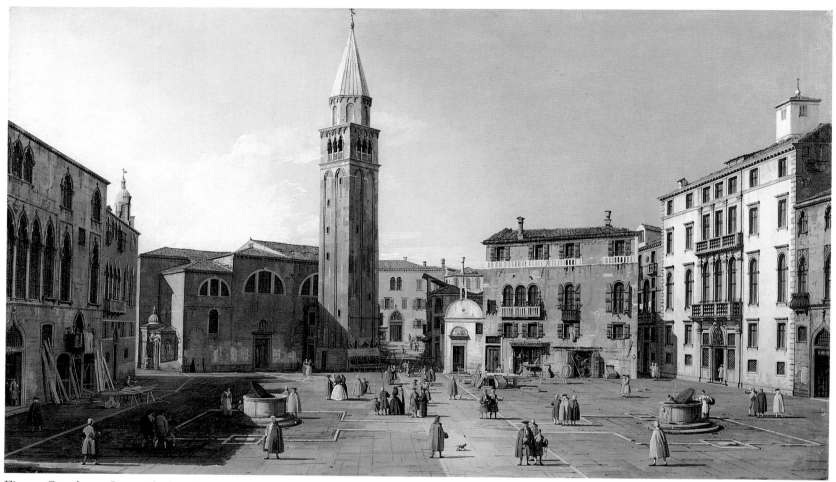

Fig. 9. Canaletto, *Campo S. Angelo*. Private Collection.

Canaletto has begun to see much further, literally and meta-phorically, and to express that vision his style had to change.

What he wanted to convey has remarkable affinities with the vision, and the technique, of late fifteenth-century Netherland-ish painters. The usually subordinate townscapes in their reli-gious pictures have a gem-like clarity and a lucent precision which seems to stem partly from an inspired identification of the medium of oil with the quality of light.

Canaletto was in pursuit of such elusive or easily missed and minute effects as that in the distance at the extreme left of *"The*

Stonemason's Yard," where a tiny, light-filled vista of facades is perceived between the great jutting wall of the foreground house and the half-shadowed apse of the Carità. Just by imaginatively setting that "detail" within the big panorama of the composi-tion, he suggests the continuous, unfolding, and ever-alluring experience of the city. Vitality is conveyed, and a sense that in a city something novel or interesting is always happening. That he responded to this activity in straightforward ways is demon-strated by his fondness for documenting not only architectural changes in Venice in his lifetime—new churches built, new pave-

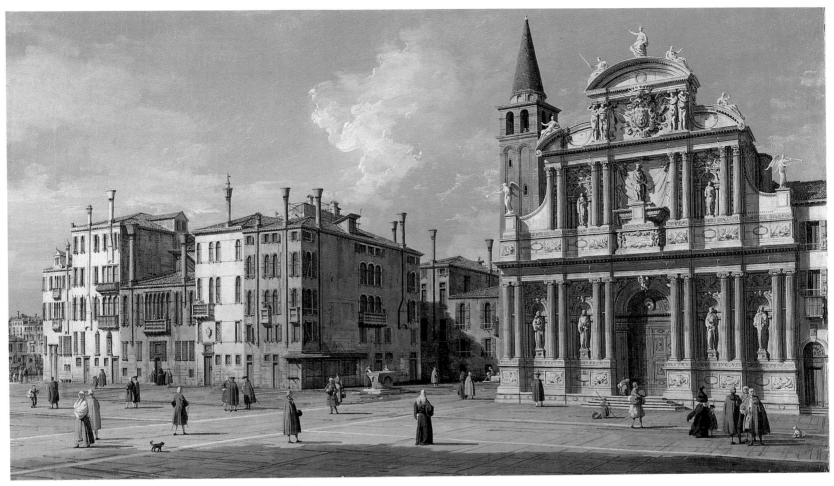

Fig. 10. Canaletto, *Sta. Maria Zobenigo*. Private Collection.

ments laid, new windows set into a facade—but all the activity of repair: scaffolding, pulleys and ladders, and the sweeping of chimneys (see the upper right of cat. no. 2). Even in the range and vivacity of Canaletto's civic architecture there are few houses of such haunting "inhabitedness" as that built out of the quay beside the waters of the Grand Canal, at the foot of the Carità's campanile, in *"The Stonemason's Yard."* Its blankest windows are invested with a sense of fascination, while other windows suggest life teeming within the blanched, irregular structure, one chimney of which is faintly smoking. To do full justice to Canaletto's

vision here would take a literary artist like Dickens, comparably absorbed by the urban spectacle. One can only note the almost surreal "aliveness" of this house, achieved by an intense, nearly delirious determination to miss no aspect of its existence.

For Canaletto's mental and visual lucidity to function best it was necessary to create in pictures an atmosphere of permanent and improbable—if not strictly unreal—sunlight. Hence the characteristic skies of his later work, from the 1730s onward, which are to be understood as having an artistic purpose apart from any tourist-propaganda one.

27

Increasingly, Canaletto set himself the problem of preserving all the impact and evidence of civic vitality—its sheer bustle—while fixing the scene with maximum firmness to convey a sense of rock-like permanence beneath. It is almost a larger version of the problem presented for him by water. The essence of the city lay in a conjunction of the fluid, everyday aspects of life—lacking which any vision of it is barren—with the solid, more timeless qualities of its buildings and architectural spaces, which are rooted in another dimension that lasts long after its inhabitants have gone to their graves. To distill and preserve that twin essence became Canaletto's goal.

How he achieved this is revealed by such small-scale, placidly ordinary views as the *Campo S. Angelo* and *Sta. Maria Zobenigo* (figs. 6, 9, 10). They, and comparable works, are as remarkable as the big, busy "feast" pictures of more obvious brilliance that are fueled by civic—indeed national—pride. It is no depreciation of one of Canaletto's most complex designs, the scene of the Bacino di S. Marco on Ascension Day (to which he would return with variations and renewed virtuosity), to find equal if not greater artistic penetration in views that mark no special occasion and show no major monuments—or show them as part of a thoroughly unglamorous, diurnal scene.

Thus in the *Sta. Maria Zobenigo*, Sardi's operatically florid, sculptural facade, although it has pride of place, is by no means the total subject and is certainly not what gives power to the composition as a work of art. One may even feel that the facade awoke no great response in Canaletto (especially in his depiction of the lower half, where the fluted columns are rather perfunctorily observed). The emphasis of the picture is on the city qua city, and on daily life lived within it. Canaletto's vision and technique lock those two aspects together indissolubly. It is as if the painter has sliced through the corporate body of Venice to present this cross section of its inner existence. Extraordinary power resides in the intimate, shadowed portion of the small *campo* to the side of the church—so quiet in mood, and in contrast to the facade of the building, with its trumpeting and gesticulating statues—where sits a solitary begging or vending figure. Most powerful of all is the breath of life in the sunny expanse of the foreground, where characteristically Venetian types pass by or pause: a woman clad in black with a boy, a gondolier, a bewigged patrician. Their environment is as vivid as they are, and much of it—like most of them—is not grandiose but ordinary and domestic, as is the architecture fondly depicted in the left half of the picture. Nor does the composition conventionally end there. Like life itself it seeks to go on. Another view is adumbrated at the very edge of the canvas, where further rows of houses appear, and the spectator enjoys the visual equivalent of a whiff of the Grand Canal winding through the center of Venice.

It was not possible for Canaletto to re-create another city with comparable penetration and conviction. Yet his best views of London show a receptivity and speed of assimilation—as well as, arguably, delight in the breadth and scale of this new urban subject—that remain astonishing. He never fails to be impressed by and to convey the extent of London. In the pair of pictures painted for the Duke of Richmond (cat. nos. 65, 66), fairly soon after Canaletto's arrival, he seems totally at ease with "plain" English architecture, and indeed fascinated by its idiom and by the idiom of a style of life different from the one that he had previously known. In some ways, *Whitehall and the Privy Garden* is the more notable picture just because of its response to a scene without any Venetian affinities whatsoever—and almost without a subject as such. Yet the portion of the stables of Richmond House (in the right foreground), an area inessential and ostensibly unrewarding, becomes the portion of the composition most keenly focused on and realized in the whole urban panorama. Within the macrocosm of this semi-aerial survey of London, the microcosm of that strongly defined, animated courtyard is rendered with intense conviction. Its resonance can be sensed reverberating all the way to the distant horizon of roofs and chimney pots.

Like the artist—or, rather, thanks to his contriving—the spectator gazes down on the sun-warmed stage of stone and tile on which unfolds a miniature, domestic, and entirely "natural" town drama: an oblong of door opened in the deeply shadowed archway and a gentleman greeted in the courtyard where a few hens peck are accompanied by such exquisitely observed minute properties as the ladder leaning against the wall and the bells inset high up on the stonework, whose existence is given additional reality in being doubled by the shadows they cast.

Perhaps nothing in the splendid river panorama of the companion picture is more vivid than the two white benches placed against the blond brick wall of Montagu House and basking in the expansive, pervasive sunlight. Their presence has real meaning. They speak of humanity, companionship, and an ideal of civilized leisure in which the visual delight of pausing to savor the cityscape has Wordsworthian anticipations:

> Dull would he be of soul who could pass by
> A sight so touching in its majesty.

Mankind built the benches, just as it built the adjoining terrace (typically animated by a man sweeping it clean), the gravel promenade, and the "Ships, towers, domes, theatres, and temples [that] lie . . . /All bright and glittering in the smokeless air."

Canaletto's instincts made it impossible for him ever to "pass by" the urban scene. Not as a mere onlooker but as its active, engaged observer and re-creator, he continued to find something in it of "majesty," however commonplace-seeming that truly was.

In the last years of his life he came back to Venice, both literally and pictorially. At some time in that period he in effect revisited the most familiar of all sites, the Piazza S. Marco, which had been the subject of one of his very earliest views (cat. no. 1) and which he had studied over the years from a variety of standpoints (cat. nos. 26, 27, 48, 55, 84). It might reasonably be assumed that he had nothing more to say on the theme, yet it was then that he produced one last, unexpected, and highly original interpretation, small in scale but of fierce clarity and compressed energy: a painting (now in the National Gallery, London; fig. 5) that offers evidence of how age only increased Canaletto's artistic assurance.

The obvious visual attractions of the Campanile and the basilica have been skillfully subordinated, as the artist daringly divides the composition between radiant open air and dark, semi-interior. In place of the usual "long shot" is a close-up in which the shadowed tunnel of the Procuratie colonnade seems to arch out of the picture and to cover the spectator, before it thrillingly shoots away in steeply diminishing perspective (a device recalling, perhaps by chance, that in Tintoretto's *Discovery of the Body of St. Mark*), culminating in a thumbnail shape of brightness—hardly bigger than a thumbnail too—that is, in fact, the beckoning prospect of a sunlit perspective of the distant Piazzetta beyond, seen as though through a glass door.

In this picture Canaletto's determination to fix his visual sensations firmly, clearly, and economically has reached a stage in which the effect resembles inspired carpentry. The strong right angle of the composition appears to be bolted to some cosmic framework of verticals and horizontals that nothing can shift. With equal craft the artist slots in his figures as if into some marquetry jigsaw, sealing them under a crystal layer formed from the fusion of vision and technique. Yet they live as vividly as ever. If anything, Canaletto now sees with even more succinct clarity. The social gamut is pungently expressed across the picture: from the elegantly cloaked man standing at the right, adroitly balancing his coffee cup as he idles pleasurably in the sunshine, to the ungainly, laboring woman at the left, who stoops to recover the contents of her basket that have spilled in the middle of the hot Piazza.

City and city existence interlock with total conviction. Life itself seems sealed in, symbolized by that golden gleam at the far end of the colonnade, like a lamp in a shrine of stone, aptly conveying the vitality and the tremendous certitude of Canaletto's mature grasp of the urban scene.

NOTES

1. Charles de Brosses, *Lettres d'Italie*, p. 399 (letter XXXI, 24 November 1739).
2. Letter from Owen McSwiney to the Duke of Richmond, Venice, 28 November 1727, published in C/L, p. 174.
3. Links, *Canaletto and His Patrons*, 1977, p. 34 n.
4. Michael Bryan, *Dictionary of Painters and Engravers*, enlarged by George Stanley (London, 1849), p. 300.

5. Letter to Carl Hårleman in Stockholm, 16 June 1736, published in Osvald Sirén, *Dessins et tableaux de la Renaissance italienne dans les collections de Suède* (Stockholm, 1902), p. 107.
6. First published in Chaloner, "The Egertons in Italy," 1950, p. 164.

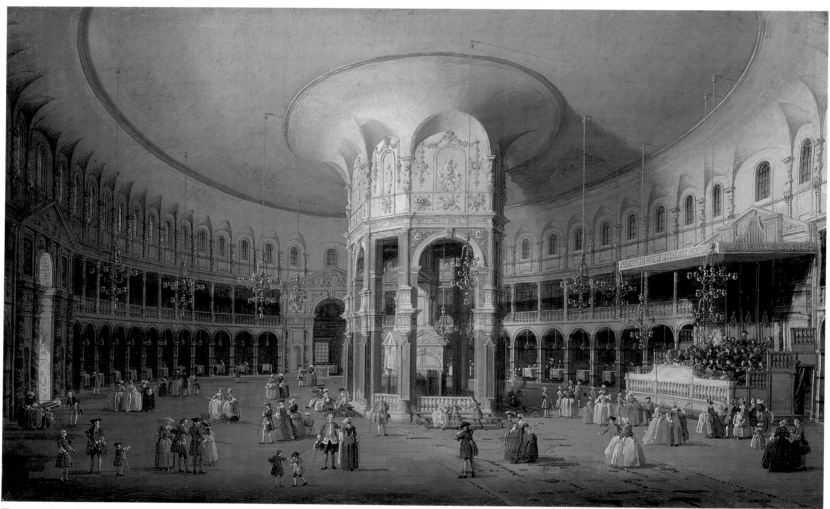

Fig. 11. Canaletto, *London: Ranelagh, interior of the Rotunda*. National Gallery, London.

THE TASTE FOR CANALETTO

by Francis Haskell

During much of Canaletto's lifetime, taste for his art went hand in hand with distaste for his character. The latter response need not concern us here, but it is worth emphasizing that the artist's supposed "whimsicality" and greed were almost certainly exaggerated by middlemen (themselves not known for their financial scruples) who were keen to obtain as much credit as possible for having succeeded in commissioning works from him on behalf of demanding and usually inexperienced clients. This same motive probably accounts for a few disparaging references to his art which we come across in his early years. Thus when in 1730—at about the time that Canaletto was producing some of his finest masterpieces—Owen McSwiney (one of the first of these middlemen) wrote sententiously about a request to Joseph Smith (who was just taking over from him in the role of intermediary) for four Canalettos that "I am, it may be, a little too delicate in my choice, for of Twenty pieces I see of him, I don't like eighteen & I have seen several, sent to London y^t I wou'd not give house room too,"[1] it is more likely that he was trying to do down rival dealers (in a manner later to be made famous by Duveen) than expressing a true opinion about quality. To judge from the very large number of works which we know that Canaletto was being asked to paint in these years, it seems that most collectors were agreed in being "amazed" by his early achievements.[2]

Several obstacles, however, stand in the way of any adequate estimate of his reputation. In the first place, Canaletto has usually been so closely associated with the subjects of his topographical pictures, especially those of Venice, that appreciation of the artist has been difficult to distinguish from that of his raw material: in this respect he is closer to a medieval maker of devotional images than to a painter working in the Age of the Enlightenment. It would certainly be of great interest to investigate how many owners of Canaletto's views of Venice in the eighteenth century had never actually been to the city. In the second place, so many pictures (which may be by him or by some imitator) are described in inventories merely as "View of Grand Canal" or even "View of Venice" that it is almost impossible to identify them. And, thirdly, by far the largest number of his pictures came to England in the eighteenth century and were little known elsewhere except through the medium of reproductive engraving; of these pictures the majority of the best have remained in the Royal Collection, since 1762 inaccessible—except at rare intervals—to all but a few. For these reasons the most revealing insights into Canaletto's art have tended to come from observers who have not been too impressed by the unique character of Venice itself and, occasionally, from connoisseurs who have been able to gauge the quality of his pictures against those of the same or similar subjects by other artists—or by Canaletto himself.

Thus—to take an example from the first of these categories—we find that by far the most perceptive comment to be made on the art of Canaletto in the eighteenth century was published (only three years after his death) by Antonio Zanetti the Younger, who spent all his life in Venice and who wrote an extremely valuable account of Venetian painting: "In his pictures Canaletto combined nature and artistic license with such skill that his works appear to be absolutely accurate to those who judge them only according to the principles of good sense; but those with real understanding will find in them great judgment in the choice of views, in the distribution of figures and space and in the arrangement of light and shade—as well as beautiful clarity and vitality and ease of color and brushwork: the effects of a serene personality and happy genius."[3] More negative, but in its own way equally significant, is the earlier observation made by George Vertue in 1749 when Canaletto was in England:

> On the whole of him something is obscure or strange. he dos not produce works so well done as those of Venice or other parts of Italy.

31

which are in Collections here. and done by him there. especially his figures in his works done here, are apparently much inferior to those done abroad. which are surprizeingly well done & with great freedom & variety—his water & his skys at no time excellent or with natural freedom. & what he has done here his prospects of Trees woods or handling or pencilling of that part not various nor so skillfull as might be expected.[4]

This is the first recorded comment on that change in the artist's style—from the bold, fresh, dramatic touch of his earlier works to his later more mannered, dry, calligraphic, bland manner—which has played such a large role in recent discussions of Canaletto, but which (as can be seen from many references in inventories, sale catalogues, and so on) was familiar enough in the eighteenth and nineteenth centuries.

However, most of the sparse written accounts of Canaletto's achievements dating from his lifetime and from the decades following his death are respectful, uninteresting, and very repetitive. He was given credit for having made use of the camera obscura and for having painted for Francesco Algarotti an art-historical fantasy of the Rialto according to the supposed designs of Palladio, and it was often claimed that Tiepolo had painted the figures in his views. The poetry of his finest paintings and even of his etchings made little impression. Canaletto was famous because he had made the appearance of the main sites of Venice more famous even than those of Rome by churning out dozens of works mass-produced for the English market. So determined were travelers to see Venice through Canaletto's eyes, and Canaletto through their experience of Venice, that even so visually sensitive and "pre-Romantic" a writer as William Beckford could note in 1780 that "I have no terms to describe the variety of pillars, of pediments, of mouldings, and cornices, some Grecian, others Saracenic, that adorn these edifices, of which the pencil of Canaletti conveys so perfect an idea as to render all verbal description superfluous."[5] Today's reader, nervously aware of the arrival on the scene of Ruskin little more than half a century later, will surely envy the happy insouciance of such connoisseurship. By 1780 Francesco Guardi had, for a generation at least, been painting scenes of Venice with a feeling for its atmosphere more in keeping—one might have thought—with Beckford's own emotions when in that city than were the

familiar views by Canaletto; but although works by the two artists were often confused, when Guardi is actually singled out for comment by his contemporaries he is nearly always stigmatized for his lack of accuracy compared to that of Canaletto. At this early stage, therefore, an awareness of Guardi served primarily to reinforce the stereotype of Canaletto as an absolutely faithful delineator of his native city.

Although the English were widely believed to enjoy a monopoly of Canaletto's pictures, a certain number (which often can no longer be traced and whose authenticity must consequently remain somewhat uncertain) are recorded as having belonged to some of the leading French collectors of the ancien régime—Jean de Julienne, the Prince de Conti, and Blondel D'Azincourt, for instance; and when in 1797, the twelve Ducal Ceremonies and Festivals, now belonging to the Louvre, were confiscated by the French government from the collection of an émigré, they were believed to be by Canaletto—although in fact they had been painted by Guardi from engravings made by Giovanni Battista Brustoloni after drawings by Canaletto. Real Canalettos, of great beauty, were to be found in the palaces of the Princes of Liechtenstein in Vienna and elsewhere, and in the royal gallery of Dresden. Very few pictures by him remained in Venice itself, although the standard reference books published there (as indeed elsewhere) always referred to him with admiration. In his later years he seems to have suffered from some neglect, but he had earlier enjoyed considerable success and he could always command high prices. And after his death pictures by him, or attributed to him, continued to do well in the salerooms.

During the nineteenth century paintings by him—including some of the best—could be seen with some ease in England. Indeed, what is by common consent his masterpiece, *"The Stonemason's Yard"* (cat. no. 32), was exhibited in the recently founded National Gallery from 1828, and was thus the first picture by him to become widely accessible, for the Canalettos in the Dulwich Picture Gallery, including the famous *Old Walton Bridge* (cat. no. 73), were only acquired some years later. Moreover, the practice of organizing loan exhibitions of Old Masters in London meant that, from 1824, there was scarcely a year when his pictures were not on view—at the British Institution

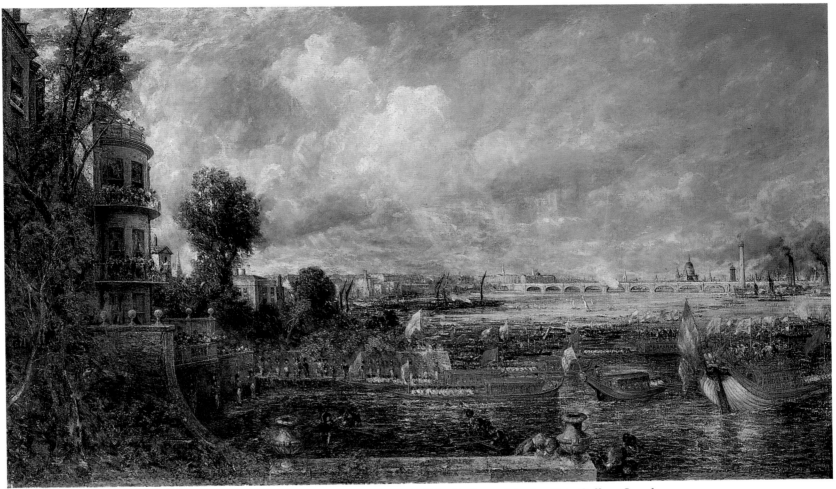

Fig. 12. John Constable, *The Opening of Waterloo Bridge seen from Whitehall Stairs, June 18th 1817*. Tate Gallery, London.

and later at the Royal Academy, and the innumerable Canalettos in country houses were diligently recorded by visitors.

Ever since the periods when Canaletto had lived in England, he had exerted a significant influence directly on topographical artists such as Samuel Scott and William Marlow and indirectly on the squiggles which Thomas Rowlandson used to such comic effect in his drawings and watercolors. It is of course obvious that it was very difficult indeed to paint any view of Venice which did not in some way reflect Canaletto's remarkable coverage of the city—as can be seen in the works of such painters as Bonington (who copied a Canaletto on one occasion),[6] James Holland, and Samuel Prout. Yet such evident debts of gifted, but minor, artists attracted little attention, whereas the two greatest landscape painters of the first half of the nineteenth century—Constable and Turner—both seem to have seen Canaletto as at once a challenge and an inspiration, even though (or perhaps just because) their pictures looked so very different from his.

33

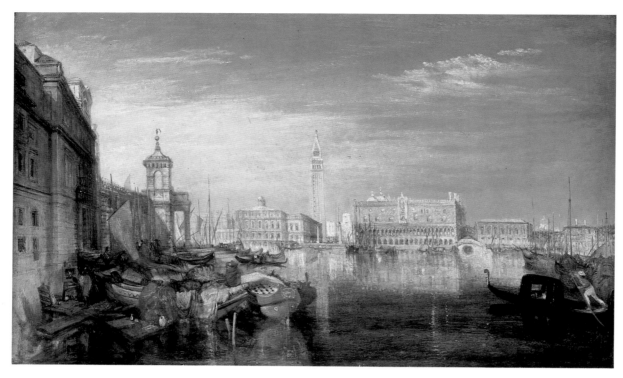

Fig. 13. J. M. W. Turner, *Bridge of Sighs, Ducal Palace and Custom House, Venice: Canaletti painting*. Tate Gallery, London.

Constable's *The Opening of Waterloo Bridge seen from Whitehall Stairs, June 18th 1817* (fig. 12), on which he began work before 1819 although he did not exhibit the full-scale picture until 1832, was the grandest view of the city to have been painted since the death of Canaletto more than half a century earlier;[7] moreover, it treated a theme which Canaletto had very much made his own: a ceremonial barge, a bridge spanning the Thames, and St. Paul's, with the spires of other Wren churches in the background. Constable was certainly familiar with Canaletto's principles of composing Venetian views because he owned the sets of engravings after them which had been made by Antonio Visentini and Giovanni Battista Brustoloni.[8] He must surely have been pleased when, in 1822, his usually rather guarded admirer Bishop John Fisher went "into raptures" over what seems to have been a large preliminary oil sketch of *Waterloo Bridge* and proclaimed that it was "equal to Cannelletti."[9] Constable's biographer and friend, C. R. Leslie, tells us that when the completed painting itself was exhibited ten years later the comparison with Canaletto was made again—but "to Constable's great disadvantage," for the style of his painting struck people as being "very unfinished" and entirely lacking in the "precision of . . . execution" for which Canaletto was then so highly admired. Leslie, whose superb *Memoirs of the Life of John Constable* appeared in the following decade, concludes his account of the reception of *Waterloo Bridge* with advice of great wisdom that has (fortunately for the writer of this essay) invariably been ignored: "I have seen it often since it was exhibited, and I will venture to say that the noonday splendour of its colour would make almost any work of Canaletti, if placed beside it, look like moonlight. But such pictures ought not to be compared, each has its own excellence, and nothing can be more true than Constable's remark that *'fine pictures neither want nor will bear comparison.'"*[10]

One year after the appearance of Constable's *Waterloo Bridge* at the Royal Academy, Turner exhibited there a painting whose link with Canaletto was even more explicit—*Bridge of Sighs,*

Ducal Palace and Custom House, Venice: Canaletti painting (fig. 13). It was well received, and *The Athenaeum* declared that Turner's style was "worth Canaletti's ten times over," but in fact the picture—for which the initial stimulus may have been provided by Bonington and Clarkson Stanfield—was certainly intended primarily as an act of homage to Canaletto.[11] The composition was derived in part from one of Canaletto's own paintings which Turner would have known through the engraving of it by Visentini,[12] although Turner radically altered (and hence rendered impossible) the vantage point from which it is supposed to be seen. The appearance of Canaletto himself, "got up like one of the Turkish sailors in his own pictures, standing on a plank in the water in front of a picture in a heavy gold frame on an easel" is—it has rightly been pointed out—"almost comic in its absurdity."[13]

Ruskin, whose life and aesthetic views were to be so intimately linked (in very different ways) with Turner and Venice and Canaletto, never once referred to this painting which combined all three. He may well have felt somewhat embarrassed by its existence, for in 1843, in the first volume of *Modern Painters*—the book that he produced to glorify the achievement of Turner (to whom his particular loyalty had been aroused partly because of savage attacks made on another of that artist's Venetian subject paintings, *Juliet and Her Nurse*)—he wrote the famous diatribes that mark a milestone in Canaletto's reputation:

> The mannerism of Canaletto is the most degraded that I know in the whole range of art. Professing the most servile and mindless imitation, it imitates nothing but the blackness of the shadows; . . . it gives the buildings neither their architectural beauty nor their ancestral dignity, for there is no texture of stone nor character of age in Canaletto's touch. . . . Let it be observed that I find no fault with Canaletto for his want of poetry, of feeling, of artistical thoughtfulness in treatment, or of the various other virtues which he does not so much as profess. He professes nothing but coloured daguerreotypeism. . . . Canaletto possesses no virtue except that of dexterous imitation of commonplace light and shade. . . .[14]

It has often been pointed out that Ruskin was only twenty-four when he published *Modern Painters* and that his knowledge of art was then very limited indeed; moreover, it has also been emphasized that in the specific case of Canaletto he was

liable to confuse that painter's works with others by imitators and followers.[15] All this is true—but it hardly matters. After all, *"The Stonemason's Yard"* had long been in the National Gallery, and in any case Ruskin continued to express the same or similar views about Canaletto well after he had acquired very wide experience of art of all kinds: as late as 1887 the best thing he could bring himself to say about the painter was that "after all, he was a good workman in oils, whereas so much of Turner's work is going to rack and ruin." The truth is that Ruskin needed Canaletto, as he needed certain other artists, as a foil to enhance the special merits which he attributed to Turner. There are some painters—one thinks of Michelangelo and Veronese, Rembrandt and Constable—whose treatment by Ruskin can cause us real surprise, but it is almost impossible to imagine him responding, under any circumstances, to that "poetry, . . . feeling, . . . artistical thoughtfulness in treatment" which, so he claimed, did not even concern Canaletto but which are surely so evident to those familiar with his finest works. Having said this, however, it must be acknowledged that Ruskin's devastating onslaughts on the "miserable, virtueless, heartless mechanism"[16] of Canaletto's technique (and hence its unfaithfulness to those variations of texture and detail which meant so much to Ruskin) do apply with real force to many of the late works and, still more, to those by Canaletto's imitators. Ruskin very rarely mentions specific paintings by Canaletto, but the chances are that during the course of his life he could have seen almost as many good as bad pictures attributed to him; that he made use of the bad ones to denigrate the good was as necessary for him as it had been for Winckelmann to visualize the greatness of Greek sculpture through the many inferior copies of it that were known to him.

It is not at all clear that Ruskin's "determined depreciation" of Canaletto seriously affected the standing of the painter with the public at large. Canaletto had in any case never figured much in the literature of art, and there does not seem to have been any significant variation in the prices paid at auction for his works. Two years after the first edition of *Modern Painters*, the *Art-Union* castigated "the mania for Canalettis, which has long proved a successful delusion to our *quasi* amateurs," and referred ominously to the "wholesale manufacture of this master existing at Richmond, in Surrey,"[17] but this comment was due to that journal's hatred for aristocratic taste and for foreign Old Masters in general rather than to any sympathy with the ideas of Ruskin: emphasizing the (certainly widespread) practice of forgery was a favorite device of the editor to encourage the purchase of modern English pictures.

The fortunes of Canaletto outside England followed a rather different course. We have seen that some pictures by him were certainly to be found in France before the end of the eighteenth century, and we also know that in 1739 Président de Brosses, who saw two *Views of Venice* by Canaletto in the Barbarigo collection in that city (very early works, presumably), thought highly of him: "This painter excels in the art of painting views in a light, lively, highly colored style with a strong sense of perspective; his pictures are becoming very expensive and are in great demand." Soon afterward he repeated this opinion and went into somewhat greater detail about Canaletto's success: "The English have so spoiled this workman [*ouvrier*] by offering him three times more than he asks for his pictures that it is no longer possible to have any dealings with him."[18] The context makes it quite clear that de Brosses is using the term "spoiled" [*gâté*] in a strictly financial sense, but by 1739 the other, even more pejorative, significance of the word was already becoming painfully apparent to those who saw Canaletto's recent work. Mariette, curiously enough, felt that the wonderful etchings which enabled Canaletto to escape (temporarily) from the tyranny of his unimaginative clients were marred "by an excessively even and unsubtle touch [*touche trop égale et trop peu délicate*]."[19] Although the opinion of this great connoisseur must always command our attention, it is difficult to follow him here—and fortunately few critics have ever done so. During the first two or three decades of the nineteenth century a certain number of pictures by Canaletto passed through the Paris salerooms, but the real vogue for his work there seems to date from about 1830. We are told by a well-informed dealer writing in 1841 that some years earlier "il y avait fureur pour les Canaletti, les Guardi, de l'école Vénitienne"[20]—the two names coupled with no distinction made between them. Nearly a quarter of a century later, in 1864, Théodore Lejeune's useful *Guide théorique et pratique de l'amateur de tableaux* explained that "the works of Canaletti

are sought after by true connoisseurs, who recognize in them the qualities which go to make up a true painter. Linear and aerial perspective, harmony and a faithful representation of appearances are all combined in his work. Canaletti rarely painted his figures; Tiepolo was nearly always entrusted with this job."[21] Lejeune's sources of information and his connoisseurship are not very reliable and the titles he gives to pictures (such as *View of Venice*) are so vague as to be useless, but the list that he provides of works believed to be by Canaletto offers some gauge of the artist's popularity all over Europe. Apart from a great many members of the English nobility and gentry, other owners of Canalettos included the Louvre and various French provincial museums; the museums of St. Petersburg, Berlin, and especially Dresden; and the galleries of the Princes Liechtenstein, Yusupov, and Esterhazy: the French Revolution had brought about some modifications, but locations had not changed very significantly from a hundred years earlier. Perhaps the most revealing aspect of Lejeune's account is the exceedingly brief reference he makes to Guardi: "A pupil of Canaletto, this painter is one of his best imitators. Were it not for the crudity of his color and its lack of harmony, it would be difficult to distinguish the master from the pupil, especially when the figures in Canaletto's pictures have been painted by Tiepolo." This attitude was to be considerably modified within a generation.

It was in the 1870s that Francesco Guardi began to attract serious attention from French writers and critics, and—as was inevitable— he was soon being compared with Canaletto.[22] By 1878 Charles Yriarte could write that "il [Guardi] est beaucoup plus piquant que lui [Canaletto]." He was a more original colorist and his talent was more personal; no one in his field could surpass Guardi when he took the trouble to follow his own ideas and carry them out. His prodigious facility and his sparkling and witty technique, combined with a sense for atmospheric transparency and light which had never been equaled, made of him a painter in a class of his own—in the face of whom even Canaletto, "so admirable in canvases such as the *Grand Canal* and the *Salute* in the Louvre, seems a cold and insipid artist." The fact that one of these pictures is certainly not by Canaletto and the other only doubtfully so hardly matters. The rise in Guardi's critical fortunes, which accompanied a general taste for an "unfinished" style of painting during the last decades of the nineteenth century, necessarily involved some depreciation of the works of Canaletto—although the process was carried out with none of the ferocity that had characterized Ruskin's championship of Turner. It was in France that in 1894 Adrien Moureau published the first book to be devoted exclusively to Canaletto[23] (an earlier German monograph had paired him with his nephew Bellotto). Moureau's short study gives a sympathetic appraisal of Canaletto's paintings, etchings, and drawings, but it is neither informative nor revealing. In the context of this essay its most significant feature is the repetition, in a slightly more sophisticated form than previously, of that confusion (which we have already come across so often) between current interpretations of Venice—the subject of Canaletto's most important paintings—and his manner of portraying the city. Thus we are told on one page that "when by chance they are not reproducing some festival or solemn ceremony, the canvases of Antonio Canal are characterized by an indefinable melancholy, like some fever exhaled from its waters" (this is eighteen years before Thomas Mann's *Death in Venice*), while—shortly afterward—Moureau explains that Canaletto was certainly no dreamer, but that "such is the magical power of Venice that we are tempted to attribute to him the poetry which is exhaled from his subjects themselves or which we add to our memories of them."[24]

It was, however, two Americans settled in Europe who, during the last years of the nineteenth century, were to make the most surprising and impressive observations regarding Canaletto. It is not clear exactly when Whistler "discovered" this painter who, a hundred years before him, had already immortalized Venice and London, but by the mid-1880s he was in thrall to him and repeatedly proclaimed his greatness as an artist (and not just as a topographer) with an inspiringly reckless conviction that has absolutely no parallels in earlier writing on Canaletto. An American visitor to London reported that as soon as he entered the National Gallery in London, Whistler "went at once to almost *smell* the Canalettos," and in 1896 we again hear of him in the National Gallery looking at the Canalettos and Guardis:

Whistler could not weary of . . . Canaletto's big red church [*The Doge visiting the Church and Scuola di S. Rocco*?; fig. 3] and the tiny

Rotunda at Vauxhall [*Ranelagh, interior of the Rotunda*; fig. 11] with the little figures, from which Hogarth learned so much. Whistler always acknowledged Guardi's influence, though it had not led him in Venice to paint pictures like Guardi or Canaletto either. And he never tired of pointing out that great artists like Guardi and Canaletto and Velasquez, who were born and worked in the South, did not try to paint sunlight, but kept their work grey and low in tone.[25]

It was some time in the first half of the 1880s that he is known to have made this most striking (yet hardly very accurate) analogy for the first time. Once again, it was an examination of Turner that led to a revaluation of Canaletto—but on this occasion the relative positions of the two artists were totally reversed (although we have seen that by now even Ruskin had been compelled to concede the superiority of Canaletto's technique). Whistler told his Australian admirer, the painter Mortimer Menpes, who was looking at the Turners in the National Gallery:

"No: this is not big work. The colour is not good. It is too prismatic. There is no reserve. Moreover, it is not the work of a man who knows his trade. Turner was struggling with the wrong medium. He ought not to have painted. He should have written. Come from this work, which is full of uncertainty. Come and look at the paintings of a man who was a true workman." So saying, he led me straight to a Canaletto. "Now," he said, "here is the man who was absolute master of his materials. In this work you will find no uncertainty." He talked of his drawing and of the crisp, clean way in which the tones were put on. "Do you know," he said earnestly and credulously [*sic*], "there are people who maintain that the figures in pictures of Canaletto were painted by another man? Now, isn't that absurd? Of course those figures were painted by the master hand of Canaletto. Only he could have painted them. But then," Whistler broke off suddenly, "after all, what's the use? His work is as little understood as mine." We looked at a Velasquez. Whistler said: "Here is another good workman. He, too, knew his trade and his tools. I place him upon the same plane as Canaletto. The two men run side by side. Their works are equally fine."[26]

In 1892, however, Henry James felt very differently about the artist whom he described as "the perfidious Canaletto," and it is worth quoting in full the extraordinary (and baffling) lines that James devoted to him:

I shall not stay to unravel the mystery of this prosaic painter's malpractices; he falsified without fancy, and as he apparently transposed at will the objects he reproduced, one is never sure of the particular view that may have constituted his subject. It would look exactly like such and such a place if almost everything were not different. San Simeone Profeta appears to hang there upon the wall; but it is on the wrong side of the Canal and the other elements quite fail to correspond. One's confusion is the greater because one doesn't know that everything may not really have changed, even beyond all probability—though it's only in America that churches cross the street or the river—and the mixture of the recognisable and the different makes the ambiguity maddening, all the more that the painter is almost as attaching as he is bad. Thanks at any rate to the white church, domed and porticoed, on the top of its steps, the traveller emerging for the first time upon the terrace of the railway-station seems to have a Canaletto before him.[27]

It is not at all clear what picture by Canaletto Henry James can have had in mind; certainly there is no existing capriccio that reincorporates the church of S. Simeone Piccolo (to which he must be referring) into some imaginary setting (although there is a rare print by Wagner after Canaletto that does so),[28] and the reproductive engravings by Visentini of Canaletto's views of the Grand Canal are all in the same sense as the originals. More interesting, however, is the fact that (unless he was utilizing some earlier source not known to me) James appears to have been —however misguidedly—the first writer to challenge the almost universally accepted notion that Canaletto's main claim to fame was that he had been a strictly accurate topographical artist who once in a while allowed himself the luxury of a witty caprice. James's attitude was certainly dismissive—but it might be argued that only thereafter could Canaletto's art begin to be treated with the seriousness it deserved.

During the twentieth century Canaletto's gifts have won increasing recognition and he is no longer omitted from general surveys of European art. A few lines had already been devoted to him in Berenson's *Venetian Painters of the Renaissance*, first published in 1894. But with few exceptions—such as the rare small exhibition, occasionally pioneering articles by W. G. Constable and Hilda Finberg (and a monograph on the drawings by von Hadeln), and the purchase by the Boston Museum of Fine Arts in 1939 of the one indubitable masterpiece by Canaletto yet to find a home in the United States (cat. no. 51)—it was not until after the Second World War that the taste for Canaletto changed in direction and intensity. We have seen that his standing has

always remained remarkably impervious to fashion or to the opinions of critics, however great, and it seems likely that the last writer of supreme eloquence to refer to his work will have made no more of an impact on the general consciousness than Mariette or Ruskin or Whistler or James. In 1946, after visiting the exhibition of Venetian paintings which had just been removed from wartime storage, Roberto Longhi wrote his dazzling *Viatico per cinque secoli di pittura veneziana*. In discussing the art of the eighteenth century he tried to reverse the received opinion that the great masters of the period had been the large-scale history painters Piazzetta and Tiepolo, both of whom he felt to have been "reactionary," and by implication almost protofascist; instead he argued the case for such "enlightened," but hitherto less-regarded, painters as Rosalba Carriera, Pietro Longhi, the "great" Canaletto, and (to a much lesser extent) Guardi. There was in fact only one Canaletto in the exhibition— the capriccio presented by the artist as a reception piece to the Academy, then (and until very recently) the sole picture remaining in his native city (cat. no. 85). Longhi uses this as his point of departure for some superbly evocative lines, which can, alas, only be travestied in my crude paraphrase. He exalted the European dimension of Canaletto's art and enrolled him in the ranks of Italian social critics: "He trained his conviction of absolute truth (so characteristic of the Enlightenment) onto the golden light, cut through by barriers of shadow, of futile afternoons in a Venice which was crumbling and cracking like the wrinkles in his wonderful etchings, and he conveys in these pictures all the stereoscopic melancholy of the images in a peep show."[29]

The great flood of international exhibitions, catalogues, and lavishly illustrated monographs that has marked artistic life during the last forty years—only a few of which events can be mentioned here—has transformed public appreciation of Canaletto, as of many other little-studied painters. The extraordinary range and quality of Canaletto's drawings and paintings in the Royal Collection have been fully revealed in catalogues by K. T. Parker (1948) and Michael Levey (1964), and in the unforgettable exhibition organized by Sir Oliver Millar in the Queen's Gallery in 1980–81. The year 1954 saw the publication by Vittorio Moschini of the first book on the artist to contain a really substantial number (about three hundred in all) of large-scale illustrations, although it was Francis Watson's volume of five years earlier that inaugurated modern research into Canaletto as a painter—research which has culminated in the two editions of W. G. Constable's full catalogue raisonné (1962 and 1976) and in the books and studies by J. G. Links, who was also responsible for revising Constable's catalogue. Volumes by Terisio Pignatti and other scholars on the drawings and by Ruth Bromberg on the etchings have helped to restore Canaletto's fame as a graphic artist—as did the exhibition of drawings by Canaletto and Guardi that was held at the Cini Foundation in Venice in 1962. Two years after that came the pioneering exhibition in Canada of paintings by Canaletto; then, in 1967, an exhibition in the Palazzo Ducale gave the city of Venice its first opportunity to see a large number of pictures by him (alongside the works of precursors, contemporaries, and followers) since

the sale to George III some two hundred years earlier of the great collection that had been built up by Canaletto's principal patron and agent, Consul Smith. This was followed in 1982 by another, carefully selected, exhibition in Venice confined to those works whose original locations could be securely documented. There have, in addition, been a few archival discoveries, some controversial reinterpretations, and the usual huge rise in auction prices (which, however, have been common to Old Masters in general, just as the decline in monetary value of his works toward the end of the last century and the first decades of this one was a feature of the market as a whole). A huge amount of information is still concealed from us (the man, incidentally, remains as inscrutable as he ever was), but we can at least claim that Canaletto's art and stature are better understood today than they were just over a hundred years ago when Whistler first proclaimed the supreme quality of his best work.

NOTES

1. Quoted in Links, *Canaletto and His Patrons*, 1977, p. 28.
2. Letter of 18 August 1725 from Alessandro Marchesini to Stefano Conti, quoted in C/L, p. 13.
3. Zanetti, *Della pittura veneziana*, 1771, p. 462.
4. *Vertue Note Books*, III, p. 149.
5. *Italy; with Sketches of Spain and Portugal*, by the Author of "Vathek," 2d ed., rev., 2 vols. (London, 1834), I, p. 101.
6. C/L 169.
7. Graham Reynolds, *The Later Paintings and Drawings of John Constable*, 2 vols. (New Haven and London, 1984), text pp. 233–34 (no. 32.1), and pl. 819.
8. *John Constable: Further Documents and Correspondence*, edited by Leslie Parris, Conal Shields, and Ian Fleming-Williams (Tate Gallery and Suffolk Records Society, 1975), pp. 28 and 37.
9. *John Constable's Correspondence: VI. The Fishers*, edited by R. B. Beckett (Suffolk Records Society, 1968), p. 93.
10. C. R. Leslie, *Memoirs of the Life of John Constable*, reprint, edited by Jonathan Mayne, of 2d ed., 1845 (London: Phaidon, 1951), pp. 207–8.
11. Martin Butlin and Evelyn Joll, *The Paintings of J. M. W. Turner*, rev. ed., 2 vols. (New Haven and London, 1984), text pp. 200–201 (no. 349) and pl. 356.
12. John Gage, *J. M. W. Turner: 'A Wonderful Range of Mind'* (New Haven and London, 1987), p. 135.
13. A. J. Finberg, *In Venice with Turner* (London, 1930), p. 80.
14. Ruskin, *Modern Painters*, I, in the *Works*, III, pp. 215–16.
15. Links, *Canaletto and His Patrons*, 1977, p. 36.
16. Ruskin, *Modern Painters*, I, in the *Works*, III, p. 214.
17. "Picture Sales of the Month, &c.," *The Art-Union*, September 1845, p. 294.
18. Charles de Brosses, *Lettres d'Italie*, pp. 216 (letter XVII, "Mémoire des principaux tableaux...") and 399 (letter XXXI, 24 November 1739).
19. Mariette, *Abécédario*, p. 298.
20. Ch. Roehn, *Physiologie du commerce des arts* (Paris, 1841), p. 78.
21. Théodore Lejeune, *Guide théorique et pratique de l'amateur de tableaux*, II (Paris, 1864), pp. 188–90.
22. See Francis Haskell, "Francesco Guardi and the Nineteenth Century," in *Problemi Guardeschi: Atti del Convegno di studi...1965* (Venice, 1967), pp. 58–60.
23. Adrien Moureau, *Antonio Canal, dit le Canaletto*, in series Les Artistes Célèbres (Paris, 1894).
24. Moureau, *Antonio Canal*, 1894, pp. 47 and 84.
25. E. R. and J. Pennell, *The Life of James McNeill Whistler*, 5th ed. (London, 1911), pp. 230 and 336.
26. Mortimer Menpes, *Whistler As I Knew Him* (London, 1904), pp. 80–81.
27. Henry James, *Italian Hours* (1909; reprint, New York: Grove Press, 1979), p. 52.
28. C/L, p. 680, no. 57.2.
29. Longhi, *Viatico per cinque secoli di pittura veneziana*, 1946, in *Opere complete*, X, p. 34: "Quella sua certezza illuministica di verità assoluta, volta alla luce dorata, a traversoni d'ombra, dei pomeriggi inutili in una Venezia che si sbriciola e screpola come le rughe delle sue mirabili acquaforti, ha la mestizia stereoscopica delle vedute del 'mondonuovo'."

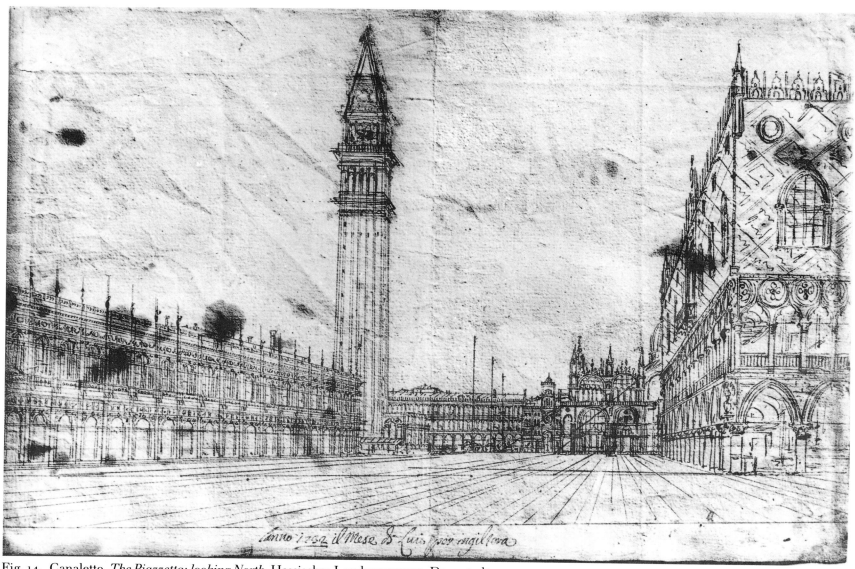

Fig. 14. Canaletto, *The Piazzetta: looking North*. Hessisches Landesmuseum, Darmstadt.

FANTASY AND REALITY IN CANALETTO'S DRAWINGS

by Alessandro Bettagno

Giovanni Antonio Canal, like many of the great eighteenth-century Venetian masters, not only was a prolific painter but also executed a considerable number of drawings, some of exceptional quality. He demonstrated through his rich and varied explorations of the graphic idiom that his poetic and artistic sensibilities in drawing match those of Piazzetta, the Tiepolos, or Guardi, not to mention Giovanni Battista Piranesi, who devoted all his energy and genius to the graphic medium. When studying a master it is always difficult to avoid the clear-cut distinction usually made between his paintings and his drawings, but for the student of drawing it is important to keep the fundamental unity of the artist's work firmly in mind. The art historian must necessarily take a tortuous and difficult road that leads from the images set down on the delicate medium of paper to the oil paintings, a path fraught with doubts and missing links but the only way of coming to a fuller understanding of a given artist's total work.

In examining Canaletto's graphic production, the preliminary questions are how many drawings can be attributed to him, and what are the particular qualities, mannerisms, and techniques to be found in this body of work. The largest group of Canaletto's drawings is in the prestigious Royal Collection at Windsor Castle. Acquired by George III in 1762 from Joseph Smith, the British Consul in Venice and a key figure in Canaletto's life, the collection consists of 143 drawings authoritatively catalogued by K. T. Parker.[1] Almost all of them are of the highest quality, and some must rank among the artist's most important graphic works. The collection does not, however, include figure studies or documentary sheets, or even preparatory sketches, but only finished drawings. Owing to his arrangement with Canaletto, Consul Smith had the pick of the Venetian artist's output, and the importance of the Englishman's holdings is beyond question. It is also reasonable to suppose that Canaletto had a vested interest in the consul's collection: after all, Smith was his principal client and patron as well as a highly useful intermediary, purveying his works to English collectors.

Among Canaletto's drawings in the Royal Library, Windsor, the ones executed during his stay in England and in his later years in Venice are perhaps less successful. On the other hand, Smith's collection included a portion of Canaletto's most brilliant graphic work and a few of the most incisive and moving Venetian drawings of any age: the paper's dazzling whiteness, the precise pen work, and the painterly handling of wash are all exceptional. Indeed, the only problem with finished drawings like those in the Royal Collection is that, in their accuracy, attention to detail, precise line, and highly transparent wash, they appear so perfect that the spectator is at a loss, technical mastery seeming almost to override the poetic content and aesthetic value of the work. Thus, at times the artist's technical skill appears to compete with his imaginative faculties, causing one to wonder whether the drawing does not lose out on one of its essential aspects: a feeling of nascent creativity.

The collection at Windsor covers the artist's range of subjects and all periods of his career from the late 1720s (cat. nos. 88, 89) to his years of artistic maturity. In fact there is evidence, such as the last great capriccio (cat. no. 118), that Smith continued to purchase Canaletto's drawings until the time he sold his collection to George III. The drawings were originally kept in an album, significantly titled *Antonio Canal Experimenta et Schedae*. Represented here by sixteen drawings, the Canalettos at Windsor are probably the most important part of Smith's extraordinary collection, described in 1929 by Detlev von Hadeln, a pioneer in this field, as "Alpha and Omega for the knowledge of Canaletto as a draughtsman.[2]

It should be noted that, while Canaletto is well represented in British collections and in a number of American museums, his work is almost completely absent from those in other countries. This resulted from his quite deliberate disposition of both drawings and paintings, based on his arrangements with Consul Smith in the late 1720s and early 1730s. The encounter with Smith was a turning point in Canaletto's career, for while his early clients had been Venetians, foreign residents of Venice, or linked in some way with the city, from then on he dealt almost exclusively with British collectors.

The catalogue raisonné of Canaletto's work examines many drawings in addition to those at Windsor, including the sheets comprising the Cagnola sketchbook (in the Accademia, Venice), as well as a few other recently identified works.[3] In all, no fewer than five hundred of Canaletto's drawings—including repetitions, different versions, and autograph copies—have come down to us. This in itself is a substantial figure, but if the artist's prolific output as a painter and his techniques as a draftsman are taken into account, his complete graphic production (finished compositions, preparatory studies, and notes for his paintings, etchings, and the drawings themselves) must have been many times greater. All this material except for the finished drawings was clearly ignored by Consul Smith but was nonetheless appreciated by other collectors such as the Venetian connoisseur, intellectual, and man of letters Francesco Algarotti: reliable sources indicate that a whole series of extremely interesting drawings belonged to him. Finally, it should not be forgotten that several numbered sheets exist (e.g., cat. no. 125) from which it can safely be assumed that they belonged to albums whose contents were dispersed, and subsequently destroyed, or lost sight of.

There must have been some hundreds of sketchbook sheets, demonstrating all of Canaletto's graphic techniques, from the simplest to the most complex. His basic tools were graphite, red chalk, and black chalk, but he also made use of pen and brush for more varied effects. K. T. Parker established a series of careful distinctions and, through a close study of the pen and ink drawings at Windsor, even managed to identify the different types of pen used: animal (including the common goose quill), reed, and metal. It is thus possible to distinguish the changes from quills (for pictorial effects and soft lines), to reed pens (with their more sparing lines), and finally to metal points, used for sharp lines and fine modulations. The latter were very rare in Canaletto's time and may have been employed only in his later years or during this stay in England.

We have no information about those "bellissimi disegni per gli scenarii" (beautiful drawings for scenery) mentioned by Anton Maria Zanetti the Younger in his biographical sketch of Canaletto in *Della pittura veneziana.*[4] Drawings of this sort would have shed some light on the artist's earliest years as a set designer. We do know that it was in Rome, where he had gone with his father, Bernardo, in 1719 to design the sets for two operas by Alessandro Scarlatti—*Tito Sempronio Greco* and *Turno Aricino*—at the Teatro Capranica, that he decided to give up this work to dedicate all his time, as Zanetti remarked, to painting views after nature.

Canaletto's earliest graphic work is perhaps the series of drawings of Roman subjects at the British Museum. Zanetti noted of the artist's experience in Rome that "he found beautiful subjects there," especially among the ruins of antiquity (fig. 15). (Twenty years later Piranesi, another young Venetian master, was so impressed by Rome on his first trip to that city that he decided to devote all his skills to portraying her antiquities.) In Canaletto's study of space in these Roman drawings, the young artist showed the effects of his training as a scenographer. This is hardly surprising, for, as Zanetti recalled, he had only recently announced his intention to "*scomunicò . . .* solennemente il teatro" (solemnly excommunicate the theater). Thus, his studies of the ancient monuments are enhanced by swiftly sketched figures in the same style as those in his early Venetian views. The Roman drawings are best considered as marking the transition between the artist's earliest scenographic work and the inventive and inspired views of the mid-1720s.

Among the drawings of this period, mention should be made of the *Grand Canal: the Rialto Bridge from the North* (cat. no. 86), Canaletto's study for the painting, number 8, commissioned by Stefano Conti of Lucca. Letters from Alessandro Marchesini to Conti indicate the date of execution, 1725, and include the valuable comment on Canaletto as a man "who inevitably amazes everyone here who sees his works, which are in the manner of Carlevaris, but light shines out from the sun."[5] The sun, seen on the water in the painting, is indicated in the lower right-

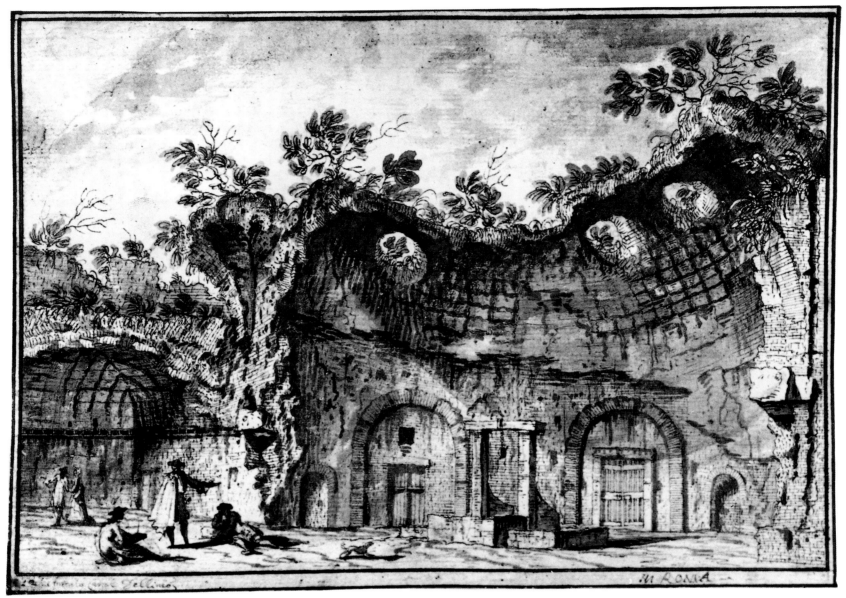

Fig. 15. Canaletto, *A Half-Domed Ruin*. British Museum, London.

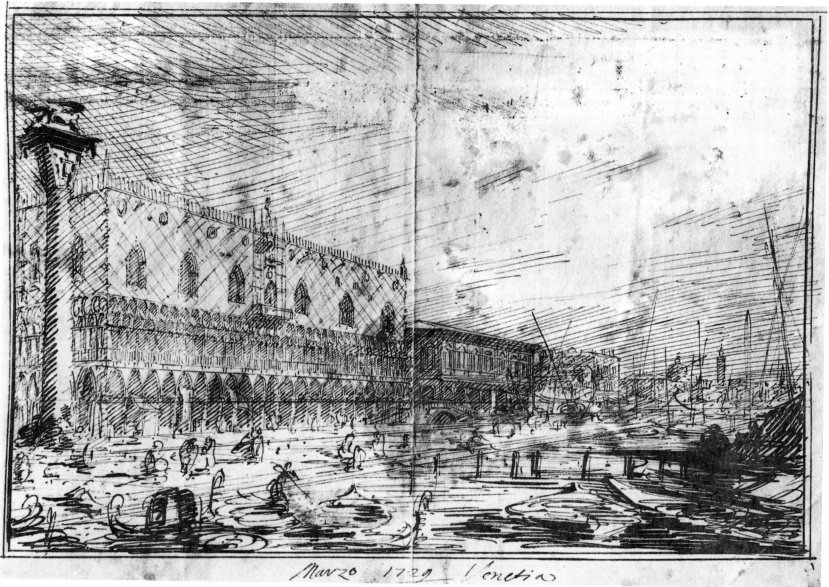

Fig. 16. Canaletto, *Riva degli Schiavoni: looking East.* Hessisches Landesmuseum, Darmstadt.

hand corner of the drawing by the note *Sole*. Marchesini also remarked that the artist painted "non con l'immaginaria mente nelle solite stanze de Pittori…ma…va sempre sul loco, e forma tutto sul vero." This observation, if not entirely correct with respect to the paintings, is pertinent to the drawings and sheds some light on how the new Venetian *vedutista* worked, how his paintings were received, and the success he achieved among his contemporaries.

Canaletto is not known to have made *bozzetti*—small preparatory oil studies for finished pictures—but he did produce works that lie halfway between the initial sketches made on the ground (e.g., in the Cagnola sketchbook at the Accademia) and the finished drawings—ends in themselves—of the sort that belonged to Joseph Smith. Examples of this type of drawing (taking the place of, and thus having much the same function as, *bozzetti*) are the one just mentioned and another which is closely related (cat. no. 87), as well as a view of *The Rialto Bridge from the South* (cat. no. 90). These drawings have a stylistic resemblance to the paintings of the 1720s and show the artist's now mature skills as a painter of *vedute*.

There is an enormous difference between Canaletto's first drawings of Roman antiquity, reflecting the highly popular *rovinismo*, or ruin painting, very much in fashion at the time, and these drawings, which reveal the true spirit of a *vedutista*. It is not always possible for the historian to check and document all of the nuances of development in an artist's work; often, as here, he must simply confine himself to the limited information that is available. From what little we know, it is clear that Canaletto's initial training in the theater, his trip to Rome, and his assimilation of different experiences helped him achieve his first successes as a graphic artist in Venice in the early eighteenth century. Luigi Lanzi noted that he "ama il grand'effetto, e nel produrlo tiene alquanto del Tiepolo" (loves a grand effect, and in this he is influenced by Tiepolo).[6] This period of Canaletto's life, the truly "Venetian" period, came to an end when he met Joseph Smith, who brought him into contact with the tastes and demands of a foreign, particularly English, clientele which led him to change his expressive idiom.

These drawings from the 1720s already demonstrate Canaletto's command of perspective and feeling for space; and although meticulous care is paid to detail, reality is not produced photographically but is interpreted freely and made to *appear* natural. This "pictorial license," as it was perceptively described by Zanetti, was referred to later by Lanzi, who remarked that Canaletto "usa qualche libertà pittoresca…in modo che il comune degli spettatori vi trova natura, e gl'intendenti vi notan arte" (takes certain pictorial liberties…so that the average observer finds nature in his work, and experts art). The effect is intensely pictorial: as the line thickens, the patches of shade become darker, contrasting sharply with the blinding brightness of the areas of paper left untouched.

Another example of Canaletto's work in the 1720s is the *Riva degli Schiavoni: looking East* (fig. 16), in Darmstadt, inscribed *Marzo 1729 Venetia*. The drawing is of great interest and is continually referred to by scholars owing to its precise date and its complex study of perspective. This interest in perspective is more commonly found in the drawings of the 1730s, many of them from Smith's collection. A sheet relating closely to the Darmstadt drawing is *The Bucintoro at the Molo*, now at Windsor and included in the present exhibition (cat. no. 92).

This preoccupation with effects of perspective is even more apparent in another quite exceptional drawing, *The Piazzetta: looking North* (fig. 14), dated 1732, and also in Darmstadt. The work is outstanding for its precision and for its abstract, almost geometric rationality: there is an unreal, illusory sense of space, and the vista is clearly outlined but appears forced. Gone are the hatching and cross-hatching, the abbreviated lines, luminous spaces, and deep shadows. This is a carefully calculated study with nothing hasty, improvised, or summary about it, in marked contrast to the drawings in the Accademia sketchbook.

Donated by Don Guido Cagnola to the Accademia in 1949, the sketchbook contains 138 drawings which form the largest group of so-called documentary sheets, and their main interest lies in their fundamental importance to Canaletto's particular and very personal working method. This preparatory work on the topographic raw material—essential for a *vedutista*—involves the problem of the so-called camera obscura. It was this technique, in fact (his use of it is much discussed and, given the available evidence, there is general agreement in critical circles), which aroused the interest of his contemporaries and

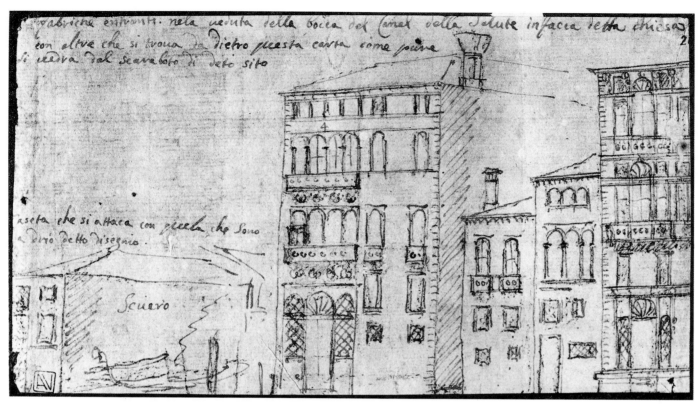

Fig. 17. Canaletto, *Grand Canal: Buildings opposite the Salute.* Gallerie dell'Accademia, Venice.

continues to be a subject of deliberation. We can now more fully understand—praise must go to Canaletto scholars—the different methods and procedures used by the Venetian *vedutista*. Always absolutely free in his approach to the problem of the point of departure for his views, Canaletto was also completely open-minded and informal in the execution of his preparatory or documentary studies. The use of the camera obscura may be seen as part of the artist's fresh approach, and the drawings based on this technique should be considered on a par with the other kinds of *scaraboti* (i.e., very quick, informal sketches), as Canaletto himself described them (see fig. 17, with the word *scaraboto* written by the artist). But it is indeed a happy coincidence that that other *camera ottica*, Canaletto's eye, was then applied to these hasty, improvised, and summary topographical notes. The content of the Accademia sketchbook is varied and includes pages dating from the late 1720s to the early 1730s

which demonstrate the painter's continuing interest in experimentation (already mentioned in connection with the Darmstadt drawings). These pages, together with others from the sketchbook, relate to views in the Bedford series (see figs. 18–21) and the Harvey series which came immediately afterward.

Thus Canaletto's explorations of style and technique marked the beginning of a decade (the 1730s) which was to be very important from the point of view of his graphic work; and as many of the finest drawings that were owned by Joseph Smith are from this period, it is obvious that the results were positive. After the previous decade of drawings rich in pictorial contrasts comes a period of works which demonstrate a more thoughtful approach to perspective. Their tighter, more vibrant handling, at times luminous and dazzling, paved the way for an increasing interest in engraving that found full expression in Canaletto's etchings of the 1740s.

The artist experimented ceaselessly, and from a preference for chiaroscuro, more or less in the manner of Marco Ricci, and to some degree reminiscent of Rembrandt (whose engravings Canaletto probably had occasion to admire in the complete collection which Anton Maria Zanetti the Elder had had in Venice since 1721), he moved on to an essentially sunlit manner, limpid with allover brightness. This particular feature of Canaletto's art was described as early as the eighteenth century by Zanetti the Younger: "una nitidezza e saporita felicità di...pennello, effetti di mente serena e di genio felice" (a brightness and a zestful facility of...stroke, the results of a serene mind and felicitous talent).[7] Canaletto scholars agree in dating to the end of the 1730s a number of extraordinary landscapes and views of the lagoon, among them *Venice from the Punta della Mota* (cat.

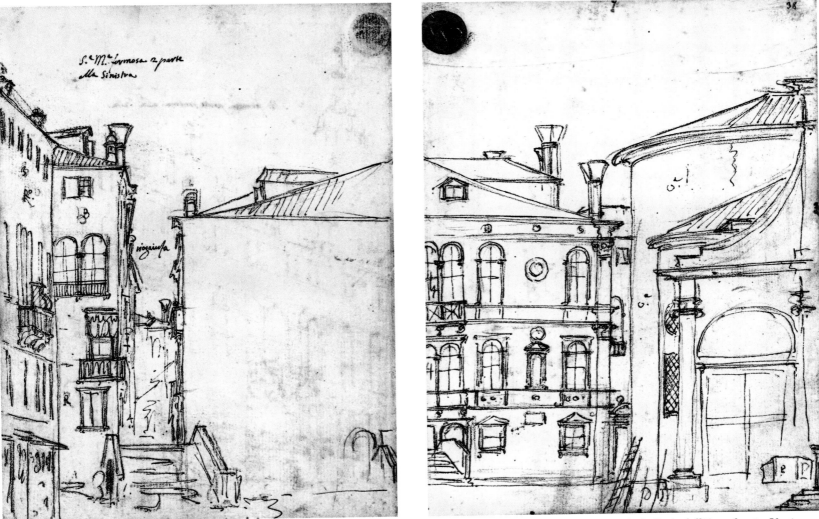

Figs. 18 and 19. Folios 37v and 38r of Canaletto's sketchbook, with studies for *Campo Sta. Maria Formosa* (C/L 278). Gallerie dell'Accademia, Venice.

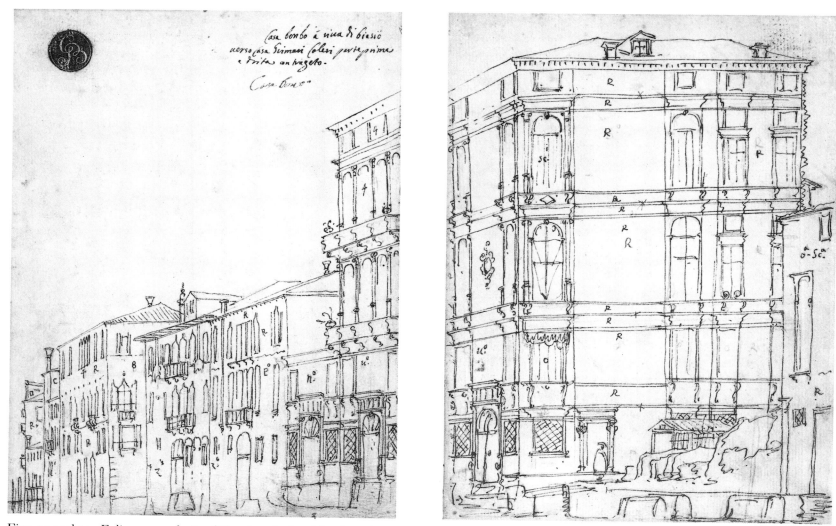

Figs. 20 and 21. Folios 47r and 46v of Canaletto's sketchbook, with studies for cat. no. 49. Gallerie dell'Accademia, Venice.

no. 101) and *The Islands of the Certosa and Sta. Elena* (cat. no. 102), both from Smith's collection and now in the Royal Collection at Windsor.

Compared with the two previous decades, which were for the young *vedutista* a period of transition from the formative years to full maturity, there were fewer contrasts in his work from 1740 to 1750: and this despite the fact that it was a very busy time for Canaletto and was also the period in which he left for England. He continued to experiment with style, something he would do throughout his life. Similarly, he never changed his well-tried working methods, even if, from the subsequent English period and the late Venetian years, there are fewer of the preparatory and documentary drawings, sketched in the characteristically rapid, abbreviated manner.

It had traditionally been thought that in the early 1740s Canaletto went to Rome. Now, however, scholars doubt that the journey ever took place, partly because of an overall reappraisal of Canaletto's oeuvre from a more general point of view, less strictly dependent upon topographical information, but also because his views of Roman subjects (both drawings and paintings) show obvious leanings toward the capriccio. Leaving aside the vexing question of the journey to Rome, the continual stylistic renewal of the artist in this period is of particular interest in the link that forms between the drawings on Venetian themes, executed before his departure for London, and the drawings of English (or Venetian) themes executed in England.

The brilliant chapter of Canaletto's etchings—closer to the spirit and the style of the 1730s—deserves special treatment, as these prints are unique in the work of the artist. There is an immediate precedent in the drawings of Roman subjects—with their strong line, clarity, and luminosity—for certain properties of style that characterize Canaletto's drawings from the 1740s, whether Venetian, Paduan, or English. (It should be noted that the journeys of Canaletto's nephew, Bernardo Bellotto, and the nature of his working relationship with his uncle are rather problematic, and this prevents a complete understanding of Bellotto before he left for Dresden in 1743, and of Canaletto in the years from 1740 to 1745.)

In this exhibition there are some fine drawings which reflect Canaletto's interest in the mainland and Padua. One of these, *A Farm on the Outskirts of Padua*, in the Royal Collection (cat. no. 107), is remarkable for a number of details reminiscent of the engravings on which the artist worked in the same years. Similarly, *Padua: Houses*, in the Kupferstichkabinett, Berlin (cat. no. 105), relates to the sheer poetry and lyricism of the etching of the same subject (although it should not be considered a "preparation" for the latter). The view *Padua: the Brenta Canal and the Porta Portello*, in the Robert Lehman Collection in the Metropolitan Museum (cat. no. 106), is smaller than the drawing of the same subject at Windsor but has the same stylistic intensity. As far as the sketches on Paduan subjects are concerned, this exhibition also provides a rare occasion to see the two famous continuous sketches of almost identical size, from the Pierpont Morgan Library and the Fogg Art Museum (cat. no. 104). The

latter bears Canaletto's signature and the date 1742 on the back. These two sketches, drawn before the motif, are of a different kind from the three drawings mentioned above, and they form the basis and point of departure for two drawings at Windsor, for the etching *A Town on a River Bank*, and for a painting in a private collection (cat. no. 58). This is proof of the importance such preparatory sketches had for the artist and of his continuing reliance upon them.

Relatively few drawings from Canaletto's English period have come down to us—despite the fact that he lived in England for almost ten years—but there are enough to allow a reasonable assessment. At present we know of only three rough sketches, made on the ground, of buildings in London: *Little Walsingham House* (C/L 736), *The Old Horse Guards and the Banqueting Hall* (C/L 735), and *A Domed Church, with a Statue, possibly St. Paul's* (C/L 849). All three, now in the Accademia, came from the Viggiano collection and had originally belonged to Algarotti. Strangely these are the only pages representing views of London from a sketchbook which was otherwise devoted to rapid studies of Venetian, Paduan, or imaginary motifs. The drawings provide a fixed point of chronological reference, and in keeping with Canaletto's usual practice, were used for various paintings during his English sojourn.

Fortunately there are many more finished drawings dating from those years, among them the five important and elegant drawings in this exhibition (cat. nos. 111–15). Horizontal compositions predominate, as had been the case with the Venetian landscape drawings considered above, and the luminous tones and meticulous attention to detail have also been maintained. Curly, serpentine lines are often employed, especially for the small figures and *macchiette*, or caricatures, which are typical of the English period but were already present in some Venetian sketches datable before 1745. The increasingly mannered style of such fascinating finished drawings as *The Thames, looking towards Westminster* (cat. no. 111) and *Old Walton Bridge* (cat. no. 115) has not always been judged favorably. Quite the contrary, some art historians have been critical of the stylized manner of Canaletto's English works. It would be wishful thinking, however, to find in the luminosity of the drawings (and paintings) of this period a certain Venetian light, or the Thames transformed into the lagoon. This would be to ignore the fact that whether in Venice or London, whether on the Grand Canal or the Thames, it was Canaletto's "genio felice" that endowed his work with a brilliant clarity of vision and harmony of tone. The subjects are different but the handling of light is the fundamental element, for therein lies the essence of Canaletto's art.

In the course of further study justice has been done, and the work of the English years is seen in more positive terms. Canaletto may have had difficulty in dealing with British clients, but it should be remembered that through Joseph Smith he had access to the wealthy and aristocratic collectors whose taste had been formed on the Grand Tour; many of them had been enthusiastic visitors to Venice and had admired the city itself, its monuments, and works of art of every kind.

After 1755, when he returned to Venice, Canaletto continued to work in his customarily prolific manner. Doubtless he brought with him much topographical raw material in the form of drawings and sketches, so that he was able to produce English views in Venice, just as he had made paintings and drawings of Venetian subjects while in England. This was also the case for views of Rome, Padua, and the terra firma in general, as well as for capriccios. Such was the nature of the relationship between topography and the imagination in Canaletto's art.

The four paintings ordered by Sigismund Streit represent the last major commission of the artist's final years. The drawing representing *Palazzo Foscari and the Campo Sta. Sofia* (C/L 596, now in the Galleria Nazionale d'Arte Antica, Trieste) is a preparatory sketch for part of one of these compositions (C/L 242): it is another of the sheets that had belonged to Viggiano and previously to Algarotti, and was part of a sketchbook containing drawings of various periods, including the late years. The free, informal line—the briefest of notations—still registers all of the information that Canaletto would require when painting the comparable part of Streit's canvas, and throughout there are color notes as reminders: *Bianco* (white), *Cenerin* (pale ash gray), *coto belo chiaro* (fine, clear brick red), etc. We are once again witness to Canaletto's continuing reliance upon well-tried working methods, and it is in his respect for and dependence upon such procedures that his greatness lies.

Canaletto's very last commission was in fact for a series of drawings: the twelve Ducal Ceremonies and Festivals. Of the original drawings (these belonged to the Hoare family and were housed at Stourhead in Wiltshire until their dispersal some years ago at auction), ten remain, and of these, two are exhibited: *The Doge Attends the Giovedi Grasso Festival in the Piazzetta* (cat. no. 122) and *The Annual Visit of the Doge to Sta. Maria della Salute* (cat. no. 123). The sheets are large and the drawings meticulously executed in pen and brown ink with modeling in gray wash. They were engraved by Giovanni Battista Brustoloni, and a number were offered for sale in 1766. This deluxe publishing venture was a commercial enterprise typical of printing and publishing houses in eighteenth-century Venice, and the publisher in this case was Lodovico Furlanetto, who had a shop at Ponte dei Baretari where books and prints were sold. To return to Canaletto's drawings, their fascination lies in their novelty and freshness, and in the absence of the slightest sign of fatigue on the part of the artist. He displays his usual interest in the setting—the details of the architecture and the handling of effects of perspective—but he focuses also on the flow of the crowd, depersonalized and anonymous extras whose festive costumes and disguises and whose gestures create a strange and fanciful effect. (For this cycle there is evidence of at least one preparatory, documentary drawing, taken from life.) These inventions, halfway between drawing and painting, are a splendid *canto* in praise of Venice, its people, and its festivals, but at the same time one senses a subtle vein of restrained melancholy. This was immediately grasped by Francesco Guardi, whose magical brush transformed the series into equally inspired compositions in a completely different language.

That same year, 1766, under a drawing of the interior of S. Marco (cat. no. 127), the artist added an inscription noting that he was sixty-eight years old, and boasted that he had completed his composition without the aid of glasses. For the moment, this work is considered to be his last. All of the drawings Canaletto made toward the end of his life demonstrate not only how lively and creative he was, but also how rich and complex was his art, which was marked by the ever-present contrast between the objective and the fanciful. The late drawings are far from the synthetic realism of his early work as a *vedutista*, and from the detachment and the contemplative aspect of his style of the 1730s and 1740s, but are closer to his output during the years spent in England. He tended increasingly toward the capriccio, the

curly, serpentine lines contributing to elaborately harmonious effects. The process of renewal was a constant factor of the art of Canaletto the draftsman.

NOTES

1. K. T. Parker, *The Drawings of Antonio Canaletto in the Collection of His Majesty the King at Windsor Castle*, 1948.
2. Detlev von Hadeln, *The Drawings of Antonio Canal, Called Canaletto*, 1929, p. 3.
3. W. G. Constable, *Canaletto*, 2d ed. rev. by J. G. Links, 1976; references to this work are given as C/L.
4. Anton Maria Zanetti, *Della pittura veneziana*, 1771, pp. 462–63.
5. Francis Haskell, *Burlington Magazine*, 1956, p. 298.
6. Luigi Lanzi, *Storia pittorica della Italia*, III, 4th ed., 1818; the Italian quoted here from Puppi, *L'opera completa di Canaletto*, 1968, p. 9.
7. Zanetti, *Della pittura veneziana*, 1771, p. 462.

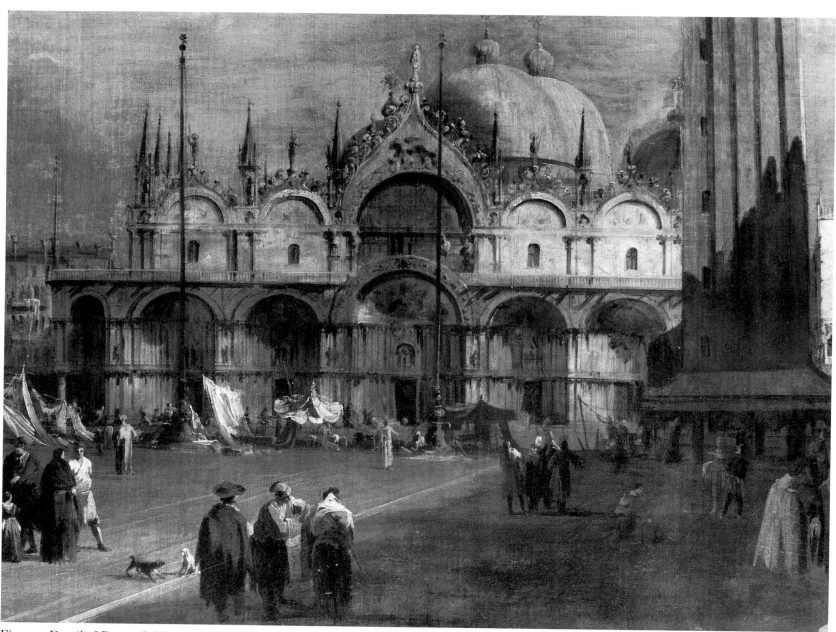

Fig. 22. Detail of *Piazza S. Marco: looking East from South of the Central Line* (C/L 12). Her Majesty Queen Elizabeth II.

THE DEVELOPMENT OF CANALETTO'S PAINTING TECHNIQUE

by Viola Pemberton-Pigott

The name of Canaletto so readily conjures up his well-known views of Venice or of the Thames in London that it is easy to overlook the transformation in style that occurs between his earliest known pictures and the familiar tourist mementos that are reproduced the world over. By comparison with the exuberance and excitement of the great early paintings of the *Piazza S. Marco* and the *Grand Canal* (cat. nos. 1, 2), the same scenes (e.g., cat. no. 84), painted toward the end of his life, may at first seem to be no more than colorful topographical views, peopled with stereotyped figures.

This repetition of subject obscures a development as masterly and innovative as that of any great artist. Canaletto never ceased to explore new methods and devices. His compositions from the outset were original and often capricious. He did not scruple to alter buildings or adapt views to suit his design. The 1720s were years of experiment and his styles of painting varied so constantly that it is hard to follow a recognizable trend until around 1730, when the single most radical development took place and his so-called mature style established itself. He carried the vivid use of impasto that had enlivened his painting of figures into his painting of architecture, and he evolved a technique of so manipulating the paint as to give an almost three-dimensional image of the structure it depicted. His compositions thus began to depend more on color and tone and the patterns they created, but the technique proved too laborious to sustain and by the late 1730s the increasing pressure of demand forced Canaletto to enlarge his workshop and simplify his style. He developed a shorthand method to convey the impression of modeling into the wet paint, and his figures gradually lost their individuality.

In the latter half of his career, the development was of style rather than technique, and his concentration was on composition. The wide horizons that he found in England opened up new concepts of design and, back in Venice, behind the familiar themes and the apparently mechanical handling there lies a constant exploration of new ideas.

Canaletto's paintings can be enjoyed in many ways, for the magic of the scene they represent and for the complexity of each design. To search for the key that carries his paintings from the bold drama of his early pictures to the meticulous patterns of the later works, one must examine the details within each painting, and appreciate how Canaletto developed the familiar themes over the decades of his working life.

The earliest paintings in the exhibition, the four great Liechtenstein canvases (cat. nos. 1–4) and the *Grand Canal: from Palazzo Corner Spinelli to the Rialto* (cat. no. 6), all datable by style to around 1723 or before, are not the work of a novice. Within these dramatic designs, Canaletto united a medley of themes into coherent compositions by devices that remind us of his experience in the theater: the dominance of blocks of light and dark, the lines of shadow cast across the scenes, and the foreground often plunged into deep shade, thus leading the eye into the picture.

The immediacy of each scene is captured as much by the quality of the paint as by the pictorial detail. The paint has been piled thickly and rapidly onto the canvas. In the *Rio dei Mendicanti* (cat. no. 4) Canaletto barely gave himself time to complete the brushstrokes; many, as in the coats of the figures, tail off with ragged wispy ends. The texture of crumbling stone and brick has been achieved by minute observation of every slight change in tone and was accurately imitated by applying different colors, brushed into each other wet-in-wet or scumbled dryly over the texture of the coarse canvas. The sun catching the white sleeve of a gondolier or the washing hanging out on the line was painted in impasto so thick that it became three-dimensional. The reflections in the water, disturbed by the waves, were painted with intricate and colorful detail. The sky, as in all Canaletto's early paintings, has been given depth and atmosphere by his use of a gray underpaint over the red priming, graded from a dark steely color to a paler shade. This underpaint was brushed on in varying thicknesses, sometimes barely covering the red ground, the two colors combining to give the impression of blue skies; the clouds were then worked into the gray with broad sweeps of color, and finally only the slightest addition of blue paint (an expensive pigment) was necessary, scumbled sparingly over the top to enhance the effect.

The tiny sketch of the *Puppet Show in the Piazzetta* (cat. no. 38) represents a microcosm of Canaletto's early style. The same marvelously vivid and spontaneous brushwork is present on the same coarse canvas, and it took only a few strokes for the cluster of crow-like tricorn hats to convey the rapt attention of the crowd below the cavorting puppets. A flight of birds appears against the clouds that zigzag upward, reminiscent of the ponderous cloud banks of Carlevaris (flocks of birds, which appear in so many of Canaletto's drawings, feature in only three or four paintings after these early works).

From Canaletto's earliest paintings of Venice, he manipulated the topography by combining two or more viewpoints so that it is rarely possible to stand in the presumed position of the painter and see each building at the angle at which it appears in the painting. To provide the framework for his compositions he changed the heights of buildings and falsified the line of the horizon. Nor did he hesitate to take liberties with such prominent features as the windows of the Palazzo Ducale or the domes of the Basilica of S. Marco itself if this would achieve the effect he desired. In a view from Smith's great series (a detail of this picture is fig. 22), similar to the *Piazza S. Marco* (cat. no. 1) but painted perhaps two years later, he enhanced the drama of the basilica facade by audaciously suppressing the left-hand dome,

lowering the one on the right, and opening up the narrow arcade at the side to the height of the adjacent three-tiered bays.

The two upright canvases from the same Smith series (cat. nos. 28, 29) are equally inventive in their amalgamation of viewpoints, but in Canaletto's use of his paint a fresh development is apparent. The figures in the background are still sparsely painted but the principal figures display a new facility: Canaletto has carried his observation of detail to a greater level of realism by applying each stroke of paint so that it follows exactly the direction and contour of the material or form he is depicting, whether it be the pleat of a coat or the twisted belt of the oriental (fig. 23). He has learned to control the viscosity of the binding medium so that the paint retains its shape and assumes the form it represents; in the white shirts of the gondoliers or the draped sails along the canal, the crest of the thick impasto mimics the sharp folds and creases of the material and catches the light falling across the surface of the canvas as would the sunlight on the figures along the quay.

This realism does not yet penetrate his painting of the architecture where he is still simulating the variety of textures and shapes by free impressionistic applications of color. All the details of each building, the windows, balconies, porticoes, and roofs, are picked out in black outlines, generally applied with the aid of a ruler.

Canaletto's use of mathematical instruments is evident at all stages of his career. Rulers and an incising instrument were employed, sometimes for laying in his design into the ground layers and sometimes for outlining or incising architectural details into the upper paint layers; dividers and compasses defined arches and roundels (the compass point is often clearly discernible); even the end of a brush or blunt instrument was used to scratch into the wet paint the details of a sculpture or architectural ornament.

The four Conti pictures from 1725–26 are crucial to the dating of Canaletto's early paintings (cat. nos. 8–11). These slightly smaller canvases emphasize his concentration on composition: the plethora of detail is subordinated within the bold shapes of the shadows, the shafts of light, and the masses of the buildings. Blocks of light and shade counterbalance each other. No wonder Marchesini wrote of Canaletto letting sun into his

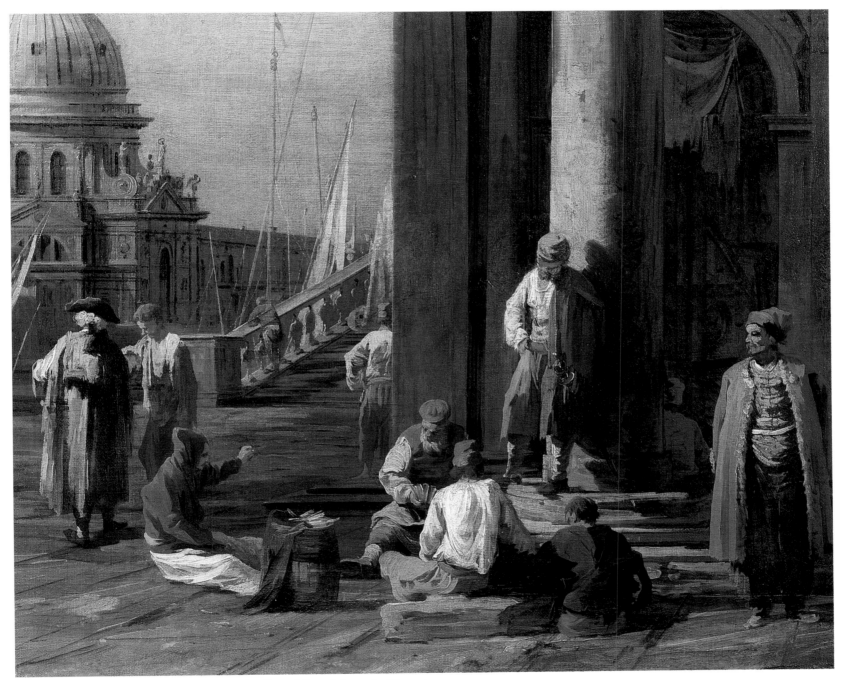

Fig. 23. Detail of cat. no. 29, *Entrance to the Grand Canal: from the Piazzetta.*

pictures.[1] The water has lost the busy ripples of the early pictures and is painted in broad green sweeps with dark shadows echoing the contrasts in the buildings. The attention to detail is, however, as vivid as ever: on the roof of the Fabbriche Vecchie di Rialto (on the right of cat. no. 8), in a virtuoso passage of paint, the late afternoon sun glances across the undulating tiles and catches the shirt of a tiny workman, precariously suspended under the eaves.

The impression of strong contrasts is heightened by the superimposed black outlining of the architecture, and the underpainting too plays a subtle role in emphasizing these contrasts. The sky, as in all his early pictures, is underpainted in gray varying from dark on one side to pale on the other; the buildings are underpainted in an orangey red and the water again in gray; some of the little figures on the quay are underpainted in black. In the distant views within these four paintings, Canaletto used a favorite touch of his early years, a rich steely gray color to suggest a misty haze over a dark form.

The correspondence from the agent Marchesini to his patron Stefano Conti describes Canaletto's progress on these paintings, and each pair, when finally under way, was completed in only four months.[2] Canaletto requested further payment for the second pair (cat. nos. 10, 11). He claimed that they had caused him more work, but the very free brushwork and comparative lack of detail would suggest the reverse, that less time was given to them. The excuses for delay were endless, including the poor quality of the priming material and, most interestingly, the expense of buying the blue pigment, "his principal color,"[3] which possibly refers to the recently invented Prussian blue, a pigment that has been identified in many of his paintings.[4]

In the middle years of the 1720s Canaletto had, "more work than he can do, in any reasonable time, and well,"[5] and his styles varied enormously, possibly according to the importance of the patron or perhaps to the size of the canvas. His output ranged from smaller views of the Grand Canal, painted in broad sweeps of color (i.e., C/L 212 and C/L 181), to such closely observed paintings as *"The Stonemason's Yard"* (cat. no. 32) with its possible pendant of *SS. Giovanni e Paolo* (cat. no. 5) which, with the treatment of the water and skies and the narrative quality of every detail, may slightly predate the Conti commissions.

The grand scale of so many of the early paintings implies that the first commissions were destined for the palaces of Venice or for those of visiting envoys. Although Canaletto established his reputation as a view painter, in the early 1720s he was also competing for the traditional demands of the home market, the market for the *veduta ideata* that he would have seen in such abundance in Rome. These capriccios with classical ruins display the stylistic hallmarks of the early views of Venice, but, as decorative pieces, they were obviously painted at a greater speed than the carefully conceived topographical views. It was, after all, as a painter of romanticized ruins and landscapes (such as Marco Ricci was supplying) that he was first engaged by McSwiney to contribute to two allegorical tomb paintings (cat. nos. 12, 13), and the earliest painting by Canaletto that was in Joseph Smith's collection is a tiny *Caprice View with Ruins based on the Forum* (fig. 24).

Smith's commission for the series of twelve views of the Grand Canal and McSwiney's for the little pictures on copper for dispatch to London span a period of about five years and show the

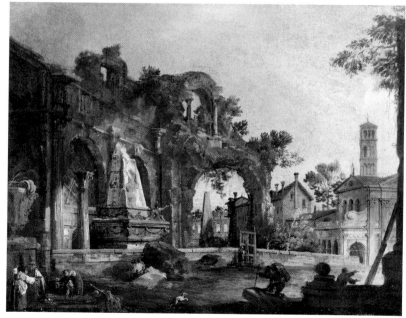

Fig. 24. Canaletto, *Rome: a Caprice View with Ruins based on the Forum.* Her Majesty Queen Elizabeth II.

artist reassessing and developing his style to suit the small format. The earliest of Smith's canal views in the exhibition (cat. nos. 39, 41), still in their original Venetian frames with a C-scroll motif though with nineteenth-century additions, resemble scaled-down versions of the Conti pictures and must be very close in date: they have the same exaggerated contrasts of light and shade in the buildings, the long dark shadows in the water, the blue-black hulls of the boats, and scrappy but animated figures on the quayside. Despite the small scale, no articulation of detail is omitted, from the faces and clothes of the tiny figures to the precise black outlining of each door or window.

These strong contrasts proved too heavy for the reduced size and, as the series progressed, Canaletto's palette lightened. In number 42 he introduced more variety of scale in the figures; the clever modeling of the impasto in the materials and sails was carried over into the boats, where the hulls were painted in long sweeping strokes that simulate the texture of the planks of wood. The water has become clearer and less turbid, the reflections more specific, and, as a final touch, white waves have been added over the top. The blue of the sky is more intense (Prussian blue was by then widely available) and the clouds too are lighter and more defined; the brushstrokes have been flicked backward to simulate the frothy edges and often there are horizontal bands of color above the skyline.

The impression of the lighter palette is subtly influenced by the color of the underpaint. Canaletto was now using a very pale beige or gray over his red ground, usually beige under the sky and gray below the water and, slightly later, a uniform layer of pale beige or gray across the canvas.[6] He also varied the texture of the canvas, selecting a weave commensurate with the size of the painting.

The other early view of the Grand Canal from Smith's series in this exhibition (cat. no. 40) was painted on finer canvas, which allowed more delicate brushwork, and the overall tonality is softened by the beige underpaint. The figures almost blend into the clear warm colors of the architecture so that they too have had to be strengthened by outlining.

The early 1730s saw the total transformation of Canaletto's technique as he extended his ability to model his figures in the wet paint into his painting of buildings. Instead of outlining

architectural details in black, he brushed the forms of doors, windows, or balconies into the wet paint. He used impasto to create the capital of a column; he could suggest a subdued reflection through a doorway by varying the density of a dark color over the pale underpaint; he modeled a wooden shutter or a shaded lintel in a single stroke by so loading his brush as to create a thick highlight down one edge and a thinned recession on the other. The tangible texture of crumbling stucco is simulated by twisting and lifting the brush off the canvas to leave a speckled area of raised paint and generate the dappled effect of peeling plaster or the sparkle of water on wet stone.

With such variety of texture in his brushstrokes, he no longer needed to imitate the impression of changing tones by the application of many colors. For a short period around 1730 Canaletto produced a small group of paintings in the palest of pastel shades that can be seen as precursors to the climax of his mature style (e.g., C/L 100, 161, 170). Pure black vanished from his palette except for the occasional strengthening of a shadow in a foreground figure or boat; the buildings are "sculpted" in misty shades of gray or brown, and even the most distant doors and windows are worked into the wet paint; the exaggerated modeling is accentuated by the shadows cast by the paint itself, as in a bas-relief. Gradually he modified this extreme subtlety of tone and reverted to greater contrasts of color throughout the pictures; he developed the use of brown washes to depict the details of architecture, often brushed on wet-in-wet.

The datable commissions of 1730 show Canaletto in the throes of mastering his technique. In the two Wicklow paintings (cat. nos. 35 and 36), the paint strokes are already fuller and more viscous, the colors are becoming lighter, and the texture of the walls and buildings is modeled into the wet paint. Much of the architecture, however, is still outlined in soft black. Less than six months later, in the pastel-toned Tatton Park pictures (cat. nos. 33 and 34), the black ruling has disappeared and the detailing of the architecture is painted in soft liquid grays. Both these paintings are very assured but show undoubted signs of being dashed off at high speed: the distant figures on the Molo are suggested by no more than calligraphic squiggles; the pale beige underpaint of the Riva is barely covered; and several areas under the arcade of the Palazzo Ducale have been left quite unfinished.

Canaletto has used his ingenious device of incising with a sharp instrument into the upper paint layers to indicate the geometric patterns on the Palazzo Ducale and the supporting rods between the arches of the arcade. In the thick paint of the sunlit facade the impasto rises into a ridge along the ruler, whereas across the shaded end and for the rods, the diamond pattern is incised through the dark paint to expose the paler underpaint below. Canaletto in fact made an error in his calculations, so that the alignment of his ruling from the top and bottom fails to meet in the middle, but he skillfully camouflaged his mistake with a few dabs of red paint over the top.

The nine little copper panels that make such a surprising appearance in Canaletto's oeuvre (cat. nos. 14–22) cover the same years of development as Smith's Grand Canal series. The earliest, numbers 16, 17, and 22, probably date from around 1726. The strong blues and blacks in the water and boats, and the broad brushstrokes that have not quite found their measure on this reduced scale, are reminiscent of earlier paintings, and the skies recall the early Smith series. The pair from Holkham (cat. nos. 20, 21; they are framed in a contemporary English version of Smith's exquisite Venetian frames for his Grand Canal views) show hints of the turbid greens from the Conti paintings, but the palette is lightening and the figures recall those from the middle of Smith's Grand Canal series. The pair from Chatsworth (cat. nos. 18, 19) display all the characteristics of the Tatton Park paintings—the pastel tones, the sketchy brushwork, the extensive incising into the wet paint, and the deft modeling of the rich impasto in the architecture and figures. They must be dated around 1731.

The Goodwood pair presents problems. The surviving letters from McSwiney[7] specify that two copper panels were sent from Venice to the Duke of Richmond in November 1727, but the stage of development of catalogue numbers 14 and 15 makes it difficult to accept that these were painted a mere eighteen months after the final Conti pictures. The paint is rich and liquid, the tonality of both veers toward the pastel shades, and the treatment of skies, water, waves, and figures seems closer to the Wicklow paintings of 1730. In number 14, the architectural de-

tailing is still outlined in black, whereas in number 15, most of the windows, doors, and balconies are modeled into the wet paint in softened grays and browns. It remains a possibility that these could be the second pair commissioned by McSwiney for the Duke of Richmond in 1727 which included a "view of the Rialto Bridge," but although there are several subsequent mentions of them as nearing completion or finished, McSwiney had apparently still not received them in September 1730, by which time Canaletto's style had progressed to the pastel shades of the Tatton Park pictures, beyond this more precise and deliberate handling.

The culmination of Canaletto's skill can be seen in every brushstroke of Smith's two festival paintings which are alive with the anticipation of the race in the *Regatta* and the pageantry in the *Bucintoro* (cat. nos. 43 and 44). Yet within each picture every smallest detail forms a perfect vignette, whether it be the tiny figure of the man on top of the Campanile who surveys the scene through his telescope, or the virtuoso description of a stuccoed wall. The sense of excitement in the *Regatta* is generated as much by the expectant attitudes of the spectators as by the sudden introduction of staccato splashes of color set against a smoother passage of paint, for instance the sharp blobs of impasto in the decorative *bissone* and their crews, or the white masks lining the balconies of the Grand Canal.

Despite the impression of color and brightness in so many of Canaletto's paintings, his range of pigments is remarkably limited, especially when considered against the rich tradition of Venetian art. Canaletto's own abbreviated color notes on the diagrammatic drawings of palaces and houses in his sketchbooks refer to colors such as *cenerino* (ash colored), *cotto* (baked or brown), *ocra zala* (yellow ocher), or *rossetto sporco* (dirty or dull reddish) and are reflected in the natural earth pigments that predominate in his works. He used his paint mainly *alla prima*, often scumbling one color or shade over another, but very rarely as a true glaze, enhancing one color by the application of a translucent layer over the top. Much of the gaiety that pervades his paintings is created by the skillful infusion of flashes of light and, when painting the figures (always added as the final item), of a few discreet touches of selectively placed vermilion or strong yellow.

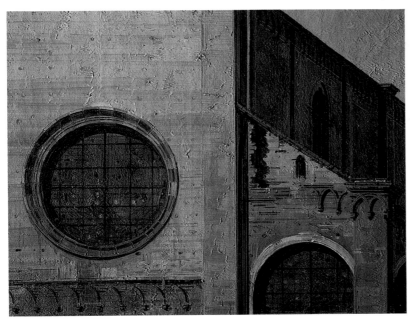

Fig. 25. Detail of cat. no. 45, *SS. Giovanni e Paolo.*

There is little evidence of struggle in Canaletto's compositions; the pentiments, apart from the major reworkings in Smith's early Piazza series, tend to be relatively insignificant, such as the narrowing of a dome or the shifting of an arm, and indicate the careful planning which went into each picture. Drawing played an essential role throughout his life, as working sketches and as finished pieces. By the mid-1730s, Canaletto had begun to introduce soft gray washes to replace the strong hatching strokes that characterized many of the early pen and ink drawings (and occasionally strayed over into his painting of figures). About the same time, a parallel development began to appear in his paintings: Canaletto explored the added potential of thinning his paint and applying it like a wash, so that it gained a translucency over the pale underpaint, and he exploited the varying degrees of shade and intensity thus obtained.

For most of the 1730s Canaletto's entire output was directed toward the English market. Perhaps to facilitate transport, the smaller sized paintings, usually on finer canvas, became standard: these included the Bedford series (see cat. nos. 48, 49; in Venetian frames with the C-scroll motif identical to Smith's Grand Canal views), the Harvey series (see cat. nos. 46, 47),

and Smith's little masterpiece, *SS. Giovanni e Paolo* (cat. no. 45). These pictures, painted about 1731–36, show the full extent of Canaletto's ability to play color and tonality against form and texture, to exploit the gamut of variety afforded by the use of rich impasto contrasted against the translucency of liquid washes of color. The church of *SS. Giovanni e Paolo* was painted in thick layers, brushed into and over each other, wet-in-wet, twisting, lifting, or smoothing out the strokes to represent the rough stucco and the courses of brick in the sunlit walls; the rose window has been incised into the wet paint with a compass, the checkered red and yellow ocher pattern around it scratched in with a blunt point, and the depth of the surrounding frame imitated by the shade lines of gray wash (fig. 25). The dark facade of the Scuola di S. Marco and the side of the church are enlivened by Canaletto's calculated use of the pale gray underpaint partially shining through; a thin incised line ruled to expose the pale underpaint provides the shimmer of light down the edge of the pilasters and the articulation around windows and bays. The impasto recreates the relief decoration on the plinth of the Colleoni monument and even models the sup-

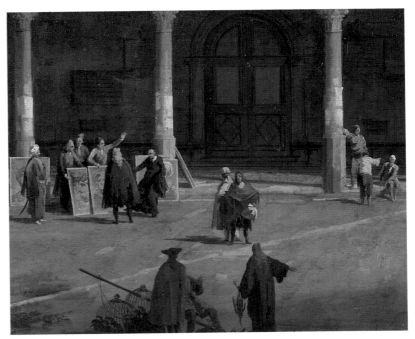

Fig. 26. Detail of cat. no. 7, *S. Giacomo di Rialto.*

porting scroll-shaped stones beneath the balconies of the houses on the right of the *campo*.

The figures are by this time treated as no more than components of his compositions, dispersed across the foreground like the windows in a facade. The narrative quality of the fleeting moment from the earlier paintings, such as the prelate, at the sale of pictures in front of S. Giacomo di Rialto, who recoils in mock horror at the sight of a grotesque caricature, perhaps of himself (fig. 26), is replaced by cameos representing recurring themes of everyday life.

Strong shadows and patches of light continue to unify the composition. The position of the shadows may be total invention, as in *SS. Giovanni e Paolo*, where the angle is unobtainable even on midsummer's day, or they may be used to provide focal points along a line of houses; it is a mark of Canaletto's inventiveness that sometimes the sun has mysteriously slid from morning to afternoon as it lights up the buildings along either side of the Grand Canal.

As the demand for paintings generated by Joseph Smith increased, Canaletto brought his nephew Bernardo Bellotto into his studio. His technique began visibly to simplify. There is less use of impasto and more skilled contrivance with thin liquid washes. He adopted time-saving illusory devices such as indicating the projection of a line of balconies merely by painting in the cast shadow, without altering the ruled lines of the balustrades. Many of the figures became mechanical and doll-like, reduced to the deft application of a couple of carefully entwined coils of light and dark paint to resemble a face, and a few precisely applied strokes to form the body. Black outlining is once more used for the architecture, softer than before, interspersed and combined with translucent wash lines. Ruling and incising were widely used for all the nuances they could provide.

There is an undeniable dullness in some of the paintings attributed to Canaletto from the late 1730s and a certain brashness of tone which must suggest studio participation, especially when compared to such a masterpiece as *The Bacino di S. Marco* (cat. no. 51). The harmonies and contrasts within the paint itself and the checkerboard patterns created by the light, the space, and the grouping of the boats across the water make this painting one of Canaletto's great achievements.

In the series of Roman views done for Joseph Smith in 1742 (cat. nos. 59, 60), Canaletto returned to the muted pastel shades, reminiscent of Carlevaris, with which he had experimented around 1730. But this time he was concentrating on the effects achieved by variations of tonality, juggling his colors within the massive forms of the ruins to create their own harmonies and patterns. Each color is introduced, modified, alternated with a new tone, and dropped—until it is reintroduced in a fresh passage elsewhere. Across the surface of *The Arch of Constantine* (cat. no. 59), for example, interwoven shades of gray on the right give way to deep and then pale golden colors, topped by the warm red of the bricks which is echoed in the maroon-colored stonework of the Colosseum on the right.

Canaletto's preoccupation with form and design gained fresh impetus on his arrival in England in 1746, where the wide-open landscapes inspired him to compositions of skies and low horizons that recall such seventeenth-century Dutch painters as Koninck or van Goyen. At first the bright Venetian light found its way to the Thames, but this soon gave way to the soft tones of England, with sometimes a hint of the pall of smoke that could afflict London. Since Canaletto was once more obliged to paint the entire picture himself, it is possible to detect passages of brushwork that relate back to almost every period, from the short staccato strokes of *Old Walton Bridge* (cat. no. 73) to the liquid washes of his views of the Thames.

George Vertue was puzzled by Canaletto's English pictures and wrote in June 1749:

> On the whole of him something is obscure or strange. he dos not produce works so well done as those of Venice . . . done by him there, especially his figures in his works done here, are apparently much inferior . . . his water & his skys at no time excellent or with natural freedom. & what he has done here his prospects of Trees woods or handling or pencilling of that part not various nor so skillfull as might be expected.[8]

No wonder Vertue was baffled. He had just recorded Canaletto's two views of Badminton, the Gloucestershire home of the Duke of Beaufort, in which the compositions are simplified to daring extremes and the staffage included as no more than an incidental element. The view of *Badminton Park, from the House*

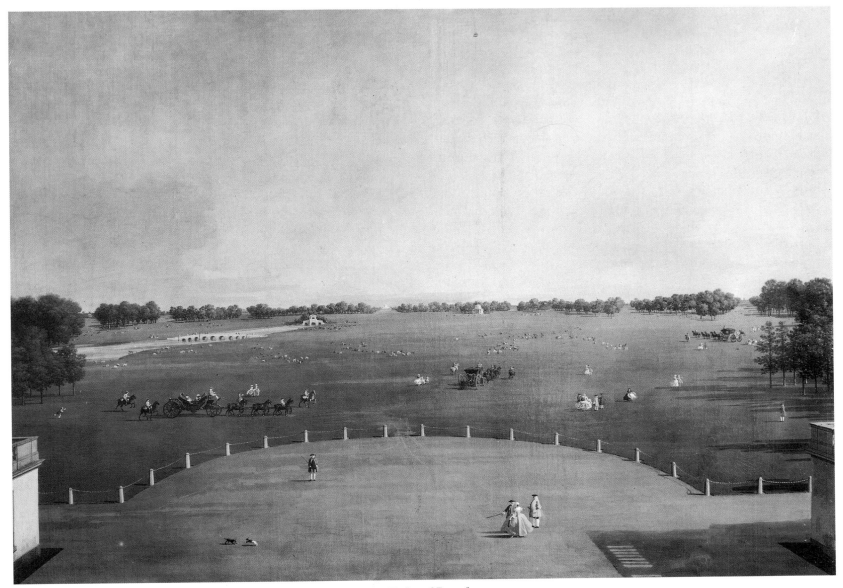

Fig. 27. Canaletto, *Badminton Park, from the House*. His Grace the Duke of Beaufort.

(fig. 27), reduced to a few geometric shapes of gravel, grass, and trees set against a low horizon, must rank as a forerunner of abstract art. Also in 1748–49, Canaletto was painting the earlier views of Warwick Castle in which, as in Smith's large Roman series of 1742, he played with the effects of modulated colors. In number 68, the imposing proportions of the castle are transformed into a composition of cubist elements; across the long south front of the castle, he used the tonal variations of a single color to produce patterns within the paint and create forms along the facade that are worthy of Cézanne. Likewise in *Westminster*

61

Abbey (cat. no. 67), recording the event of 20 June 1749, Canaletto, in a similarly arresting design, contrasted the sweep of red-robed figures against the verticals of the abbey. The detailing of the architecture is now, once again, entirely outlined in black, with evident use of the compass and ruler.

The last paintings from Canaletto's years in England are as diverse as *Old Walton Bridge* (cat. no. 73) with its rare view of storm clouds—and birds in flight—or as the bland washes of color of the Lovelace capriccios (cat. nos. 75–80). He relied more and more on the inflections he could obtain from translucent washes to substitute for the texture that he had previously worked into each brushstroke, and he resorted to an ever more perfunctory shorthand of bright blobs and squirls. This device, which he had first adopted to give sparkle to the decorated barges on the Grand Canal and to the golden ornamentation of the Bucintoro (e.g., cat. nos. 8 and 44), he now used throughout his pictures, integrating figures, landscape, and even clouds into a mosaic of color and pattern.

Back in Venice in 1756, Canaletto reassessed the familiar scenes, sometimes reducing them by his extreme stylization to a pattern of abstracts, as in the two night views that belonged to Sigismund Streit (cat. no. 83 and C/L 360), combining them with a sizable output of ever more inventive capriccios.

Even in the 1760s, the last decade of his life, Canaletto retained the urge to experiment. In the capriccio that he painted as his reception piece to the Accademia in 1765 (cat. no. 85),

glimpses of the old virtuosity of handling are to be seen; his sense of composition is undiminished, creating through the architectural forms and the strong contrasts of light and shade a powerful pattern of diagonals and geometric shapes. Equally remarkable are the extreme distortions of his wide-angled views such as number 84, dated 1763, or the capriccios in which the entire painting is reduced to a hieroglyphic shorthand of blobs and squiggles (e.g., C/L 493).

The craftsman within Canaletto never waned. The excellent state of preservation of so many of his paintings is testimony to the soundness of his technique and his attention to the quality of his materials; despite the rich use of impasto and the liquid washes, barely a hint of craquelure mars the flow of his paint or confuses the design.

It may be hard to find compensation in the decorative shorthand of Canaletto's later pictures for the exhilarating brushwork of his early work or the masterly control of paint in his mature period, but behind the confines of his range of subjects, his search for new techniques and ideas was continuous. As he evolved the ability to manipulate and model the substance of his paint, he deliberately rejected the brand of realism that had characterized his early painting. He passed from the meticulous observation of every detail to exploring the scope of composition within color, pattern, and texture, and the extreme stylization of his later works became a further stage of Canaletto's unflagging creativity.

Canaletto's Painting Materials

Canaletto's pigments and media have been analyzed and published.[9] The following is a brief summary:

Media

Drying oil: linseed oil in the ground layers; linseed or possibly walnut oil in the upper paint layers.[10]

Pigments

Blue
Prussian blue (ferric ferrocyanide). Samples analyzed so far from the skies and water of paintings from all periods have shown Prussian blue to be the only blue pigment used except in catalogue number 1, in which ultramarine (lapis lazuli) was identified in the sky. Samples taken from the sky of number 6, about 1723, were also identified as

Prussian blue,[11] which represents a very early use of this synthetic pigment in Venice.

Green
Green earth (terre verte), natural marine clay containing glauconite.

Yellow
Naples yellow (lead antimony oxide).

Red
Vermilion (mercuric sulfide); red lake (a natural dyestuff deposited on an inorganic substrate).

Earth colors
A range of naturally occurring red, yellow, and brown ochers and umbers.

Black
Charcoal black; bone black.

White
Lead white (basic lead carbonate).

Support

Apart from nine paintings on copper panels (cat. nos. 14–22), painted about 1726–30, Canaletto's known output is on canvas. The weave varies from very coarse to fine, both plain and twill. The paintings from the early 1720s are mostly on coarse canvas, including very small sketches. Thereafter the coarseness of the canvas generally relates to the size of the painting.

Paint-Layer Structure

Invariably consists of priming or ground, underpaint, and upper paint layers.

Priming
Canaletto used the traditional Venetian red ground of the period, applying two or more layers. Usually strong red, but for a period in the mid-1720s, an orangey red occurs.

Underpaint
Up to about 1727–28 Canaletto varied the color of his underpaint for sky, buildings, and water: gray under the sky, with the gray graded in the early paintings from dark to light, usually from one side to the other; clouds are often indicated in the underpaint but the positions are not always followed in the final paintings. Red or orange under the buildings. Gray under the water.

Around 1728 a pale beige underpaint was introduced, often used in combination with a pale gray.

From about 1729–30 onward the underpainting is simplified to a uniform overall layer, usually pale beige, sometimes pale gray, though a combination can sometimes be found in the larger or the more carefully worked paintings. Occasionally pendants are painted one on beige, one on gray (e.g., C/L 68 and 85, dated 1743). The impression of a pink underpaint in some paintings from the 1730s onward is given by the red ground showing through the thin beige underpaint.

From the 1740s onward the upper paint layers sometimes appear to be painted directly onto the red ground.[12]

Sequence of Laying in the Painting

The sky was completed first, then the architecture and water, finally the figures and boats were added.

NOTES

1. Haskell, *Burlington Magazine*, 1956, p. 297.
2. Haskell, *Burlington Magazine*, 1956, pp. 296–300.
3. Haskell, *Burlington Magazine*, 1956, p. 298.
4. See "Canaletto's Painting Materials" at the end of this essay.
5. Letter from Owen McSwiney to the Duke of Richmond; see "McSwiney's Copperplates," preceding cat. nos. 14–19.
6. See "Canaletto's Painting Materials."
7. See "McSwiney's Copperplates" with cat. nos. 14 and 15.
8. *Vertue Note Books*, III, p. 149.
9. Pamela England, "An Account of Canaletto's Painting Technique," in *Canaletto*, 1980, pp. 27–28; and David Bomford and Ashok Roy, "Canaletto's 'Venice: The Feastday of S. Roch,'" *National Gallery Technical Bulletin* 6 (1982), pp. 40–44.
10. Bomford and Roy, "Canaletto's . . . 'Feastday of S. Roch,'" 1982, p. 42.
11. I am indebted for this information to Frau Gerti Sacher, Conservation Department, Staatliche Kunstsammlungen, Dresden.
12. In cat. no. 67, only a gray ground and underpaint were found, similar to most English paintings of the 1740s; Canaletto possibly used a commercially prepared canvas.

PAINTINGS

Four Paintings Formerly in the Collection of the Princes of Liechtenstein

1. Piazza S. Marco: looking East along the Central Line

Oil on canvas, 54¼ × 80½ in. (140.5 × 204.5 cm)
Thyssen-Bornemisza Foundation, Lugano
C/L 1

EXHIBITED
Canada 4; Venice 79

NOTES
1. Pallucchini, *Pittura veneziana*, 1960, p. 74, first proposed a
   date for this canvas in function of the repaving of Piazza S.
   Marco. His suggestion, a milestone for the chronology of
   Canaletto's earliest work, has been the subject of critical
   commentary. See Levey, *Burlington Magazine*, 1961, p. 139;
   Allen Rosenbaum, *Old Master Paintings from the Collection
   of Baron Thyssen-Bornemisza*, exh. cat. (Washington, 1979),
   pp. 86–87; and Filippo Pedrocco, in *Canaletto & Visentini*,
   1986, p. 31, who wishes to separate the Grand Canal views
   from the others of this series by as much as four or five years.
2. Anton Maria Zanetti the Younger, *Della pittura veneziana*,
   1771, p. 463.
3. See Bettagno, in *Canaletto*, 1982, pp. 56–57; and Bettagno,
   "In margine a una Mostra," 1983, pp. 222 and 224.
4. Rudolf Heinemann, in *Sammlung Thyssen-Bornemisza*
   (Castagnola, 1971), pp. 64–65.

This is the quintessential Venetian view: the earliest in date, the largest in size, and the most famous of Canaletto's paintings of the city's best-known artistic subject, Piazza S. Marco. The Piazza, trapezoidal in plan and opening outward toward the facade of the Basilica di S. Marco, is a vast open-air salon and theater, the center of Venetian life. The basilica and the adjoining urban space are dedicated to the Evangelist Mark, patron saint of Venice. Immediately to the south, and to the right of the Campanile, is the Palazzo Ducale, until Napoleonic times the residence of the Doge and the seat of government. The arcades of the Procuratie Vecchie and the Procuratie Nuove —so-called because they were intended to house the Procurators or magistrates, and referred to as "old" and "new" because they were completed about 1532 and in 1640 respectively—enclose the square to the north and south. The Torre dell'Orologio (Clock Tower), at the eastern end of the Procuratie Vecchie, opens into the Merceria, which leads in turn to the Rialto, center of Venetian commercial life.

Traditionally held views and oft-repeated assertions to the contrary, it has been amply demonstrated in recent years that Canaletto, throughout his career, subordinated topographical considerations to pictorial effect. Such is the case with the present early canvas. The artist insisted upon the precise regularity, and the too rapid diminution in scale, of the flattened, arcaded facades of the Procuratie, an effect of theater. The architectural detail, though drawn without the aid of a rule, is relatively monotonous, particularly by comparison with the free, ragged brushwork and delicate coloring of the facade of the basilica. Filtered sunlight animates the domes and spires of S. Marco, and plays upon the awnings and umbrellas that shelter the merchants and their clientele and provide shade for the colonnade and many of the windows of the Procuratie Vecchie. Gentlemen and officials in full wigs and gowns, men in the traditional costume of cape and three-cornered hat, laborers, vendors, and other exotics people the square, and beneath the Torre dell'Orologio goats wander among the potted plants displayed for sale. The lowering clouds wreathing the Campanile and the fitful brightness of the light convey a sense of urgency, and drama.

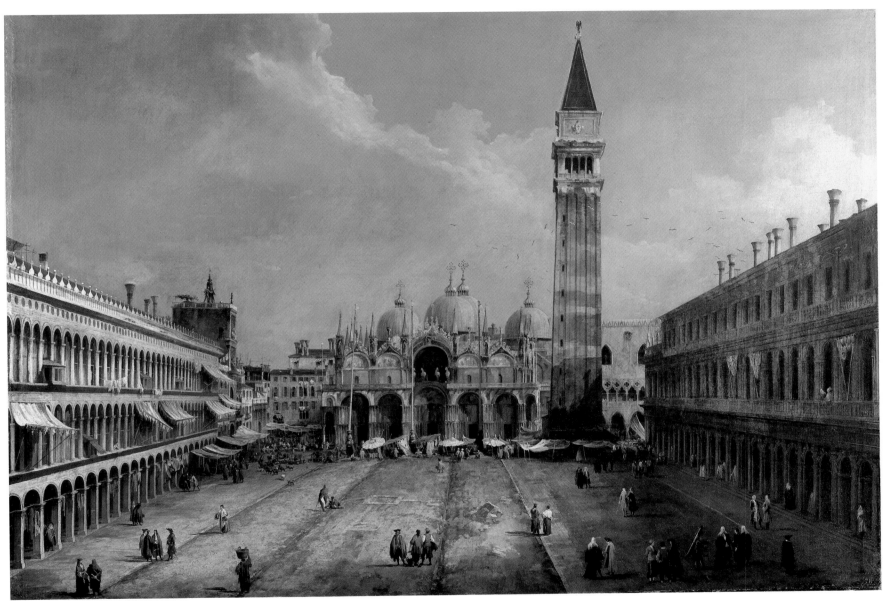

I.

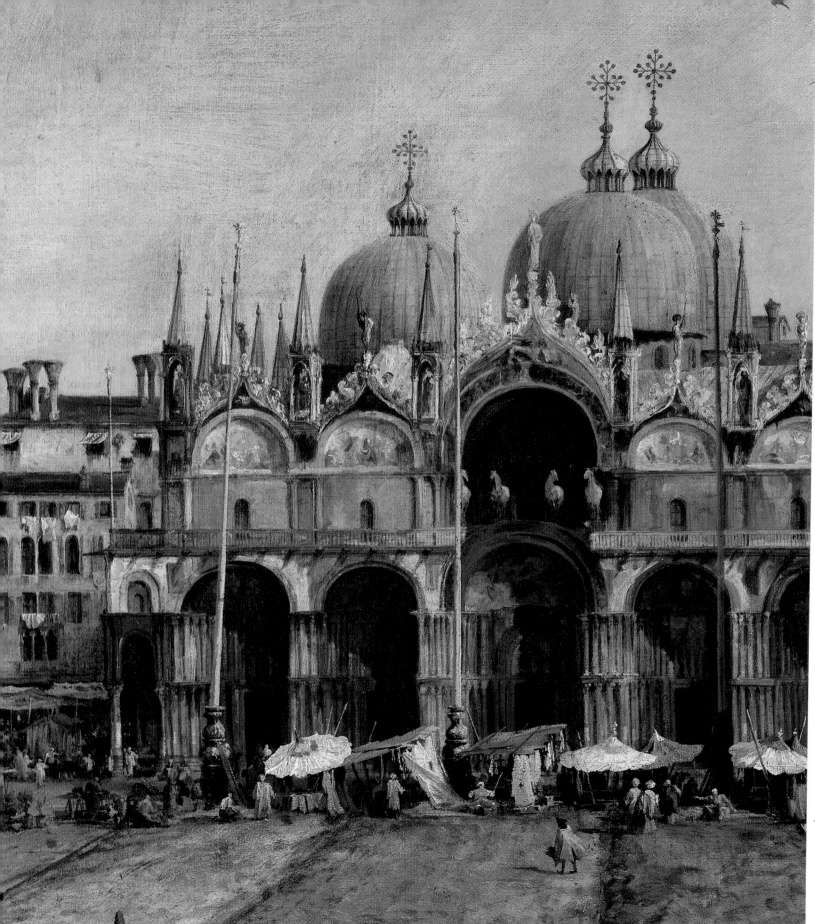

Detail of 1.

A third of the square on the southern side, roughly coinciding with the shaded area, has been paved, perhaps also the northernmost part, between the drainage channel and the Procuratie Vecchie, and herein lies the only evidence for the date of the picture, as this pavement with its white marble geometrical design was laid by Andrea Tirali in 1723.[1] Previously Piazza S. Marco had been paved with brick, punctuated with drainage channels running east and west of which several still remained. Canaletto may therefore have had the present canvas upon his easel in 1723, and the series, to which three other canvases (cat. nos. 2–4) belong, may constitute the earliest record of his independent activity as a Venetian view painter.

With his father, Bernardo, Canaletto is identified as a set designer for two Alessandro Scarlatti operas performed in Rome in 1720, but meanwhile, according to the younger Zanetti's biographical note, published in 1771, Giovanni Antonio "solemnly excommunicated the theater" with the intention of devoting himself entirely to views after nature.[2] It is difficult to imagine that these four canvases, so large in scale and dramatic in content, would have been painted on speculation. More likely, they were commissioned, and as they belonged until quite recently to the Princes of Liechtenstein it has been assumed, in the absence of documentary evidence, that they were painted for Joseph Wenzel von Liechtenstein (1696–1772), reigning prince from 1748, soldier, diplomat, connoisseur and patron of the arts, and Canaletto's almost exact contemporary. If indeed the pictures were ordered by Joseph Wenzel, then Anton Maria Zanetti the Elder, with whom he was on terms of friendship by the 1720s, might have acted as intermediary.[3] (As part of the private collection of Joseph Wenzel, acquired previous to 1748, they need not have figured in Vincenzo Fanti's complete account of the gallery of painting and sculpture of the reigning prince, published in 1767.) The series might, on the other hand, have been commissioned by a Venetian connoisseur and then offered for sale by an agent at an as yet undetermined, but relatively early, date. The four paintings are first inventoried in the Liechtenstein collection in 1806.[4] All were sold to the same private collector in Italy: the view of Piazza S. Marco and that of the Grand Canal from Palazzo Balbi (cat. no. 3) in 1956, the others (cat. nos. 2, 4) three years earlier, in 1953. This canvas and catalogue number 2 were acquired by their present owner in 1956.

2. *Grand Canal: looking East, from the Campo S. Vio*

Oil on canvas, 55¼ × 80½ in. (140.5 × 204.5 cm)
Thyssen-Bornemisza Foundation, Lugano
C/L 182

Exhibited
Canada 3; Venice 80

Note
1. Levey, *Burlington Magazine*, 1961, p. 139 and fig. 13.

Among the most spectacular of the Grand Canal views is this one, which is taken from a point above the water and beside the Campo S. Vio, looking toward the Bacino di S. Marco. On the opposite side of the canal, toward the left center of the picture, is Palazzo Corner della Ca' Grande. The pierced openings of the grandiose marble facade are neatly painted but do not hold the artist's interest by comparison with the delicately tinted expanse of the plastered side wall facing west, with many windows irregularly spaced and a roof line dotted with chimney pots. Smaller buildings, varying in elevation from one to five stories, cling to this noble edifice. Palazzo Barbarigo, also seen from the side and in very steep perspective, anchors the composition at the right. A sweep in a tattered cloak, his ladder propped against the chimney upon which he stands, is silhouetted against the sky, and a maidservant leans over the balcony of a second-story window. Four men, rather ill-dressed and ill-favored, take their ease in the sunny *campo*. Behind them, on the wall of the palace, is a casual drawing of a large and elegant barge, flags flying fore and aft.

Above the palaces along the south side of the canal is the dome of Sta. Maria della Salute, and, as pointed out by Michael Levey, the presence of scaffolding upon the dome may be connected with the record of repairs to the dome authorized in 1719, suggesting that this canvas may be the earliest of the series.[1] A sailing boat with two masts rides high on the water at the center of the picture, beside a more heavily laden barge with a tattered, discolored sail. The masts of the larger boat and of many other craft in the distant *bacino* pierce the irregular skyline of the Riva degli Schiavoni. The darkest shadows and brightest highlights animate the waters of the canal in the foreground.

This was to be Canaletto's favorite view of the Grand Canal and there are variations in the many versions, including changes to the windows of the Palazzo Barbarigo. He must therefore have returned to the site many times. A smaller and somewhat later view of the same subject—less chaotic and dramatic in effect—is that in the collection of Viscount Coke (cat. no. 20).

Detail of 2.

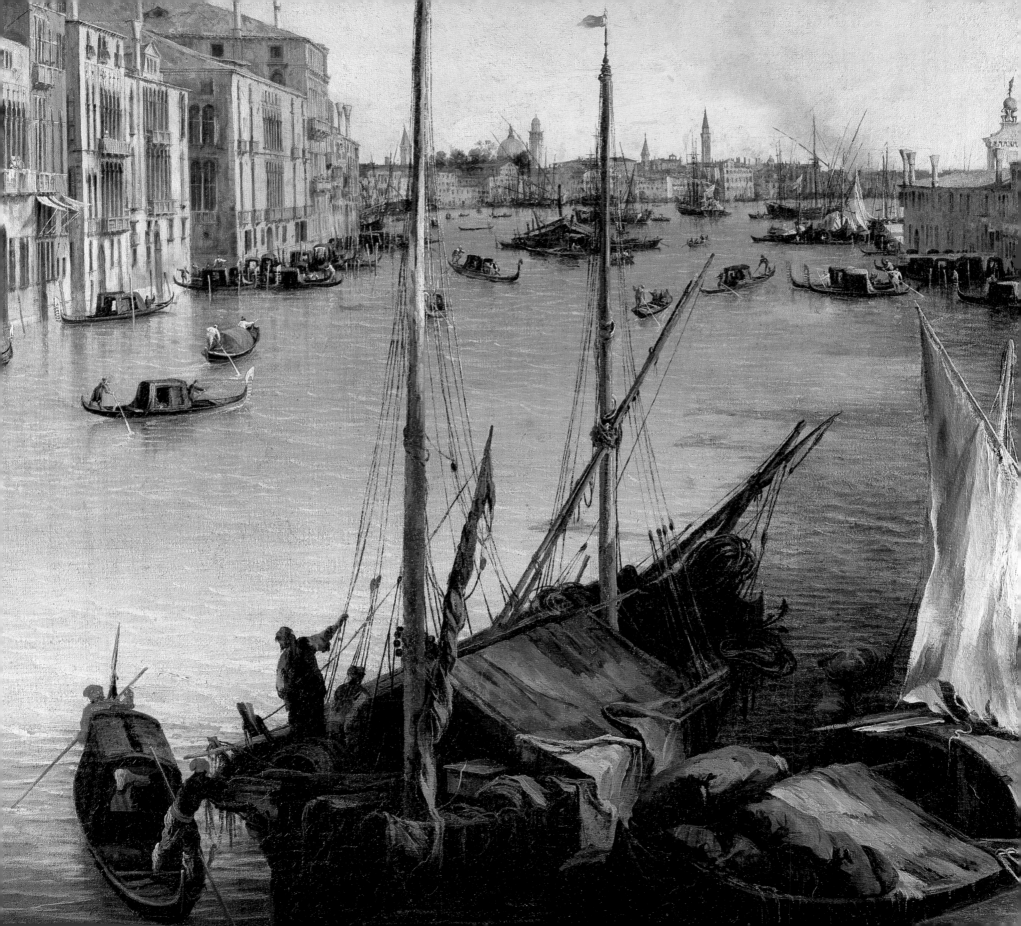

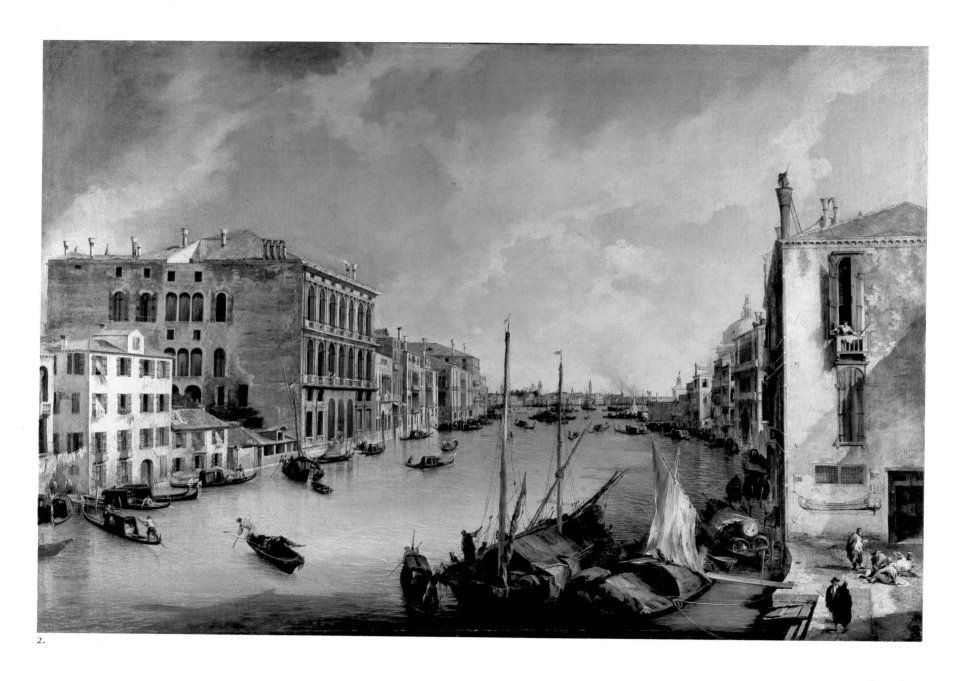

2.

Opposite
Detail of 2.

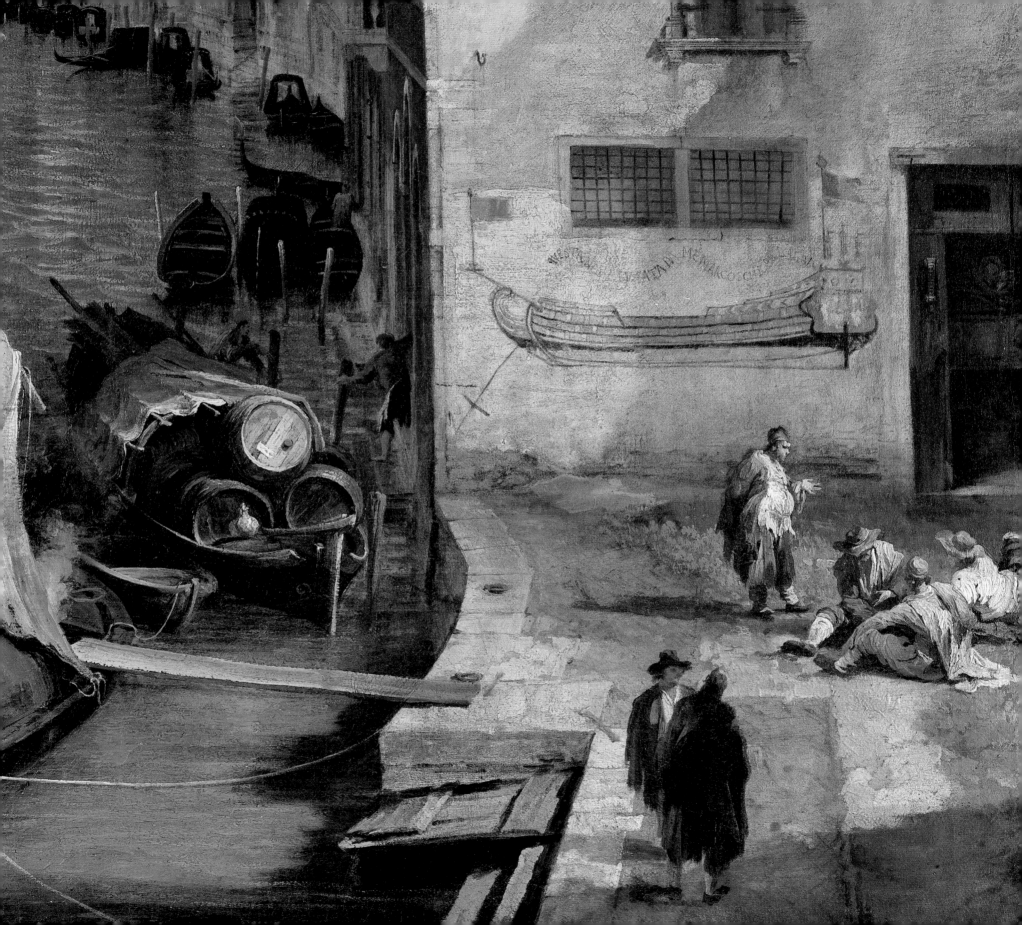

3. Grand Canal: looking Northeast from the Palazzo Balbi to the Rialto Bridge

Oil on canvas, 56¾ × 79⅛ in. (144 × 207 cm)
Ca' Rezzonico, Venice
C/L 210

EXHIBITED
Venice 82

Canaletto here represents the broadest possible expanse of water: the reaches of the canal turning at Palazzo Balbi toward the northeast and the Rialto Bridge in the far distance. The sun illuminates the obelisk, roof line, and upper story of the late sixteenth-century facade of Palazzo Balbi and all of the facades on the westward bank, leaving in shadow the buildings opposite: from the right, the Palazzi Erizzio (now Nani Mocenigo) and Contarini dalle Figure, and the four palaces of the Mocenigo family, where Byron lived later. The roof and dome of SS. Giovanni e Paolo are at the center, to the right and above a partial view of the Rialto Bridge. In the near distance the canal is relatively free of shipping; the few gondolas and sailing boats are small in scale and are shown from above in very steep perspective. The ominous sky—brighter toward the north, at the center of the picture—occupies half of the canvas, and the vast expanse of water the greater part of the other half, its greenish color in strangely menacing contrast. It was from approximately this viewpoint that Carlevaris painted, about 1709, his *Regatta in Honor of King Frederick of Denmark*, which Canaletto followed in his own regatta paintings (see cat. no. 43).

No occurrence in the well-chronicled history of Venetian architecture offers any specific evidence as to the date of this picture, which is among Canaletto's most evocative depictions of the Grand Canal. Numbers 3 and 4 were acquired by the city of Venice in 1983, shortly after the close of the Canaletto exhibition at the Fondazione Giorgio Cini, and are now displayed at Ca' Rezzonico.

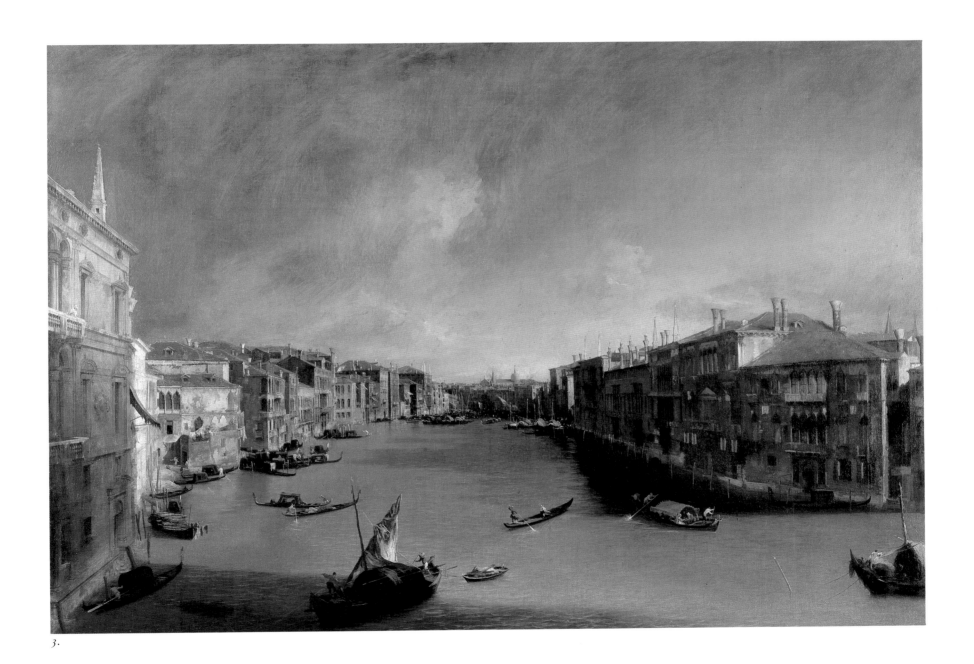

3.

4. Rio dei Mendicanti: looking South

Oil on canvas, 56¼ × 78¾ in. (143 × 200 cm)
Ca' Rezzonico, Venice
C/L 290

EXHIBITED
Venice 81

NOTE

1. V. Fanti, *Descrizzione completa di tutto ciò che ritrovasi nella galleria di pittura e scultura di Sua Altezza Giuseppe Wenceslao del S. R. I. Principe Regnante della casa di Lichtenstein* (Vienna, 1767). Neither does this series figure in J. Dallinger, *Description des tableaux et des pièces de sculpture, que renferme la gallerie de Son Altesse François Joseph chef et prince règnant de la maison de Liechtenstein* (Vienna, 1780), published in the reign of Joseph Wenzel's successor.

The view of the Rio dei Mendicanti toward the south is, as has often been remarked, quite unique in Canaletto's oeuvre. This canvas represents a place which would have been little visited, and a perspective not often seen, by travelers, and it does not include any major landmark. The view, slightly elevated, is taken from a point near the Fondamente Nuove with, at the left, the wide *fondamenta* or footway running along the facade of S. Lazzaro dei Mendicanti. A blind man with a stick, his outstretched hand touching the wall, makes his way along the *fondamenta*, and another suns himself in a warm corner, nearby. Beyond the wooden footbridge is the Ponte del Cavallo; to the left, and out of sight, the *campo* and church of SS. Giovanni e Paolo. Canaletto focuses on the wooden shacks, gondolas, and lively figures working in the *squeri*, or boat builders' yards, to the right, and on the rather unprepossessing buildings behind, aflutter with multicolored streams of laundry which is everywhere hung out to dry. The festival effect of these colored banners is mitigated by the many small, darkened windows against which they hang—suggestive of the squalid conditions of life within. The buildings, faced with discolored plaster, do not appear to rest upon firm foundations, but rather to sink into the waters of the canal. Undatable except by association with other canvases belonging to the same series, the picture is more fascinating by comparison with the view of Piazza S. Marco, with which until recent years it must always have hung.

No paintings by Canaletto are recorded in the description of the Liechtenstein gallery published by Fanti in 1767, five years before the death of Prince Joseph Wenzel, but Dallinger records a number of smaller canvases—of which catalogue number 54 is an example—in his catalogue of 1780.[1] These are now widely dispersed. Number 54 is labeled twice on the reverse: in German, with the artist's name and a date, 1740, and in French, with a note that it belonged to Joseph Wenzel. It is thus likely that this painting among others by Canaletto was acquired by the prince no later than 1740, that is, shortly before the outbreak of the War of the Austrian Succession. The small, tranquil, and readily salable Canalettos of the thirties may conceivably have entered the Liechtenstein collection at the same time—or even before—the more dramatic early views that are the subject of these entries.

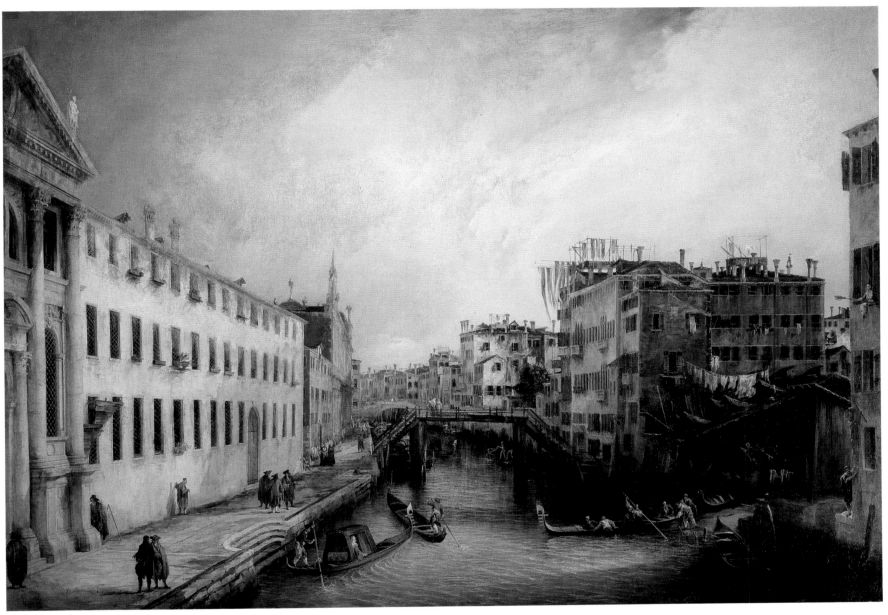

4.

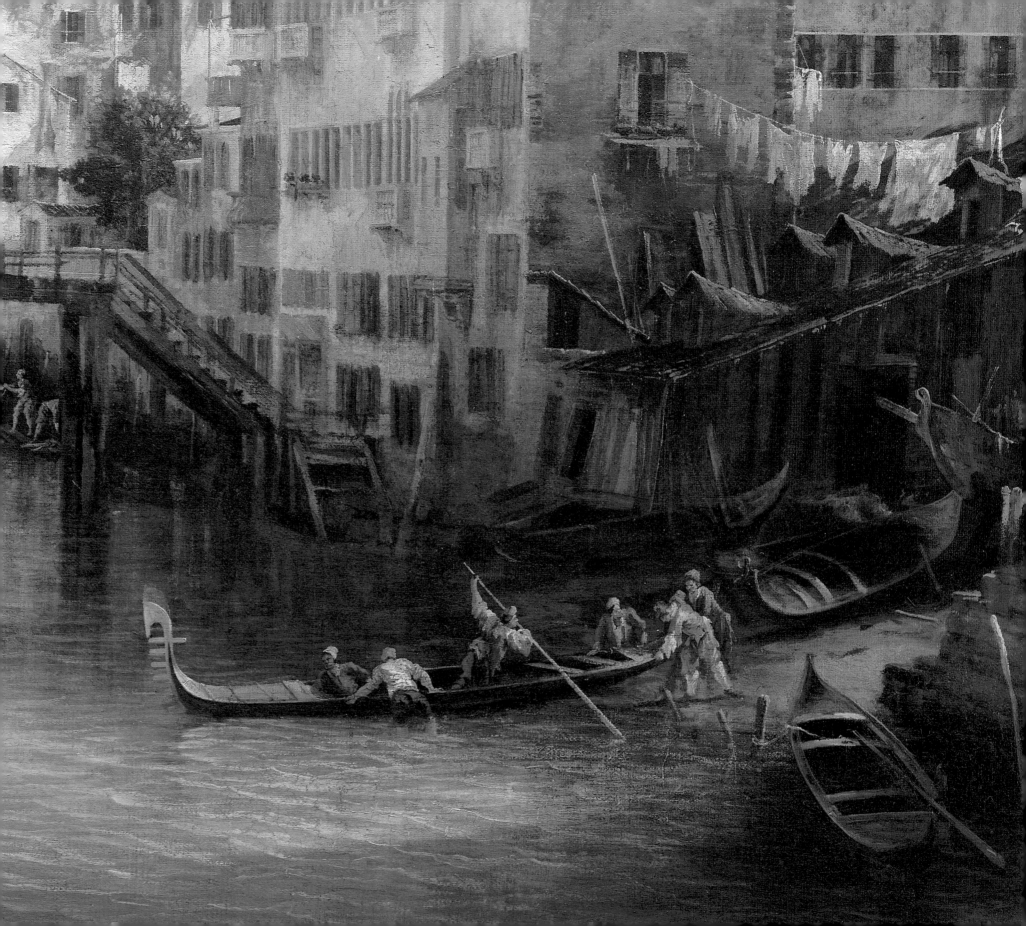

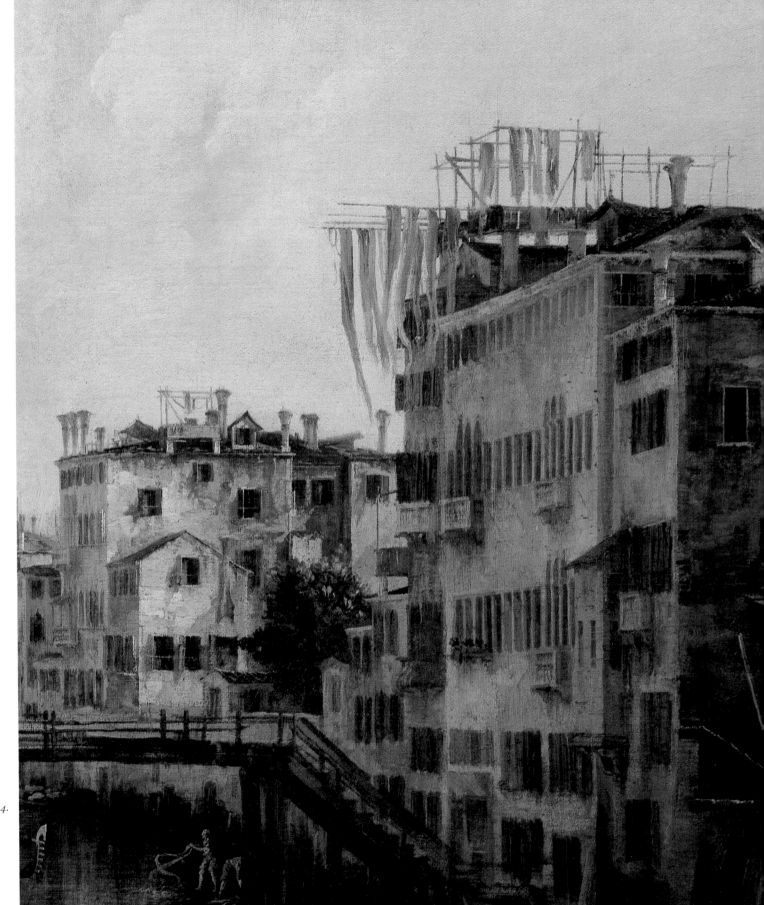

Details of 4.

5. SS. Giovanni e Paolo and the Scuola di S. Marco

Oil on canvas, 49¼×65 in. (125×165 cm)
Gemäldegalerie Alte Meister, Staatliche Kunstsammlungen,
Dresden
C/L 305

The Scuola Grande di S. Marco was one of the six principal charitable institutions of its kind in the city. SS. Giovanni e Paolo is the main Dominican church, and the *campo* is second in size only to Piazza S. Marco. The subject is likely to have been of greater interest to an Italian—more especially a native Venetian—than to a foreign client.

By tradition, open-air exhibitions of paintings were held annually in the Campo S. Rocco on 16 August, the feast day of the saint.[1] Pictures were also shown and sold in Piazza S. Marco and in Campo di Rialto (see cat. no. 7), but the exhibition at S. Rocco was the most important event of the kind in eighteenth-century Venice, timed as it was to coincide with the annual visit of the Doge, his retinue, the Senators, and foreign ambassadors. Most of the leading painters of the day exhibited at S. Rocco: Canaletto showed a canvas there in 1725—it may have been this one—and later he commemorated the feast day in the splendid painting belonging to the National Gallery, London (fig. 3). On 18 August 1725 Alessandro Marchesini, who was acting as agent for the purchase by Stefano Conti of four paintings commissioned from Canaletto (cat. nos. 8–11), gave the following account:

> Il giorno di S. Rocco espose al Publico una sua Veduta di S. Gio. e Paolo che fece meravigliare tutti. L'Ambasciadore dell'Imperatore se La Levò, e ne fece l'Acquisto avendone un altra di maggior grandezza....[2]

> (On St. Roch's Day he exhibited to the public one of his views, of SS. Giovanni e Paolo, and everyone marveled at it. The Ambassador of the Emperor took it, and acquired it having another of larger size....)

Conti's view of the same church and *scuola* (cat. no. 10) was ordered in December 1725 and completed before 15 June 1726, and if Marchesini's account is relevant, then the canvas that is the subject of this entry would have had to have been painted ten months or so before the Conti picture, rather than a little later, as is generally thought to have been the case. The Dresden painting is the larger of the two; there are two or three boats on the canal rather than one, and many more figures; the left half of the picture is taken from a point farther toward the right and omits the distant view of the

NOTES

1. Francis Haskell and Michael Levey, "Art Exhibitions in 18th Century Venice," *Arte Veneta* 12 (1958), pp. 181–83, 185.
2. Haskell, *Burlington Magazine*, 1956, p. 298.
3. *Katalog der Staatlichen Gemäldegalerie zu Dresden* (Dresden and Berlin, 1927), pp. xvii, xviii, 63, 65–66.
4. Rizzi, *Carlevarijs*, 1967, pp. 65, 88, 103, and pls. 143–45.

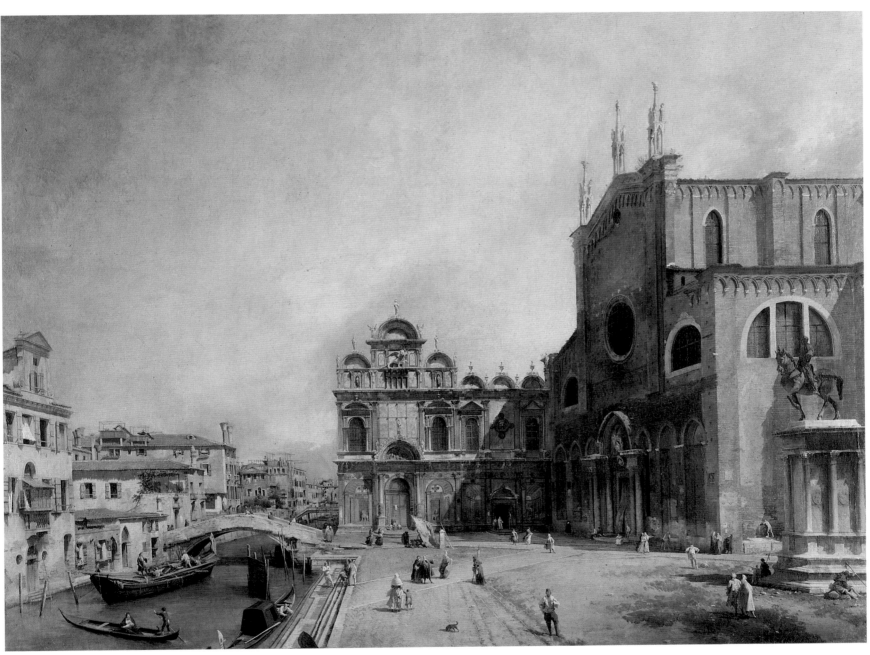

5.

mainland; and rather more of the south elevation of the church is shown.

There are five Canalettos in the Gemäldegalerie at Dresden: all are from the 1720s, and all were acquired after the death in 1733 of Augustus II, Elector of Saxony and King of Poland.[3] The pair of Grand Canal views (C/L 168 and 183) were among 268 paintings bought from the Wallenstein collection at Dux (Bohemia) in 1741. The remaining three—and coincidentally the only Carlevaris—are first recorded in the inventory of Augustus III's collection which was compiled in 1754 by Matthias Oesterreich. Carlevaris's canvas represents the triumphal entry on 3 April 1726 of Charles VI's ambassador to the Serenissima, Giovanni Battista, Conte di Colloredo (1656–1729), who probably commissioned that painting and could also have been the first owner of this view and of the other two exhibited (cat. nos. 6, 7).[4] Members of the family, which had its origins in Udine, lived from time to time in Venice; there was also an Austrian branch, and the Colloredos were long associated with the Imperial Court at Vienna.

6. Grand Canal: looking Northeast from near the Palazzo Corner Spinelli to the Rialto Bridge

Oil on canvas, 57½ × 92⅛ in. (146 × 234 cm)
Gemäldegalerie Alte Meister, Staatliche Kunstsammlungen, Dresden
C/L 208

The view is from a point farther up the Grand Canal than catalogue number 3 and from the opposite bank. The landing stage of the S. Angelo *traghetto*, or gondola ferry, is at the right, and beyond the quay is the corner of Palazzo Corner Spinelli. The sailing barge moored on the far side of the canal to the left lies just in front of Palazzo Barbarigo della Terrazza; the bell tower of S. Polo projects above the roof line. The sun shines on the facade of Palazzo Cappello, later the home of the English ambassador and collector Sir Henry Layard.

Canaletto rearranged the topography, widening the canal so that the water occupies the foreground from one side of the canvas nearly to the other, and giving more than half the picture surface to the sky. The palette is subdued, with few touches of local color, the canal gray-green, the sky ominous, nearly black in some passages. The view is animated by the working boats rafted together in the foreground, which are of remarkable variety and interest. Wisps of smoke from a bargeman's pipe, from a small fire aboard another boat, and from the chimneys of several of the palaces on the opposite bank suggest a fitful breeze.

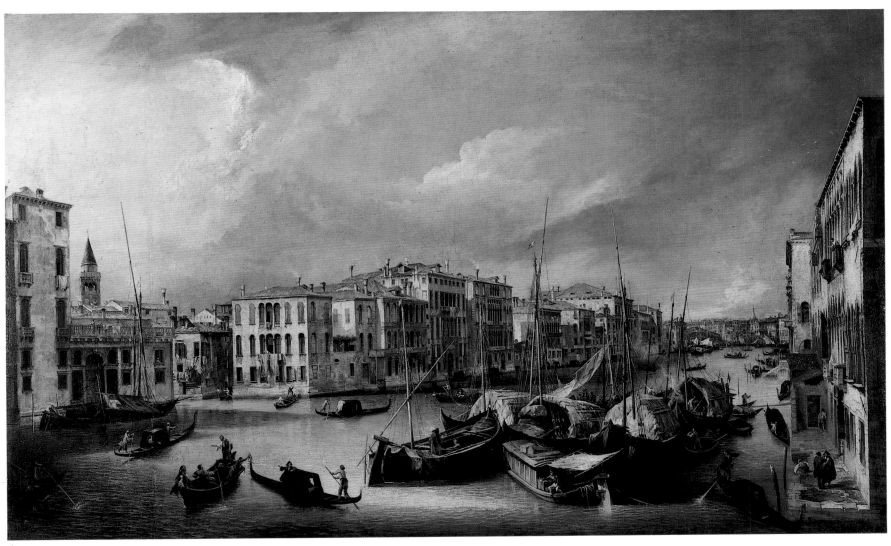

6.

The theatrical effect of the picture is unparalleled for Canaletto's work of the period and for view painting in general, and it would be interesting to know how this canvas was received by its first owner. If it is to be identified with the larger painting owned by the Imperial ambassador, then this view of the Grand Canal must have been finished by the summer of 1725, and it could be significantly earlier. Very probably, it has not been seen with the early views from Ca' Rezzonico and the Thyssen collection and from the Conti series since leaving the artist's studio, if then.

7. S. Giacomo di Rialto

Oil on canvas, 37⅝ × 46⅛ in. (95.5 × 117 cm)
Gemäldegalerie Alte Meister, Staatliche Kunstsammlungen, Dresden
C/L 297

The Rialtine islands were the first to be settled, and S. Giacomo di Rialto is thought of as the oldest church in Venice, though the building that is the subject of the present picture dates from the twelfth century, and was restored in 1531, in 1601, and again shortly after the middle of the eighteenth century.[1] The *campo* has always been the banking and trading center of the city. The gold- and silversmiths traditionally occupied the shops along the Ruga degli Orefici, to the right and leading to the Rialto Bridge, while beyond the bridge and the buildings on the opposite side of the canal is the spire of S. Bartolomeo. Left of the facade of S. Giacomo is a partial view of the Palazzo dei Camerlenghi.

The figures are beautifully painted and of much interest: street urchins, officials, orientals, vendors of objects in precious metals, picture salesmen, and bird sellers and their clientele, among them a gentleman in a full wig and a long black cloak, a dead bird suspended by the legs from his hand. The canvas, carefully composed, is precisely bisected by the column supporting the right corner of the church portico; the *campo* and the facade of the church are in sunlight, while the street and the Palazzo dei Dieci Savi are in deep shade and steep perspective.

The subject is one to which Canaletto would return, but not for some twenty or perhaps even thirty years. This picture and, by comparison, the later works relating to it demonstrate the variety and extent of Canaletto's manipulations of topographical fact. In the painting of the same subject at the National Gallery of Canada, Ottawa (C/L 298), the bell tower is smaller in proportion to the facade, the windows differ in scale and position, and the

NOTES
1. Michael Pantazzi, in *European and American Painting, Sculpture, and Decorative Arts, 1300–1800: Catalogue of the National Gallery of Canada* (Ottawa, 1987), pp. 51–55, provides a full account of the various representations of S. Giacomo di Rialto, giving details of the history of the church and *campo*.
2. Corboz, *Canaletto*, 1985, p. 56.
3. For the etching, see Bromberg, *Canaletto's Etchings*, 1974, p. 161, no. 30.

84

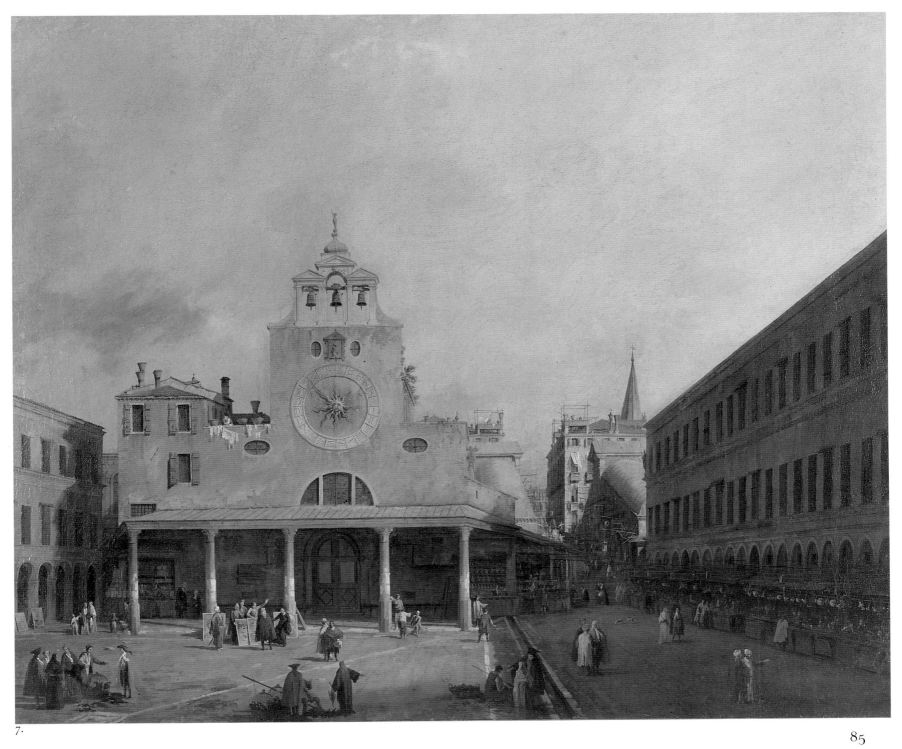

7.

portico has four columns instead of (as in fact) five; the figures are also much larger in proportion to the architecture around them. Two drawings in public collections—the principal version in the Courtauld Institute Galleries, London (C/L 611), and a replica in the Kupferstichkabinett, Berlin-Dahlem (C/L 611 note)—and a third whose present location is unknown show the portico with six columns and two more semicircular windows not otherwise represented by Canaletto. Corboz observes that while the facade of the church in Canaletto's various representations appears to be perpendicular to the Ruga degli Orefici, the angle is in fact oblique.[2] Neither can the Palazzo dei Camerlenghi and the Rialto Bridge be seen at the same time, as shown here, by someone standing in the *campo*; the scene is accurately observed but from two different viewpoints. The Ottawa picture has traditionally been dated between 1740 and 1746, but may have been painted after Canaletto's return from England ten years later, and the chronology of the drawings is also problematic, though they are probably later still—the repaving of the *campo* and replacement of the spire of S. Bartolomeo notwithstanding. The existence of a capriccio view of S. Giacomo di Rialto among the etchings of the early 1740s serves only to complicate the matter further.[3]

No precedent is known for this view, and even though it is not recorded in Dresden until 1754 the artist is unlikely to have retained it for long. It seems likely that years later some sort of rough drawing or *modello* served to remind him of his early design. Until 1918 the *S. Giacomo di Rialto* had as a pendant a now-lost view of *Piazza S. Marco: looking East along the Central Line* (C/L 10).

Stefano Conti's Commission

In July 1725 Stefano Conti, a textile merchant in Lucca, was advised by his agent, the Veronese painter Alessandro Marchesini, who was then living in Venice, to order two paintings from Canaletto, whose work had astonished those who had seen it, rather than from Carlevaris, three of whose pictures Conti already owned. A pair of paintings was contracted for from Canaletto on 2 August 1725 and, although work on them did not begin until September, the two canvases were completed by 25 November of that year. Meanwhile, and before the first two were finished, Conti ordered a second pair, Canaletto acknowledging receipt of an advance for them on 22 December. On 2 February 1726 Canaletto was about to begin; in late May the third picture—representing SS. Giovanni e Paolo—had been completed, and by 15 June the fourth was also finished and the artist had been paid in full. Canaletto received ninety *zecchini*, having at the outset asked thirty *zecchini* for each of the first pair, and then agreed to accept between twenty and twenty-five, leaving to the favorable cognizance of Marchesini and Conti the difference between. Canaletto's certificates and receipts, first published by W. G. Constable in 1923, have always remained with the paintings and are exhibited here (see Appendix).[1]

Owing to the researches of Francis Haskell, detailed information about Conti's activity as a patron and Marchesini's as his agent has also come to light, the correspondence having been copied into a notebook which is preserved in the Biblioteca Governativa at Lucca.[2] Marchesini's comments are detailed and place the works precisely in context. He mentions and reaffirms what can only be called a fascinating but unlikely hypothesis: that Canaletto painted "sopra il loco," that is, out-of-doors and before the motif.[3] He addresses and attempts to justify the matter of Canaletto's failure to begin work in timely fashion, describes other projects, the critical response to certain of Canaletto's early pictures, and many more practical details, such as the difficulty of securing blue pigment of good quality, and Canaletto's thoughts on the subject of suitable frames.

Conti died in 1739 and his Canalettos passed by descent to Marchese Boccella of Lucca, who in 1832 sold them to Robert Townley Parker. Parker's grandson, Reginald A. Tatton, consigned them to Christie's for sale on 14 December 1928: they made considerable sums, records for the artist's work.[4] In June 1929 the entire series was acquired from Knoedler by a Canadian collector. The Conti Canalettos are the milestone and point of reference for the artist's early development.

NOTES

1. The paintings and the documents reprinted in the Appendix were published by W. G. Constable some forty years before the catalogue raisonné: "Some Unpublished Canalettos," *Burlington Magazine* 42 (1923), pp. 284–88. The pictures had been mentioned previously by Hilda Finberg, "Canaletto in England," 1920–21, pp. 23–24.

2. Haskell, *Burlington Magazine*, 1956, pp. 296–300, quoting extensively from MS. 3299; and Haskell, *Patrons and Painters*, 1980, pp. 226–28.

3. Haskell, *Burlington Magazine*, 1956, p. 298.

4. Three were sold to P. and D. Colnaghi and the fourth—representing SS. Giovanni e Paolo—to the Savile Gallery. The next several months saw various combinations of joint ownership in the art trade.

8. Grand Canal: the Rialto Bridge from the North

Oil on canvas, 35⅜ × 53 in. (90.5 × 134.6 cm)
Private Collection
C/L 234

EXHIBITED
Canada 6

NOTE

1. For a photograph of the document and an approximate translation of the whole, see the Appendix.

Canaletto's own description of this picture is dated 25 November 1725:

> ...the Bridge of the Rialto on the side looking towards the Germans Warehouse which is opposite the Palace of the Magistrates of Camerlinghi and other Magistrates besides, looking down upon the Vegetable Market where they land all kinds of Vegetables and fruits to be shared amongst the dealers in the City. In the middle of the Canal is painted a Peotta Nobile with figures in it, and four Gondoliers going at full speed and close to it a Gondola having the Livery of the Emperors Ambassador.[1]

The corner of a palazzo of three stories, with an awning extended at the uppermost window, provides a vertical accent and closes the composition at the left. The building is probably Palazzo Civran. This compositional device was quite often used by Canaletto to structure his views, and was later employed also by Francesco Guardi in, for example, a painting of the same subject in the Metropolitan Museum. Just to the right, in full sun, is the Fondaco dei Tedeschi, originally a residence and warehouse for the German traders congregating in the area. At the beginning of the sixteenth century, after a fire, the *fondaco* had been rebuilt in traditional style, and the facade facing on the canal had been decorated with frescoes by Giorgione, which were engraved as late as the 1750s by Anton Maria Zanetti the Younger. The frescoes are not distinguishable in this painting. The Rialto Bridge, the Palazzo dei Camerlenghi, which was occupied by the city treasurers, and the Fabbriche Vecchie di Rialto are in shadow. The *campo* then as now occupied in the early morning hours by the Naranzeria and Erberia, the fruit and vegetable markets, lies between and is brightly illuminated. In the center foreground there is a private barge, rowed by four gondoliers and carrying a party of ladies and gentlemen seated at a table under an awning.

Two later variations on the same theme are exhibited here (cat. nos. 15 and 24), together with a preparatory drawing (cat. no. 86) for the picture. The composition of the drawing is identical to that of the painting in all important respects; the cloud masses are in the same place, and the diagonal hatchings conform with the shaded areas. As has been noted, Marchesini told Conti that Canaletto, unlike Carlevaris, painted at the site, but this is unlikely to have been the case: there is no single viewpoint from which the buildings represented in this canvas can be seen in the relationships shown.

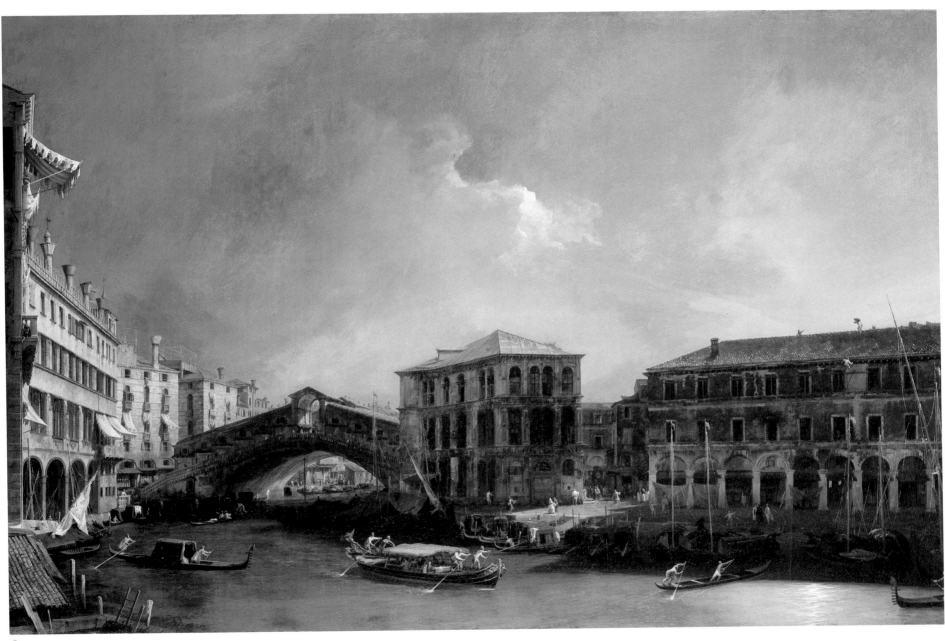

8.

9. Grand Canal: looking North from near the Rialto Bridge

Oil on canvas, 35¼ × 51¾ in. (89.5 × 131.4 cm)
Private Collection
C/L 230

EXHIBITED
Canada 5

NOTE
1. For the document and full translation, see the Appendix.

In the same document of 25 November 1725 Canaletto describes the second painting as follows:

> ... pursuing the same Canal looking down to the Fish market the Palazzo Pesaro and in the distance the Campanile de S. Marcola, on the other side of the Canal but near is the Palazzo de Casa Grimani and in succession other Palaces, as Rezonico, Sagrado and many more.[1]

At the extreme left in this canvas is a sunlit corner of the market previously described, and beyond the Fabbriche Vecchie di Rialto, which are in shadow and partially clad in scaffolding toward the north, is the open-air fish market. Ca' Pesaro, outlined against the sky, is the most distant palace visible on the far bank of the canal. The larger of the palaces opposite in the foreground are Michiel dal Brusà and Michiel dalle Colonne; a little farther along is Ca' d'Oro, and near the end of the vista is the palace Canaletto calls Grimani, better known as Vendramin Calergi, where Richard Wagner died in 1883. Zaccaria Sagredo, the great connoisseur who is recorded as having been one of Canaletto's first patrons, lived in one of the palaces shown, and the Rezzonico family owned one of them until they built the celebrated palace lower down the Grand Canal that still bears their name.

As with the companion painting, there is no single viewpoint which presents the scene as depicted here. By a remarkable coincidence the drawing which must have been preparatory to this painting has also been preserved and appeared recently in the salerooms (cat. no. 87). Drawing and painting clearly show scaffolding on the building in front and to the left of Ca' Pesaro, scaffolding which was put up in connection with the rebuilding of the Palazzo Corner della Regina, begun in 1724. The scaffolding does not appear in any of the several later versions of the subject, by which time the new palace must have been finished. Of the later versions of this pair, the first must have been those painted for the Duke of Richmond (cat. nos. 14, 15), and among the most interesting is the one painted, and altered, for Consul Smith (cat. no. 41).

90

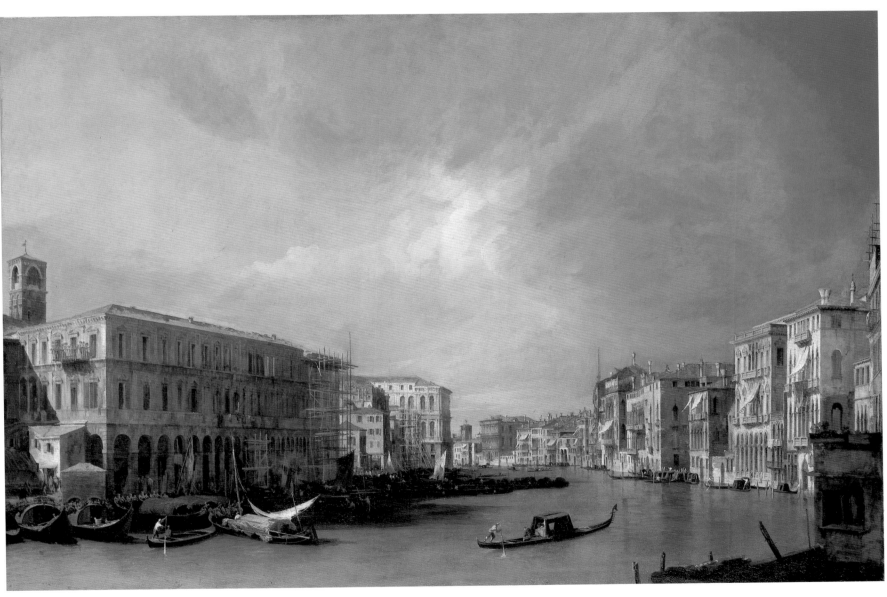

9.

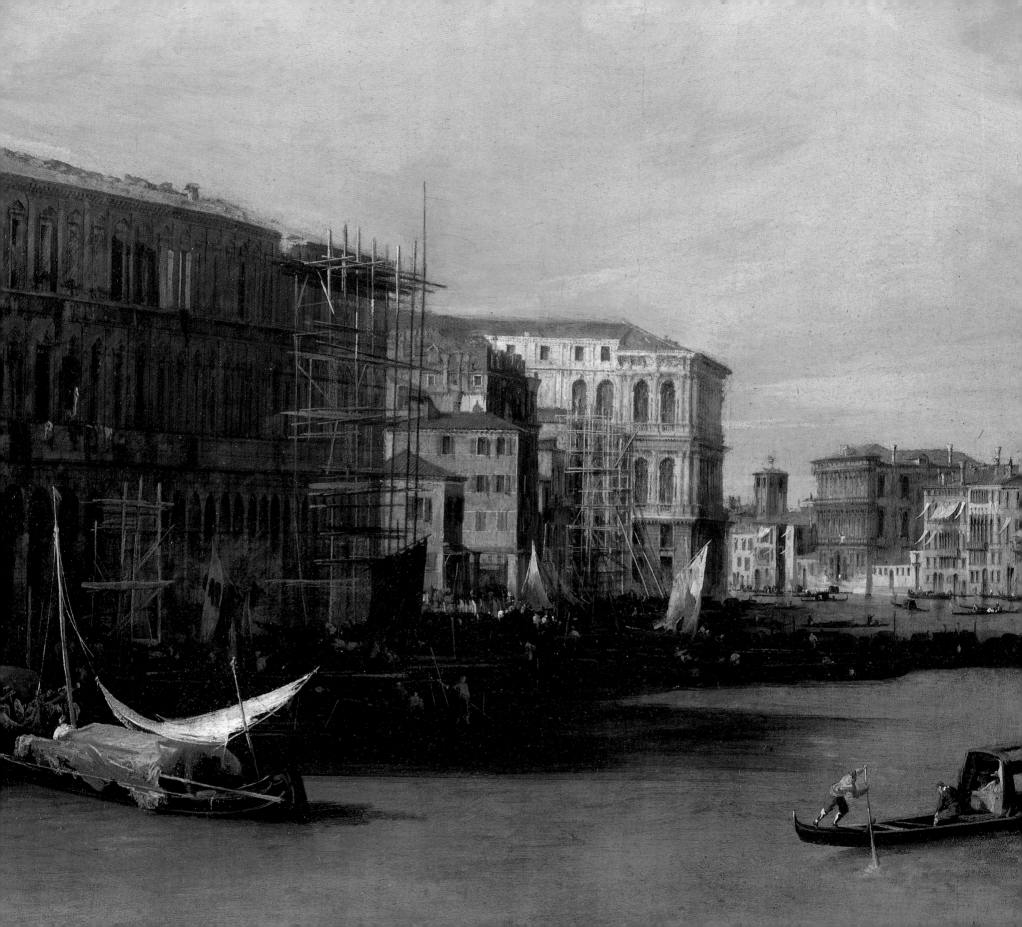

10. SS. Giovanni e Paolo and the Scuola di S. Marco

Oil on canvas, 35⅝ × 53½ in. (90.5 × 135.9 cm)
Private Collection
C/L 304

EXHIBITED

Canada 8

NOTE

1. For the document and full translation, see the Appendix.

Detail of 9.

Several subjects were considered as possibilities for Stefano Conti's second pair, and he was not told that the church of SS. Giovanni e Paolo was to be represented in one of them until the canvas was completed in May 1726. On 15 June Canaletto supplied the following description:

> ...a View of the Church of S.S. Giovanni e Paolo with the Square and the Equestrian Statue of General Bartolomeo da Bergamo and various other figures, namely a Counselor in a Red Gown going into church an other of a Domenican friar and different other figures.[1]

This view is taken from a point looking north along the same canal, but from the opposite direction as the *Rio dei Mendicanti* (cat. no. 4). The *rio*, the Ponte del Cavallo, and the wooden footbridge beyond are to the left; at the center, across the *campo* and in partial shadow, is the Scuola di S. Marco, and to the right, the shaded facade and sunlit south elevation of the great Dominican church of SS. Giovanni e Paolo. Verrocchio's monument to the famous *condottiere* Bartolomeo Colleoni is in the right foreground. A distant view of the mountains of the mainland can just be seen at the end of the canal. Except for the fact that the farthest buildings along the Rio dei Mendicanti are backlit, the view is much the same as the one now in Dresden (cat. no. 5).

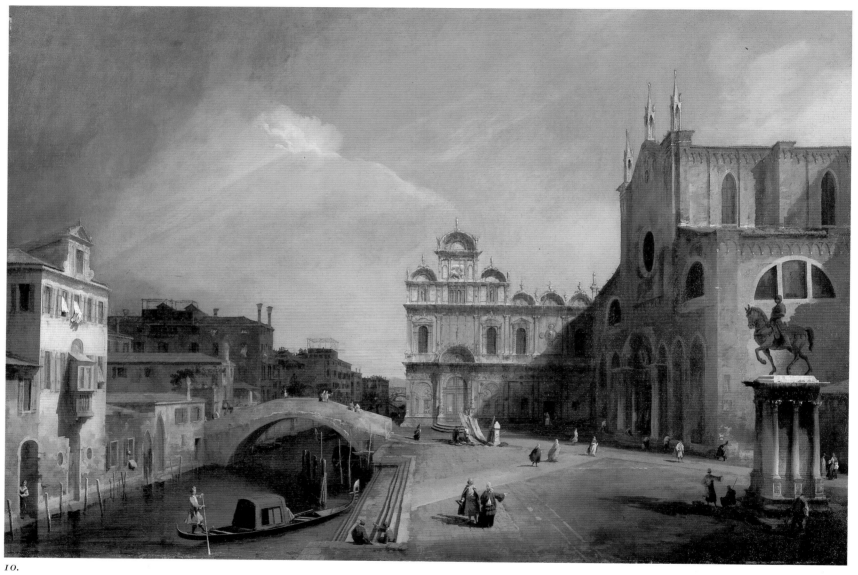

10.

94

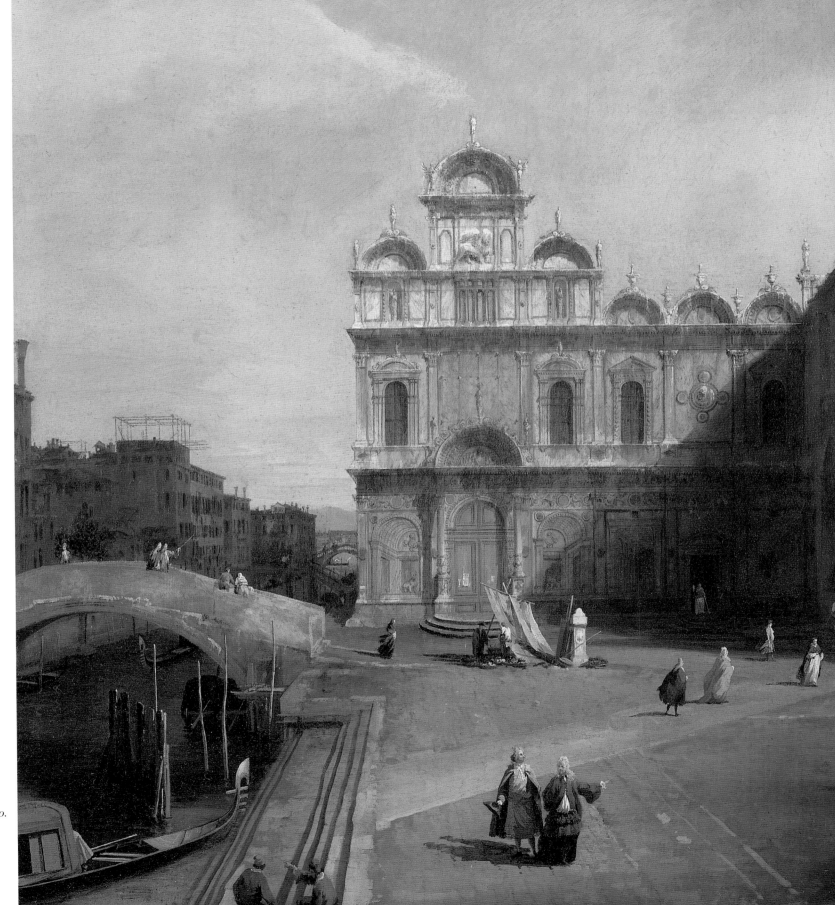

Detail of 10.

11. Grand Canal: from Sta. Maria della Carità to the Bacino di S. Marco

Oil on canvas, 35¼ × 51¾ in. (89.5 × 131.4 cm)
Private Collection
C/L 194

EXHIBITED
Canada 7

NOTES
1. For the document and full translation, see the Appendix.
2. Haskell, *Burlington Magazine*, 1956, pp. 299–300, who notes that as a patron of the arts Conti was representative of the "man in the street." It is of interest that, during the same years, Marchesini was negotiating on Conti's behalf with Marco and Sebastiano Ricci and also considered, but rejected, Cimaroli.

Canaletto referred to the church as that of the Rocchetini, or Lateran canons, and to the *campo* as the piazza where he disposed many small figures, among which, in a little group of three, two fathers of the order talking with a Savio, or learned man, in a violet-colored robe. Canaletto also noted that the view extends as far as the Riva degli Schiavoni in the distance.[1]

The church of Sta. Maria della Carità is now part of the museum of the Accademia and is thus well known to visitors to the city, though from a different perspective, as the buildings of the museum are now most often approached by a wooden bridge, recently rebuilt (the first, iron, bridge was built in 1854, and the original wooden bridge in 1932). The smaller canal in the foreground of the Conti picture has been filled in. The campanile, which fell in the early 1740s, can also be seen in *"The Stonemason's Yard"* (cat. no. 32); on the other hand by the time *"The Stonemason's Yard"* was painted the building at the extreme left in this view had been demolished in order to make a garden for the adjoining palace, Palazzo Franchetti.

The present picture and the preceding one are more broadly painted than Conti's earlier pair, the view of Sta. Maria della Carità depending for its effect on marked contrasts of light and deep shade. Canaletto shows the quay in the foreground in need of repair. In a later variant (C/L 195) it has fallen into even greater disrepair, and in a third, for Smith's Grand Canal series (cat. no. 40), it has been rebuilt. By that time, though, the statue on the pinnacle at the right of the church facade had fallen off.

With respect to the subjects Canaletto chose for Conti's second pair, each had evidently been painted before. By Marchesini's account, a view of SS. Giovanni e Paolo had been publicly exhibited at S. Rocco, on the 16 August 1725 feast day, and had been bought on that occasion by the Imperial ambassador. As to the Carità, Marchesini noted that a picture of the church with different figures belonged to the distinguished collection at Ca' Sagredo. Canaletto himself, or Marchesini, may have concluded that association with such luminaries would be pleasing to Stefano Conti who was, as Francis Haskell points out, an elderly gentleman of conventional taste.[2]

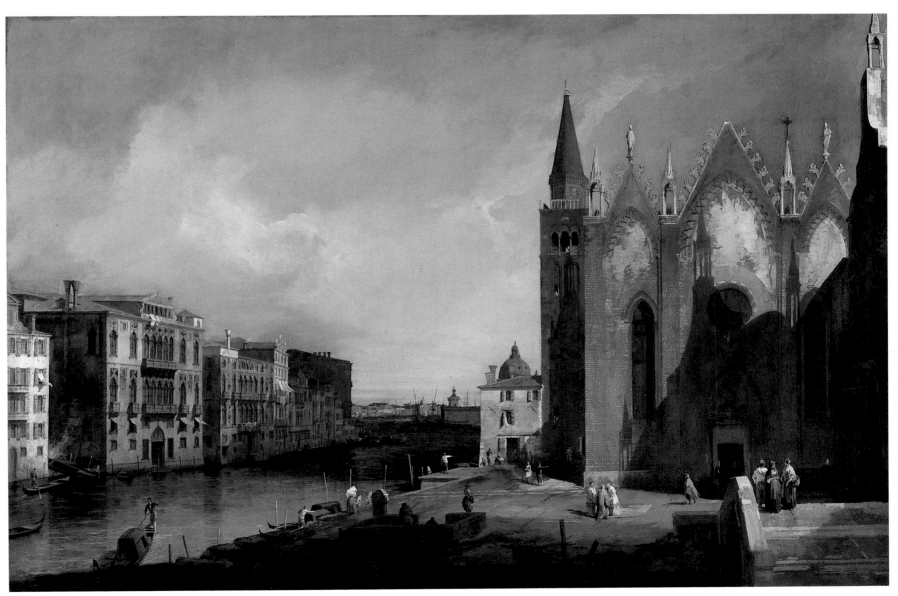

II.

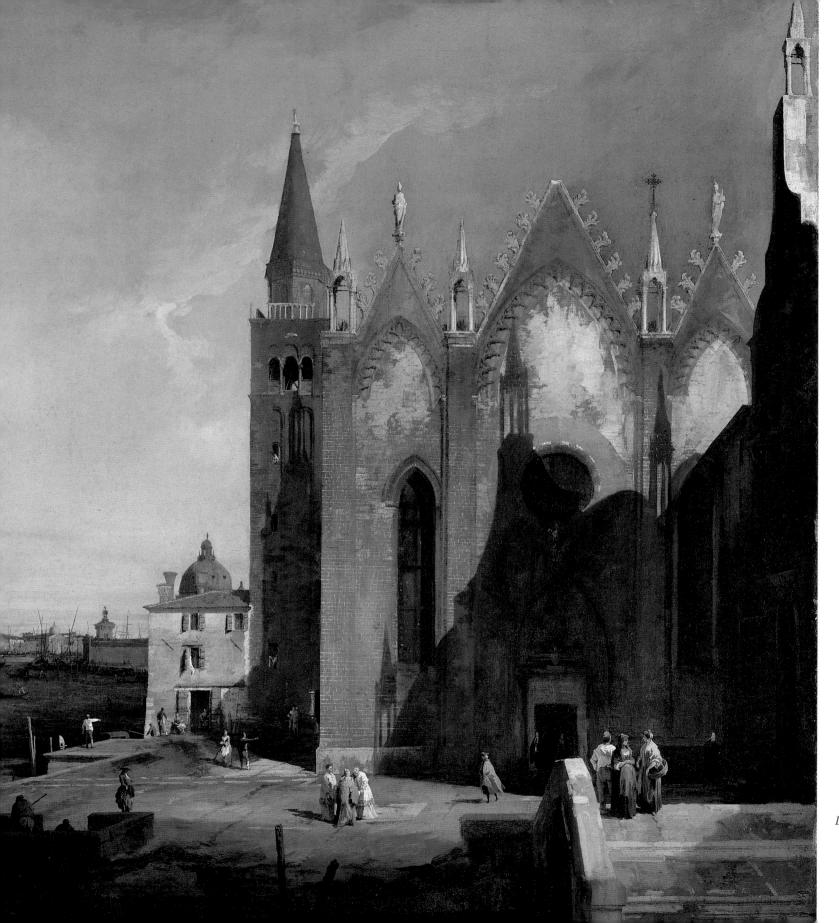

Detail of 11.

McSwiney's Allegorical Tomb Paintings

It was through the good offices of Owen McSwiney that Canaletto—as he called the painter—received his first commissions for paintings destined for the English market.[1] In the early years of the eighteenth century McSwiney, who was Irish, enjoyed a brief moment of success as a theatrical performer and impresario in London, but bankruptcy soon drove him into exile on the Continent. While in Venice McSwiney was associated in business with the English merchant Joseph Smith, who later became Canaletto's principal patron. Acting probably for the second Duke of Richmond (who had succeeded to the title in 1723), McSwiney commissioned from a number of Venetian and Bolognese painters of the day a series of very large pictures representing allegorical tombs, each of which was intended to commemorate one of the heroes of modern English history with particular reference to the Glorious Revolution of 1688. McSwiney intended that each picture should be the work of three artists charged respectively with painting the landscape, the buildings and other ornaments, and the figures. The scheme, and the list of subjects to be represented, probably grew over time. The series eventually numbered twenty-four canvases and, based upon these canvases, reductions in grisaille from which engravings were to be made.

By 8 March 1726 McSwiney was able to report to the Duke of Richmond that, of fifteen pictures commissioned, six were finished (the date the project got under way is unfortunately not recorded). In the event ten of them were sold to the duke for installation in the dining room at Goodwood, where Vertue saw them and described them in 1747, and where they remained until the late eighteenth century when the room was redecorated.[2] The balance went to Sir William Morice, who had bought them by November 1729. McSwiney meanwhile issued a pamphlet about the allegorical tomb paintings, and a number of them were engraved by French engravers; these prints were published in London in 1741, as a volume entitled *Tombeaux des Princes grands capitaines et autres hommes illustres, qui ont fleuri dans la Grande-Bretagne vers la fin du XVII et le commencement du XVIII siècle*. Canaletto's role in the tomb project was a rather minor one: he contributed to two of the pictures (cat. nos. 12, 13). Why would Canaletto have accepted so minor a commission if by this time, as Marchesini reports, he was so busy and well known?[3] Perhaps he wished to be associated with such older and yet more famous artists as Marco and Sebastiano Ricci, who contributed to the project, or perhaps, as an established view painter, he already anticipated the benefits that might be associated with foreign patronage.

NOTES

1. For a brief account of the entire project see Haskell, *Patrons and Painters*, 1980, pp. 287–91. There is a catalogue of the series, including much related material, by Mazza, "La vicenda dei 'Tombeaux des Princes,'" 1976, pp. 79–102 and pls. 141–51.
2. *Vertue Note Books*, V, pp. 149–50, with a floor plan suggesting that the tomb pictures were closely hung, and that there were in addition two overdoors by the English painter John Wootton.
3. Haskell, *Burlington Magazine*, 1956, p. 298.

Canaletto, with Giovanni Battista Pittoni, and Giovanni Battista Cimaroli

12. Capriccio: Tomb of Archbishop Tillotson

Oil on canvas, 87 × 55 in. (221 × 139.7 cm)
Private Collection
C/L 517

EXHIBITED
Venice 78

NOTES
1. See Jeffery Daniels, in *Canaletto*, 1982, p. 56, no. 78.
2. The date of the letter, misrecorded as 1722 by Constable, *Burlington Magazine*, 1954, p. 154, was corrected to read 1726 by Jeffery Daniels, *Sebastiano Ricci* (Hove, 1976), p. 17.
3. For Pittoni (1687–1767), see Franca Zava Boccazzi, *Pittoni* (Venice, 1979), pp. 60, 134–35, no. 83, p. 137, no. 92, p. 150, no. 143, and p. 221.
4. Watson, *Burlington Magazine*, 1953, p. 365. See also Watson, *Burlington Magazine*, 1953, pp. 205–7 and figs. 46, 47, and 51; Morassi, "Saggio su Giambattista Cimaroli," 1972, pp. 167–76; and John Pope-Hennessy with Laurence B. Kanter, *The Robert Lehman Collection: I. Italian Paintings* (New York and Princeton, 1987), p. 256, no. 103, and pl. 103. The pictures thus far identified are almost all of mainland subjects.

John Tillotson (born 1630), a celebrated theologian and preacher, was Archbishop of Canterbury from 1691 until his death in 1694.[1] He was remembered for the influence he exerted upon Queen Anne in the matter of the Protestant succession. On the pedestal of his allegorical tomb is a group representing Charity, and below are single figures of Hope, with an anchor, and Faith, with a chalice and a cross. Tillotson's coat of arms is displayed, and a miter and scepter lie upon the altar, which is surrounded by priests and acolytes carrying candles and smoking censers. Classical ruins are disposed in the middle distance against a mountain landscape, and to the right the composition is closed by the trunk and spreading branches of a tree in full leaf.

In his letter of March 1726, McSwiney referred to the picture as "A Bishop Tillotson's perspective and landscape (finished) by *Canaletto* and Cimaroli. Figures (now painting) by *Jean Battista Pittoni*."[2] On 11 October and again on 1 November, the picture was described as finished, but owing to the delay in the completion of the chiaroscuro—a grisaille reduction preparatory to an engraving—it was not dispatched to England until 25 February 1727. The painting hung at Goodwood and seems to have had as its pendant the allegorical tomb of the Duke of Devonshire by Sebastiano and Marco Ricci. The grisaille reduction (Louvre, Paris) is generally, though not universally, ascribed to Pittoni, and a variant, larger in size, may be by Pittoni and his workshop. The engraving published in 1741, which relates most closely to the grisaille, is inscribed *J. B. Pittoni. et A. Canal et J. B. Cimaroli Pinx.—D. Beauvais Sculp. D. M. Fratta delin.*

The figures are judged to be entirely by Pittoni and accord stylistically with their recorded date.[3] To Canaletto are ascribed the tomb, the ruins, and rather more of the landscape than McSwiney's comment seems to indicate. As to Cimaroli, he is an artist about whom very little is known, and perhaps, as Sir Francis Watson suggested, he contributed little more than the foliage.[4]

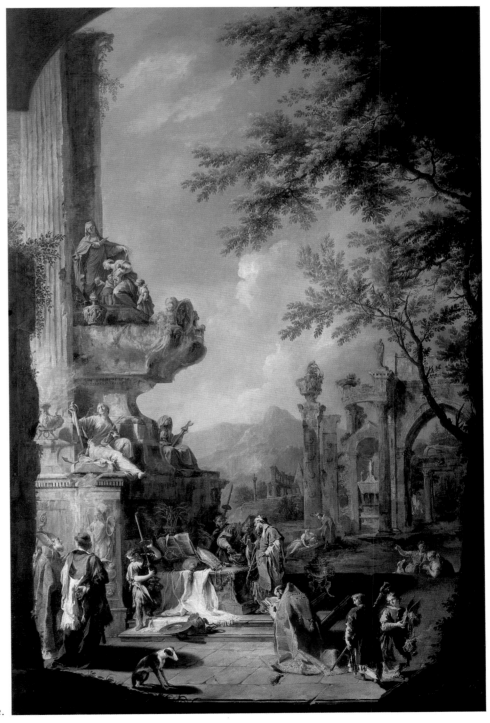

12.

Canaletto, with Giovanni Battista Piazzetta, and Giovanni Battista Cimaroli

13. Capriccio: Tomb of Lord Somers

Oil on canvas, 110 × 56 in. (279.4 × 142.2 cm)
Viscount Windsor
C/L 516

The tomb is surmounted by allegorical figures of Justice and Peace, and below there is a fountain and a basin of water. Among the ecclesiastical figures at the center are two bishops, one of them carried upon a litter. In the absence of a coat of arms the key to the rather obscure subject matter—and ultimately to the attribution—of the picture is provided by the still life in the foreground: the mace, woolsack, and purse of the Lord Chancellor of England, and the sword of the Sergeant-at-Arms. As Sir Francis Watson first pointed out, these can only refer to John, Lord Somers (1651–1716), Lord Chancellor from 1697 until 1700, who was famous for his eloquent defense of the Whig cause during the Trial of the Seven Bishops (1688).[1] Watson's identification of the subject was immediately confirmed by Constable, who published the letter from McSwiney to the Duke of Richmond dating from 8 March 1726:

> That of Ld Sommers is a sacrifice or Religious Ceremony (at his monument) in acknowledg^mt of the service done the Church, for his pleading the cause of the Bishops etc, The perspective and lands^cps are painted by *Canaletto* & Cimeroli. The figures by Geo. *Battista Piacotta*.[2]

There are no further references to this painting in the correspondence. It is not recorded in the dining room at Goodwood, and must therefore have been among the tomb paintings bought by Sir William Morice by 29 November 1729. Francis Russell notes that a reduction was sold by Lord Harewood at Christie's on 2 July 1965; there is no record of an engraving. The picture was lost from sight from the time of the presumed sale to Morice until sold by a London dealer about 1880 to a member of the family of the present owner.

As noted by McSwiney, the figures are by Piazzetta and were evidently finished while Pittoni was still working on the figures in the Tillotson picture.[3] If, as seems likely, Cimaroli painted little more than the foliage, then Canaletto did the lion's share of the work and this picture was for him the more important of the two, the essential point of reference against which the capriccios ascribed to him and thought to date from the 1720s must be judged. The vaults and arches overgrown with exuberant foliage anticipate certain much later imaginary views (see cat. no. 79).

EXHIBITED

Canada 1

NOTES

1. Watson, *Burlington Magazine*, 1953, pp. 362–65; and see also Francis Russell, in *The Treasure Houses of Britain*, exh. cat. (Washington, 1985), p. 251, no. 171.
2. Constable, *Burlington Magazine*, 1954, p. 154, where the date is misquoted.
3. For Piazzetta (1682–1754), see Adriano Mariuz, *L'opera completa del Piazzetta* (Milan, 1982), p. 83, no. 32.

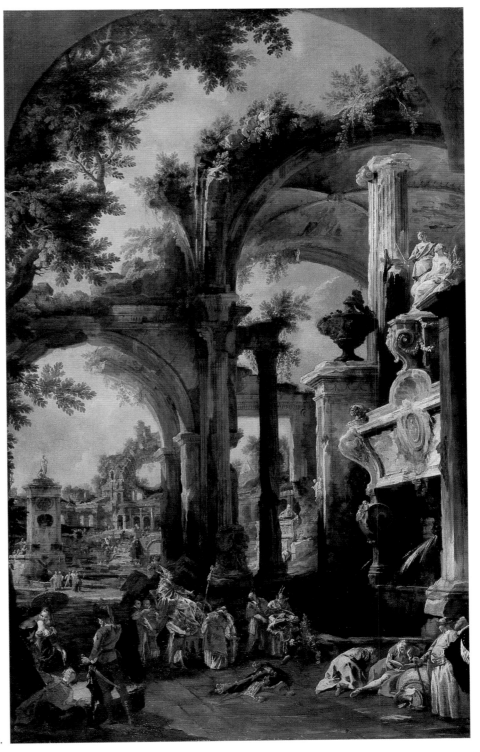

McSwiney's Copperplates

On 28 November 1727, in a letter to the Duke of Richmond dealing mainly with the progress of the allegorical tomb paintings (cat. nos. 12, 13) and the duke's complaint of delay in sending pictures long since paid for, McSwiney first mentioned buying view paintings from Canaletto.[1] The passage reads as follows:

> The pieces which Mr. Southwell has, (of Canals painting) were done for me, and they cost me *70 sequeens*. The fellow is whimsical and vary's his prices every day: and he that has a mind to have any of his work, must not seem to be too fond of it, for he'l be yᵉ worse treated for it, both in the price and the painting too. He has more work than he can doe, in any reasonable time, and well: but by the assistance of a particular friend of his, I get once in two months a piece sketch'd out and a little time after finished, by force of bribery.
>
> I send yʳ Grace by Captain Robinson (Commandʳ of the Tokeley Gally) who sails from hence tomorrow, *Two of the Finest pieces*, I think he ever painted and of the same size with Mr. Southwells little ones (which is a size he excells in) and are done upon copper plates: *They cost me two and twenty sequeens* each. They'l be delivered to yʳ Grace by Mr. John Smith, as soon as they arrive in London.

Finally he writes that he will have a view of the Rialto Bridge "done by Canal in twenty days" and that he has "bespoke another view of Venice for by the by." He refers several times in subsequent letters to the two copperplates which had been sent, hoping to hear that the duke liked them, but by 1 October 1729 the second pair are still only promised, although McSwiney acknowledged receipt of payment several months before.

Mr. Southwell could have been Edward Southwell, father or son: both were in Italy in the 1720s. The wording of the letter gives the impression that the duke knew Mr. Southwell, had seen his pictures, and had asked McSwiney about them, but too much should not be read into this. Of one point, however, there can be no doubt: that McSwiney had sold the Duke of Richmond two views on copper, which had been finished by Canaletto and packed up for shipment on 29 November 1727. As late as September 1730 McSwiney wrote the letter to John Conduitt, quoted above in "A Biographical Sketch," from which it is apparent that the duke's second pair had still not been delivered. He refers once again to the duke's first pair, to Mr. Southwell's pair, and to "Two of Sir Wᵐ Morice" as in Canaletto's "buon gusto—nay compare these with any other you know & you'l soon discern yᵉ difference."

Nine copperplates in all are known to have survived, of which two pairs can be identified with near certainty. Some role in the change of style that Canaletto's copperplates represent must be attributed to McSwiney, who may

NOTE

1. C/L, p. 174; excerpts from McSwiney's correspondence with the Duke of Richmond were first published by Hilda F. Finberg in her pioneering account of Canaletto's English period, "Canaletto in England," *Walpole Society* 9 (1920–21), pp. 22–24.

have conceived the notion that sunny views of well-known sites—the Grand Canal, the church of Sta. Maria della Salute, the *bacino*, and the Riva degli Schiavoni—would appeal to milords, to other grand tourists, and even to those who had not visited Venice but knew of its major monuments. The copperplates are quite small, and portable, a matter of some convenience to McSwiney, who also acted as forwarding agent for his clients, as was customary. The entire series of surviving copperplates is here exhibited together for the first time (cat. nos. 14–22).

14. Grand Canal: looking North from near the Rialto Bridge

Oil on copper, 18 × 24 in. (45.7 × 61 cm)
The Trustees of the Goodwood Collections
C/L 232

15. Grand Canal: the Rialto Bridge from the North

Oil on copper, 18 × 24 in. (45.7 × 61 cm)
The Trustees of the Goodwood Collections
C/L 235

The subjects are the same as those of Stefano Conti's first two paintings (cat. nos. 8, 9), which had been completed by 25 November 1725 and sent to Lucca shortly thereafter. A related view of the bridge is catalogue number 24, and one of yet another pair of early date now at Schloss Pillnitz, near Dresden (C/L 231), shows more or less the same stretch of the canal looking northward.

The viewpoints for these two copperplates have been changed, and the compositions are more narrowly focused, partly no doubt in function of the smaller scale of the pictures. It is probable that the drawings—none of which survive—would have been done from Campiello del Remer, close to S. Giovanni Grisostomo, and that the building on the right of number 14 is Palazzo Lion. For parts of these compositions, sketches from a boat would have been necessary. Number 14, showing the campanile of S. Giovanni Elemosinario and the Fabbriche Nuove di Rialto, is lit from the left, leaving the focus and center of the picture largely in shade (likewise its pendant, which is taken and lit from the opposite direction, so that the bridge is in shadow). The gondolas and other boats and the figures that occupy them are at eye level. The Fabbriche Nuove, by contrast, are seen as if from a higher viewpoint: in the comparable Conti view the roof looks shallow and its line is quite straight, whereas in this painting the contour is broken by numerous chimney pots and dormer windows, no doubt to increase the interest of a silhouette so important to the overall composition.

The water, flat and opaque in number 14, is clear in number 15, and, despite its rippling surface, reflective, picking up the contours and the shapes of the window openings of the nearest buildings. Local color is mostly red,

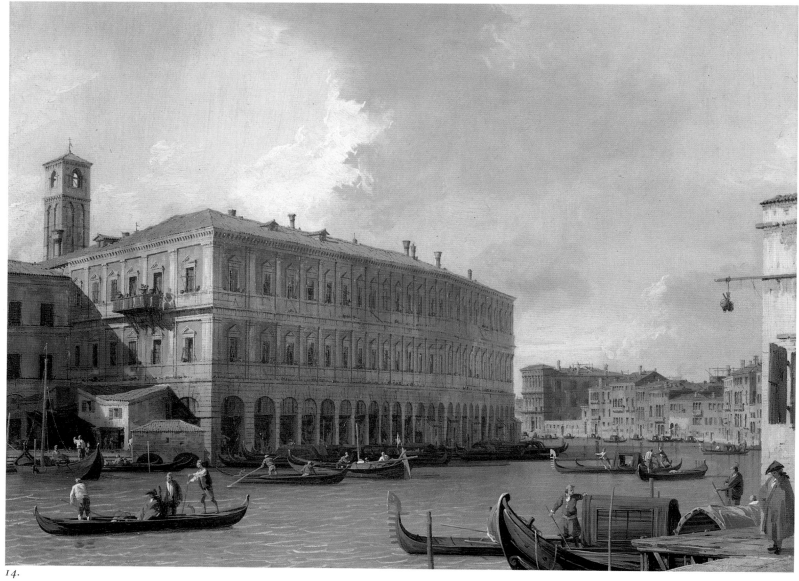

14.

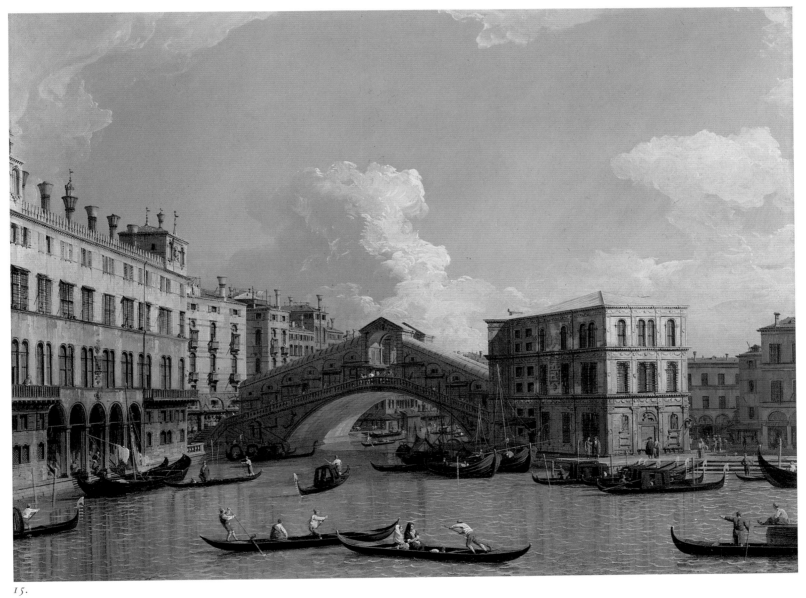

15.

107

for the gondoliers' hats, and in number 14, for the *felze* of the boat in the right foreground. The corner of the building just to the right serves as a repoussoir and draws attention to the still, cloaked figure of a man in a cape and tricorn.

These paintings are assumed to be the ones sent to the Duke of Richmond in November 1727, although it is surprising that McSwiney promises "a view"—rather than *another* view—of the Rialto Bridge for future delivery. For other questioning factors see the discussion by Viola Pemberton-Pigott in "The Development of Canaletto's Painting Technique." The duke either refused or never received his second pair of Venetian subjects. He bought nothing else until, some twenty years later, he commissioned the two paintings of London from Richmond House terrace (cat. nos. 65, 66).

16. Riva degli Schiavoni: looking East from near the Mouth of the Grand Canal

Oil on copper, 17½ × 23½ in. (44.5 × 59.7 cm)
Private Collection
C/L 117

17. The Molo: looking West, Ducal Palace Right

Oil on copper, 17½ × 23½ in. (44.5 × 59.7 cm)
Private Collection
C/L 89

NOTES

1. Corboz, *Canaletto*, 1985, pp. 48–49.
2. Rizzi, *Carlevarijs*, 1967, pp. 87–88 and pls. 28 and 143.
3. The document is quoted by Haskell, *Burlington Magazine*, 1956, p. 297.
4. Sir William Morice, it may be remembered, had bought from McSwiney the tomb paintings not taken by the Duke of Richmond.

The pair must be among Canaletto's earliest representations of these famous sites, and the present picture of the Riva degli Schiavoni is in fact more or less unique, as Canaletto generally painted the eastward view as if from a point nearer to the Piazzetta. Here he shows at the left the Granai, or Public Granaries—eventually torn down and replaced by a garden—and the Campanile of S. Marco behind. With respect to the Granaries, André Corboz points out that Canaletto varies the number of windows: there are fewer of them than there were in fact toward the eastern end of the building, which strengthens the effect of diminution.[1] Beyond are the Zecca, or Mint; Sansovino's famous library, Biblioteca Marciana; the columns of St. Theodore and St. Mark; and the Palazzo Ducale. With the prison the Riva degli Schiavoni begins, and it can be seen to almost its full extent. In the foreground at the left is a small harbor formed by high walls on the quay and posts in the water (see also cat. no. 22). A boat lies at anchor within, its mast lowered and supporting a blue and white striped cover, and at the far end of the Molo the Doge's much larger covered and masted galleon is moored. The viewpoint is not as high as that of the companion picture and would have been attainable from a boat or a pier.

Number 17 is a bird's-eye view, taken from a point which is imagined to be above the corner of the quay. Beyond the palace and the two columns are the Library, the Mint, the Granaries, and, closing the perspective, the Fonteghetto della Farina. The Fonteghetto was occupied by the Magistrato della Farina, the official responsible for the Granaries, and then for some fifty years from 1756 by the Venetian Accademia di Pittura e Scultura (later transferred to the Carità); it is now the Capitaneria di Porto. Across the Grand Canal is Longhena's basilica of Sta. Maria della Salute, and to the left the Dogana, or Customs House, the Giudecca Canal, and the island of the Giudecca.

Canaletto painted the Molo toward the west many times, always from a high viewpoint, and often paired with a view in the opposite direction. The uneven light and the flickering shadows that play across the pink and white facade of Palazzo Ducale distance this early copperplate from the later and more prosaic paintings of the same subject. The prow of a gondola enters the picture space at the lower left corner and, silhouetted against the opaque surface of the water, brings to mind the expanse of the *bacino* extending outward from the Molo toward S. Giorgio and beyond.

This is a subject that Carlevaris also favored. His many paintings of the Molo are generally twice as wide as they are high, and embrace the *bacino*, which is usually crowded with shipping. In 1707 he had painted the official entry of the British ambassador, the Duke of Manchester, who disembarked from his gondola at the corner of the Molo, and nearly twenty years later the same panorama, but this time on the occasion of the arrival of the Imperial ambassador, the Conte di Colloredo.[2] By the mid-1720s Carlevaris and Canaletto are thought to have been rivals, the work of the younger artist replacing that of the elder because, as Marchesini remarked, you can see the sun shining in it.[3] Carlevaris's paintings are not without sunlight and cast shadows, but scenographic reportage and an element of artifice outweigh the effects of nature and art that brought Canaletto fame and the English patronage upon which, at this time, he came to depend.

Catalogue numbers 16 and 17 are identified with the pair that McSwiney, writing to Conduitt in September 1730, reported having sold to Sir William Morice—at a date which unfortunately is unknown.[4] Sir William's second cousin Humphrey inherited his estate in 1750, and in 1786, after Humphrey Morice's death, the copperplates and the balance of the collection from The Grove, Chiswick, were bought by the second Earl of Ashburnham, in the hands of whose descendants they remained until 1953. After the Sotheby's sale of 24 June of that year the pictures disappeared for a time until, having been removed from a West Country house, they were acquired by their present owner at Christie's in 1986. Considerations of style suggest that the Morice copperplates may well be earlier in date than those commissioned by the Duke of Richmond and remaining at Goodwood.

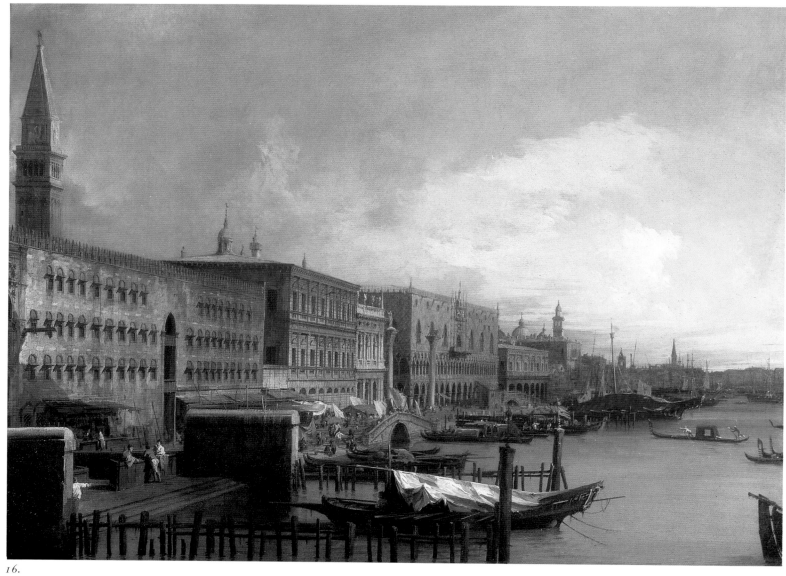

16.

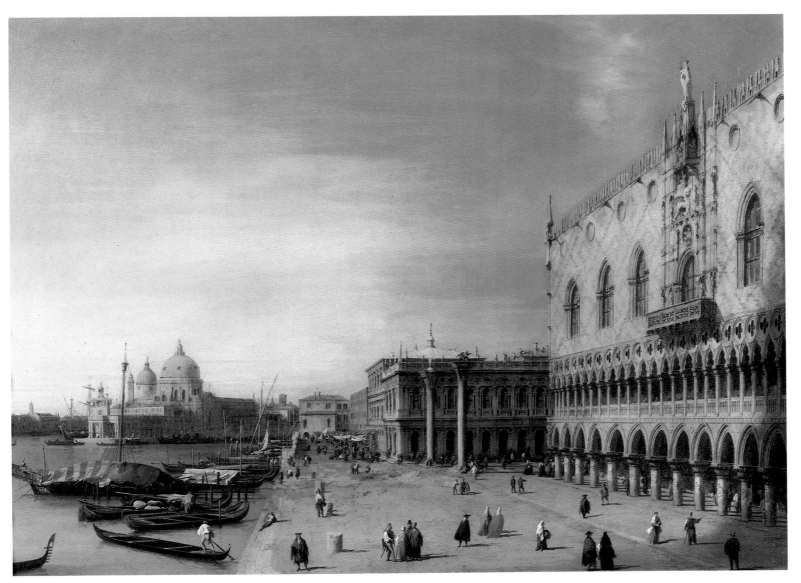

17.

18. Riva degli Schiavoni: looking East

Oil on copper, 17⅜ × 23½ in. (44.1 × 59.7 cm)
The Duke of Devonshire and the Trustees of the Chatsworth Settlement
C/L 115

19. Entrance to the Grand Canal: from the Piazzetta

Oil on copper, 18 × 24 in. (45.7 × 61 cm)
The Duke of Devonshire and the Trustees of the Chatsworth Settlement
C/L 149

Note

1. John Julius Norwich gives an account of the Doge's murder in *A History of Venice*, 1985, pp. 105–7.

112

These copperplates offer rather less sweeping views of the panorama from the Molo than the ones first owned by Sir William Morice (cat. nos. 16, 17). In the painting representing the Riva, the column with the lion of St. Mark is silhouetted against Palazzo Ducale, and the rain spouts cast well-defined shadows on the facade. The coloring of the pink and white bricks and the irregularities of the surface are conveyed by thickly applied and carefully worked pigment. Between the Prisons and Palazzo Dandolo, its roof a maze of chimney pots, are some rather unprepossessing structures: from 1172, when Doge Vitale Michiel II was murdered there, until 1948 no more permanent structure in stone could be built upon the site.[1] There are many small figures, and boats crowd the quay as far as can be seen. As is usual, Canaletto's viewpoint is high and over the water.

The tower—no longer standing—of Palazzo Venier dalle Torreselle lies at the center of the pendant painting with, at the left, the Customs House and Sta. Maria della Salute and, at the right, the Fonteghetto della Farina, the Granai, the Zecca, and the corner of the Biblioteca Marciana. The bridge is the Ponte della Pescheria, named after the fish market which was located there. The portico of the Dogana, the crenellations atop the adjoining warehouses, the ribbed domes and sculptural decorations of the Salute, and some very small figures are minutely described, and illuminated with tiny blobs of light-colored pigment. In general, the details of the architecture have been painted with a nearly hallucinatory precision.

In the Devonshire copperplates very strong light brings every three-dimensional object, whatever its size, into sharp relief, but the artist's eye for incidental detail—such as the weeds sprouting from the tops of the columns dedicated to the patron saints of the city—does not compromise the integrity and coherence of the whole. The clouds are slightly in relief, and the pigment varies in thickness, denying the smoothness of the surface.

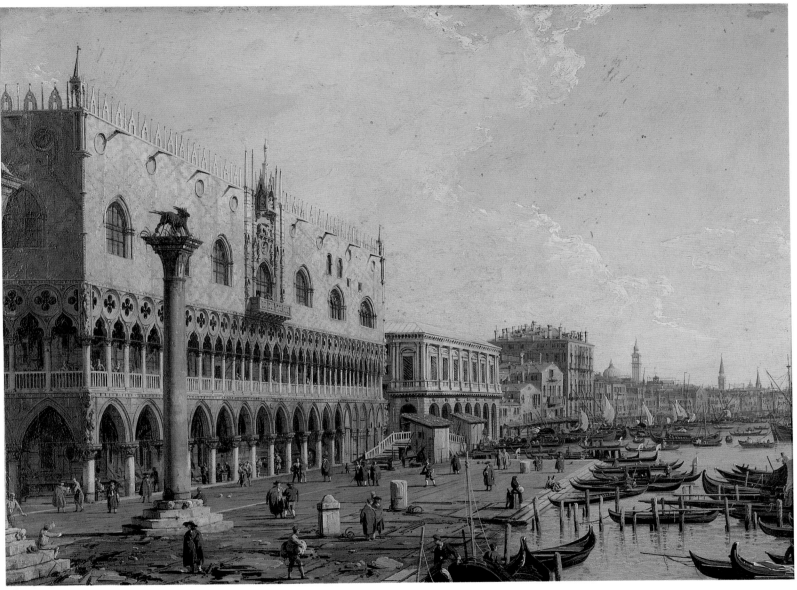

18

113

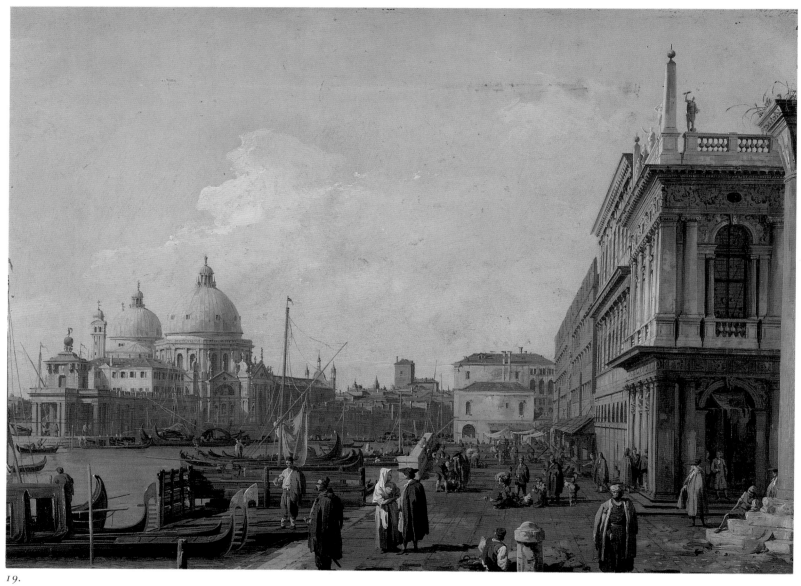

19.

The Tatton Park pictures (cat. nos. 33, 34) are the first documented examples of these subjects but, as it is probable that all of the copperplates were painted within a short interval of time, the Chatsworth pair may precede them chronologically. It would be reasonable to assume that McSwiney handled them, but they are unlikely to have been, on account of their style, Mr. Southwell's, which were painted in 1727 or earlier, nor—since there is no Rialto Bridge—can they have been the second pair promised to the Duke of Richmond but undelivered in 1730. The date of their arrival at Chatsworth is not recorded; they are not in the 1792 inventory, and their early history remains entirely a matter for speculation.

The Baudin Group

Of the twelve paintings copied and published by Joseph Baudin, eight have been traced and six (cat. nos. 20–24, 26) are here exhibited. Baudin was himself an artist: of his work we know only that by Vertue's account he painted fans and, in his later years, was much given to imitating Canaletto. He was born in 1691, entered Kneller's Academy in 1711, married in 1726, and died in 1753 or 1754. At his death he was living in London at Durham Yard, St. Martin-in-the-Fields. Baudin evidently made gouache copies, uniform in size, of each of the twelve Canalettos that he subsequently published as engravings. Six of his gouaches have thus far been identified. Complete sets of the engravings are extremely rare: they combine six views by Louis-Philippe Boitard published in London in 1736, and six by Henry Fletcher published in 1739, also in London. Gouaches (or paintings perhaps) were exhibited by Baudin at his studio in 1740.

All of the known paintings by Canaletto are very much earlier than the prints; they seem in fact to date from the 1720s, and several are on copper. It is probable that they formed a single collection, and a candidate as owner is Elizaeus Burges, English Secretary-Resident in Venice from October 1719 until March 1722, and from December 1728 until his death in November 1736. According to an eighteenth-century label on the back of one of the paintings that was later engraved by Fletcher, a view of the Canale di Sta. Chiara (C/L 269), Burges himself is shown in the picture entering his residence on the *fondamenta*.

Mrs. Finberg's pioneering researches on the Baudin series, published in 1932, have led to further discoveries by Antonio Morassi, F. J. B. Watson, W. G. Constable, and J. G. Links, but even now four of Canaletto's paintings have not been accounted for.[1]

NOTE

1. The prints are mentioned in passing by Ashby and Constable, *Burlington Magazine*, 1925, p. 299. See principally Finberg, *Burlington Magazine*, 1932, pp. 204–7; Morassi, *Burlington Magazine*, 1955, pp. 349–53; Watson, *Burlington Magazine*, 1955, p. 353; Links, *Burlington Magazine*, 1967, pp. 405–9; and Watson, *Burlington Magazine*, 1967, pp. 410–13. Four of the Baudin gouaches may be found, under an attribution to Francesco Guardi, in *Catalogue des tableaux composant la Collection Ch. Sedelmeyer* (Paris, 1907), p. 148, nos. 137–40, and figs. 137–40.

20. Grand Canal: looking East, from the Campo S. Vio

Oil on copper, 18⅛ × 24⅝ in. (46 × 62.5 cm)
Viscount Coke & the Trustees of the Holkham Estate
C/L 192

21. Grand Canal: the Rialto Bridge from the South

Oil on copper, 17⅞ × 24⅝ in. (45.5 × 62.5 cm)
Viscount Coke & the Trustees of the Holkham Estate
C/L 226

NOTES

1. Corboz, *Canaletto*, 1985, p. 55.
2. The front cover of the inventory reads "An Extract account of the furniture in Holkham House / bought by Lady Leicester to compleat the apartments and / what part she brought from Russell Street, and also the / furniture she has removed to different Rooms. She has / left a copy of this to be delivered to Wenman Coke Esq. / February ye 9th 1774." Russell Street was the London home of the family. This information was kindly communicated by Mr. F. C. Jolly, Administrator at Holkham. The Earl of Leicester's son predeceased him, and in 1759 the estates devolved on his nephew, Wenman Roberts, who assumed the name of Coke.
3. *Catalogue des tableaux composant la Collection Ch. Sedelmeyer* (Paris, 1907), p. 148, no. 138, and fig. 138.

The style differs radically from that of the four early pictures formerly in the Liechtenstein collection (cat. nos. 1–4), but the subject of number 20 is the same as one of them, and it will be seen that the sketch of a boat under the barred windows of the side wall of Palazzo Barbarigo in that painting has disappeared. The windows of the upper stories of the palace have also been realigned, as the present picture is on a much smaller scale and the panorama has been compressed. There are other minor topographical simplifications, fewer chimneys and fewer windows, for example.[1] The water is calmer and more evenly lit, its color a dull turquoise, and the clouds and sky above the horizon are of a rosy pink. A fat man in a black cap and gown directs activities on the boat lying just off the quay at S. Vio; the boat is also black, with a small white pennant flying from the mast and a striped awning shading the stern.

For number 21 the viewpoint is low enough to afford a glimpse of the palaces along the Grand Canal beyond the Rialto Bridge. The Fondamenta (then called Riva) del Ferro runs across the foreground. On the far side of the canal is the Riva del Vin, where barrels of wine were unloaded. These *fondamente* are among the widest in the city and have always been heavily traveled because, until the middle of the nineteenth century, the bridge at the Rialto was the only one spanning the Grand Canal. The building with the arched openings is the Palazzo dei Dieci Savi; above the bridge and to the left is the roof of Palazzo dei Camerlenghi, and to the right, the upper stories of the Fondaco dei Tedeschi. In the immediate foreground to the left is a black boat, the sail lowered, the stern draped in blue and white. A man urinates in the sunny corner where the stairs angle downward from the bridge to the *fondamenta*.

The pictures were almost certainly bought by the Earl of Leicester (died 1759), as in 1760 they were removed by his widow from London to Holkham.

116

In the household accounts there is an inventory in the hand of the Dowager Countess bearing the date 9 February 1774, and listing on folio 12, which is headed "The pictures brought from Russell Street to Holkham. June 1760," two views on copper by "Canaletti."[2] As one represents the Rialto Bridge, it is tempting to suggest that they might be the paintings promised by McSwiney to the Duke of Richmond in 1727 but undelivered three years later; on the other hand it is difficult to imagine that they were painted after 1730. The Holkham copperplates could have been sold to Burges, or to some other collector living in Venice, and later resold after having been copied by Baudin. His gouache of the Rialto Bridge from the south is among the four identified by Sir Francis Watson as having been sold, under an attribution to Francesco Guardi, at the Sedelmeyer Gallery in Paris in 1907.[3] Engravings of both compositions are among those by Fletcher, published in London in 1739.

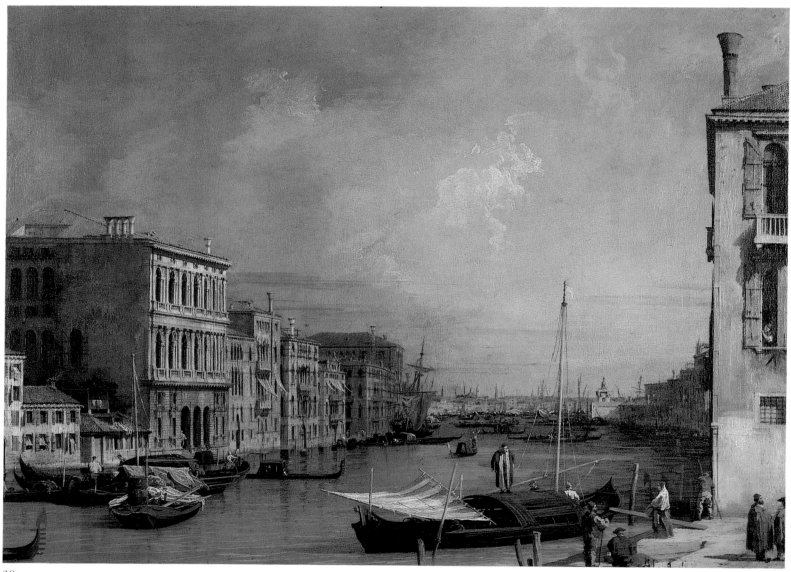

20.

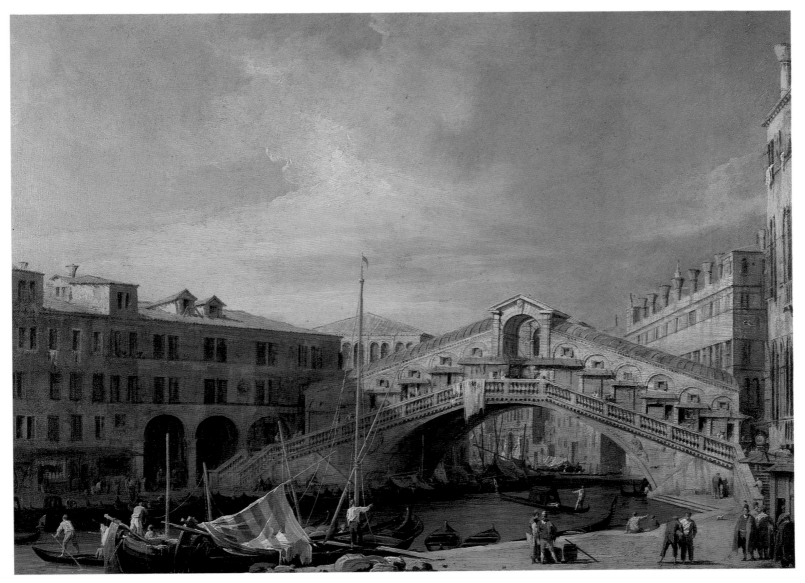

21.

22. *Entrance to the Grand Canal: from the West End of the Molo*

Oil on copper, 17¾ × 23⅝ in. (45 × 60 cm)
Musées de la Ville de Strasbourg, Musée des Beaux-Arts
C/L 152

NOTES

1. See Pierre Rosenberg, *Catalogue de la donation Othon Kaufmann et François Schlageter au Département des peintures, Musée du Louvre*, exh. cat. (Paris, 1984), p. 82, no. 25, ill., who records an inventory number—*R* and *n° 51*—on the reverse, suggesting a possible connection with the Duke of Richmond. Rosenberg compares this copperplate to the canvas of the same subject (C/L 151) belonging to the Musée des Beaux-Arts, Grenoble.
2. Mr. Southwell figures among those who owned a pair of copperplates, as recorded in McSwiney's 1727 letter to the Duke of Richmond, referred to above.
3. Watson, *Burlington Magazine*, 1967, p. 410 and fig. 36.

In the background, from left to right, are the island of the Giudecca with Palladio's church of the Redentore, the Giudecca Canal, the Dogana and the Salute, and the entrance to the Grand Canal. The small harbor in the foreground can be seen from the opposite direction in catalogue number 16. At the right, across the Molo, is the Fonteghetto della Farina. The sky, a bright blue, glows pink toward the southwest, while the buildings and the pavement are in carefully modulated shades of gray. A brilliant red is Canaletto's local color of choice, and is used for the jackets and hats of several of the boatmen, for the *felze* of the gondola at the center, and for the robe of a Procurator climbing the steps toward the entrance to the Salute.

This is the only copperplate for which there is no known companion.[1] The picture is first recorded under number 112 in the catalogue of a sale held at the Dorotheum in Vienna from 19 to 21 July 1938. It might possibly be the survivor of the pair McSwiney sold to Mr. Southwell.[2] It is one of the six pictures engraved in 1736 by Boitard for Joseph Baudin; the originals of three are missing, and the pendant to this painting, also on copper, is presumably among them. Baudin's gouache was published by F. J. B. Watson.[3] Gouache and print omit the half-figure in the immediate foreground of the painting; the gouache also shows rather more of the man at the right edge of the picture, while in the engraving that figure is complete.

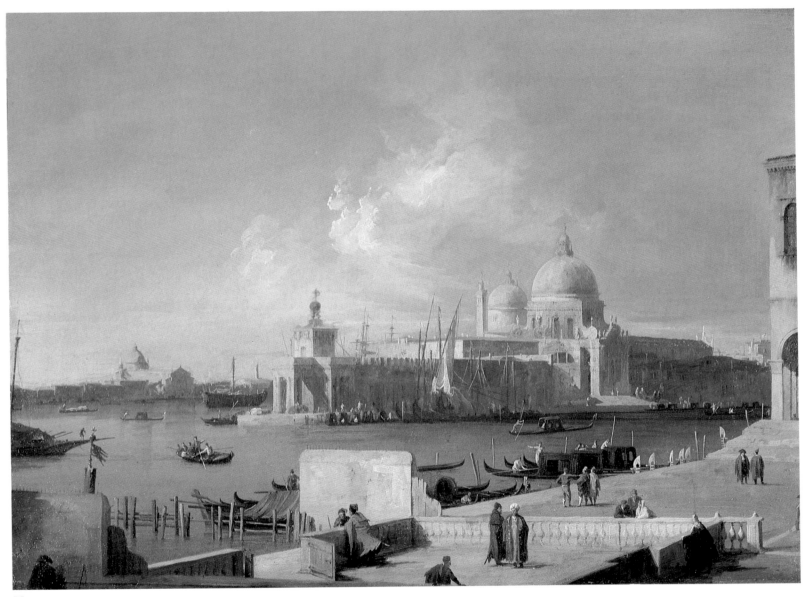

22.

23. Grand Canal: looking Northeast from the Palazzo Balbi to the Rialto Bridge

Oil on canvas, 26⅛ × 38½ in. (66.5 × 97.7 cm)
Ferens Art Gallery: Hull City Museums and Art Galleries
C/L 214

The view is roughly that of catalogue number 3, but taken as from a point farther away and to the right, so that the whole of the facade of Palazzo Balbi can be seen, together with part of the side wall and part of the adjoining house. This house is in fact on the Rio Foscari, which is not apparent from the painting. Canaletto shows five arches instead of three at the center of each of the upper floors of Palazzo Balbi, while in his earlier and later views incorporating this palace its appearance is in general more accurately recorded. To the right of center a large, decorated *peota* with a red canopy emerges from the shadows cast by the palaces on the opposite bank: it looks like the same barge, painted from the same angle, as the one in the early picture formerly in the Liechtenstein collection. A partial view of two gondolas and a sailing boat in deep shade, silhouetted against the water, is at the lower right. The picture is freely and thinly painted, on a dark ground, and it is invested with a sense of drama generally associated with Canaletto's earliest work.

The Ferens Gallery Canaletto must certainly date from the 1720s. It may be later than the comparable painting at Schloss Pillnitz, near Dresden (C/L 211), but is certainly earlier than the Duke of Bedford's view of this subject (C/L 215) or any of the pictures representing the regatta on the Grand Canal, such as catalogue number 43. The engraving after this composition is by Louis-Philippe Boitard, of 1736. The picture was acquired from a London dealer in 1948 by Mrs. Richard Warde, who in turn bequeathed it to the museum. At that time it was ascribed to Francesco Guardi.

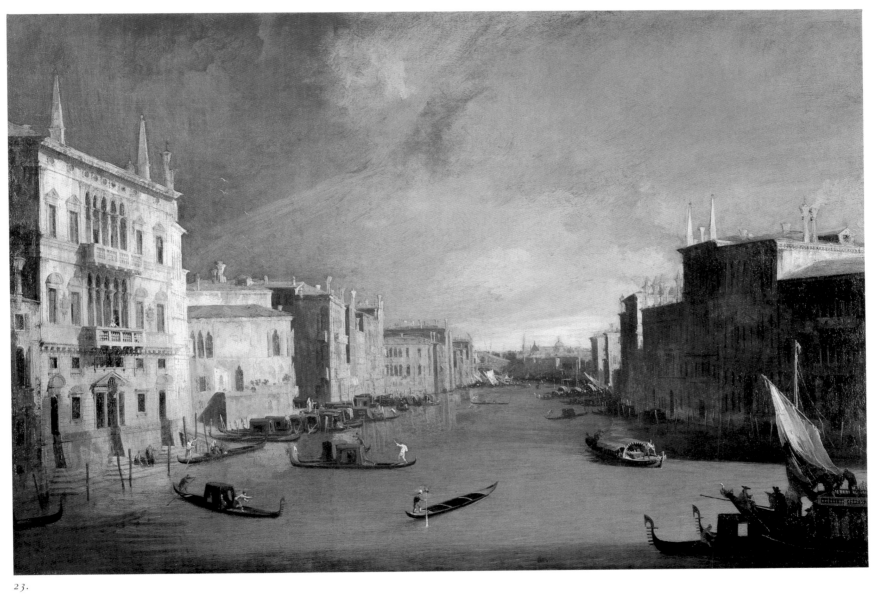

23.

24. *Grand Canal: the Rialto Bridge from the North*

Oil on canvas, 22⅞ × 33½ in. (58×85 cm)
Private Collection
C/L 238*

25. *Riva degli Schiavoni: looking East*

Oil on canvas, 22⅞ × 33½ in. (58×85 cm)
Private Collection
C/L 111*

NOTE
1. Links, *Burlington Magazine*, 1967, pp. 405–9.

Stefano Conti's painting of the Rialto Bridge from the north (cat. no. 8) was completed by November 1725, and the Duke of Richmond's copperplate (cat. no. 15) is assumed to have been sent to him in November 1727. Catalogue number 24 is also an early work but, as it belongs to the series copied and published by Baudin, it is documented but not dated with precision.[1] The view as represented here has been expanded to take in more of the quay in the left foreground and more of the Fabbriche Nuove di Rialto, on the opposite bank of the canal and to the right. The lighting is in general the same: the Fondaco dei Tedeschi and the Palazzo dei Camerlenghi are in sunlight, the rest in shadow.

The Baudin gouache has not come to light; the engraving of the composition is in this case by Boitard and its date of publication 22 April 1736. The engraving extends the view represented in the painting at both sides and at the bottom, and there are a few other minor discrepancies with respect to the number and distribution of the figures and architectural details. Canaletto's original has been relined, and while it is therefore possible that the canvas was slightly cut down to match precisely in size the view of the Riva degli Schiavoni with which it is paired, this cannot be proven. On the other hand, Boitard may simply have copied the composition as enlarged by Baudin. Precedent suggests that a view of the Rialto Bridge from the north would originally have had as a pendant the panorama looking northward from the same bridge: this subject was also engraved, but by Fletcher rather than by Boitard, and three years later, in 1739.

The *Riva degli Schiavoni* (cat. no. 25) was not engraved. It is close in composition—but for the placement of the column of St. Mark—and in handling to the undated copperplate of the same subject at Chatsworth (cat. no. 18). The figures are equally lively and individually observed, and in both the paving of the Molo seems to be in poor condition, and perhaps under repair. A knife grinder works in the shade of a tattered curtain by the hut at the near

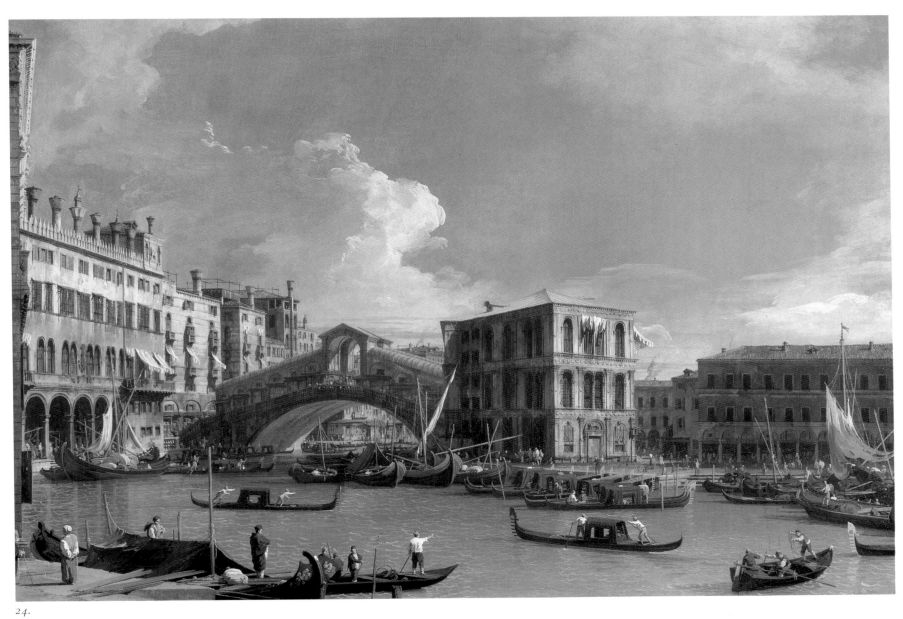

24.

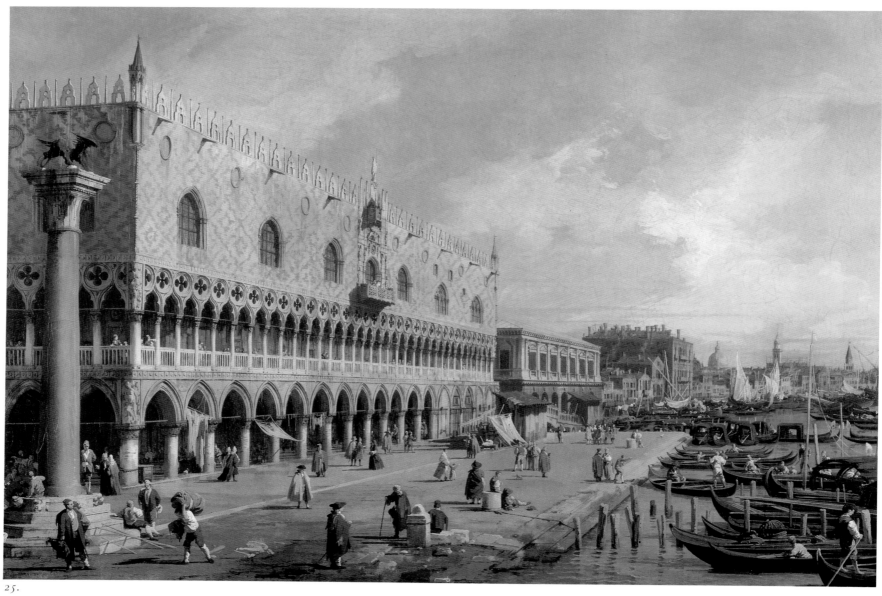

25.

end of the Ponte della Paglia. Another closely similar picture, in which every detail of the architecture of Palazzo Ducale is painted with the same immaculate precision, is catalogue number 33, which was painted for Samuel Hill in 1730.

A more likely companion to this painting would have been a view from the Molo toward the west—similar to the Chatsworth copperplate (cat. no. 19) or to number 34, from Tatton Park. Catalogue numbers 24 and 25, which until 1941 belonged to the ninth Earl of Jersey and hung at Osterley Park, are both of high quality and early date, but they do not seem to have been intended as a pair.

26. Piazza S. Marco: looking North

Oil on canvas, 20¾ × 27¾ in. (52.7 × 70.5 cm)
The Nelson-Atkins Museum of Art, Kansas City, Missouri;
Nelson Fund
C/L 43

NOTES

1. Morassi, *Burlington Magazine*, 1955, pp. 349–53.
2. Corboz, *Canaletto*, 1985, pp. 41–42, 86, and 178.
3. Morassi, *Guardi*, [1973], pp. 237–38, 377–78, nos. 353–60, and figs. 378–84, catalogues eight views by Francesco Guardi of the Torre dell'Orologio.
4. *Catalogue des tableaux composant la Collection Ch. Sedelmeyer* (Paris, 1907), p. 148, no. 137 and fig. 137, and, after the pendant, no. 139 and fig. 139.

Coducci's Torre dell'Orologio was built at the very end of the fifteenth century; the wings were added at the beginning of the sixteenth century, and were subsequently raised—but this was about 1755, long after the present picture was painted. On the terrace at the top of the tower are the great bronze bell and the Moors—so-called because of their dark patination—that strike the hours. Below are the lion of Venice, the Virgin and Child, and an elaborate clock giving the time of day, the phases of the sun and moon, and the corresponding signs of the zodiac. The passageway at the base of the tower leads by the Merceria to the Rialto.

Insofar as is known, this is the only view by Canaletto of the Torre dell'Orologio from the northern edge of the Piazzetta with, at the left, the lower part of the Campanile and Sansovino's Loggetta, and opposite, the last two bays of the facade of the Basilica of S. Marco.[1] The *campo* in shadow to the right is that of S. Basso. There are many stalls with shed roofs, canvas booths, figures of all types, including children, and a number of dogs. Certain details were incised with dividers or with a sharp point, and some of the contours were laid in with a straightedge. The coloring is cool and subdued.

This is a canvas that well illustrates Canaletto's habit of adjusting the topography of the city in the interest of design and pictorial effect.[2] The small windows of the Campanile have been moved from left to right, the last bay of the facade of S. Marco is inaccurately represented as open to its full height, and the Clock Tower is westward of its true location and parallel—

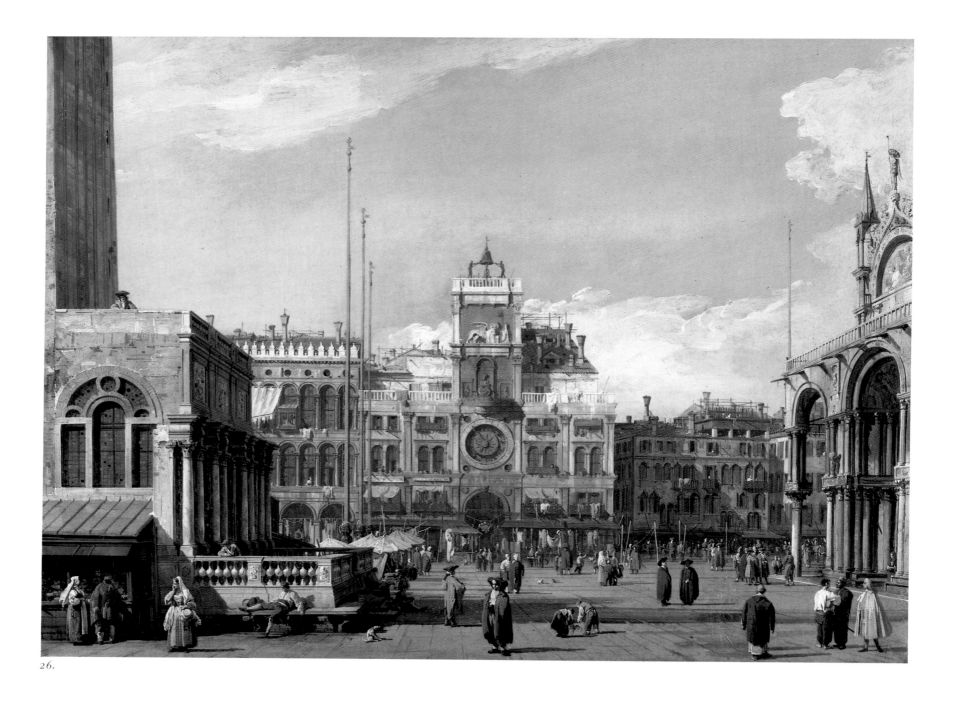

26.

rather than at an oblique angle—to the picture plane. Francesco Guardi was to paint the Torre dell'Orologio many times in later years; his views, as Antonio Morassi remarks, are by comparison topographically correct.[3]

Catalogue number 26 is among the Canaletto paintings engraved by Henry Fletcher and published by Joseph Baudin in London in 1739. There was the usual intermediate source: a copy by Baudin in gouache, which was sold in 1907, as lot 137, at the Sedelmeyer Gallery in Paris.[4] Baudin tidied up Canaletto's picture in certain details, and Fletcher followed Baudin more or less exactly. On balance, the material now available for comparison would seem to suggest that in this case, and in general, neither one of the engravers need have had access to Canaletto's originals.

The Kansas City picture differs considerably in style from other paintings published by Baudin. Its high quality places it within the period of Canaletto's maturity but before his studio was under pressure, that is, from about 1730. Perhaps the view of the Torre dell'Orologio was a direct commission from the owner of the Baudin group. The painting first appeared at public auction in 1923 with, as its pendant, a view of the *Entrance to the Grand Canal: looking West* (C/L 167). Baudin's copy of the pendant was lot 139 of the Sedelmeyer sale, and an engraving after it by Fletcher was also published in 1739.

27. Piazza S. Marco: looking East along the Central Line

Oil on canvas, 27 × 44¼ in. (68.6 × 112.4 cm)
The Metropolitan Museum of Art, New York; Purchase,
Mrs. Charles Wrightsman Gift, 1988
C/L 2

The subject is that of the larger and earlier view in the Thyssen collection (cat. no. 1), which shows the Piazza only partly paved with stone, and is on that account dated in or about 1723. Here Tirali's pavement with its white geometric design is complete. The air is clear, and the sunlight even and bright, the base of the Campanile, the Procuratie Nuove, and part of the Piazza lying in luminous shadow. The windows of the Campanile are fewer in number and more widely spaced than they should be, and the flagstaffs are too tall, but otherwise Canaletto took few, if any, liberties with the topography. He used a straightedge as a guide when ruling many of the perspective lines and verticals. Blue and white awnings project at odd angles from the facade of the Procuratie Vecchie, and lengths of tattered fabric propped on short poles protect the colonnade below from the sun. Canaletto does not tire of detail: potted plants, birdcages, weeds sprouting from the ledges of the buildings, the hem of a man's cloak caught by a slight breeze, and in all more than a hundred animated figures. The sky is freely painted, especially where the brushwork abuts the Campanile, and for the clouds the white pigment is thickly applied and projects slightly in relief. The loose, ragged brushwork and heavy impasto in the lights, and the high key, combined with the neatly ruled perspective lines and the presence of so much closely observed detail suggest a date in the late 1720s.

The painting was not engraved, nor is there any evidence of a pendant. Until its recent acquisition by the Metropolitan Museum it had not been exhibited, except perhaps in 1939–40, when it was on the London art market. Robert Barlow bought it from Colnaghi in 1940, and that dealer gave W. G. Constable what little information we have about its earlier history: according to the former owner of the picture, W. G. Hoffmann of Berlin, it had been acquired for his grandfather by Wilhelm Bode.

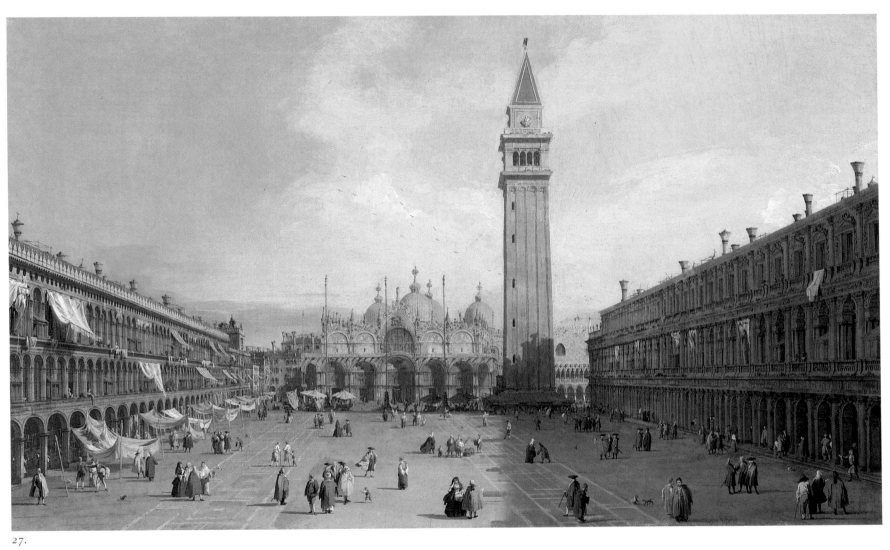

27.

131

Canaletto, Joseph Smith, and the Royal Collection

McSwiney's first letter to the Duke of Richmond mentioning Canaletto as a view painter, dated 28 November 1727, refers to the difficulty of getting pictures from the artist in reasonable time and adds, "by the assistance of a particular friend of his, I get once in two months a piece sketch'd out and a little time after finished, by force of bribery."[1] Although not mentioned by name, the "friend" must have been Joseph Smith, long resident in Venice as a successful businessman and collector. The first documentary record of Smith's association with Canaletto is dated two years later, but by that time the first, and probably the greatest, commission he gave the artist must have been almost or completely finished.

This was for six very large paintings of the Piazza S. Marco and the Piazzetta, four upright and two of landscape format, possibly all for the decoration of a single room. For each painting there was a drawing which may well have been the basis of a discussion between Canaletto and Smith as to the form the painting would take. Two of the paintings are shown as well as the two corresponding drawings (cat. nos. 28 and 29, 88 and 89).

The paintings in this series are the earliest works by Canaletto in the collection of Her Majesty Queen Elizabeth II. With the sale in 1762 of Smith's collection to George III, the Crown holdings of paintings, drawings, and prints by Canaletto came to be absolutely preeminent.[2] The artist has been brilliantly served by those who have catalogued the Royal Collection: Sir Karl Parker, Sir Michael Levey, Sir Oliver Millar, and Charlotte E. Miller.[3]

NOTES

1. Finberg, "Canaletto in England," 1920–21, p. 23.
2. Vivian, *Il Console Smith*, 1971, and, for a brief account, Levey, *Later Italian Pictures*, 1964, pp. 28–35. Among painters of the—then—modern Venetian school, Francesco Zuccarelli (1702–1788) and Sebastiano and Marco Ricci are splendidly represented. It should be remembered that Smith also owned many Flemish and Dutch paintings, uneven in quality but including, under an attribution to Frans van Mieris, the great Vermeer, *The Music Lesson*.
3. Parker, *Drawings of Canaletto*, 1948; Levey, *Later Italian Pictures*, 1964, pp. 31–33, 54–68, nos. 367–420; Millar and Miller, in *Canaletto*, 1980; and Miller, *Fifty Drawings by Canaletto*, 1983.

28. The Piazzetta: looking North

Oil on canvas, 67¾ × 53⅛ in. (172.1 × 134.9 cm)
Her Majesty Queen Elizabeth II
C/L 63

EXHIBITED
Canada 10; London 1

NOTE
1. Levey, *Later Italian Pictures*, 1964, p. 57, no. 381, and see also pp. 56–57, no. 378; Millar, in *Canaletto*, 1980, pp. 31–32, no. 1.

To the left is the Biblioteca Marciana with the Campanile and the Loggetta beyond; to the right, part of the column of St. Theodore and the facade of the Basilica of S. Marco. In the background are the east end of the Procuratie Vecchie, the three flagstaffs, the Torre dell'Orologio, and the buildings along the north side of the Campo S. Basso. As Sir Oliver Millar points out, Canaletto has raised the Campanile and set the flagpoles incorrectly in order to heighten the drama of the scene.[1] As in the case of the drawing, he has also greatly widened the interval between the Library and the column. The perspective is steep, and the Clock Tower much diminished in scale, so that it appears farther away than it is in fact. The Loggetta partly obscures the Clock Tower from Canaletto's chosen viewpoint, so he has taken a second viewpoint, well toward the right, from which it can be seen in its entirety. In the foreground are a Procurator and his attendant, the former dressed in scarlet and overbearing in demeanor, the latter in black, self-effacing, and bowing obsequiously.

This canvas and all of the others in the series are broadly painted, and architectural detail is suppressed. The compositions are extremely bold, and in each Canaletto employs sharp diagonals and areas of deep shade. In three of them the emphasis is on the left, in the other three on the right, and in all the palette is subdued, so that the silhouette of the buildings against the sky, which in each case occupies more than half of the picture surface, becomes an important component of the design. Throughout the series a straight-edge was used in ruling out perspective lines and contours. Given the existence of what might be called compositional studies (for which, in this case, see cat. no. 88), it is not difficult to imagine that the set of paintings was intended for a specific location, the layout and lighting of which would have influenced Canaletto's scheme.

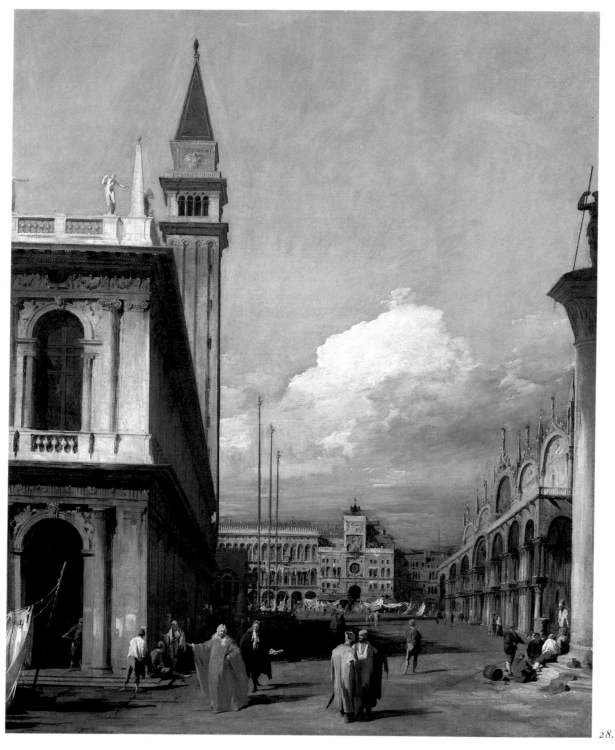

28.

*Opposite
Detail of 28.*

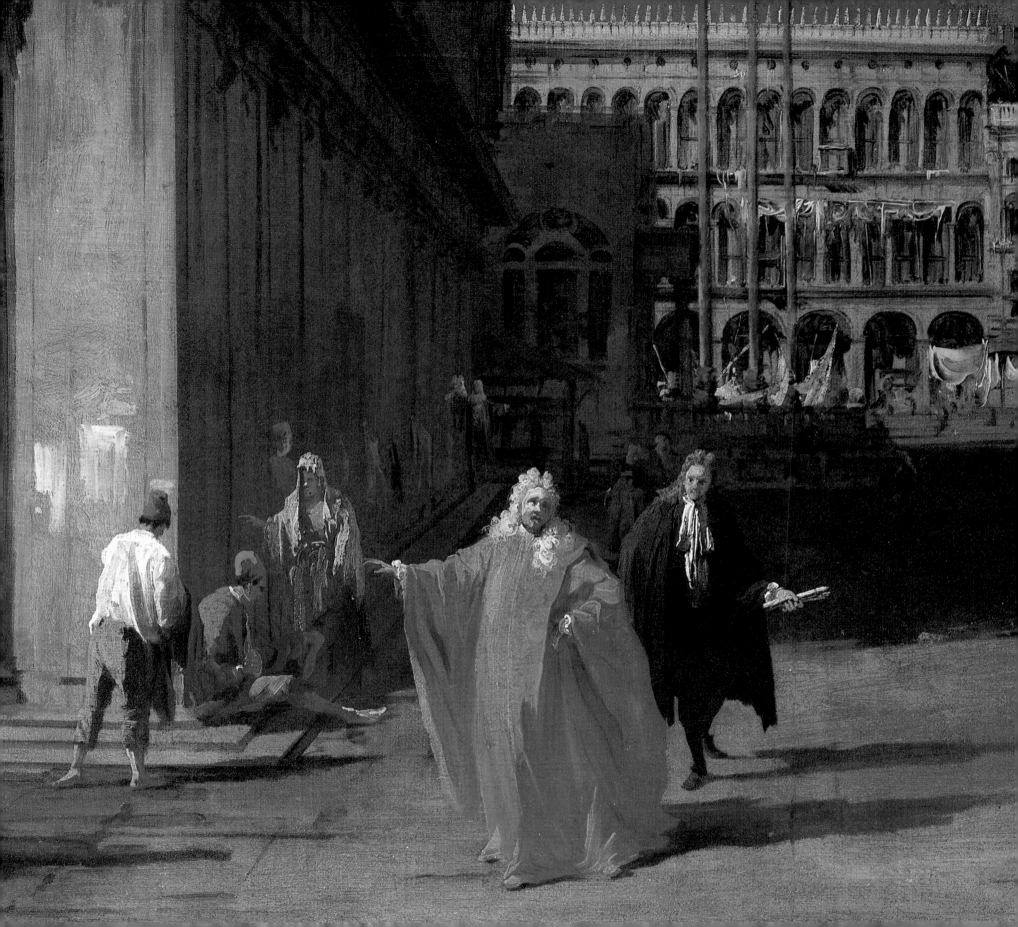

29. Entrance to the Grand Canal: from the Piazzetta

Oil on canvas; 67¾ × 53⅝ in. (172.1 × 136.2 cm), including additions of ½ in. (ca. 1.3 cm) on the left and ⅝ in. (1.6 cm) on the right
Her Majesty Queen Elizabeth II
C/L 146

EXHIBITED
London 5

NOTES
1. Levey, *Later Italian Pictures*, 1964, p. 57, no. 383; and Millar, in *Canaletto*, 1980, p. 36, no. 5.
2. The onion-shaped steeple was in its turn replaced, after 1774, with the one that may be seen today.

Three of the paintings in the set represent the Piazza: as seen from the west, with the facade of S. Marco (C/L 12); from the east, with the church of S. Geminiano (C/L 32); and from the southeast, an angled view showing the Procuratie Vecchie to its full extent and the corner of the basilica (C/L 33). The corresponding views of the Piazzetta are taken toward the north (cat. no. 28), toward the south and the *bacino* (C/L 55), and—in the present canvas—diagonally toward the southwest and the church of Sta. Maria della Salute.[1] The water can be seen only in this picture and one other, and it plays a minor role.

Seldom has Canaletto so drastically rearranged the topography to suit his composition. For the column of St. Theodore to appear level with the Library roof the viewpoint would have to be far back along the Molo. The steps of the bridge have been brought forward. The Dogana has been moved closer to the Salute than it should appear, and both are much too close to the Library. In the related drawing (cat. no. 89) Canaletto omits the column of St. Theodore but includes that of St. Mark, on the extreme left. Sir Oliver Millar notes that in this picture "it at first occupied the same position, but was painted out, presumably so as to concentrate the weight of the design on the right, and was only partly replaced by the mast and slackened sail." The outline of the dome of the Salute is drawn with dividers, and a ruling instrument has been much used. The silhouettes of the buildings and certain other details were painted over the sky, and there are numerous pentimenti in the area encompassing the bridge and the lower part of the column. Canaletto's brilliant painting of figures is exemplified in both this and the previous picture.

One topographical detail confirms the generally accepted dating of the series in the late 1720s: the conical steeple of S. Giorgio Maggiore, which can be seen in the view of the Piazzetta toward the south (C/L 55), was demolished between 1726 and 1728, and an onion-shaped steeple replaced it.[2]

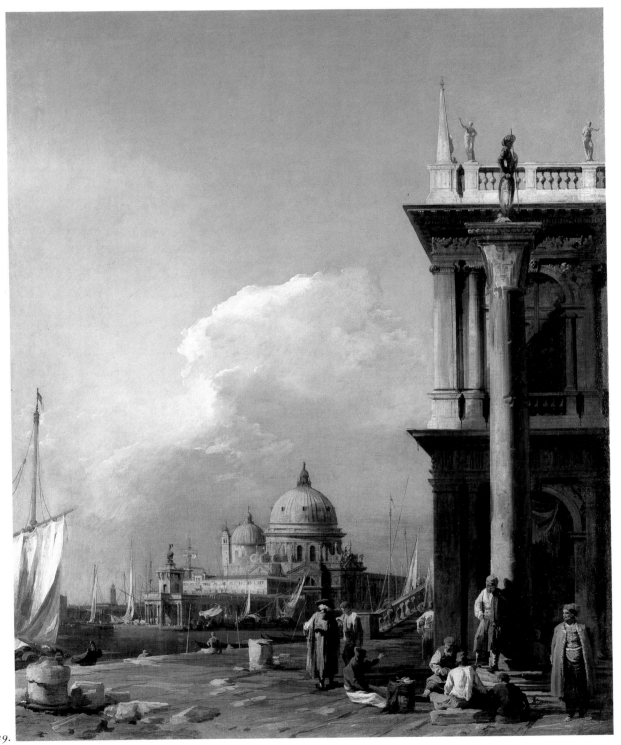

29.

137

30. S. Cristoforo, S. Michele, and Murano from the Fondamente Nuove, Venice

Oil on canvas, 56 × 59¼ in. (142.2 × 150.5 cm)
Dallas Museum of Art; Foundation for the Arts Collection,
Mrs. John B. O'Hara Fund
C/L 365(a)

NOTES

1. Levey, *Later Italian Pictures*, 1964, pp. 66–68, no. 419;
   Millar, in *Canaletto*, 1980, pp. 77–78, no. 44; Clovis
   Whitfield, *Views from the Grand Tour*, exh. cat., Colnaghi
   (New York, 1983), pp. 14–16, no. 4.
2. *Exhibition of Works by the Old Masters, and by Deceased
   Masters of the British School* (London, 1877), p. 46, no. 260,
   as Francesco Guardi, *Venice: Storm Clearing Off*, lent by J. H.
   Hutchinson, Esq. An attribution to Guardi was at one time
   proposed for the companion views in the Royal Collection.
   See F. J. B. Watson, "Venetian Paintings at the Royal
   Academy 1954–55," *Arte Veneta* 9 (1956), pp. 260–61, and
   "Canaletto or Guardi?" *Arte Veneta* 10 (1956), pp. 203–4.
   It cannot as yet be proven that the painting which is
   the subject of this entry belonged to John Strange, who in the
   later eighteenth century was British Resident in Venice.

138

Predicted Discoveries

Occasionally the existence of a copy or an engraving indicates that there must once have been a certain picture which may yet be found. Following are two interesting examples of paintings that until recently were known from copies.

This is an unusual subject: a view toward the north, taken from a point on the Fondamente Nuove westward of the Rio dei Mendicanti (for which see cat. no. 4), and showing in the background at the left the island of Murano and the hills of the mainland. In the mid-distance, center and right, are the islands of S. Michele and S. Cristoforo, which were then separated by a canal, but which were joined in the early nineteenth century to form the cemetery island. S. Michele still stands, serving as the cemetery church. In the foreground the steps of a bridge descend to the quay, and beyond, a timber raft from the mainland crosses the lagoon. The shallow, opaque surface of the water reflects in a zigzag pattern the vertical contours of the island buildings, and the sky above the darkening horizon is suffused with light. The figures are large and sketchy, with impasto used for the whites.

The Royal Collection contains a slightly smaller variant together with a companion, a version of catalogue number 31: their origin is unknown but they did not come from Smith's collection, and may perhaps have been received as a gift. The unusual design of the Royal Collection *S. Cristoforo* (C/L 365), particularly, was long greatly admired. However, in 1964 Michael Levey, having "studied the picture over a period of years," concluded that it was not by Canaletto but might be a copy of a lost work or a pastiche from an early view of the same subject in the Hermitage (C/L 366).[1]

The present canvas was included in the first edition of W. G. Constable's catalogue raisonné as perhaps by Canaletto, but it had not been seen by the author, nor was it reproduced. Constable further noted that it might be identical with a painting that had been in the Aguado collection, sold in 1843, and previously engraved by Larbalestier. The picture was on one occasion exhibited: in 1877, at the Royal Academy, as the work of Guardi.[2] *S. Cristoforo, S. Michele, and Murano* was consigned to Sotheby's by the Earl of Wharncliffe in 1982, and on its appearance in the salerooms it was generally recognized as the original by Canaletto of the work in the Royal Collection, painted, as Michael Levey had suspected, in the 1720s.

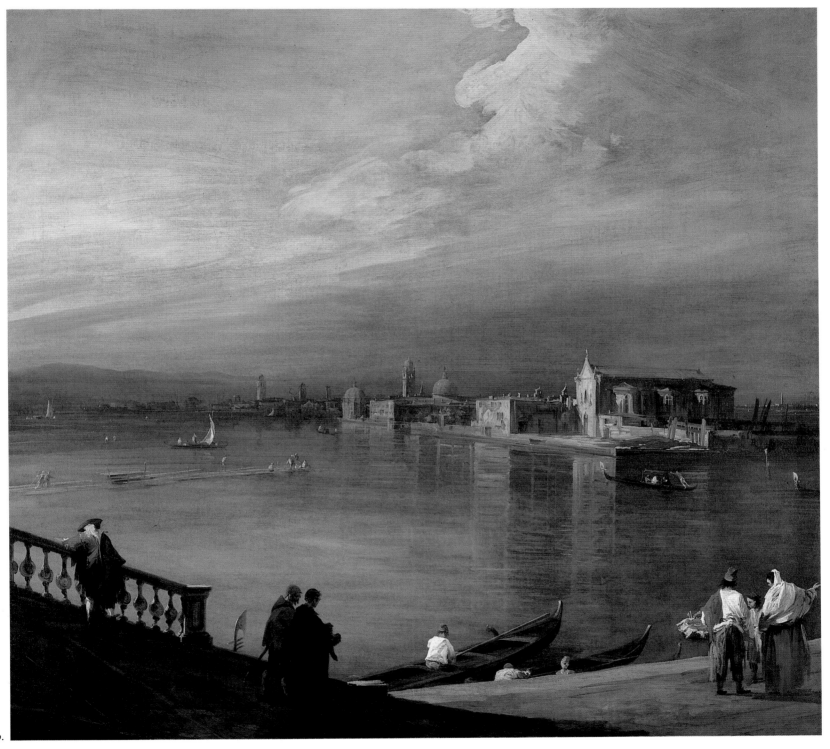

30.

31. Entrance to the Grand Canal: looking East

Oil on canvas, 43 ½ × 54 ¼ in. (110.5 × 137.8 cm)
Mr. and Mrs. A. Alfred Taubman
C/L 177* (1989 ed.)

NOTE

1. Levey, *Later Italian Pictures*, 1964, p. 68, no. 420, who suggested that the missing, subsidiary dome might appear in the original. This did not prove to be the case.

The imagined viewpoint is above the Grand Canal to the north and east of S. Vio, and the palaces at the left, the nearest of which is Palazzo Corner, are the ones that can be seen in the Thyssen picture (cat. no. 2), though here they are shown in deep shadow and differ somewhat in detail. The dome of Sta. Maria della Salute rises above the smaller houses on the opposite bank. The theatrical quality of this view is enhanced by the slanting rays of sunlight breaking through the clouds overhead. The brushwork is broad and fluid, the window openings indicated by one or two parallel strokes of gray or black. Canaletto captures the differing poses and lost profiles of the three figures in the rowboat. A beautiful passage is the slackened sail of a larger boat anchoring the composition at the lower right, its stern and mooring line silhouetted against the waters of the canal.

As has been noted, there is another version (C/L 177), more vertical in format, in the Royal Collection. It was first recorded at Windsor about 1790, and has for long been regarded as by the same hand as the view representing S. Cristoforo (C/L 365), and of the same, unknown, origin. Levey, in 1964, described it as a copy or imitation.[1] The present painting, then unknown and presumably in the collection of W. A. Shand, since deceased, was offered for sale by Sotheby's in 1985, only three years after catalogue number 30 appeared on the market. Recognized as Canaletto's original, upon which the Royal Collection copy was based, it should also be dated in the 1720s.

In this picture and in the one now in Dallas, the handling of the sky is exceptionally dramatic, and they must have been painted within a short interval of time. On the other hand, the present canvas differs significantly in size and proportions from the view of S. Cristoforo, and the two need not have formed a pair. The existence of the two copies, evidently by the same hand and in the same collection since about 1790, militates in favor of the two originals having belonged to the same owner at some earlier date. A candidate is Giovanni Berzi of Padua, who in 1783 had four Canalettos, including both of these subjects.

A fine ink drawing (cat. no. 94) is closely similar in composition.

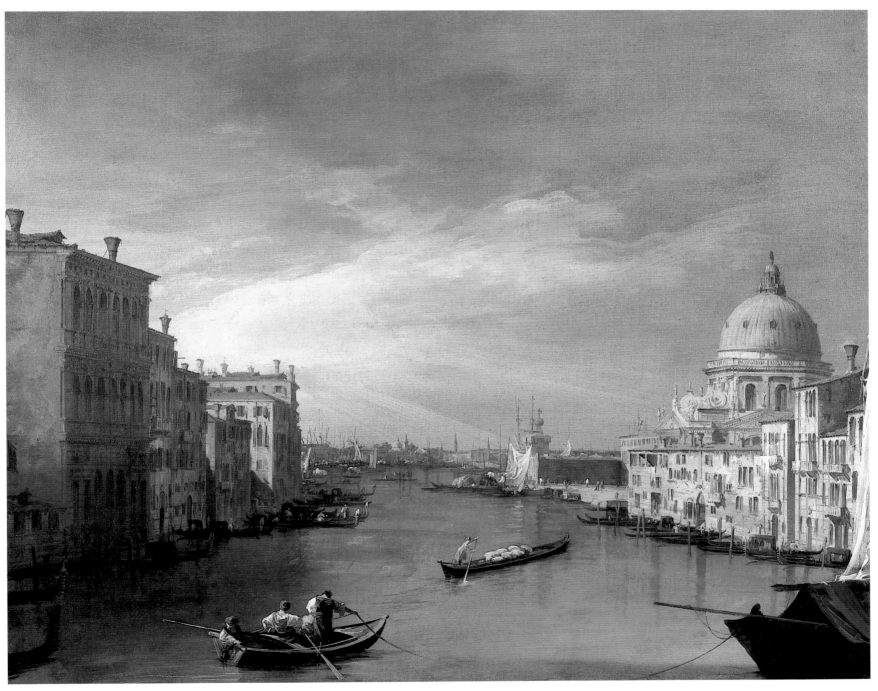

31.

32. *"The Stonemason's Yard"*

(Sta. Maria della Carità from across the Grand Canal)
Oil on canvas, 48¾ × 64⅛ in. (123.8 × 162.9 cm)
The Trustees of the National Gallery, London
C/L 199

NOTES

1. Levey, *Eighteenth Century Italian Schools*, 1956, pp. 11–14, no. 127.
2. Levey, *Eighteenth Century Italian Schools*, 1956, p. 13. See also his discussion in "Canaletto as Artist of the Urban Scene" in this catalogue.
3. Links, *Canaletto and His Patrons*, 1977, p. 36.

142

Venice is relatively little changed since the eighteenth century, but many who look at this famous picture will find that at first sight its subject seems unfamiliar. The viewpoint is from Campo S. Vitale—or S. Vidal—looking across the Grand Canal to the church and *scuola* of Sta. Maria della Carità. The church was secularized in Napoleonic times and the complex is now mainly occupied by the galleries of the Accademia. The facade of the church, only the top of which can be seen in this picture, is shown in its entirety in one of Stefano Conti's paintings (cat. no. 11), and some of the crockets visible in the earlier view are missing from this one. The campanile of the Carità toppled in the 1740s. The entrance to what was then the *scuola* and is now the museum was replaced later in the eighteenth century, and the building adjoining it to the right was torn down. The Accademia bridge now spans the canal at this point. The house at the left was destroyed to make way for the garden of Palazzo Franchetti, or Cavalli. The houses to the right and the wellhead can still be identified, and the bell tower in the background to the right of center is that of S. Trovaso.

There is no record as to how the picture acquired the title by which it is universally known, and it is unlikely that there was ever a stone yard in the *campo*: probably the stone that is shown there was used for the rebuilding of the church of S. Vitale.[1] A drawing at Windsor Castle (C/L 586) shows the site cleared and the hut removed.

By 1808 *"The Stonemason's Yard"* belonged to Sir George Beaumont, a founding trustee of the National Gallery, London, but nothing is known of it before that date. A promised gift in 1823, the picture has been displayed at the National Gallery since it opened to the public in 1828. There has been much discussion as to the date of the painting with a consensus placing it in or just before 1730. "Part of the difficulty in dating" it, writes Michael Levey, "is due to its uniquely high quality. It is perhaps the product of a moment of fusion between Canaletto's early and mature styles, both of which seem present in it."[2]

"*'The Stonemason's Yard'*...is Canaletto at his finest, the Canaletto that might have been perpetuated but for the pressures of the English dukes and their representatives in Venice, and it must be assumed to have come out of the studio at much the same time as the Duke of Richmond's 'copperplates', however incomprehensible such a confusion of endeavour may appear.... The light falls on the various textures of wood, stone, brick and stucco revealing the individuality of each. The shadows unobtrusively give the picture coher-

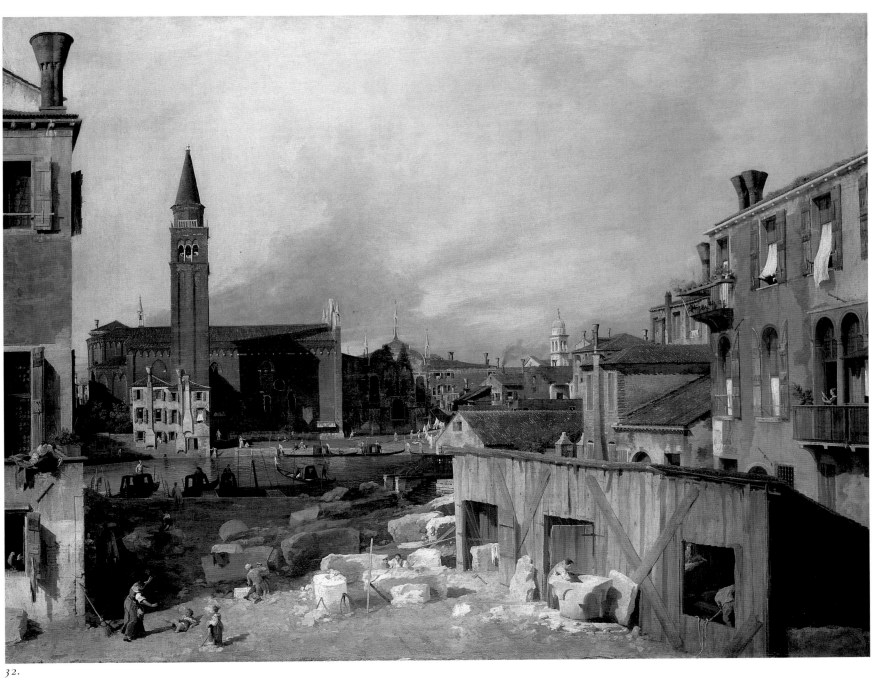

32.

ence in a way that must have been considered by the artist although there is no trace that they are there for any reason other than that they *were* there. This noble picture moved Ruskin to confess, on coming out of the National Gallery in 1887, that he now admired Canaletto 'after all'—that is, after the 'determined depreciation' with which, to use his own words, he had for so long pursued him. Even then it was primarily the fact that Canaletto's pigments endured that brought about the recantation. Ruskin was in fact incapable of recognizing a Canaletto: of the only three works he mentions specifically, one (in the Louvre) proved to be a Marieschi, another (in the Academy, Venice) a Bellotto and the third (in the Manfrini collection, Venice) of so little consequence that it has been allowed to disappear without trace. On the other hand Whistler, whom Ruskin attacked as bitterly but who was still alive to answer back, considered *'The Stonemason's Yard'* worthy of Velasquez. In the late nineteenth century no higher praise was possible and Whistler added: 'Canaletto could paint a white house against a white cloud and to do that you have to be great.'"[3]

Smith's Commission for Samuel Hill

Of the few surviving documents concerning Canaletto, none is more important than the letter of 17 July 1730 from Joseph Smith to Samuel Hill of Staffordshire, England: it offers a rare, direct comment by Smith himself on the nature of his relationship with the artist.[1] Smith asks how Hill likes Lodovico Ughi's new plan of Venice published in 1729 (see fig. 2 for a later edition), and, in Smith's view, overpriced at two sequins. Continuing in a similar vein, he writes:

> At last I've got Canal under articles to finish your 2 peices within a twelvemonth; he's so much follow'd and all are so ready to pay him his own price for his work (and which he vallues himself as much as anybody) that he would be thought in this to have much obliged me, nor is it the first time I have been glad to submitt to a painter's impertinence to serve myself and friends, for besides that resentment is lost upon them, a rupture with such as are excellent in their profession resolves 'em either not to work for you at all, or which is worse, one gets from them only slight and labour'd productions, and so our taste and generosity is censured—tho' both unjustly.

Hill's nephew, Samuel Egerton, was apprenticed to Smith, and on 15 December of the same year he took up the subject again, explaining that Smith

NOTE

1. Chaloner, "The Egertons in Italy," 1950, p. 164. For the Tatton Park pictures, see also St John Gore, in *The Treasure Houses of Britain*, exh. cat. (Washington, 1985), pp. 248–49, nos. 167–68, and on the collection and a portrait of Samuel Egerton, pp. 258–59, no. 178.

"had att last prevailed with Canal to lay aside all other business till he had finished the 2 pictures you order'd when you was last here...." The pictures were to be completed and sent by the next ship, though the date is not recorded. Samuel Egerton outlived his elder brother, inheriting his uncle's estate, and the pictures were transferred to the family seat, Tatton Park, Cheshire, which was bequeathed with its contents to the nation by the fourth Lord Egerton in 1958. It is the property of the National Trust.

33. Riva degli Schiavoni: looking East

Oil on canvas, 23 × 40 in. (58.4 × 101.6 cm)
The National Trust, Tatton Park; Egerton Collection
C/L 111

Among the most famous sights that Venice affords is that of Palazzo Ducale, the Ponte della Paglia, and the Riva degli Schiavoni extending into the distance, and it is not surprising that by 1730 Canaletto had painted the view several times for English clients. The scene is similarly represented in a copperplate at Chatsworth (cat. no. 18) and in a canvas formerly belonging to the Earls of Jersey (cat. no. 25), which is also taken from a point farther to the right along the Molo, so that the arches of the Palazzo Ducale appear—as in fact they are—more widely spaced. In the present picture, as in number 25, the column of St. Mark has been arbitrarily moved, so that it stands against the shaded, west facade, rather than the south facade, as it should. At some distance along the Riva is the church of the Pietà and, beyond, the dome and campanile of S. Pietro di Castello (for which see cat. no. 83). The quay in the foreground is in disrepair. The *bacino* at the Riva is more than ever crowded with shipping, the masts and rigging of the sailing vessels forming a web of finely drawn lines that contributes to the chaotic effect. There are a great many figures of all types, including, at the corner of the Piazzetta, a crowd of officials in long black gowns issuing forth from Palazzo Ducale.

A sketch by Canaletto of this eastward view of the Riva, which was among those retained by Smith and is now at Windsor (cat. no. 93), is related to this painting and may have been a preparatory drawing. In both, the prow of the Doge's galleon anchors the composition at the lower right.

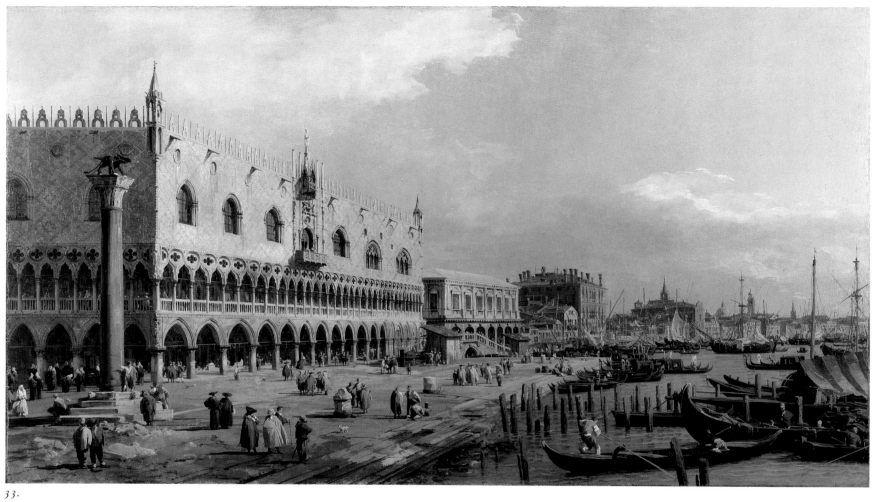

33.

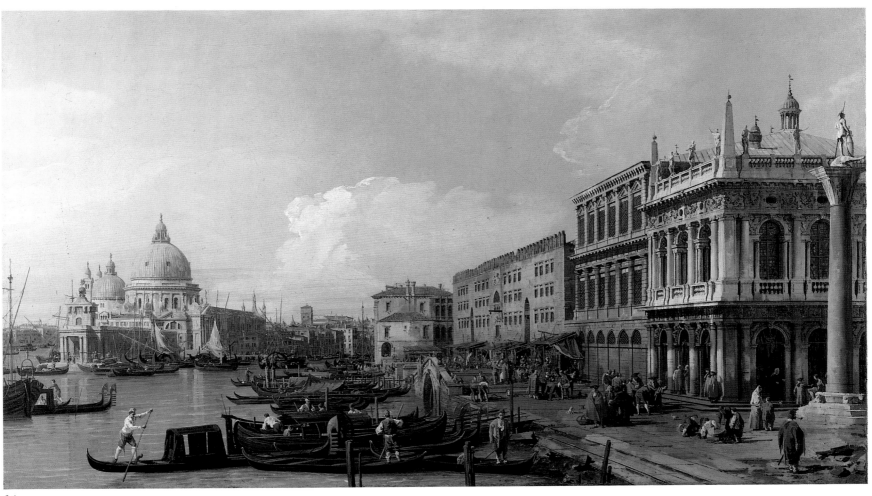

34.

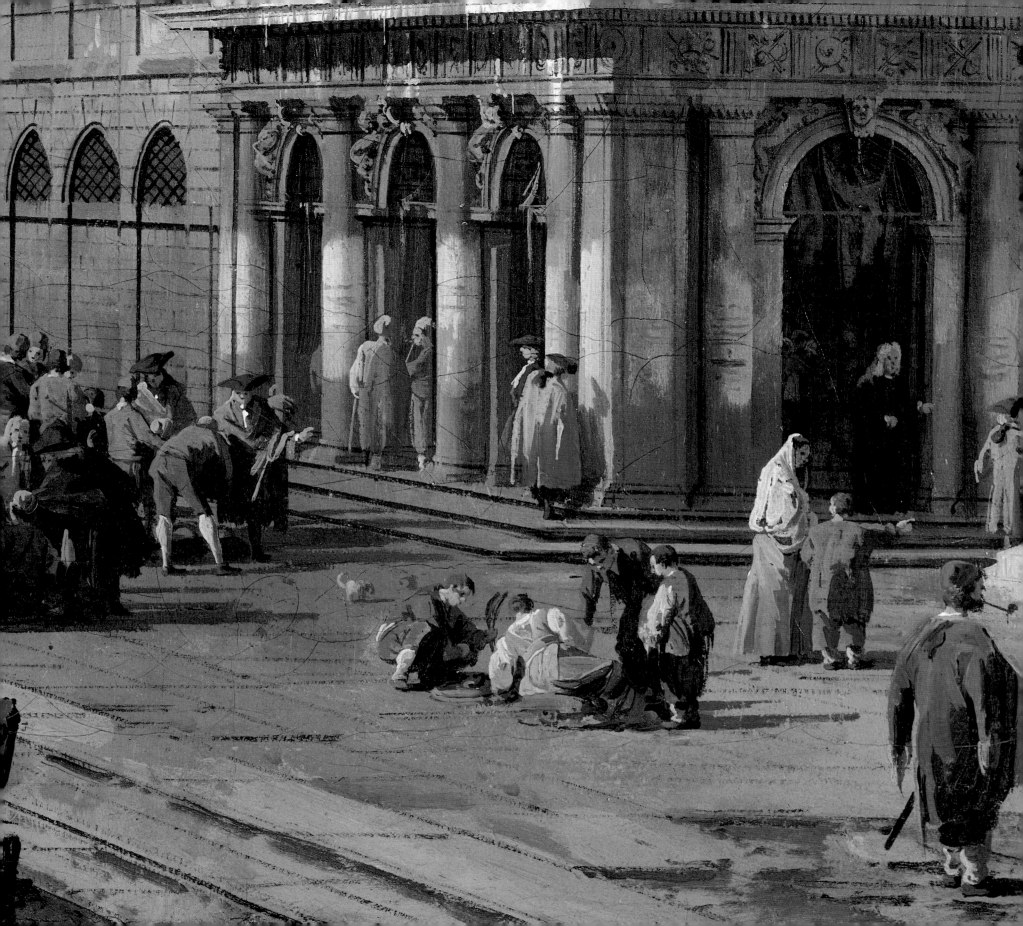

34. The Molo: looking West, Library to Right

Oil on canvas, 23 × 40 in. (58.4 × 101.6 cm)
The National Trust, Tatton Park; Egerton Collection
C/L 97

As in the case of the pendant to the copperplate view of the *Riva degli Schiavoni*, the companion to number 33 shows the Molo in the opposite direction. However, Canaletto has chosen a viewpoint over the water, not the land as in number 19, and farther away so that more is seen of the Library, the Mint, and the Granaries. Untidy booths with slat roofs line the facade of the Granaries, attracting a crowd. A boy in tattered clothes stands at the bow of the nearest small boat, which is beached in the mud at the Molo: he gazes idly out at the viewer.

The drawing inscribed *Veduta della pescharie* (View of the fish markets, cat. no. 91) appears to be a preparatory sketch, either for this painting or for a more elaborate drawing (C/L 565) in the Royal Collection.

The Wicklow Paintings

Until 1955 catalogue numbers 35 and 36 belonged to the Earls of Wicklow in whose family archive is a copy of a memo which reads:

Aug 22 1730 Recd two pictures of Canaletti from Venice

	£	s	d
Pd Mr Smith Mercht 35 Venn. Zecni	18	7	11
Freight	0	11	0
Custom	2	0	0
Charges		8	0
Frames		1	14	0
	23	0	11[1]

The pictures were probably ordered by Hugh Howard, whose descendants were the Earls of Wicklow, and the memorandum is of exceptional interest as revealing Smith's methods. As well as commissioning the pictures from Canaletto, he arranged for them to be framed, packed, and sent to London, where no doubt his brother John cleared them through customs and saw that they were delivered to Ireland. The price of 35 sequins for two pictures just under twenty inches high may be compared with 90 sequins for four pictures a little over thirty-five inches high, paid by Stefano Conti in 1726.

Opposite
Detail of 34.

149

NOTES

1. Links, *Canaletto and His Patrons*, 1977, p. 33.
2. Finberg, "Canaletto in England," 1920–21, p. 23.

McSwiney, in 1727, told the Duke of Richmond that he had paid 70 sequins for Mr. Southwell's copperplates but only 22 sequins each for the duke's own (the copperplates were the smallest of all). Although by 1730 Canaletto's work was much in demand, and his patrons said to be willing to pay what he asked, the sums in question seem not to have risen. Perhaps, though, there was some justification for McSwiney's charge (28 November 1727, to the Duke of Richmond) that "the fellow is whimsical and vary's his prices, every day."[2]

35. Entrance to the Grand Canal: looking West

Oil on canvas, 19½ × 29 in. (49.5 × 73.7 cm)
The Museum of Fine Arts, Houston; The Robert Lee Blaffer Memorial Collection, Gift of Sarah Campbell Blaffer
C/L 166

The church of Sta. Maria della Salute is at left center with, in the foreground, part of the Dogana, and beyond, the nave and the reverse of the facade of S. Gregorio, the tower of Palazzo Venier dalle Torreselle and, at the bend, the campanile of the church of the Carità. Two Senators climb the steps to Sta. Maria della Salute. In the foreground to the right is a partial view of Palazzo Tiepolo, now part of the Hotel Europa and Britannia. The buildings are strangely narrowed and crowded together, suggesting that perhaps, under the terms of the commission, specific dimensions were required and the artist failed to take the requirement sufficiently into account.

The boats in the foreground constitute something of a perspective tour de force, but they are, on the other hand, rather perfunctorily painted, their masts and spars radiating outward in an awkward, irregular semicircle. The figure of a monk seated in the bow of a rowboat, gazing toward the viewer, is observed with interest, but several of the gondoliers seem for the first time to have been drawn from a stock repertory. The ripples are picked out in an unvarying pattern of a lighter color over the opaque blue surface of the canal.

Perhaps the earliest of the many versions of this perennially popular subject, the present canvas and its pendant typify the views of the Grand Canal from the Salute to the Rialto which were to become Canaletto's principal stock in trade.

EXHIBITED
Canada 11

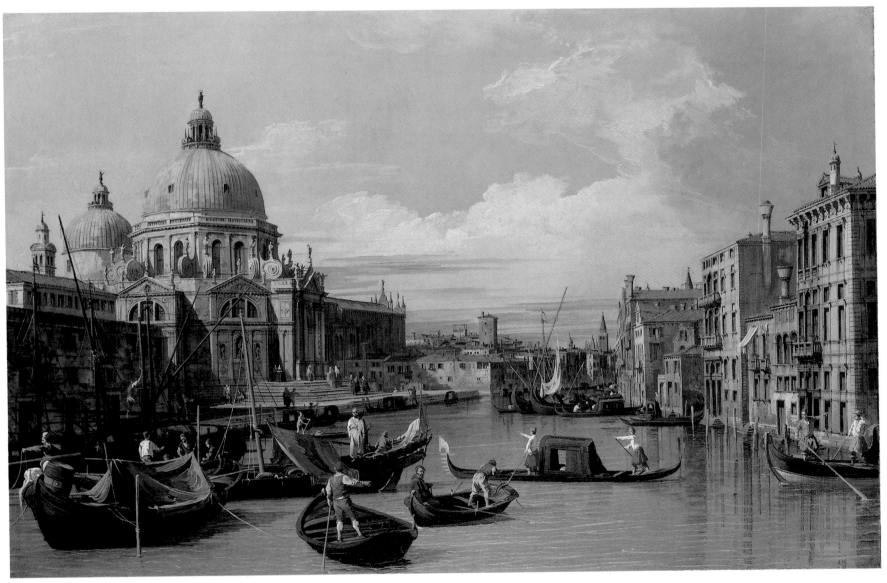

35.

36. Grand Canal: looking Southwest from the Rialto Bridge to the Palazzo Foscari

Oil on canvas, 19⁹⁄₁₆ × 28¾ in. (49.6 × 73 cm)
The Museum of Fine Arts, Houston; The Robert Lee
Blaffer Memorial Collection, Gift of Sarah Campbell Blaffer
C/L 220

EXHIBITED
Canada 12

To the left is part of the Riva del Ferro, now called the Pescheria (fish market) di S. Bartolomeo, with, beyond, the Palazzi Dolfin Manin and Bembo and the huge Palazzo Grimani, now the Court of Appeals. Lottery tickets were sold from the hut on the quayside which is visible here and in some other views from the Rialto Bridge to the south. Ca' Foscari is in the far distance, at the turn of the canal. The gondoliers rowing down the center of the canal are elaborately dressed in the sort of costume often worn for the regatta; ripples lap neatly at the hull of the boat as it passes.

The picture is closely similar to catalogue number 39, which was retained by Smith and is in the Royal Collection.

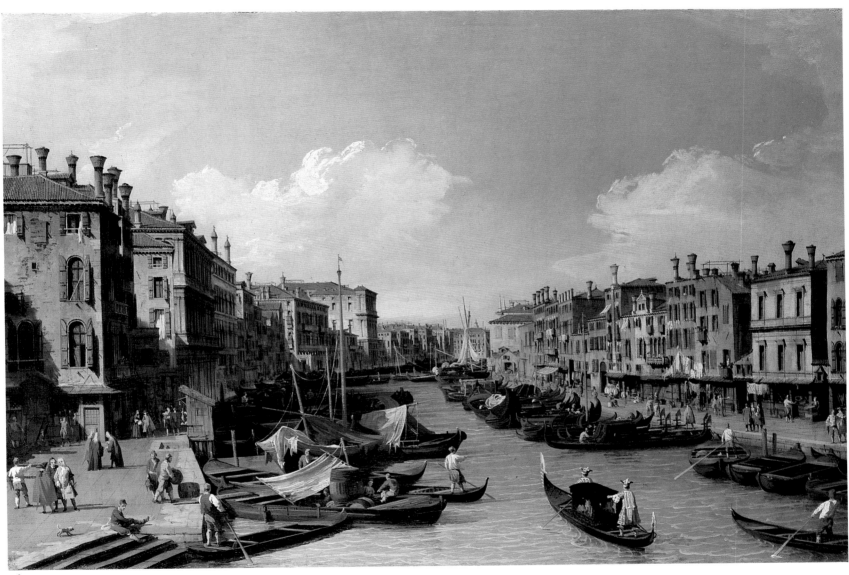

36.

37. S. Marco: the Crossing and North Transept

Oil on canvas; overall 13 × 8⅞ in. (33 × 22.5 cm), painted surface 11¼ × 7¾ in. (28.6 × 19.7 cm)
Her Majesty Queen Elizabeth II
C/L 77

EXHIBITED
London 27; Venice 87

NOTES
1. Millar, in *Canaletto*, 1980, p. 58, no. 27.
2. Parker, *Drawings of Canaletto*, 1948, pp. 34–35, nos. 30–31; and Levey, *Later Italian Pictures*, 1964, p. 62, no. 398. For the Orseolo reliquary, see also Succi, in *Canaletto & Visentini*, 1986, p. 216, no. 1 (Visentini's print).

The picture is titled by Constable *S. Marco: An Evening Service*, following an entry in a manuscript list of pictures bought by His Majesty in Italy as "Inside of S¹ Marks Church with Innumerable figures by Night."[1] Sir Oliver Millar has questioned the association with this entry: "The play of light...is immensely dramatic, but the strength of light at certain points seems greater than could ever have been obtained by candlelight and perhaps suggests shafts of daylight pouring into the Basilica in the late afternoon or evening." Innumerable solutions to the problem of the specific iconography of the picture have been proposed: that it should be identified with another entry in Smith's list, and shows the church on Good Friday; that it was intended to recall the services of Tenebrae sung during Holy Week; that the tabernacle where the Sacrament is reserved from Maundy Thursday until Holy Saturday is shown in the north transept; or rather that a sarcophagus is represented and that the picture documents the reception on 7 January 1732 of the relics of the Blessed Pietro Orseolo.[2] Each has been rejected, on liturgical or other more practical grounds.

A date in the 1730s seems likely. A drawing of the north transept (cat. no. 99) probably came later. Canaletto seldom painted interiors and almost never worked on so small a scale, and it is probable that the picture resulted from Smith's direct order. Another view of the interior of S. Marco toward the high altar (C/L 78, also in the Royal Collection) was one of Smith's last commissions to Canaletto, after the artist returned to Venice about 1755. A version of this later view is catalogue number 81.

The crossing and north transept are shown from a point toward the south and beneath the Cupola di S. Leonardo. The interior spaces have been narrowed, and the illusion of height is reinforced by the thread-like chain from which the lamp is suspended. Light plays over the cross hanging above the opening of the sanctuary, the architrave of the iconostasis supporting fourteen statues and a gilt crucifix, and the pulpits, two of them heavily draped and crowded with figures. Canaletto captures the mystery and solemnity of the ancient building and of the rites celebrated therein, and the personal qualities of the picture have endeared it to all who have seen it on the few occasions it has been exhibited.

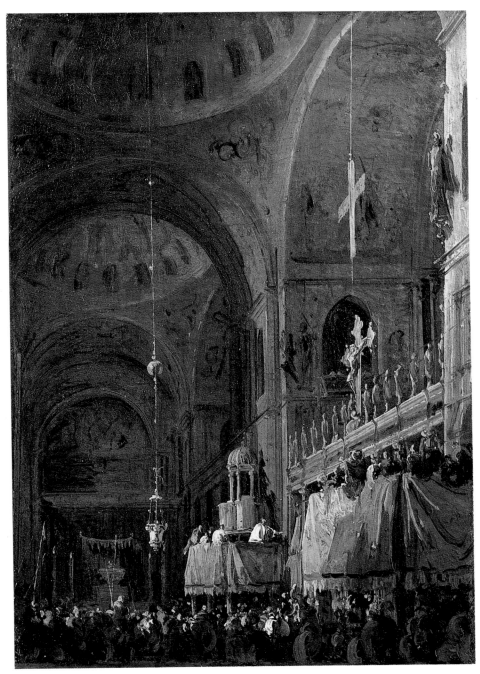

37.

155

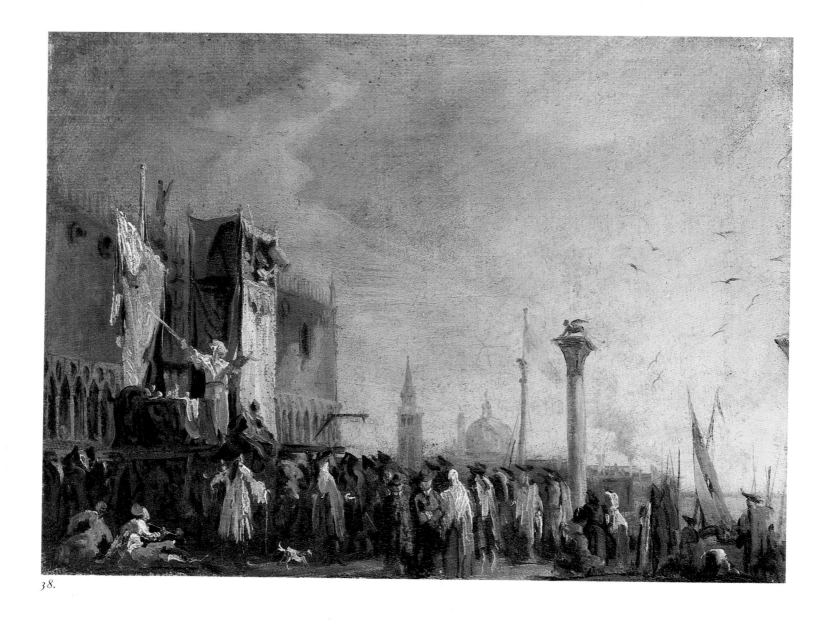

38.

38. A Puppet Show on the Piazzetta

Oil on canvas, 9½ × 12½ in. (24 × 31 cm)
The Ashmolean Museum, Oxford
C/L 363

NOTE

1. Pallucchini, "Per gli esordi del Canaletto," 1973, p. 177; and see also Viola Pemberton-Pigott, "The Development of Canaletto's Painting Technique."

On the left is the Piazzetta facade of the Palazzo Ducale in front of which a tall booth for puppets has been erected (also shown in much the same position in a considerably later work, C/L 71), together with a platform on which stands a man apparently reading and pointing with a stick. He has the attention of a small crowd but two men in brown, perhaps in uniform, face the viewer. Right of center is the column of St. Mark and, extreme right, part of the column of St. Theodore. In the background are the campanile and dome of S. Giorgio Maggiore, exaggerated in size, the campanile with the straight-sided steeple it had until about 1726.

Rodolfo Pallucchini described the painting as a sketch of a type representative of Canaletto's earliest period.[1] W. G. Constable had found no parallel in Canaletto's oeuvre for the very ragged brushwork and the romantic feeling of the painting and suggested the possibility of a late eighteenth-century work when the spire of the campanile had again been rebuilt with straight sides after a long period of being onion shaped. To eyes more accustomed to the early paintings shown in the present exhibition an attribution to Canaletto seems justified.

NOTES

1. Chaloner, "The Egertons in Italy," 1950, p. 164.
2. See Links, *Views of Venice*, 1971; Succi, *Venezia nella felicità illuminata delle acqueforti di Antonio Visentini*, 1984; and *Canaletto & Visentini*, 1986.
3. There was an earlier edition, published about 1717 and entitled *Il Gran Teatro di Venezia ovvero raccolta delle principali vedute e pitture che in essa si contengono*. See Succi, in *Da Carlevarijs ai Tiepolo*, 1983, pp. 230–32. We are appreciative of the advice of Eleanor Garvey on this matter.

Prospectus Magni Canalis Venetiarum: Views of the Grand Canal in the Royal Collection

In his letter of 17 July 1730 to Samuel Hill, Joseph Smith remarked upon another project with which he was associated: "The prints of the views and pictures of Venice will now soon be finish'd. I've told you there is only a limited number to be drawn off, so if you want any for friends, speak in time."[1] The voice is that of the man of commerce looking for trade, and the wording suggests that Smith was reminding Hill about a matter of which he had previously been informed. Smith referred to a set of engravings by Antonio Visentini after twelve Grand Canal subjects by Canaletto entitled *Prospectus Magni Canalis Venetiarum*, hereafter cited as *Prospectus*.[2] In the event, the engravings were not published until 1735, prints of two festival paintings (cat. nos. 43, 44) having been added meanwhile. The publisher is not indicated but must have been Giovanni Battista Pasquali, whose name appears on the part-title page to the second, definitive edition of 1742. In each case, the frontispiece incorporates a portrait of Canaletto after a drawing by Giovanni Battista Piazzetta (see fig. 1), and a self-portrait of Visentini.

The publication—and illustration—of luxury books often intended for foreign markets was a specialized business in Venice, and many such must have been sold to tourist visitors at local shops. *Prospectus* followed well-established precedent: *Le Fabriche e Vedute di Venetia*, a vastly more extensive compendium by Luca Carlevaris, was issued in 1703, and Domenico Lovisa's *Il Gran Teatro delle Pitture e Prospettive di Venezia*, incorporating engravings after famous monuments and paintings, was published in 1720.[3] All of the paintings by Canaletto reproduced as engravings for the first edition of *Prospectus* are in the Royal Collection; all were owned by Smith, who might well have commissioned them. According to the title pages of the two earliest editions, Canaletto's originals were *in Aedibus Josephi Smith Angli*, in the house of Joseph Smith, of England: Smith in this way engaged in a form of advertising, no doubt in the hope of capturing future clients. Of the fourteen paintings reproduced in all, four, of the Grand Canal (cat. nos. 39–42), and the two festival pictures (cat. nos. 43, 44) are here exhibited (in the catalogue entries, comparison is to the engravings of the 1742 edition of *Prospectus*).

39. Grand Canal: looking Southwest from the Rialto Bridge to the Palazzo Foscari

Oil on canvas, 18½ × 31⅛ in. (47 × 79.1 cm)
Her Majesty Queen Elizabeth II
C/L 219

EXHIBITED
London 7

NOTE
1. Levey, *Later Italian Pictures*, 1964, pp. 57–58, no. 384; and Millar, in *Canaletto*, 1980, pp. 39–40, no. 7.

The engraving of this painting was the first in *Prospectus*, whose views followed a course down the Grand Canal to Sta. Maria della Salute, then back to the Rialto Bridge for a trip to the end of the Canale di Sta. Chiara. The print bears an explanatory inscription, *Ex Ponte Rivoalti ad Orientem, usque ad Aedes Foscarorum, cui respondet Ripa Vinaria.*—which mistakenly describes the view as toward the east. It is unlikely that all of the Grand Canal views were painted in or before 1730, but some of them certainly were, and the order of the engravings may to some extent reflect the order in which Canaletto's pictures were finished.[1] The subject is the same as that of one of the Wicklow pair (cat. no. 36), which were delivered to their original owner in August 1730, but the viewpoint is a little lower—that is to say, the artist had descended some additional steps of the Rialto Bridge. The format chosen for this canvas and the others of the series differs from that adopted

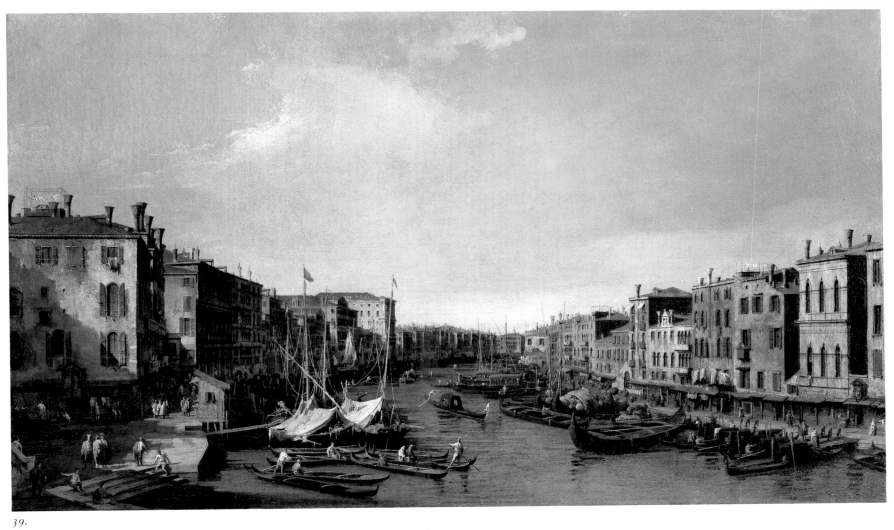

39.

for the Wicklow views: the picture surface is wider in proportion to its height, and the distant buildings are proportionately smaller. Many of the compositions engraved as the first twelve plates of *Prospectus* are taken from two viewpoints, but not this one, though even here Ca' Foscari appears nearer than in fact it is. The dull, slate gray-blue color of the water is unusually convincing, and Canaletto has also captured the look of the faded and discolored plasterwork of many of the old houses near the Rialto, and the effects of filtered sunlight and deep shadow. The evocative, fugitive quality of the light is reminiscent of his work of the mid-twenties, and the picture must be significantly earlier than number 36. Inevitably, Visentini failed even to approximate the subtlety of handling, and his engraving is prosaic by comparison.

40. Grand Canal: from Sta. Maria della Carità to the Bacino di S. Marco

Oil on canvas, 18⅞ × 31½ in. (47.9 × 80 cm)
Her Majesty Queen Elizabeth II
C/L 196

This is a later variant of one of Stefano Conti's second pair of paintings, number 11, of 1726.[1] The church of the Carità is shown as from a point farther to the left with the result that the campanile is here visible in its entirety, as is the building between it and the church. The Grand Canal bending toward the *bacino* can be seen to be wider than it appeared in Conti's picture, and the upper part of the facade and the drum and dome of the Salute are visible. All of the buildings are proportionately smaller in scale. The quay in the foreground was crumbling in the Conti view, and in a state of abandonment, the water washing over the loose stones, in a picture of intermediate date now belonging to the Kimbell Art Museum, Fort Worth (C/L 195); by the time the present picture was painted it had been rebuilt. In both of the later versions the brickwork of the facade of the Carità—neatly bisected by the shadow of the adjoining *scuola*—seems also to have undergone repair, though in the meantime a statue and some crockets had fallen off the pinnacle at the right. The fine Gothic building on the opposite bank is Palazzo Cavalli, which later underwent extensive rebuilding. Next to it are the Barbaro palaces, where Henry James was to stay as guest. As Sir Oliver Millar noted, a ruling instrument was used extensively, especially for the buildings on the left. The few figures, nearly all of them seen from behind, are of high quality. The sky, no longer ominous, is a bright blue with light summer clouds. Today, the presence of the Accademia bridge spanning the Grand Canal at this point, and the transformation of the church and the

EXHIBITED
London 9

NOTE
1. Levey, *Later Italian Pictures*, 1964, p. 58, no. 386; and Millar, in *Canaletto*, 1980, p. 40, no. 9.

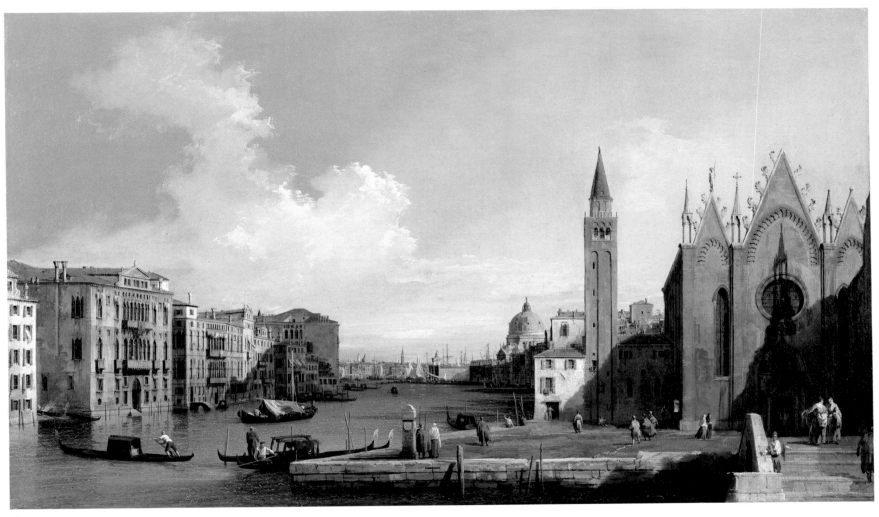

40.

adjoining *scuola* into a museum, have combined to make what was once a peaceful *campo* one of the liveliest in all Venice.

Visentini's engraving is the third in *Prospectus*. He does not show the shadow of the pinnacle of the *scuola*, which in the painting intersects the window at the center of the church facade. The first three views of the series (see, in addition to cat. no. 39, C/L 203) embrace the length of the Grand Canal from the Rialto Bridge to the Bacino di S. Marco. The subjects of the fourth, fifth, and sixth views (C/L 184, 170, and 161) overlap, so to speak: the fourth shows the *bacino* from S. Vio, the fifth the *bacino* from the Salute, and the sixth the Dogana and the Salute from the opposite direction. Sir Oliver Millar has suggested that the last two, incorporating Sta. Maria della Salute, are the latest of the six, from the early 1730s, and that they may have been conceived as a pair. The duplication of subject matter might weigh in favor of this pair's addition to the series at a relatively late date.

41. Grand Canal: looking North from near the Rialto Bridge

Oil on canvas, 18¾ × 31½ in. (47.6 × 80 cm)
Her Majesty Queen Elizabeth II
C/L 233

EXHIBITED
London 14

NOTE
1. Levey, *Later Italian Pictures*, 1964, p. 59, no. 391; and Millar, in *Canaletto*, 1980, pp. 44–46, no. 14.

Three of the subjects that Canaletto had painted for Conti reappear among the Grand Canal views engraved by Visentini.[1] The view from the Rialto toward the north was one of the earlier pair, completed in 1725, and Canaletto's description appears in the entry for number 9. The work on Palazzo Corner della Regina had meanwhile been finished and the scaffolding removed: this palace is the one immediately in front of Ca' Pesaro, which lies at the bend of the canal on the opposite bank. In the foreground, at the right, is part of the approach to the Rialto Bridge. The second palace beyond is the Ca' da Mosto, an ancient building which had been from the sixteenth century and was still in Canaletto's time a famous hotel, the Leon Bianco.

The fourth house that is visible on the right is the Palazzo Mangilli Valmarana, which was leased and later bought by Joseph Smith. As Sir Michael Levey pointed out, it is shown with a new facade designed by Visentini, which is not known to have been completed until 1751. The painting had to have been finished before 1735 when the engraving after it was published as plate VIII in *Prospectus*. Since in the engraving the palace has its old facade, the explanation must be that the old facade was overpainted by Canaletto to show the new one, presumably at the owner's request. The present picture is probably one of the earliest of the series, dating from before 1730, so this commission must have been carried out more than twenty years later.

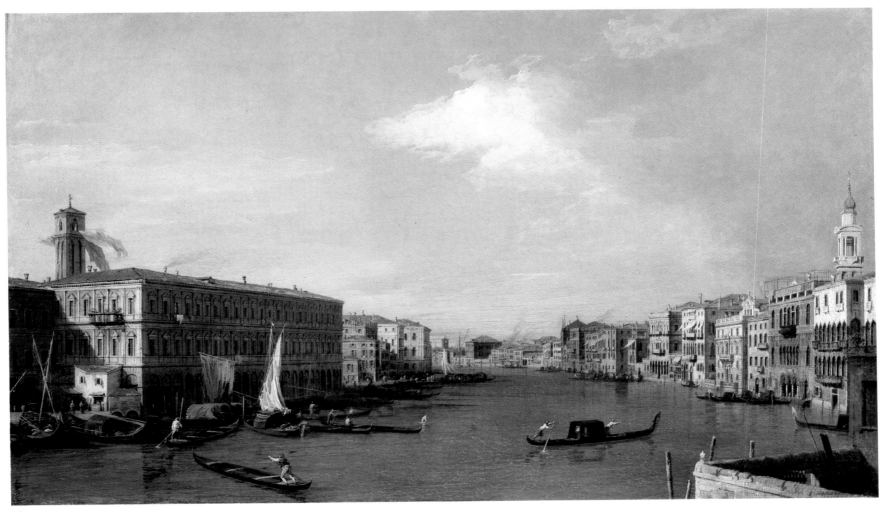

41.

In his engraving of this painting (and in one or two others of the series) Visentini transcribed plumes of smoke issuing from a number of the chimneys, a rare suggestion of cold weather since, generally speaking in Canaletto's views, as in most views of Venice, it is impossible to tell the season. The picture engraved as plate VII (C/L 236) shows the bridge from the north, a subject often paired with the view from the bridge in the opposite direction.

Sir Oliver Millar noted that when Canaletto reworked the facade of Smith's palace, he drew detail in the wet paint. Earlier, he made extensive use of a straightedge for the Fabbriche Nuove, the largest structure on the opposite bank of the Grand Canal.

42. Grand Canal: looking Northwest from the Palazzo Vendramin Calergi to S. Geremia and the Palazzo Flangini

Oil on canvas, 18⅝ × 31¼ in. (47.3 × 79.4 cm)
Her Majesty Queen Elizabeth II
C/L 250

EXHIBITED
London 15

NOTE
1. Levey, *Later Italian Pictures*, 1964, p. 59, no. 392; and Millar, in *Canaletto*, 1980, pp. 46–48, no. 15.

The visitor is now assumed to be on the second stage of his journey from the Rialto Bridge to the far end of the Grand Canal.[1] Beyond the two palaces with obelisks, at the left, are two with crenellated roofs. The first of these was the Deposito del Megio, a public granary in addition to the one already seen on the Molo. The second is the Fondaco dei Turchi, originally built in the thirteenth century and later used as a warehouse by the Turkish merchants. The two buildings in strong light just beyond have been added as a compositional device but would not in reality be seen. In the right foreground is the Palazzo Vendramin Calergi (which Canaletto called Grimani: see cat. no. 9). There are several inaccuracies in the architectural details of this palace, surprisingly, since Canaletto drew the building correctly in his sketchbook, which is now in the Accademia (f. 48r). Visentini corrected these in his engraving, plate IX of *Prospectus*, and Canaletto, in a much later painting of the palace (C/L 326), corrected them himself. In the distance, right, are the campanile and the church of S. Geremia, at the entrance to the Cannaregio Canal. Different viewpoints were necessary to include all of the buildings shown, and the curve of the canal in the distance had to be reduced.

The tour—paintings and engravings—continues with views of the entrance to the Cannaregio Canal (C/L 251), and of the churches of the Scalzi and S. Simeone Piccolo (C/L 258), and concludes with the Canale di Sta. Chiara opening into the distant lagoon (C/L 270). The relevant plates are numbers X through XII of *Prospectus*.

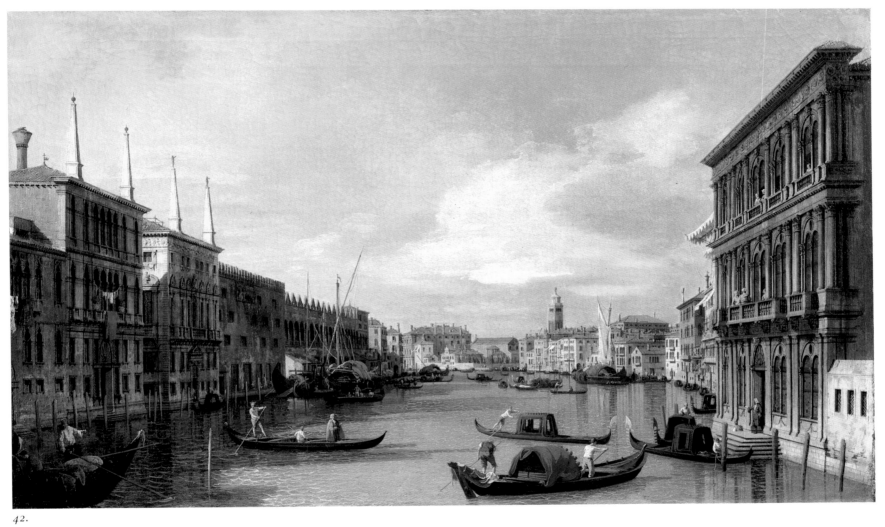

42.

43. A Regatta on the Grand Canal

Oil on canvas, 30⅜ × 49½ in. (77.2 × 125.7 cm)
Her Majesty Queen Elizabeth II
C/L 347

EXHIBITED
London 19

NOTES

1. Levey, *Later Italian Pictures*, 1964, pp. 60–61, no. 396; and Millar, in *Canaletto*, 1980, pp. 50–51, no. 19. For a fuller treatment of the subject of the regatta, see Levey, *Eighteenth Century Italian Schools*, 1956, pp. 18–19 and 26–29, with reference to similar paintings in the National Gallery, London (C/L 350 and C/L 348a).
2. Levey, *Burlington Magazine*, 1953, p. 366.
3. Rizzi, *Carlevarijs*, 1967, pp. 51, 88, and 93, pls. 35, 38, and 39; and "Acquisitions/1986," *J. Paul Getty Museum Journal* 15 (1987), p. 187, no. 51.
4. See Morassi, *Guardi*, [1973], pp. 199–203, 366–67, nos. 298–302, and figs. 326–29 and 334.

Engravings of two festival subjects concluded the first edition of *Prospectus*; both paintings, larger than the preceding twelve Grand Canal views, are here exhibited.[1] The title page refers to them as *addito Certamine Nautico et Nundinis Venetis*, making it clear that the nautical contest and its companion piece were additions, by implication the latest of the series. At the left is the *macchina della regata*, a temporary structure erected upon a barge or floating platform which was positioned between Palazzo Balbi and Ca' Foscari, where the Rio Foscari joins the Grand Canal. Here colored flags and prizes of money were distributed to the winners. Customarily, the *macchina* was ornamented with a coat of arms, either that of the distinguished visitor in whose honor the regatta was held, or that of the Doge, in the present case Carlo Ruzzini, who reigned from June 1732 until his death in January 1735.[2] This would seem to constitute irrefutable evidence for the date, bearing in mind the publication in 1735 of the first edition of *Prospectus*.

From the beginning of the fourteenth century rowing races were held on the Grand Canal on 2 February, the feast of the Purification of the Virgin, and the regatta was associated with the carnival season, which began on 26 December, St. Stephen's day. Some of the figures wear carnival costume, and the picture must show either the regatta of 2 February 1733 or that of the following year. Several races were held—this one is rowed in light gondolas by single gondoliers—and the course was from the east of Venice, through the *bacino* and the Grand Canal to its far end, and then back to the Volta di Canal (the turn in the canal) and the *macchina*, represented here.

The source for the specific iconography of this picture and many others representing the regatta is to be found in the work of Luca Carlevaris.[3] In 1709 a regatta was held to honor a royal visitor to the city, Frederick IV, King of Denmark and Norway, and this event occasioned Carlevaris's canvas, which was presumably painted immediately thereafter and taken back to Denmark by the king. It is now at Frederiksborg Castle, near Copenhagen. A variant, now belonging to the J. Paul Getty Museum, Malibu, is dated in the following year. Canaletto may never have seen either of the paintings, but he would certainly have known the reproductive print by G. Baroni after the 1710 picture. Carlevaris had taken a closely similar viewpoint, from the Volta di Canal, but at the left he incorporated the corner of Ca' Foscari, in shadow, and at the right he showed only the first two Gothic windows of Palazzo Erizzio, which is now called Nani Mocenigo. In Carlevaris's paintings the racing gondoliers have only the narrowest passage: except for an

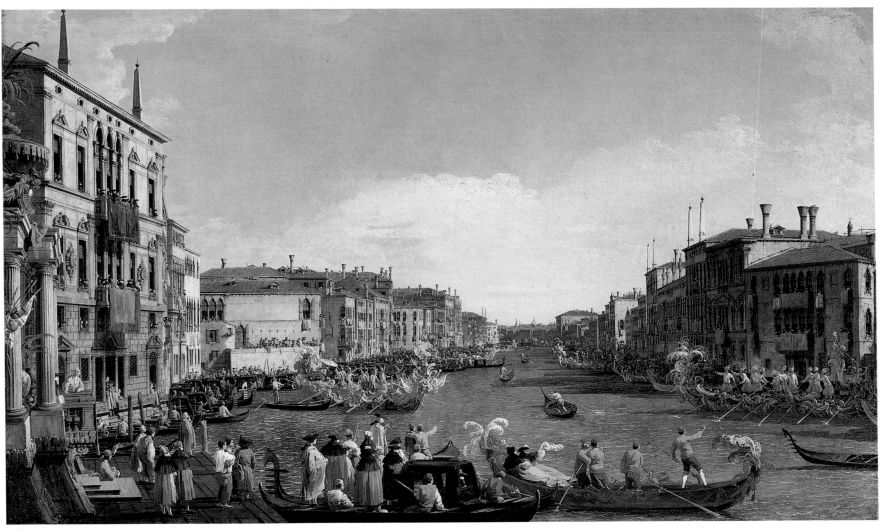

43.

167

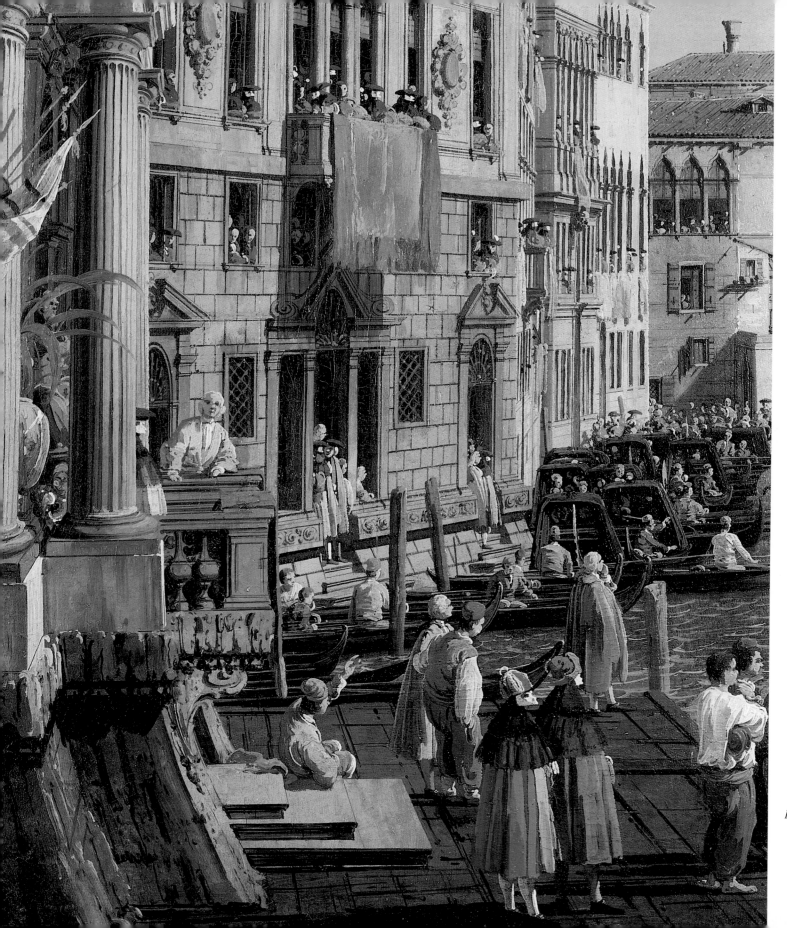

Details of 43.

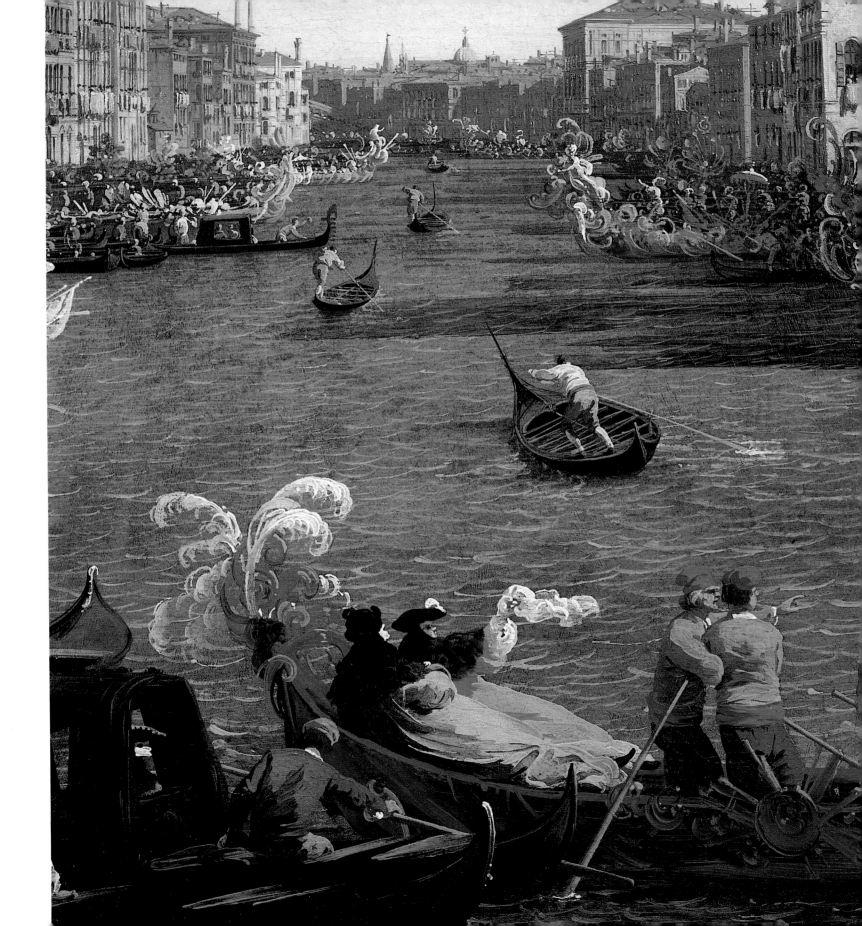

opening directly in front of the *macchina della regata*, the Grand Canal is crowded with very elaborately decorated boats, many of them *bissone*, rowed by eight or ten oarsmen. Gondolas and other small boats, water to the gunnels because of the number of spectators, occupy the immediate foreground.

Perhaps Canaletto's earlier views of the Grand Canal toward the northeast, from Palazzo Balbi to the Rialto, had also been influenced by Carlevaris's regatta composition. The paintings now at Ca' Rezzonico (cat. no. 3) and the Ferens Art Gallery, Hull (cat. no. 23), are closely similar in layout, though taken from a higher viewpoint. These are remarkable, by contrast to number 43, for their sobriety: because the canal is still and opaque, largely free of shipping, effects of weather and reflections on the water assume greater significance. In *A Regatta on the Grand Canal* the architecture gives the impression of having been painted with assurance and precision, but nevertheless there are the usual slight differences among these canvases, and variations from topographical fact. The sky is bright, by comparison with the earlier views, and the water is blue-green, flecked with ripples. Four gondolas follow a northward course, and a wider path has been left for them than was the case in Carlevaris's paintings. Colored hangings are at the windows and balconies and, as always, every window with a view is crowded with spectators.

Some of the smaller boats and the *bissone*, which belonged to the great Venetian families, are decorated, and the oarsmen are either in costume or in uniform. A number of the spectators, notably those in the more elaborate boats and at the windows of Palazzo Balbi, wear a domino of white mask and black cape, often combined with a tricorn, the costume of carnival. The *macchina della regata*, incorporating trophies of arms, is crowned with a parasol shielding the coat of arms of the Doge (his hat, the *corno*, may be more closely seen in the Visentini print, where the arms cannot be read). Two small balconies project at the center, in a position of honor. In the nearer one, partially hidden by a column, stands an anonymous figure in hat, mask, and cape, his arms covered by his cloak, watching the race. From the more distant balcony a figure in yellow confronts the spectator: this figure has the look of a minute portrait, and seems to play some special role, quite apart from the event which is the subject of the picture. It is amusing to imagine that he might be Smith, whose appearance is not recorded. The man looks to be middle aged. Smith, at this time, was about sixty but, it must be assumed, youthful, as he lived to be well over ninety.

In general the foreground figures have a wonderful sense of presence and individuality. The handling is bold, the narrative lively and unforced; this picture and its pendant are of exceptional quality, the style perfectly adapted to the subject matter and differing from that of the earlier Grand Canal subjects that were likewise engraved. As Sir Oliver Millar has noted, they should probably be dated about 1734. The variants of the subject by Canaletto (and from his shop) are later, as Sir Michael Levey demonstrated, and the subject was also painted on several occasions by Francesco Guardi.[4] The Royal Collection regatta was engraved by Visentini—with the title *Nauticum Certamen cum Prospectu ab Aedibus Balborum, ad Ponte Rivoalti.*—as plate XIII of *Prospectus*.

44. The Bucintoro Returning to the Molo on Ascension Day

Oil on canvas, 30¼ × 49⅜ in. (76.8 × 125.4 cm)
Her Majesty Queen Elizabeth II
C/L 335

EXHIBITED
London 20

NOTES

1. Levey, *Later Italian Pictures*, 1964, p. 61, no. 397; and Millar, in *Canaletto*, 1980, pp. 51–52, no. 20. For additional information about Ascension Day views, see Levey, *Eighteenth Century Italian Schools*, 1956, pp. 24–26, on a painting in the National Gallery, London (C/L 333).
2. Rizzi, *Carlevarijs*, 1967, p. 93 and pl. 43; and "Acquisitions/1986." *J. Paul Getty Museum Journal* 15 (1987), p.187, no. 51.
3. For this picture, the only example of its type catalogued by Morassi, see *Guardi*, [1973], pp. 192–93, 362–63, no. 281, and figs. 310–12. Francesco Guardi's preference was for views of the state barge crossing the *bacino* on its way to or from the Lido, for which see Morassi, *Guardi*, [1973], pp. 193–99, 363–65, nos. 282–88, 292, and figs. 313–17, 321, and 324.
4. Norwich, *A History of Venice*, 1985, pp. 54–55, and see also pp. 51–53 and 116.
5. For a further account of this painting and its pendant, see Pietro Zampetti, in *Canaletto*, 1982, pp. 59–61, nos. 83–84.

The picture commemorates a moment in an annual ceremony of great antiquity, the Sposalizio del Mar, symbolic of Venetian seafaring supremacy, specifically in the Adriatic by way of which her naval forces reached the Mediterranean and the East.[1] However, by the eighteenth century the ceremony was conducted with a view to the entertainment of grand tourists and other visitors. Smith would have had such visitors in mind as future clients, and to one or more of them he may have sold later variants of this composition by Canaletto, as well as copies of *Prospectus*. The subject was in every way a suitable conclusion to the Grand Canal series, and to the first edition of Visentini's engravings after Canaletto. Carlevaris had painted the state barge at the Molo only once, in 1710 (the painting is in the J. Paul Getty Museum with its pendant, his second version of the regatta, referred to above).[2] The resemblance is little more than generic, and the present composition should thus be regarded as Canaletto's invention. There is a fine painting of the subject by Francesco Guardi, which is closely related thematically, though very different in handling.[3]

In the year 1000, or thereabouts, Doge Pietro Orseolo II undertook an expedition into the Adriatic, his object to subjugate the Slav pirates of the Dalmatian coast who were endangering free passage of Venetian ships and thus her mercantile interests. The fleet weighed anchor on Ascension Day, and the expedition was notably successful. John Julius Norwich describes as follows the pageantry of the symbolic marriage of Venice to the sea:

And so there was added to the Doge's other honorifics the mellifluous title of *Dux Dalmatiae*; and in further commemoration of the expedition it was decreed that on

171

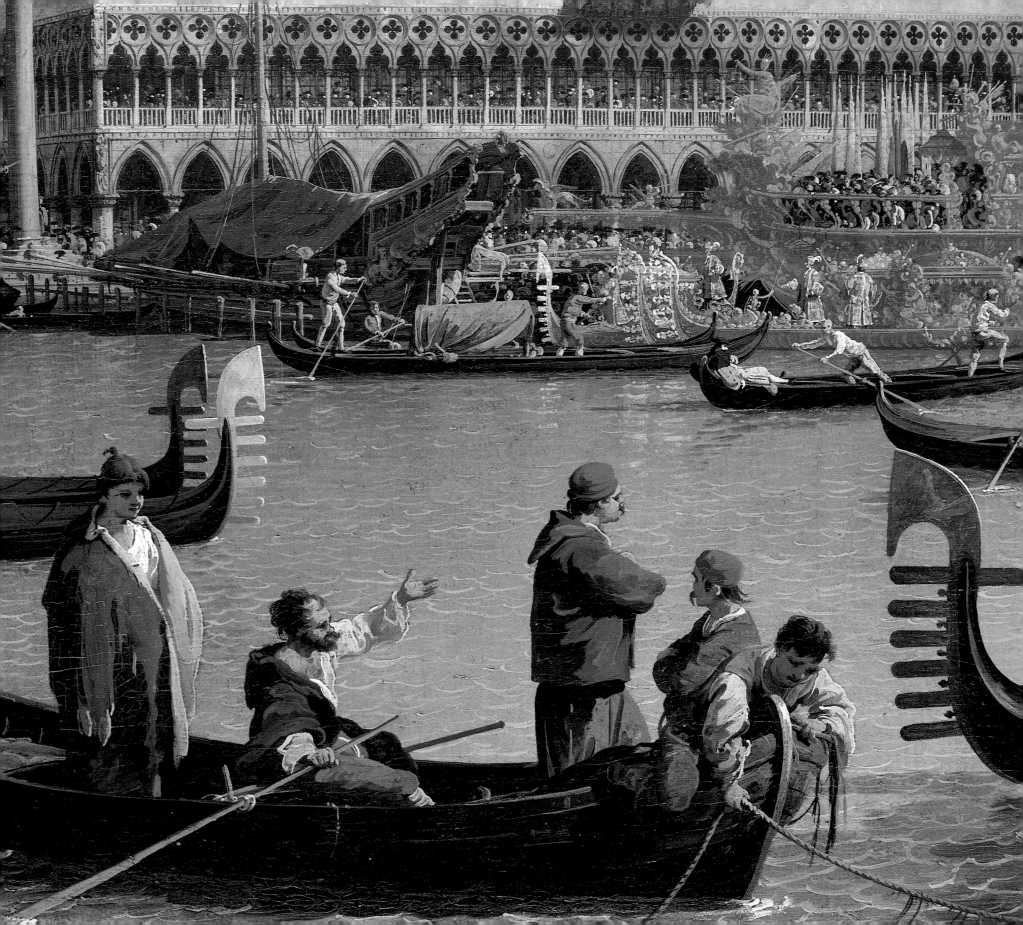

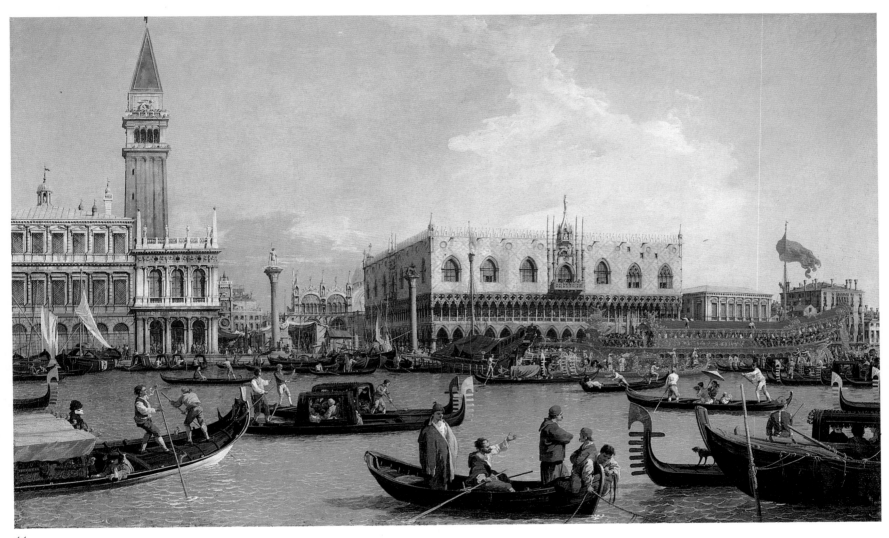

44.

Detail of 44.

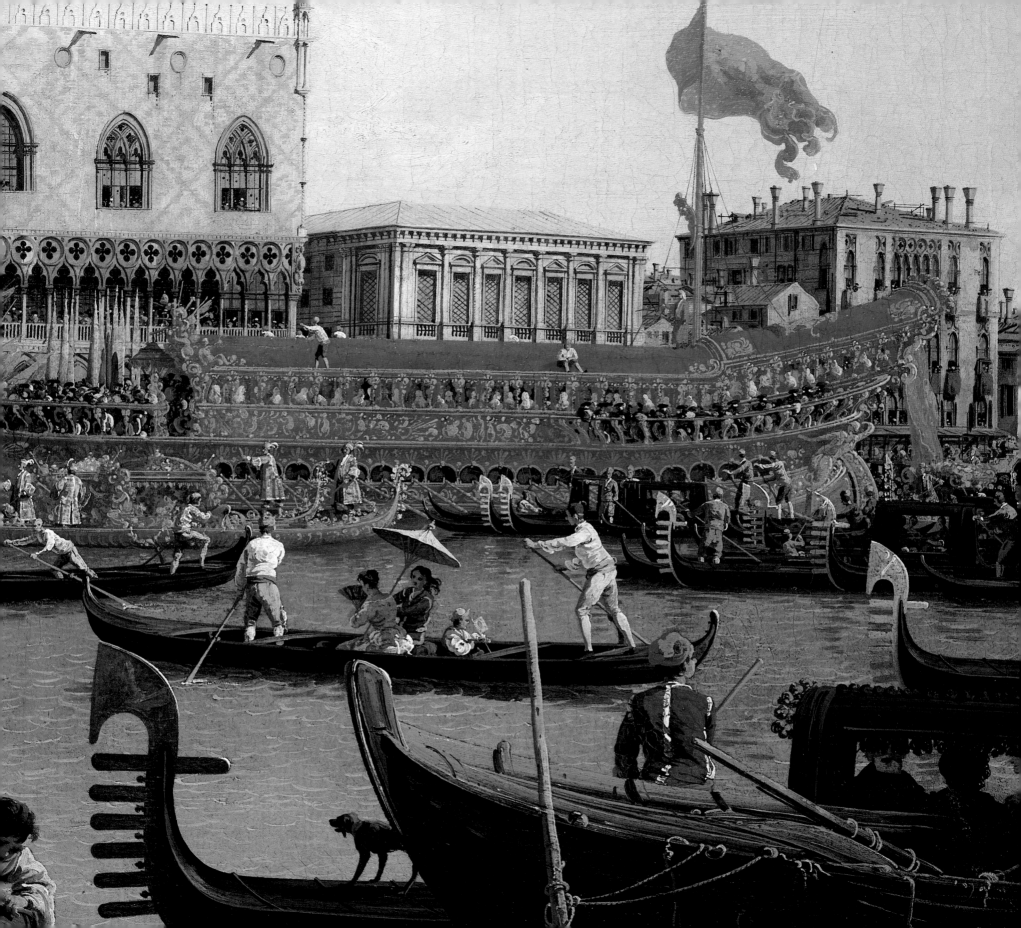

every succeeding Ascension Day—the anniversary of the fleet's departure—the Doge, with the Bishop of Olivolo and the nobles and citizens of Venice, should sail out again by the Lido port into the open sea for a service of supplication and thanksgiving. In those early days the service was short and the prayer simple, though it asked a lot: "Grant, O Lord, that for us and for all who sail thereon, the sea may ever be calm and quiet." The Doge and his suite were then sprinkled with holy water . . . and what was left of the water was poured into the sea. Later, as the tradition grew more venerable, so the ceremony grew more elaborate, and included the casting of a propitiatory golden ring into the waves; thus it was slowly to become identified with a symbolic marriage to the sea—the *Sposalizio del Mar*—a character that it was to retain till the end of the Republic itself.[4]

Canaletto showed the Zecca (Mint) and the Library with the Campanile rising behind them; the Piazzetta with the columns of St. Theodore and St. Mark, and part of the Clock Tower and S. Marco, beyond; the Palazzo Ducale, the Prisons, the roofs of the wooden buildings (see cat. no. 18), and the Palazzo Dandolo, now the Hotel Danieli. The temporary buildings on the Piazzetta are explained by the title page of *Prospectus* where the picture is described not as a ceremony but as *Nundinis Venetis*, a Venetian market. Evidently to the Venetians this was an important part of the celebrations. To the right and facing westward is the Bucintoro, the state barge, which had only recently been built, although it had had a number of predecessors, each expected to last a century or more. This was the last Bucintoro: no new one had been built when Venice fell to Napoleon more than half a century later, in 1797. The galleon with the red and gold striped awning was called *la fusta* and was kept in reserve for the Doge's protection; the oars are raised in waiting, and there is what may be a coat of arms (blue) at the stern. This boat is frequently seen in Canaletto's work and must often have stood at the Molo.

There are many variations on this theme by Canaletto and by his followers, some showing the Bucintoro before it set out for the Lido. In certain of the later versions—in the National Gallery, London (C/L 333), and at Woburn Abbey (C/L 332), for example—the viewpoint is imagined to be well to the east, off the Riva degli Schiavoni. Closest in style and composition is a painting in a private collection in Milan (C/L 336), which is larger, even more elaborate (though omitting the market on the Piazzetta), and presumably earlier in date.[5] Both are related to a drawing in the Royal Library, Windsor (C/L 642). In the foreground at the left of the present painting, in the Royal Collection, a collision is threatened between two gondolas; in the picture in Milan it is in fact taking place. The oarsmen leaning back upon their oars to slow the motion of the ongoing boats are closely similar in the

Detail of 44.

175

two views, as, in general, is the figure style throughout. The Bucintoro painting in Milan has as its pendant the *Reception of the Imperial Ambassador, Count Giuseppe Bolagnos, at the Doge's Palace* (C/L 355), an event which took place on 29 May 1729. It must be assumed that the ambassador commissioned the pair, and that they were painted before his death on 26 January 1731.

The scene as depicted in the canvas in the Royal Collection is less chaotic than the version in Milan. In the foreground there are no more than a dozen boats, some carrying elegant passengers a few of whom wear the white mask and black cape generally associated with carnival. The expanse of the *bacino* is a brilliant blue, flecked with white, and in the foreground the blades of the oars may be seen beneath the surface of the water. To the west of the Doge's galley, gondolas and working boats are moored at the Molo. The passageway between the booths in the Piazzetta is overhung with awnings, and through the opening, in the dim light, touches of color suggest the goods for sale. The top of the Campanile is crowded with spectators, some of whom have climbed over the railings and are seated on the parapets, their legs silhouetted against the sky, but the interest of the onlookers is perhaps not so great—nor are they so numerous—as the audience for the regatta. The Bucintoro has been accompanied on its return from the Lido by several elaborate small boats and a number of gondolas. The shadowy presence of the oarsmen, four to each oar, may be glimpsed through the openings of the lower deck, their red and gold oars at rest. The admiral stands on the roof and the participants in the ceremony are still on board: bewigged officials, in red, are seated in the cabin, and other distinguished guests crowd the deck, the colored flags and gold parasol signaling the presence of the Doge who is about to disembark. The picture was engraved as the fourteenth and final plate of the first edition of *Prospectus: Bucentaurus et Nundinae Venetae in die Ascensionis.*

Prospectus: Paintings and Engravings for the Edition of 1742

The second edition of *Prospectus*, published in 1742, contained twenty-four additional engravings by Visentini, organized in two parts.[1] Part II comprises ten further views of the Grand Canal—arranged to follow a more or less regular course from the Canale di Sta. Chiara to Palazzo Corner della Ca' Grande, a little below Campo S. Vio—and concludes with views of the Molo looking east and west. Part III describes ten of the *campi*, or city squares, and ends with Piazza S. Marco from the east and the west, the view of the basilica being the thirty-eighth and final illustration in the album. The words *Elegantius recusi* on the title page document the recutting of the original plates. By 1742, Canaletto's most productive and successful years were over, and the War of the Austrian Succession had interrupted the flow of foreign visitors to Venice. Smith still owned the fourteen paintings upon which the first set of engravings had been based, and the title page of the second edition retained the words *in Aedibus Josephi Smith Angli*. However, with one exception (cat. no. 45), the paintings on which the twenty-four new engravings depended had almost certainly been sold: eight (or more probably nine) of them among a group of twenty-one perhaps to the grandfather of the first Duke of Buckingham (the so-called Harvey series, since dispersed), three among twenty-four to the fourth Duke of Bedford (these are still at Woburn Abbey), three among seven or more to the Duke of Leeds (sold in the 1920s), and two of eight to Earl Fitzwilliam; not all of the others can be traced. Buyers could still choose their subjects from the engravings if they wished to order paintings, but few appear to have done so, compared with those who had ordered from the fourteen paintings engraved for the 1735 edition. Between 1730 and 1742 Smith must have sold many other pictures by Canaletto which were not engraved. There are also enough known or suspected cases of buyers dealing directly with Canaletto, or possibly with other agents, to establish that Smith did not, as was suggested at the time, have a monopoly of the artist's services. A selection from the work of the 1730s follows, and four of Canaletto's pictures engraved for the 1742 edition are among them (cat. nos. 45–47, 49).

NOTE

1. Visentini's engravings are illustrated in Links, *Views of Venice*, 1971.

45. SS. Giovanni e Paolo and the Monument to Bartolomeo Colleoni

Oil on canvas, 18⅜ × 30⅞ in. (46 × 78.4 cm)
Her Majesty Queen Elizabeth II
C/L 308

EXHIBITED
London 21; Venice 96

NOTES
1. Levey, *Later Italian Pictures*, 1964, p. 63, no. 402; Millar, in *Canaletto*, 1980, pp. 52–54, no. 21; and Millar, in *Canaletto*, 1982, p. 67, no. 96.
2. Morassi, *Guardi*, [1973], pp. 233, 421, nos. 594–95, and figs. 564 and 566.

178

The Dominican church of SS. Giovanni e Paolo, of which the west facade, the south transept, and the greater part of the dome may be seen, had for centuries been the main resting place for the Doges.[1] At the left is the elaborate trompe l'oeil marble facade of the Scuola di S. Marco, then one of the principal *scuole*, or guilds, of Venice, and since its suppression under Napoleon, the main hospital of the city. To the right of the church, the celebrated monument to Bartolomeo Colleoni, designed by Verrocchio, stands upon a high marble pedestal. (Colleoni, a mercenary soldier from Bergamo and a defender of the Venetian Republic who died in 1475, bequeathed his fortune to the city; it had been his requirement that the equestrian monument should stand in Piazza S. Marco but, this being prohibited, Venetian ingenuity prevailed, and it was installed instead outside the *scuola* dedicated to St. Mark.) The horizontal provided by the quay and the water stairs along the Rio dei Mendicanti anchors the composition in the foreground. Among the figures in the square are many elegantly attired ladies and gentleman and several Dominican monks. The Rio dei Mendicanti, from the north, figures prominently in number 4 in this exhibition and the facade of the *scuola* and the church, from the south, in numbers 5 and 10.

The composition is in a general way reminiscent of an engraving by S. F., published in Lovisa's *Gran Teatro* of 1720, and is rather more closely similar to the print by Carlevaris that figures in his *Fabriche e Vedute* of 1703, though Carlevaris omitted the *rio* and gave a more prominent role to the Colleoni monument. The same sources were used by Guardi, who would also have known Canaletto's view through Visentini's engraving.[2] Smith owned no drawing by Canaletto of the subject, perhaps an indication that he always intended to keep the picture. There are, however, four pages (ff. 52r–50v) in Canaletto's sketchbook at the Accademia in Venice containing drawings of the lower part of the facade of the church, the side elevation, the monument, and the buildings to the south.

One of the upper windows of the house nearest the canal, shown here and in the related sketch, must have provided Canaletto's viewpoint for his pictures toward the north (cat. nos. 5, 10). For this painting, however, at least two widely separated viewpoints were required, and even then the artist significantly adjusted topography in the interest of pictorial effect. The bold, convincing composition is strengthened by the diagonal shadow lines—figuring also in the S. F. print and in one pair of Canaletto's sketches—which have

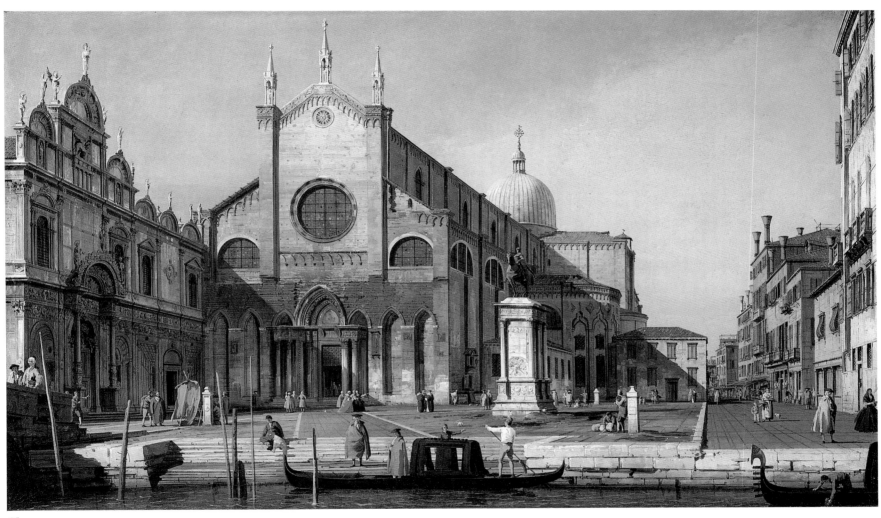

45.

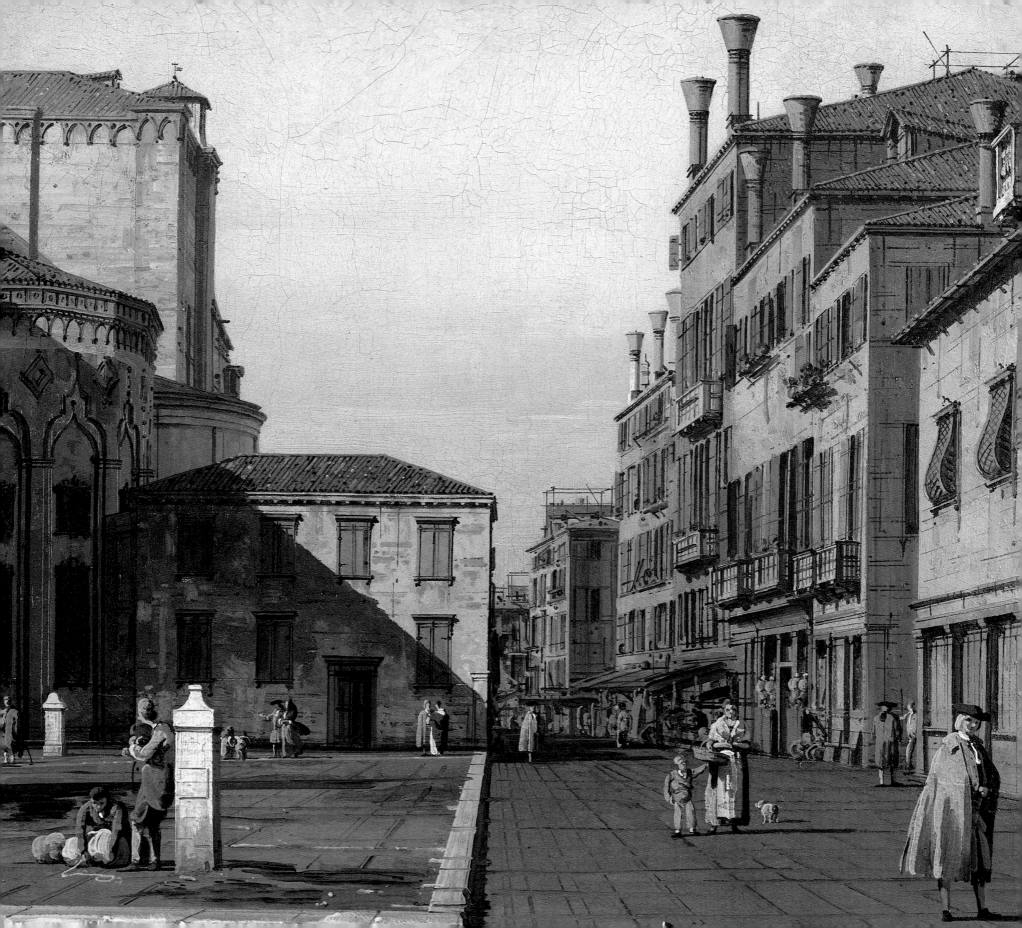

no basis in observation and are entirely fanciful. The dome of the church has been raised, its shape changed significantly.

The painting is engraved as plate 1 of the third part of the 1742 edition of *Prospectus*. While the size of the canvas is roughly that of the first twelve Grand Canal views, the style corresponds to later work. The main door of the church was rebuilt in 1739, and since Canaletto showed the old door, the picture may have been painted between the years 1735 and 1738.

Paintings Formerly Owned by Sir Robert Grenville Harvey

The Harvey group of twenty-one paintings of the Grand Canal and the churches and *campi*, all of the same size, is second in importance only to the twenty-four views bought by the fourth Duke of Bedford.[1] There can be no reasonable doubt that both groups passed through Smith's hands, and the fact that no subject is duplicated suggests that in some way he controlled their production. Eight or nine of the paintings engraved by Visentini for the 1742 edition of *Prospectus* were the property of Sir Robert Grenville Harvey, who died in 1931 and whose trustees dispersed them about 1957. It is a remarkable fact that their earlier history is undocumented. Sir Robert was a kinsman of the last Duke of Buckingham, who in 1839 inherited an income of £100,000 a year, but within ten years was bankrupt. There is probability, though no real evidence, that the duke owned the pictures, but it is almost impossible that he could have bought them himself in Venice, as has been stated. The original purchaser may have been George Grenville (1712–1770), whose grandson became the first Duke of Buckingham in 1822. Possibly it was the wish to conceal some of the last duke's assets from his creditors that contributed to the mystery surrounding the series. Readers of Sir Michael Levey's essay in this catalogue will be conscious of the unique attraction of such intimate scenes of inner Venice.

NOTE

1. Two of this series are exhibited (cat. nos. 46, 47), and two are reproduced in Michael Levey's essay (figs. 6, 9, 10); in addition see C/L 188, 198, 217, 221, 240, 241, 246, 257(d), 260, 262, 267, 275, 276, 277, 294, 295, and 314.

Detail of 45.

181

46. Campo S. Polo

Oil on canvas, 18¼ × 30⅜ in. (46.3 × 77 cm)
Private Collection
C/L 281

The *campo* is among the largest in Venice and for many centuries was the scene of fetes, tournaments, bullfights, and military reviews.[1] The church of S. Polo is behind the spectator and adjoins the house on the extreme left. The large house with most of the windows shuttered, in the background to the left, is the Palazzo Corner Mocenigo. A *rio*, or small canal, ran in front of the palaces on the right, around which parapets had been built and flat bridges leading to the entrances. The nearest of these is one of several belonging to the Tiepolo family, and beyond are two Gothic palaces owned in Canaletto's day by the Soranzos:

> In 1746, some ten to fifteen years after the picture was painted, the celebrated libertine Giacomo Casanova, then twenty-one, was, in his own words, "one of the fiddlers making up one of the several orchestras for the balls which were given for three days in the Palazzo Soranzo" on the occasion of a family marriage. As he left on the third day, an hour before dawn, he was befriended by a man who was seized by a stroke within a few minutes. Casanova saved the life of this man, who proved to be the highly influential Senator Bragadin and who adopted Casanova as a son—"which raised me at one bound from the base role of a fiddler to that of a nobleman," he wrote later.[2]

The picture is full of ordinary incident of a sort recorded in each of the paintings of the *campi*. Water is being drawn from the well, and a maid wearing an apron carries two buckets that have been filled. Men and women gather in the foreground at the right, leaning over to inspect some merchandise for sale. Patterning the skyline are the chimney pots and roof terraces of the houses at the far side of the square.

The engraving by Visentini, number IV in the third part of *Prospectus*, corresponds closely in detail.

EXHIBITED
Venice 89

NOTES
1. James Byam Shaw, in *Canaletto*, 1982, p. 64, no. 89.
2. Links, *Views of Venice*, 1971, p. 74.

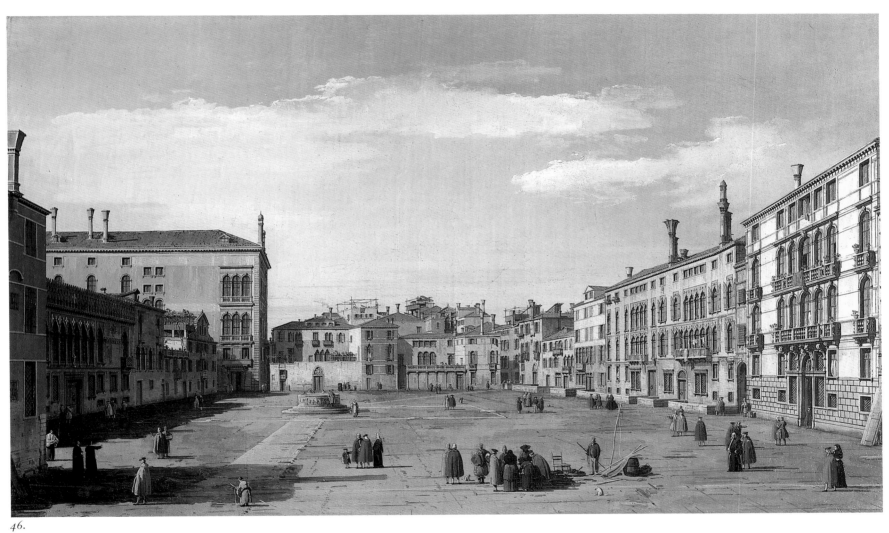

46.

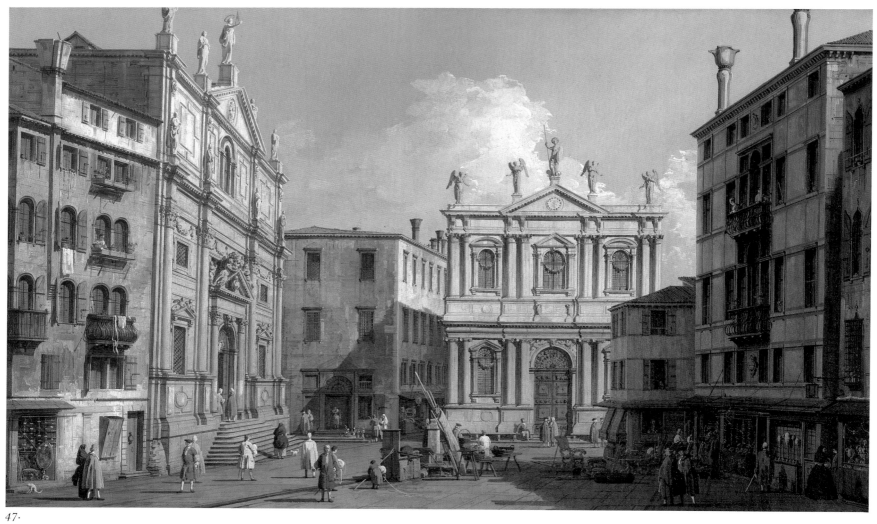

47.

47. Campo S. Salvatore

Oil on canvas, 18⅜ × 30½ in. (46.8 × 77.5 cm)
Private Collection
C/L 283

EXHIBITED
Venice 88

NOTE
1. James Byam Shaw, in *Canaletto*, 1982, p. 64, no. 88; and Links, *Views of Venice*, 1971, p. 72.

At the left is the church of S. Salvatore, and at the center, the Scuola di S. Teodoro, dedicated to the first patron saint of the city.[1] In contrast to the Campo S. Polo, this *campo* is well known to visitors to Venice since it is traversed by those walking through the Merceria, the busiest shopping street, on the way from the Piazza S. Marco (reached by turning left at the house between the church and the *scuola*) to the Rialto Bridge, which is behind the spectator. In the shops around the *campo* stylish furniture, wigs, metalwork, and other goods are offered for sale; at the center there is a whetstone, and vegetables are displayed in baskets atop trestle tables, as they still are today.

Belonging with number 46 to the Harvey group, the painting was engraved by Visentini as number III of Part III of *Prospectus*. The view is similar to a print by Carlevaris in *Le Fabriche e Vedute*. No other autograph paintings by Canaletto of Campo S. Polo or Campo S. Salvatore are recorded.

The Duke of Bedford's Views

Splendidly installed at Woburn Abbey are twenty-two views and two larger festival subjects, recorded in a 1771 inventory as divided between the Little Eating Room and the Large Dining Room of Bedford House, London. It has long been assumed and very recently confirmed that these were bought by the fourth Duke of Bedford, who succeeded his brother in 1732. Records relating to the purchase, from Smith, were found among documents at the Bedford Office, and have been published by Francis Russell.[1] These are in the form of bills drawn on the duke by "JosSmith" and payable to his brother John, who endorsed them as received; the bills are dated 27 February 1733, 7 January 1735 (1732 and 1734 Venetian style), and 27 April 1736. As Francis Russell notes, the total sum of just over £188 is less than might have been expected, in view of the price of the Howard pictures; perhaps payment for the two larger festival paintings was not included. Although Canaletto's name does not appear in the documents, the connection with him is beyond any reasonable doubt, and the inescapable conclusion is that most if not all of the Woburn Abbey pictures were completed by 1736. They are thus roughly coeval with the 1735 edition of *Prospectus*, and had long left Smith's hands by 1742 when three of them were published in the second edition as to be seen "in Joseph Smith's house."

NOTE
1. Russell, "The Pictures of John, Fourth Duke of Bedford," 1988, pp. 402–6.

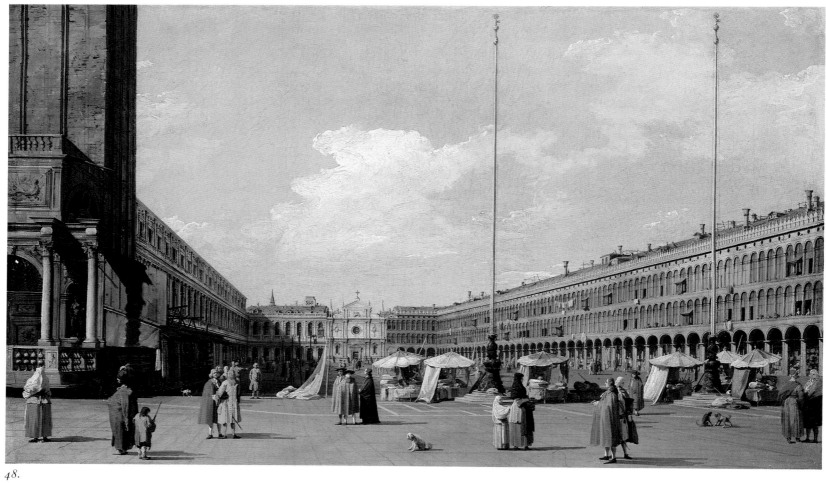

48.

48. Piazza S. Marco: looking West from South of the Central Line

Oil on canvas, 18½ × 31½ in. (47 × 80 cm)
The Marquess of Tavistock, and Trustees of the Bedford
Estates, Woburn Abbey
C/L 27

Sansovino's Loggetta, the base of the Campanile, and a shed along its north side are at the left with, in the foreground, merchants offering their wares in the shade of colored umbrellas. The flagstaffs, of which two may be seen, appear to have been displaced to the right to give an unimpeded view of the facade of the church of S. Geminiano, which stood opposite the basilica and was demolished with the west end of Piazza S. Marco on Napoleon's order, to be replaced by the Ala Napoleonica (the Napoleonic wing). The Procuratie Nuove are in shade and deep perspective, while the greater part of the Procuratie Vecchie may be seen, in sunlight.

The view toward the west is the subject of one of the six early canvases (C/L 32) that belonged to Smith and are in the Royal Collection. A related composition, engraved by Visentini as number XI of Part III of *Prospectus*, has descended since the eighteenth century in the Fitzwilliam family.

49. Grand Canal: looking East from the Palazzo Bembo to the Palazzo Vendramin Calergi

Oil on canvas, 18½ × 31½ in. (47 × 80 cm)
The Marquess of Tavistock, and Trustees of the Bedford
Estates, Woburn Abbey
C/L 256

At the right, in shadow, a man stands at the end of the footpath along the Riva di Biasio, looking across the *rio* to Palazzo Bembo, which was demolished at the beginning of the nineteenth century. At the extreme left is a quay with a gateway from which a man looks onto the Cannaregio. Although not apparent from this part of the painting, which has been oddly truncated, the Cannaregio is by far the widest of the canals leading off the Grand Canal, and it was from near this point that many visitors disembarked upon arrival in Venice.

On the far side of the Cannaregio is a small house with a loggia which has not been identified. It has been wrongly described in the catalogue raisonné and elsewhere as the unfinished Palazzo Querini, that is, the building appearing on the extreme right of the drawing, number 96. This small house can also be seen in one of the paintings of the Harvey group (C/L 257[d]), taken from a point a little farther up the Grand Canal, and in that view the

NOTE

1. J. G. Links has amended the transcription of the inscription in the left margin of the drawing as follows: *Casa che va nela veduta di Canèrio [Canèrro?] in fazzia S. Gier/mia la prima.* For the "word which might be 'Venezia,'" read *z[c]enerin,* or ash colored.

187

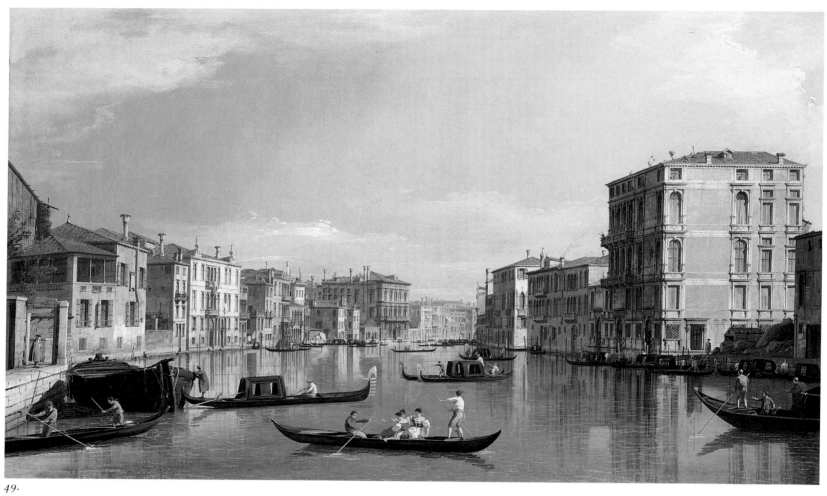

49.

Palazzo Querini, already completed, is shown in shade beside it, separated only by low buildings. In the mid-distance, near the center of the picture, is the Palazzo Vendramin Calergi, referred to as Grimani by Canaletto, almost the first Renaissance building in Venice, although not finished until 1509. It is seen from the opposite direction in number 42, which was engraved for Part I of *Prospectus*.

Six sheets of Canaletto's sketchbook now in the Accademia, Venice, show nearly all of the buildings along both sides of the Grand Canal that are represented in the present canvas (ff. 49v–46v; see figs. 20, 21). They end with the small house with the loggia, but Sir Michael Levey has pointed out that a drawing from another sketchbook (C/L 624.[*]) in fact shows the Palazzo Querini, which would be the next building to those drawn on folio 49 verso.[1] The unusually awkward perspective of the Cannaregio entrance in both this painting and the one belonging to the Harvey series may possibly be related to the separation of the Palazzo Querini drawing from the other preparatory sketches.

The present painting was engraved by Visentini and published as number 4 in Part II of the 1742 edition. It does not show any of the major landmarks and, like some of the other compositions of the second Grand Canal series, would not have been readily recalled by the occasional visitor; perhaps for this reason it seems not to have been repeated. By contrast, the familiar view from the Riva di Biasio toward S. Geremia and the entrance to the Cannaregio was painted by Canaletto more than once (C/L 251 and 252); a drawing of the subject is at Windsor (cat. no. 96); and a print by Visentini figures in the first part of *Prospectus*.

50. Grand Canal: looking South-west from the Palazzo Grimani to the Palazzo Foscari

Oil on canvas, 22½ × 36½ in. (57.2 × 92.7 cm)
Private Collection
C/L 218

At the extreme left is the Palazzo Valmarana, dwarfed by its neighbor, the Palazzo Grimani. To the right are the Palazzi Businello and—the one with the obelisks—Coccina Tiepolo. (The larger, Grimani palace was built in a show of face by the son-in-law of the wealthy owner of the Coccina, or so it is said.) In the distance, facing up the canal, is Ca' Foscari and to the right of it Palazzo Balbi, seen in the opposite direction in numbers 3, 23, and 43. The Rialto Bridge is some distance behind the imagined viewpoint. As was the case with number 49, Canaletto made unusually detailed preparations for this picture in his sketchbook now in the Accademia (ff. 54v–57r), which includes studies for all of the buildings at the left, as far as Ca' Foscari, and also for the barges at right center (ff. 57v–58r). In the sketches, the rigging extends far above the roof of Ca' Foscari, and during the restoration of the present painting it was discovered that the rigging had been included but then painted over.

The picture was owned by the second Earl of Normanton early in the last century. Smith may well have handled it, but Visentini's engraving for number 9 of Part II of *Prospectus* is from another version, not identified with certainty. The same drawings might have been used for both, this perhaps being an instance of a painting commissioned by someone who admired the Visentini engraving, or Canaletto's original upon which it was based.

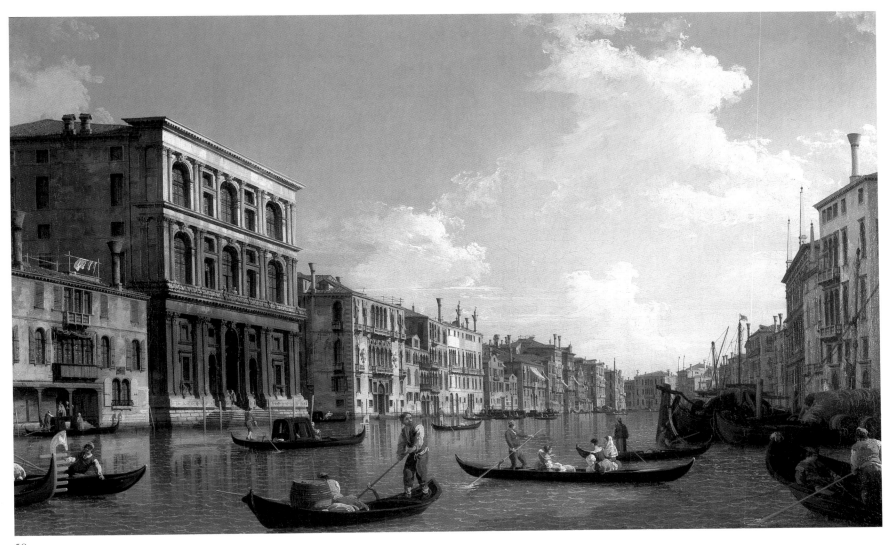

50.

51. The Bacino di S. Marco: looking East

Oil on canvas, 49 × 80½ in. (124.5 × 204.5 cm)
Museum of Fine Arts, Boston; Abbott Lawrence Fund,
Seth K. Sweetser Fund, and Charles Edward French Fund
C/L 131

EXHIBITED
Canada 18; Venice 85

NOTES
1. Walter Muir Whitehall, *Museum of Fine Arts, Boston: A Centennial History* (Cambridge, Mass., 1970), II, pp. 448–49.
2. For an account based on remarks by Vertue and Lady Oxford, and on an article published by H. Ellen Browning in 1905, see C/L 40. This entry touches on the various problems presented by the Castle Howard pictures (C/L 40, 50, 85[b], 131, 154, 171, 236[d], 262[b], and 334). Three of those catalogued had been destroyed by fire about 1940; several are apparently not autograph.
3. G. F. Waagen, *Works of Art and Artists in England* (London, 1838), III, p. 206.
4. Bettagno, "In margine a una Mostra," 1983, pp. 225–28, stating that the date suggested by the presence of the scaffolding, which was first noted by Giorgio Ferrari, depends from archival documents for the church of S. Antonin, housed at S. Giovanni in Bragora and reviewed by Silvano De Tuoni.

The view is from two points on the quay surrounding the Dogana, or Customs House. One of them takes in the whole of the Molo from the Granaries at the left to the Castello district, the *sestiere* farthest to the east; the other the island, the monastic buildings, and the great sixteenth-century Palladian church of S. Giorgio Maggiore, with the end of the Giudecca at the extreme right, and the church of S. Giovanni Battista, since demolished. The island of S. Giorgio is now also the home of the Fondazione Giorgio Cini, and it was here that the first Venetian exhibition ever devoted to the work of Canaletto was held in 1982. A small boat with four oarsmen, towing a barge, passes betweeen S. Giorgio and the Giudecca. Beyond may be seen one of the smaller lagoon islands and a Gothic church, and on the horizon, the Lido, its banks fringed with trees silhouetted against the sky. There are many sailing and smaller working boats, gondolas (one of which is rowed by oarsmen in red uniforms), a *peota* with a red awning, and a little pleasure boat with a blue and white sail hoisted to catch the breeze. There are examples of almost every kind of vessel that used the *bacino*, and some fly the flags of Venice, England, France, or Denmark. The picture is uniquely suggestive of the historic vitality of the maritime enterprises of the Serenissima. Delicate reflections color the rippling turquoise surface of the water and, in the clear air, the image of the city and the southward islands may be read in every detail. There are a few other paintings of the panorama offered by the city of Venice and its anchorage, but none as observed from the Dogana, and none approaching this canvas in its unique quality and interest.

The name of W. G. Constable will always be associated with Canaletto studies, and he should perhaps be permitted to enter the picture for a moment.[1] A British art historian, he resigned his post as director of the Courtauld Institute, London, in 1937, and was then invited to assume the position of curator of paintings at the Museum of Fine Arts, Boston, where he remained until 1957. Having taken up a fellowship for the further study of Canaletto in Venice, he arrived in Boston only in March 1938, and among his first recommended purchases, in 1939, was the *Bacino di S. Marco*, which is one of the artist's most brilliant works, and without question the finest in any American collection.

The painting came from Castle Howard, in Northumberland, the home of the Earls of Carlisle, and it may or may not have been among the "several views of Venice by Canaletto lately put there," which Lady Oxford recorded seeing in 1745. Nothing more is known of the collection of Canalettos at

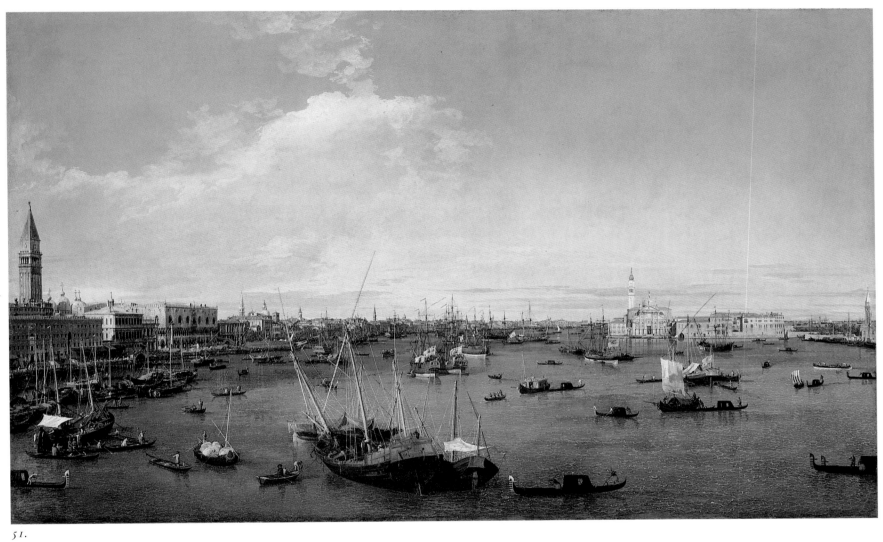

51.

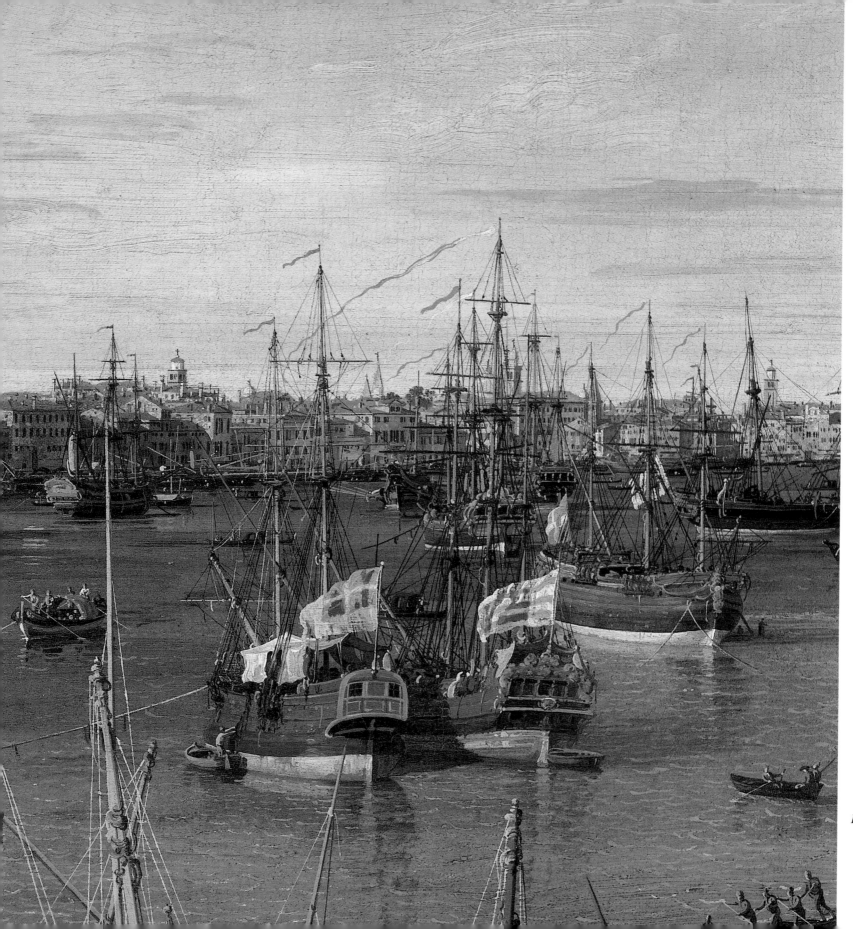

Details of 51.

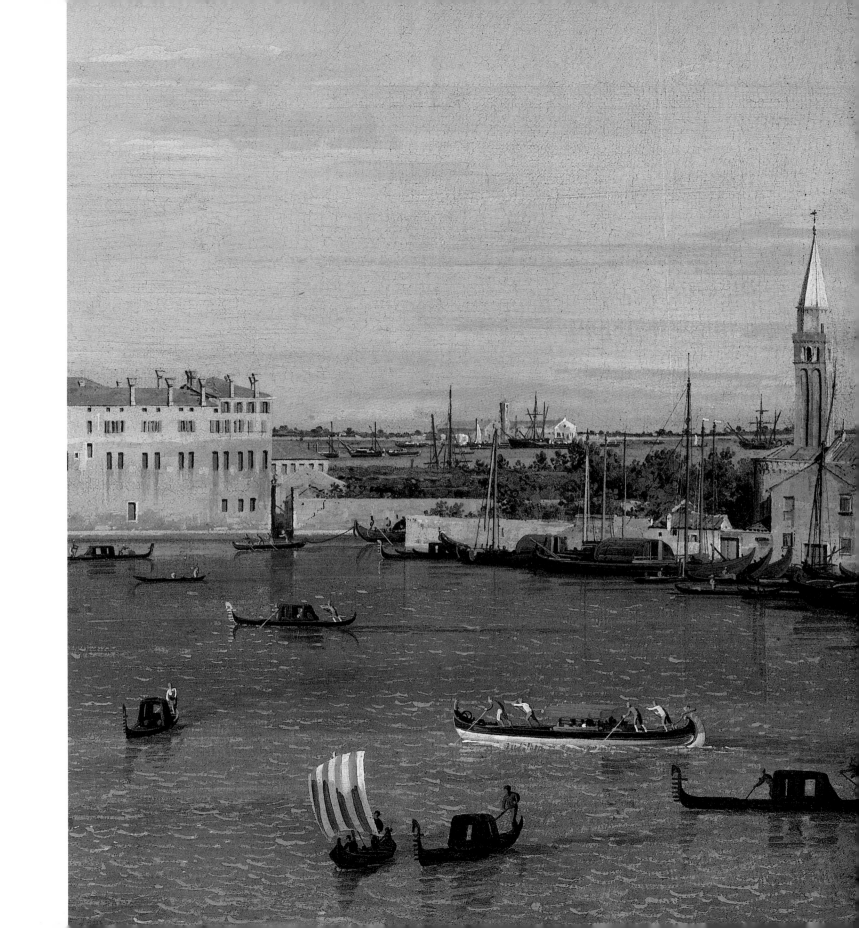

Castle Howard until early in this century, when it included this acknowledged masterpiece, two signed paintings now in Washington (C/L 50, 154), and a number of less important pictures, several perhaps from the workshop.[2] Probably not all were bought at the same time. On the other hand, if in fact there were Canalettos lately installed in 1745, it seems likely that the fourth earl, who died in 1758, bought the fine paintings and some much less fine, either directly from the artist or from some agent other than Smith, whose offerings to his English clients seem to have been more consistent in quality and kind. The verdict offered by the influential German critic Gustav Waagen 150 years ago—"in every respect one of the capital works of this master, whose extraordinary merit is not to be appreciated except in England"—has been endorsed by all those who have seen this celebrated painting.[3]

The Bacino di S. Marco is undocumented and has been variously dated from the early 1730s to about 1740. Topographical evidence for a date toward the end of the decade has been published by Alessandro Bettagno: among the many bell towers silhouetted against the skyline of the Riva degli Schiavoni is that of the church of S. Antonin, and the new campanile, for which final payment was made in the autumn of 1738, is shown with scaffolding still in place around its onion-shaped dome.[4]

52. The Molo: looking West, Column of St. Theodore Right

Oil on canvas, 24½ × 39⅞ in. (62.3 × 101.3 cm)
Kimbell Art Museum, Forth Worth, Texas
C/L 96

NOTE
1. Corboz, *Canaletto*, 1985, p. 48.

The composition is closely similar to that of Samuel Hill's painting of the same subject (cat. no. 34), but the view is from a point just above the water's edge, so that the buildings along the Molo recede even more sharply. Three bays of the Library can be seen (the statues along the roof line differ between the two pictures, as Corboz has observed); the Punta della Dogana is here omitted.[1] Such a viewpoint was not attainable, and the perspective must have been worked out in the studio, as with so much of Canaletto's work. On the drawing now belonging to the Philadelphia Museum (cat. no. 91) Canaletto described the area as the *pescherie*, or fish markets, but in his paintings, which are particularly lively, much more seems to be taking place than the selling of fish. Though the angle of the Molo is different and the viewpoint lower, the Philadelphia drawing could have served as an aide-

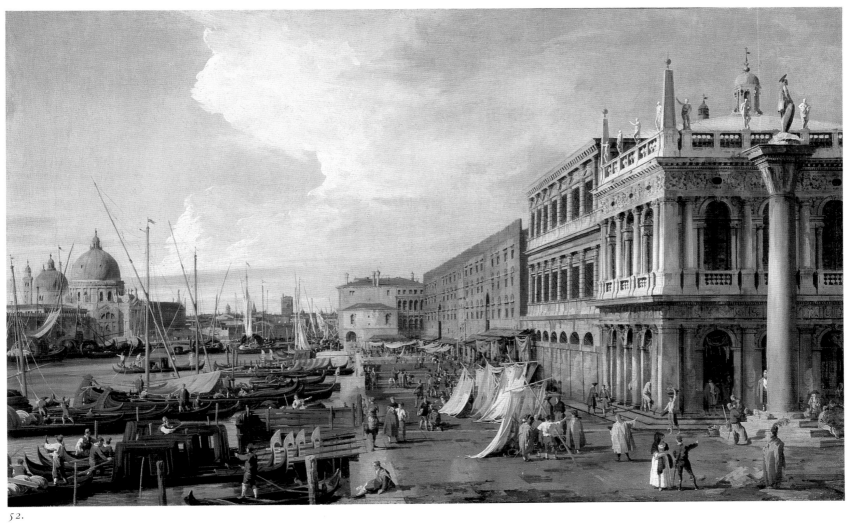

52.

mémoire for the Fort Worth picture: the angles of the masts at either side of the Salute are not dissimilar. The booths are numerous, and the figures —especially the man with a feathered turban in the foreground at the right —are observed with interest. The painting is unlikely to be many years later in date than the one at Tatton Park (cat. no. 34). It belonged until 1955 to the Earl of Rosebery.

53. Riva degli Schiavoni: looking East

Oil on canvas, 22½ × 36½ in. (57.2 × 92.7 cm)
Mr. and Mrs. John J. Pomerantz
C/L 112 note

For a description of the scene see number 18, which also shows the column of St. Mark against the south facade of the Palazzo Ducale. In only one other painting of this particular view—in the Wallace Collection, London (C/L 112)—do both columns appear, but that picture has little else in common with this one, and the placing of the columns is anyway arbitrary since Canaletto did not alter the perspective of the backgrounds according to whether he included one or both of them.

The galleon with the red and gold awning, *la fusta*, was at the Doge's disposal; here the oars are raised as it departs from—or arrives at—its mooring on the Molo. The figures are quite similar to the ones in the view of the northeast corner of Piazza S. Marco (cat. no. 55). In several early versions of the Molo and Riva the quay by the water's edge appears in need of repaving. By the time the present canvas was painted the work seems to have been taken in hand and, with Canaletto's interest in accuracy in such matters, this might well indicate a later date. It can be seen that the *fondamenta* along the Riva degli Schiavoni, beyond the Ponte della Paglia, was narrow; this *fondamenta* was not widened until 1780. When the painting was in the collection of the Earl of Normanton it was paired with number 50.

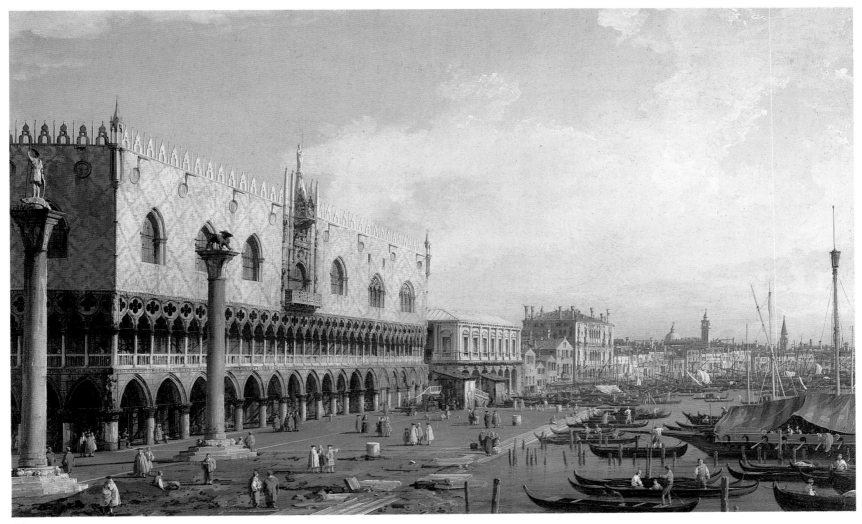

53.

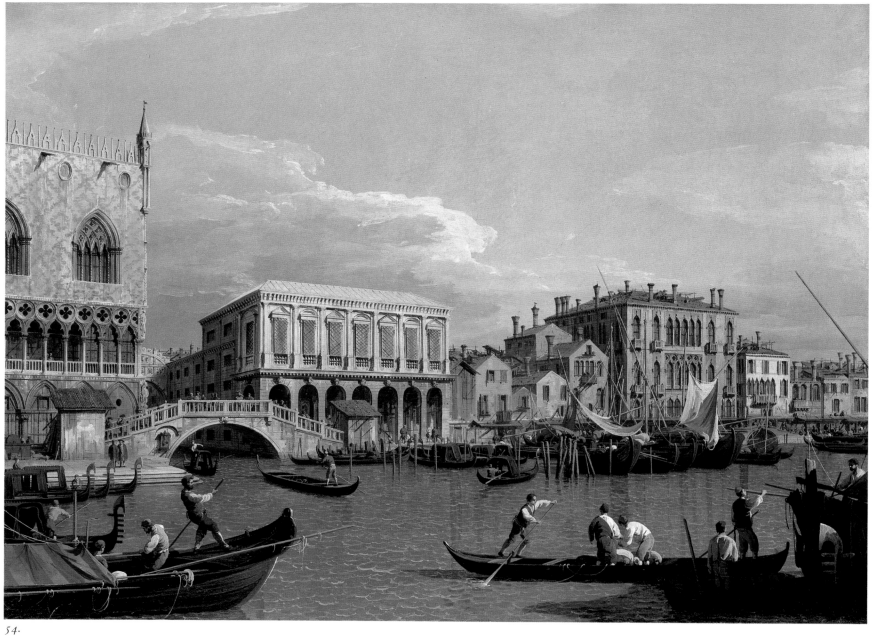

54.

54. Molo and Riva degli Schiavoni: from the Bacino di S. Marco

Oil on canvas, 18½ × 24⅞ in. (47.1 × 63.3 cm)
The Toledo Museum of Art; Gift of
Edward Drummond Libbey
C/L 118

NOTE

1. *European Paintings*, Toledo Museum of Art (Toledo, 1976), p. 34. William Hutton kindly supplied a photocopy of the labels.

The Palazzo Ducale, the Prigioni (Prisons), and the Riva are often seen in Canaletto's work, but not from this viewpoint, which he did not adopt for any other painting. Part of the Ponte dei Sospiri (Bridge of Sighs), behind the Ponte della Paglia, has now come into view and the buildings between the Prisons and the Palazzo Dandolo are closely observed (see cat. no. 18 for their history); these and the building beyond Palazzo Dandolo appear differently than in number 53. The knife grinder's stall on the extreme left is more clearly shown than in other pictures.

Two handwritten labels removed in recent years from the old lining canvas of the Toledo painting read, "Anton Canale./M...zu Venedig./ a 1740." and "N° 191/ Tablau Apertenant/au Prince Joseph/Wenceslau de/ [Liechten]stein/... 73."[1] The painting is among the smaller pictures formerly in the Liechtenstein collection and now widely dispersed, having been paired, according to Constable, with a view from the Piazzetta (C/L 126) that shows the onion-shaped dome of the campanile of S. Giorgio. It may, as one of the labels suggests, have been acquired by 1740, more certainly by 1780.

55. Piazza S. Marco: the Northeast Corner

Oil on canvas, 52¼ × 65 in. (132.8 × 165.1 cm)
National Gallery of Canada/Musée des beaux-arts
du Canada, Ottawa
C/L 45

At the extreme left is a bay of the Procuratie Vecchie, and next to it the Torre dell'Orologio; the church of S. Basso is among the smaller buildings beyond.[1] To the right is a partial view of the facade of S. Marco. Above the doorway toward the north—the so-called Sant'Alipio arch—is the only original mosaic that survives on the exterior: Canaletto transcribed in outline the old facade of the basilica as it appears in the mid-thirteenth-century mosaic, but omitted the figures, and thus the narrative subject, the Transposition of the Body of St. Mark. The brightly colored mosaics of the arch above are loosely painted and illegible, especially by comparison with the otherwise crisp detail. The corner of the Piazza at the northeast, here in shadow, is sometimes called the Campo S. Basso but more often the Piazzetta dei Leoncini, after the two red, Verona-marble lions that were installed there in 1722. Canaletto never showed them. On the other hand he was always ob-

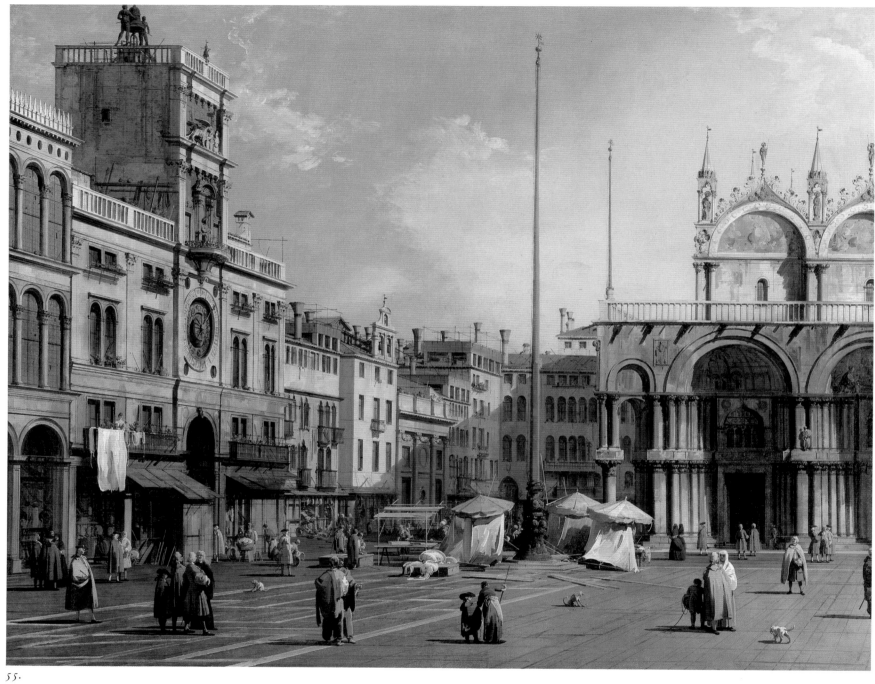

55.

servant of the merchandise in the shops, and he must have been particularly fascinated by the ones along the north side of the Campo S. Basso, as can be seen in a remarkable drawing from Berlin (cat. no. 125), and another like it (C/L 541) whose present whereabouts is unknown.

The Royal Collection has an elaborate drawing of the northeast corner of the Piazza (C/L 539), which is substantially the same in its general design, though differing in many details, and taking in several more bays of the arcade of the Procuratie Vecchie at the left. The drawing belonged, of course, to Smith, and it is sufficiently close to the Ottawa painting to have served as Smith's record, suggesting that he may have acted as agent for William Holbech, of Farnborough Hall, Warwickshire, who was the first owner of the painting. There were four pictures in Holbech's set (C/L 38, the presumed companion, C/L 128, and C/L 173), which was dispersed in 1930. The tradition is that this view and the one showing Piazza S. Marco looking west from the Piazzetta were painted in Venice, and the other pair while Canaletto was living in England, from 1746. All were installed in the dining room at Farnborough by 1750.

Number 55 and the painting thought to have been its pendant are on a coarse-weave Venetian canvas, whereas the other two—which are generally dated later—are on a canvas of fine weave. There is much incising; a straight-edge was used as a guide, and a compass for the outlines of the portals of the basilica.

EXHIBITED

Canada 15; Venice 90

NOTE

1. J. G. Links, in *Canaletto*, exh. cat., 1982, p. 65, no. 90, and see also pp. 64–66 and nos. 91–93; Michael Pantazzi, in *European and American Painting, Sculpture, and Decorative Arts, 1300–1800: Catalogue of the National Gallery of Canada* (Ottawa, 1987), pp. 48–51, inv. no. 3718; see also Bettagno, "In margine a una Mostra," 1983, p. 225.

On the Brenta Canal

In the early 1740s Canaletto made a trip to the mainland, traveling along the Brenta Canal and probably going no farther than Padua. The route was by way of Fusina to Dolo, and onward, and may also have included stops at Marghera and Mestre. The journey to Padua could be made by *burchiello*—a small passenger barge with a cabin—and the distance is no more than forty kilometers. A number of drawings (see cat. nos. 104–7) and twenty-three of a total of thirty etchings represent real or imagined mainland subjects.[1] Most of the etchings were published as a series dedicated to the ubiquitous Joseph Smith, and on the title page Canaletto identified Smith as Consul of His Britannic Majesty to the Republic of Venice, a post the English merchant had long sought and to which he was finally appointed on 6 June

NOTES

1. On the question of the number of prints published in or after 1744 as a volume dedicated to Consul Smith, see Bromberg, *Canaletto's Etchings*, 1974, pp. 15–21.

2. Kozakiewicz, *Bernardo Bellotto*, 1972, I, pp. 15–28, 38, 41, and 53–55. From August 1743 onward Bellotto was often absent from Venice, working elsewhere in northern Italy, and in the summer of 1747 he departed for Dresden and the court of Augustus III. He never returned to his native city.

3. See Morassi, *Michele Marieschi*, 1966; Toledano, *Michele Marieschi*, 1988; and Succi, in *Da Carlevarijs ai Tiepolo*, 1983, pp. 235–41.

1744. With the exception of two paintings of Dolo, the prints—one of which is dated 1741—and the few terra firma pictures were probably completed after Canaletto's mainland visit.

It is at this moment that Canaletto's nephew Bernardo Bellotto assumes an identifiable role as an independent artist, and there can be no doubt, given the subject matter of some of his earliest drawings, that he accompanied Canaletto on the mainland journey. Bellotto was born in Venice on 30 January 1721, his mother the eldest of Giovanni Antonio's three sisters.[2] The young Bellotto was enrolled in the register of Venetian painters in 1738, and it is probable that at the time he had already served a period of apprenticeship in his uncle's studio. He would have been about twenty years old at the time of the visit to the Brenta, which was most likely in 1740 or 1741.

A number of reasons may be imagined for Canaletto to have sought a change of scene: the diminution in the number of foreign visitors to Venice owing to the War of the Austrian Succession, a desire for new subjects and a fresh source of inspiration, and the example of earlier print-making ventures that had been successful, such as Visentini's series after Canaletto's views of Venice. Michele Marieschi, a talented view painter and etcher who must have been seen by Canaletto as a rival, published his twenty-one views as a volume entitled *Prospettive di Venezia* in 1741.[3] (Born in Venice in 1710, he was to die at an early age in 1743.) It seems reasonable to assume that Smith played some role in Canaletto's decision to visit the mainland at this time, and to take up print making. While Venice is not much changed since the eighteenth century, the terra firma has suffered the ravages of industrial development, so that little remains of what Canaletto saw in the course of his tour of the Brenta.

56. Dolo on the Brenta

Oil on canvas, 31¾ × 38 in. (80.5 × 96.5 cm)
Staatsgalerie Stuttgart, loan of Daimler-Benz AG
C/L 371 note

For *Dolo on the Brenta* Canaletto chose a viewpoint looking eastward, that is toward Venice, and above the sluice gates at Dolo on the Brenta Canal, with the towpath on the left. The picture therefore represents the view opposite to that of the etching entitled by the artist *Al Dolo*, and at right angles to the one called *Ale Porte del Dolo*.[1] The campanile of S. Rocco is visible in all three views; the *squeri*, or boatyards, partly hidden by trees, and the Villa Zanon Bon, formerly called Andruzzi, in two of them. In its composition, which is exceptionally felicitous and was to be much imitated, the painting anticipates that of the etched view of Mestre. Small boats lie at various

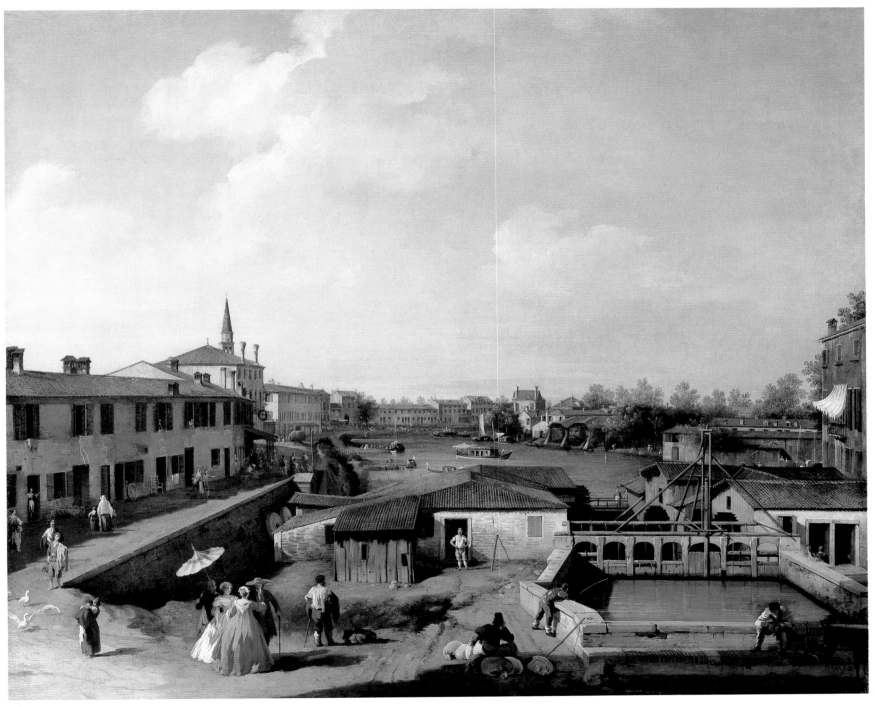

56.

NOTES

1. Bromberg, *Canaletto's Etchings*, 1974, pp. 54–64, nos. 4 and 5, ill.
2. *Pictures from the Grand Tour*, exh. cat., Colnaghi (London, 1978), no. 28.
3. Kozakiewicz, *Bernardo Bellotto*, 1972, II, pp. 27 (ill.), 29, no. 29; Morassi, *Guardi*, [1973], pp. 253–54, 434–35, cat. nos. 669–71, and figs. 625–27. Guardi also painted the Torre di Marghera and the Porta del Dolo.

disembarkation points along the towpath, and in the middle of the canal a *burchiello*, the open deck behind the passenger cabin shaded by a striped awning, heads toward the locks. The figures in the foreground are large in scale, closely observed, and colorful.

The composition has long been known from the version given in 1855 to the Ashmolean Museum, Oxford. When the present canvas was first exhibited in 1978, it was found to be not only of very high quality but also in a much better state of preservation.[2] Some of the figures are different, and the picture surface is higher in proportion to its width. It was probably painted a little after the Oxford version, but it is difficult to date either with confidence, for neither seems to be related to Canaletto's journey of the 1740s. Bellotto might have been inspired to paint his canvas of the subject after that trip, and Francesco Guardi painted his own versions, but much later.[3] On grounds of style, Canaletto's two views of Dolo from the west might have resulted from a brief stay on the mainland in the late 1720s.

57. Padua: the Brenta Canal and the Porta Portello

Oil on canvas, 24⅝ × 43 in. (62.5 × 109 cm)
National Gallery of Art, Washington; Samuel H. Kress Collection
C/L 375

The view is taken from the south bank of the canal, looking westward toward the Porta Portello and the skyline of the city of Padua, with the church of Sta. Maria del Carmine in the distance.[1] The road from Venice and the east still passes under this gate, which was designed by Il Bergamasco in 1518, and although the tower has lost its cupola the building is otherwise unchanged, and the piers of the bridge also remain. Canaletto was drawn not so much to the Porta Portello as to the relatively tranquil ambient of the outskirts of a mainland town, and the crumbling masonry of the wall in the foreground captured his attention as much as anything. The use of local color is limited, the palette being largely confined to earth tones and greens. There are only a few boats and, among the small figures in the distance, a cart drawn by bullocks.

Of several drawings by Canaletto (and Bellotto) representing the Porta Portello, the closest is Canaletto's finished pen and ink drawing at the Albertina, Vienna (C/L 676): the topography is the same in detail, though the figures and boats differ. For the other drawings, whether by Canaletto or Bellotto, the imagined viewpoint is higher, and farther to the north, over the canal (see cat. no. 106 and C/L 675 which is at Windsor).[2]

NOTES

1. Fern Rusk Shapley, *Catalogue of the Italian Paintings*, National Gallery of Art (Washington, 1979), pp. 103–5, inv. no. 1605.
2. For Bellotto's drawings, see Kozakiewicz, *Bernardo Bellotto*, 1972, II, pp. 28 (ill.), 30, no. 34.

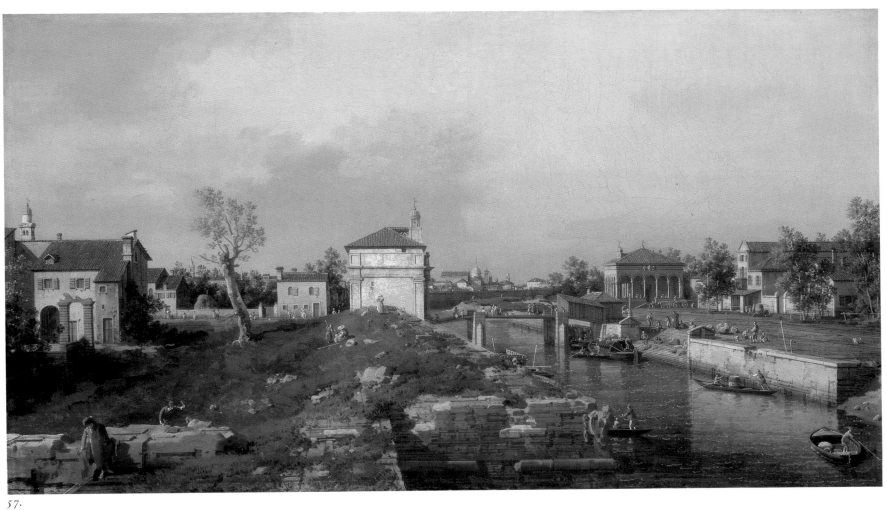

57.

58. View on a River, perhaps at Padua

Oil on canvas, 19½ × 32¾ in. (49.5 × 83.2 cm)
Private Collection
C/L 377

EXHIBITED
Canada 72

NOTES
1. Bromberg, *Canaletto's Etchings*, 1974, p. 9.
2. Bromberg, *Canaletto's Etchings*, 1974, pp. 78–81, no. 9, ill.
3. Kozakiewicz, *Bernardo Bellotto*, 1972, II, p. 458, no. Z296, lists number 58 under rejected attributions.

With some uncertainty, Constable called this painting a view at Padua, but it has since been proposed that the campanile is that of the church of S. Rocco at Dolo on the Brenta, which may also be seen in the background of number 56.[1] The picture derives from a panoramic sketch, made on the ground and dated 1742; the two halves of the drawing are at the Pierpont Morgan Library and the Fogg Art Museum and are here reunited as catalogue number 104. Two finished drawings from Smith's collection, at Windsor (C/L 696 and C/L 697), are related to the left half, and the panoramic sketch also inspired an etching, in reverse but otherwise topographically similar to the present work, though different in feeling.[2] Ruth Bromberg has questioned the authenticity of the inscription on the right half of the drawing, but this is not critical to consideration of the painting which, given the mannerisms of the brushwork, should probably be dated not long before Canaletto left Venice for England in 1746.[3]

By comparison with the drawing and the print, the painting has fewer buildings—for example, a large house beyond and to the right of the footbridge was replaced by trees—and in general the view has been simplified in the interest of clarity. Perhaps following the print, the composition is organized around the diagonal provided by the gnarled trunk and few leafy branches of an old tree which, together with the plank bridge and narrow gully, the fence, the swans, and the figures, has been invented as a suitably bucolic foreground. There is some strong local color to highlight the figures, and the reflections take the form of wide strokes of pastel shades laid over the blue-green surface of the water. The picture evokes rather than transcribes the atmosphere of its mainland subject, which the artist seems to have recalled with pleasure and, like the Windsor drawings, this canvas must have been worked up in the studio at a date subsequent to Canaletto's visit to the terra firma.

After he came back from England about 1755 Canaletto painted a smaller version (C/L 377* [1989 ed.]) with more houses at the end of the bridge and on the right, perhaps indicating that he returned to the site.

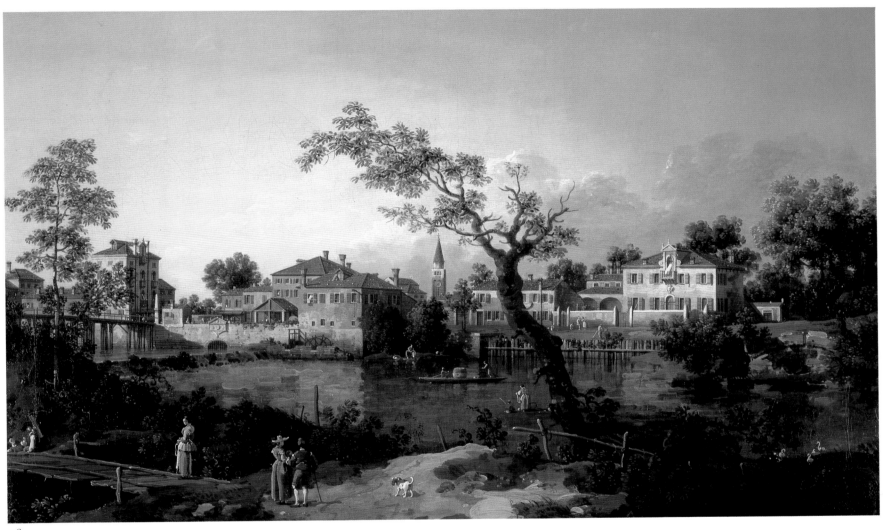

58.

Roman Views

In 1742 Canaletto signed and dated five upright canvases, all of the same exceptionally large size and representing famous ancient monuments in Rome:[1] a view of the Forum toward the Capitol (C/L 378), the Arches of Septimius Severus, Titus, and Constantine (C/L 384, C/L 386, and cat. no. 59), and the Pantheon (cat. no. 60). These can only have been commissioned as a set, and by Smith, to whom they belonged until they were sold to George III. It is not difficult to imagine that they, like the earlier views of Piazza S. Marco and the Piazzetta (see cat. nos. 28, 29), were designed for a particular location, perhaps a room in the palace on the Grand Canal then occupied by Smith and now called Mangilli Valmarana after other owners. The signatures and dates are among the earliest known.

The existence of these views, and a limited number of other paintings and drawings of Roman subjects by or attributed to Canaletto, has given rise to a debate as to whether Canaletto might have gone to Rome again at this time. The question has not been settled, the consensus holding that he did not. An alternate source for the Roman views is a series of twenty-three numbered and inscribed drawings (C/L 713) of much earlier date, by or perhaps copied after Canaletto, all but one (which belonged to Bellotto and is now at Darmstadt) in the British Museum.[2] Further, the Venetian printmaker Giovanni Battista Brustoloni engraved most of these subjects, twenty-two in number according to a document of 1781 in which he sought sole privilege of publishing them. According to this document Brustoloni owned the originals, having received them from Canaletto's heirs. Three of the five Royal Collection views of ancient Roman monuments relate to drawings in the British Museum series, but the other two subjects chosen for the paintings do not figure among the drawings. More recently, an entirely different source for the painting representing the *Arch of Constantine* has been identified, for which see number 59.

While Canaletto probably did not go to Rome during this period, Bernardo Bellotto almost certainly did, stopping in Florence and Lucca in the course of the same journey, and returning to Venice in 1742 or 1743.[3] A few paintings and drawings of views and monuments in each of the three cities are now ascribed to the young Bellotto with some degree of certainty. To illustrate the complexity of the problem it may be noted, for example, that the ruins of the Forum as seen looking toward the Capitol are the subject of one of Canaletto's 1742 pictures, two or more other paintings by or from the studio of Canaletto (which may suggest the intervention of Bellotto), a draw-

NOTES

1. For the series in general and the three canvases not exhibited, see Levey, *Later Italian Pictures*, 1964, pp. 54–55, nos. 369, 372, and 373, and Millar, in *Canaletto*, 1980, pp. 60–64, nos. 29–31.

2. In recent years these drawings have been accepted by James Byam Shaw and Alessandro Bettagno as autograph early works: James Byam Shaw, *Disegni veneti della collezione Lugt*, exh. cat. (Vicenza, 1981), p. 81; Bettagno, in *Canaletto*, 1982, p. 35, nos. 1, 2; and James Byam Shaw, *The Italian Drawings of the Frits Lugt Collection*, Institut Néerlandais (Paris, 1983), p. 300.

3. See Kozakiewicz, *Bernardo Bellotto*, 1972, I, pp. 33–38 and 69–70; II, pp. 38–59, nos. 52–81 (ill.), for Bellotto's paintings and drawings of Florence, Lucca, and Rome, which may be approximately dated 1742–44.

4. C/L 378, 379, 379(a), 379(b), and 713 (224); and Kozakiewicz, *Bernardo Bellotto*, 1972, I, p. 222 (ill.); II, pp. 50–52, no. 69 (ill.), and pp. 464–65, nos. z317–318 (ill.).

ing in the British Museum series, an engraving by Brustoloni, and a painting now attributed to Bellotto but once thought to be by Canaletto.[4] The Roman views in the Royal Collection are the milestone against which all such works must be judged.

59. The Arch of Constantine

Oil on canvas, 73 × 41⅝ in. (185.4 × 105.7 cm)
Signed and dated (lower left): ANT· CANAL FECIT / ANNO MDCCXLII
Her Majesty Queen Elizabeth II
C/L 382

EXHIBITED
London 33

NOTES
1. Levey, *Later Italian Pictures*, 1964, p. 55, no. 370; and Millar, in *Canaletto*, 1980, p. 67, no. 33.
2. Corboz, *Canaletto*, 1985, p. 69; and see Antoine Desgodetz, *Les Edifices antiques de Rome dessinés et mesurés très exactement* (Paris, 1682), pp. 230–31, who, it should be noted, reproduced the north face of the Arch of Constantine only.

Most famous of the arches in Rome, the Arch of Constantine was built in the second decade of the fourth century by the Emperor Constantine in celebration of his victory over Maxentius. As may be seen, it is of white marble, and stands near the Colosseum, in what was in Canaletto's time a more or less rural environment.[1] W. G. Constable pointed out that while the inscription, the friezes, and the reliefs painted by Canaletto are from the north face, the view is that in the opposite direction—from the south.

A drawing in the British Museum series (C/L 713 [222]) is from the same viewpoint and also reverses the arch, showing it in a roughly comparable state of disrepair. The composition of the painting follows that of the drawing, allowing for the adjustments necessary to convert a horizontal image into a vertical. The position of the wall abutting the arch at the left was changed, perhaps also in the interest of a more pleasing effect, and the angle of recession of the wall was sharpened; the buildings on the opposite side were narrowed, and the ruins of the Colosseum moved inward. André Corboz has identified a source upon which Canaletto may have depended for the details of the decoration of the arch: an engraving of the north face from Antoine Desgodetz's *Edifices antiques de Rome*, published in Paris in 1682.[2] Corboz draws attention to certain discrepancies shared by the painting and the print. In both, and as described by Desgodetz in his text, the statues are without heads or hands, whereas in fact these were restored in 1732, ten years before Canaletto's picture was painted. In other respects Desgodetz's print does not show what the picture describes as the ravages of time: the exposed brickwork and broken cornice, from which grow leafy branches and blades of meadow grass.

There are other views by Canaletto of the Arch of Constantine, among which are a highly finished, inscribed drawing in the Petit Palais, Paris (C/L 716), and a signed painting at the J. Paul Getty Museum, Malibu (C/L 383). The Paris drawing is in general similar in layout to the one in the British

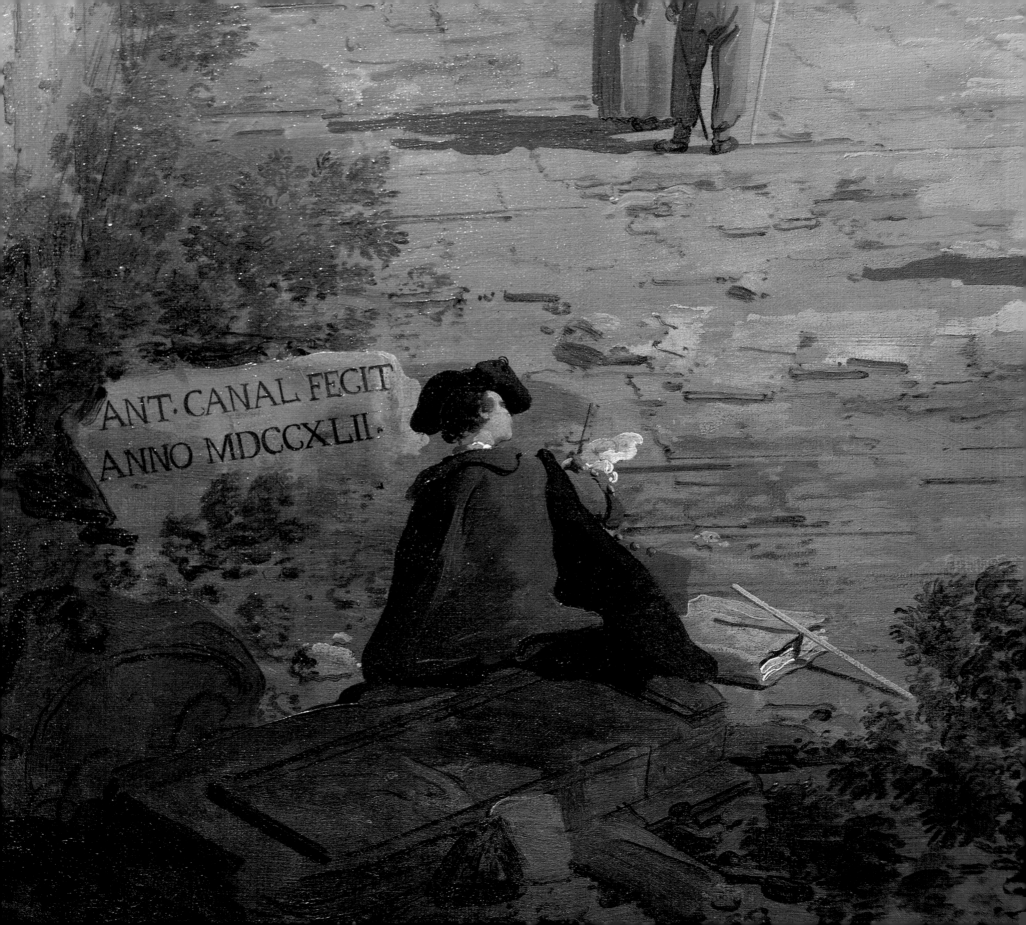

Detail of 59.

59.

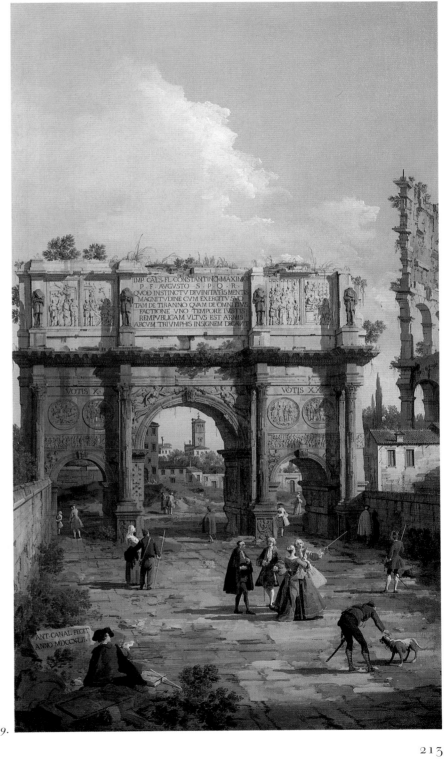

Museum. In the Getty Museum painting, a horizontal like the drawings, the Colosseum has been moved well toward the center, so that it may be partly seen through the central bay of the triumphal arch. Nothing by Bellotto of this subject is known, though he did paint the Arch of Titus, which is also among Canaletto's subjects for the Windsor series (C/L 386).

Canaletto took pride in his work, as evinced by the bold signatures and dates. Here the stone with its inscription draws further attention to a seated man, writing or drawing, his back to the spectator, his folio and ruler beside him. Surely Canaletto intended an association with this figure, even if it is not in any other sense a self-portrait. The people represented seem otherwise to comprise tourists enjoying the sights, and local people looking for those who might be in need of guidance (upon payment of a small fee, perhaps, for services rendered). The artist's interest would seem to have been deliberately decorative. He concentrated on the scale, mass, and grandeur of the ancient monuments, which are brought closely into focus, and on the wonder and delight of those who confront them for the first time. Perhaps Smith had the idea that old clients and future visitors might take up Canaletto as a painter of Roman views. In the event, despite the brilliance of the Windsor series, demand proved limited.

Sir Oliver Millar notes that throughout the series, as in this canvas, there is much ruling and incising of the architecture. For the medallions and the round heads of the arches, dividers were used. In the working up of the surface, the drawn contours were often softened in the interest of pictorial effect.

60. The Pantheon

Oil on canvas, 72⅛ × 41½ in. (183.2 × 105.4 cm)
Signed and dated (lower right): ANT· CANAL FECIT / ANNO
MDCCXLII
Her Majesty Queen Elizabeth II
C/L 390

EXHIBITED
London 32

NOTES
1. Levey, *Later Italian Pictures*, 1964, p. 55, no. 371; and Millar, in *Canaletto*, 1980, p. 67, no. 32.
2. For the bell towers, formerly attributed to Bernini, and other seventeenth-century modifications to the building and the piazza, see Franco Borsi, *Bernini Architetto* (Milan, 1980), pp. 96, 99, and 294–95.
3. Arisi, *Gian Paolo Panini*, 1986, pp. 195, 340–41, 349, and 373, nos. 218–21, 236–37, and 282, ill. The exterior of the Pantheon (without the bell towers) and the Arch of Constantine also figure in Pannini's views, both real and imaginary.
4. Levey, *Later Italian Pictures*, 1964, p. 54.

A trip to the Pantheon has always figured on the agenda of visitors to Rome: built by Hadrian to replace a sanctuary founded by Agrippa, the second-century temple was consecrated in 609 to the Virgin Mary and the Martyrs, becoming the church of Sta. Maria Rotonda, and it is thus part of the ancient and modern fabric of the city.[1] As one of the few buildings of pagan antiquity converted to Christian use, it was provided in the thirteenth century with a campanile, which was replaced in the course of a seventeenth-century refurbishing by the small bell towers visible in the present painting.[2] The basin in the piazza is shown as it appeared before 1711, when an Egyptian obelisk was installed at its center.

The Pantheon is chiefly famous for its interior, until recently the largest domed structure in the world. This particular subject was the province of Giovanni Paolo Pannini, who was by a few years Canaletto's senior, and by whom there are a number of dated canvases of the decade of the 1730s.[3] Pannini's views very often included tourists, generally guided by a cicerone, but in the Pantheon interiors the guide was more often a cleric. The visitors are easily identifiable by their elaborate dress and enthusiastic gestures. Sir Michael Levey found "something un-Canalettesque" in Canaletto's Roman pictures, "especially in the groups of figures and in the relationship of these to the architecture," and indeed the figures are different from the ones in the Venetian views.[4] They are larger and more prominent, but at the same time they play the passive role of onlookers. Levey has suggested the influence of Pannini, perhaps on Bellotto and so indirectly on Canaletto. It is not surprising that at the hands of a Venetian painter the elaborate coach and the rearing white horses with their inadequate trappings convey an air of fantasy.

Although André Corboz has not identified a print source for the present composition, there must be one. Given Canaletto's talent for conveying a sense of place, he would have been able to invest with light, atmosphere, and human presence an image of a Roman building that he probably had not seen for over twenty years.

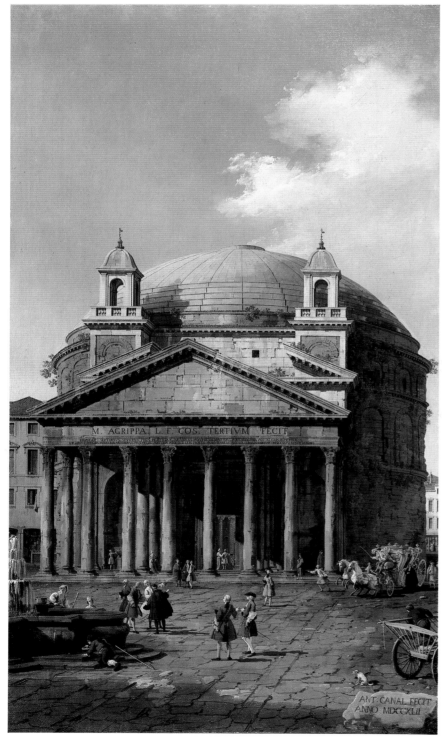

60.

Detail of 60.

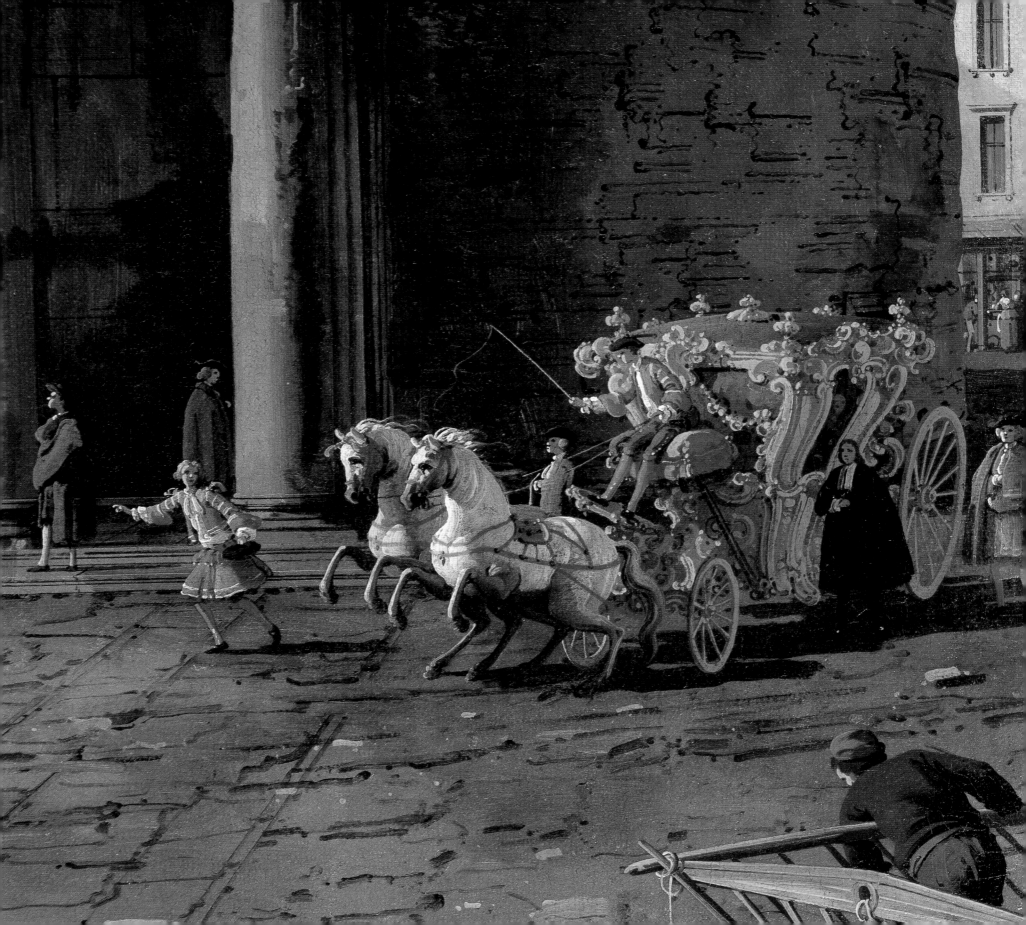

The Overdoors

Smith, who by 1743 was virtually Canaletto's only patron, proved to be a friend in need. After the drawings of the mainland near Venice and the ones of Roman subjects, which were in great part taken by the English merchant, and the painted views of Rome (for which see cat. nos. 59, 60), he commissioned some new Venice views for engraving (C/L 37, 48, 68, and 85).[1] These are signed and dated 1743 and 1744 and were engraved as usual by Visentini, presumably, as Sir Michael Levey pointed out, before June 1744 when Smith was appointed consul. Smith also conceived the idea of a series of paintings to go over doors: they were intended as a tribute to Palladio and, again, were perhaps for the palace on the Grand Canal that was his residence, if not for his country house at Mogliano.[2]

In the event, Palladio's buildings were sometimes overlooked in the thirteen overdoors (for which see C/L 451), nine of which are still in the Royal Collection, and the alterations to Smith's palace were not completed for several years. The overdoors are more or less uniform in width, if not in height, and are consistent in style. Some are signed and dated, and the series was most likely painted in 1743–44. Of the paintings by Canaletto bought by George III the overdoors are listed in a note apart, and they are associated with a series representing English Palladian-style buildings in imagined settings which were done by Visentini and Francesco Zuccarelli during the same period and to Smith's order.[3]

NOTES

1. Among the Royal Collection drawings are cat. no. 107 and C/L 666, 680, 689, 714, 717, and 728.
2. Levey, *Later Italian Pictures*, 1964, pp. 64–66, nos. 408–16, figs. 166 and 168–74; and Millar, in *Canaletto*, 1980, pp. 67–70, nos. 34–37. See also C/L 374 and C/L 460.
3. Levey, *Later Italian Pictures*, 1964, pp. 104–5, nos. 669–76, and figs. 183–90.

61. Capriccio: a Palladian Design for the Rialto Bridge

Oil on canvas, 35½ × 51¼ in. (90.2 × 130.2 cm), with a strip measuring 1½ in. (3.8 cm) at the bottom that may at one time have been turned over or covered
Signed (lower right): *ACanal* (AC in ligature) *F.*
Her Majesty Queen Elizabeth II
C/L 457

Men at first made bridges of wood, as being attentive to their present necessity only; but since they have begun to have a regard for the immortality of their name, and when riches gave them spirit, and conveniency to do greater things, they began to build with stone, which is more durable, of greater expence, and of more glory to the builders.

Andrea Palladio[1]

And so it was in Venice in the sixteenth century. Palladio's design—reproduced in chapter XIII of Book III of *I quattro libri dell'architettura*—was published in 1570, when the old wooden bridge at the Rialto was in urgent need of replacement. He described this design as "well adapted to the place where

218

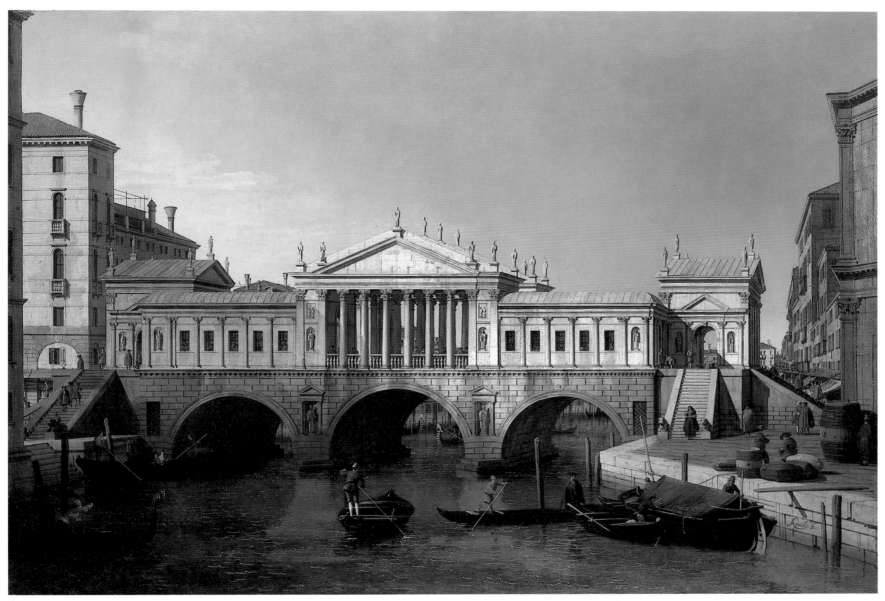

61.

219

EXHIBITED
London 37

NOTES
1. Andrea Palladio, *The Third Book of Architecture* (London, 1738), reprinted in *Andrea Palladio: The Four Books of Architecture*, with introduction by Adolf K. Placzek (New York, 1965), p. 68.
2. Palladio, *The Third Book of Architecture*, 1738 (1965), pp. 70–71 and pls. 9–10.
3. Levey, *Later Italian Pictures*, 1964, p. 64, no. 408; Millar, in *Canaletto*, 1980, p. 70, no. 37; Barcham, "Canaletto and a Commission from Consul Smith," 1977, pp. 385–93; and Corboz, *Canaletto*, 1985, p. 36.
4. There are variants (see C/L 458 and C/L 459) in which the same bridge is shown between two well-known buildings in Vicenza. In 1759 Francesco Algarotti, the critic and collector, wrote a letter giving the impression that he had recently had the idea of just such a painting and commissioned Canaletto to execute it for him. This has caused much speculation, particularly as the Algarotti picture cannot be identified among the several versions, which seem to be earlier in date. It is significant that Algarotti was in Venice in 1743–45 and may well have seen Smith's overdoors. For the text of Algarotti's letter see Gio. Bottari, *Raccolta di lettere sulla pittura, scultura ed architettura*, VII (Milan, 1822), pp. 427–36.

it was to have been built; which was in the middle of a city, that is one of the greatest, and of the most noble in *Italy*, and is the metropolis of many other cities, and where there is a very great traffick carried on, almost from every part of the world." Without mentioning Venice or the Rialto, he continued: "The river is very broad, and the bridge would have been in the very spot where the merchants assemble to treat of their affairs."[2] The old bridge was not in fact replaced for some years. Designs were submitted by a number of architects in December 1587 and, the commission having been awarded to Antonio Da Ponte, the work was undertaken in 1588. The bridge, of a more practical design than that envisaged by Palladio, was largely completed by 1590.

Smith and the members of his circle were obsessively interested in Palladianism, and the project he devised for Canaletto is in no way surprising, though the artist may have found the idea less sympathetic than did his patron.[3] There is nothing Palladian about a view of the Molo toward the west, showing the flagstaffs removed from Piazza S. Marco and aligned beside and between the columns of SS. Theodore and Mark (C/L 453), which was one of Canaletto's chosen subjects. By contrast the painting of the bridge is the finest of the series, on account of the clarity and lucidity of its handling and design. Canaletto followed Palladio's elevation closely, adding only some statuary to the roof line. The view is down the Grand Canal with, at the right, the corner of a building that seems to be Palazzo dei Camerlenghi, standing at the correct location. Opposite are some buildings bearing no resemblance to reality, scaled to balance the composition. The canvas is exceptionally well suited to its function as an overdoor, the more so by comparison with others of the same set.[4]

62. *Capriccio: an Island in the Lagoon, with a Pavilion and a Church*

Oil on canvas, 20⅛ × 27 in. (51.1 × 68.6 cm)
The Saint Louis Art Museum
C/L 488

Of the imaginary views inspired by the lagoon this painting and its pendant (C/L 487) are certainly among the finest. The pair is said to have been bought by the first Lord Boston (1707–1775) and remained in the family until sold at Christie's in 1942. In the present picture there are reminiscences of the terra firma: for the pavilion, Porta Portello or another of the gates at Padua; for the campanile, that of S. Rocco at Dolo, as seen in the untitled etching of houses along a river bank; for the chapel, the cottage beside the water mill in the imaginary etched view of Padua; perhaps also the divided plate whose

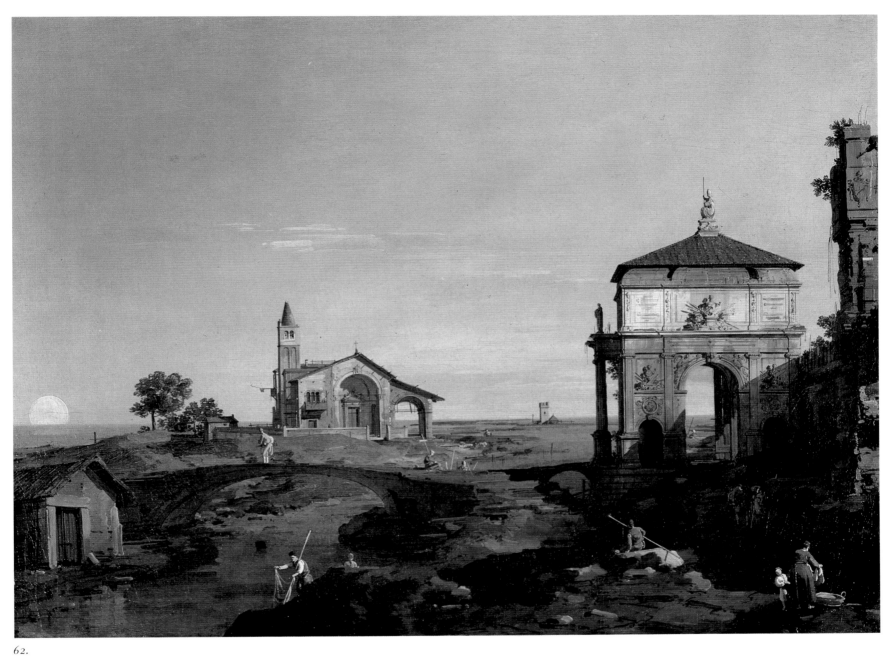

62.

221

two parts are known as *The Wagon Passing Over a Bridge* and *The Little Monument*.[1] The motif of the tower and the crenellated wall in ruins, at the right, must have been inspired by something on the mainland, so too the slender statue standing upon an equally slender column.[2]

The companion painting is *Capriccio: an Island in the Lagoon, with a Church and a Column*. In that painting the sluice gate is represented as from an angle similar to the lock in the etching called *Le Porte del Dolo*, and the distant domes and towers were perhaps inspired by the skyline of Padua. Of the Venetian churches the closest may be S. Simeone Piccolo. The pyramid, prominent here and figuring also in the companion piece, appears in Canaletto's etchings, in a drawing which must be an alternate for the title plate to the etchings (C/L 818), and among the British Museum studies of Roman subjects (C/L 713 [230]).

The atmosphere of the lagoon and its islands is most vividly conveyed in a famous series of drawings in the Royal Collection (cat. nos. 101, 102; and C/L 523, C/L 649), where the shallow water and the porous earth merge, and the buildings cling like barnacles to their footings. There are also a few very rough sketches that convey the same sense of a fresh encounter with the lagoon environment: a church or pavilion at the water's edge (C/L 657, in the Royal Collection), a bridge under the moon (C/L 661), a house and quay beside a sandbank (C/L 663).

The painting belonging to the Saint Louis Art Museum has been ascribed to Bellotto.[3] Kozakiewicz, however, accepts only two views of this type, *Capriccio with a Roman Gate* and *Capriccio with a Roman Triumphal Arch*.[4] While Bellotto's pictures are related to works by Canaletto in the material upon which they draw, they are land based and more archaeological in feeling, which is not surprising given Bellotto's relatively recent encounter with the Roman cityscape. The figures in them (sometimes given to Francesco Zuccarelli) also differ dramatically in their type and handling. The first of Bellotto's two paintings should be compared to a drawing by Canaletto of closely related motifs, at Windsor (C/L 780).

NOTES

1. See cat. no. 106, C/L 682, and Bromberg, *Canaletto's Etchings*, 1974, pp. 78, 88, and 164, pls. 9, 11, 32, and 33.
2. Further to this subject, see Corboz, *Canaletto*, 1985, pp. 259, 278 n. 217, 290, 298, 306, 368, and 437.
3. The attribution to Bellotto was suggested by Terisio Pignatti and Francesco Valcanover in 1976 (information communicated by the Saint Louis Art Museum).
4. Kozakiewicz, *Bernardo Bellotto*, 1972, II, pp. 95–98, nos. 127, 128.

Canaletto's First Visit to England

It is assumed, in the absence of documentary evidence, that Canaletto's journey to England in 1746 must have been brought about by a continuing scarcity of visitors to Venice and Smith's inability to support the artist with further commissions. Canaletto may have been influenced by the success in England of his friend Jacopo Amigoni, who had spent ten years there, returning to Venice in 1739, and by members of the preceding generation who had worked there as scene painters, decorators of country houses, history painters, and portraitists to prominent members of the nobility, including Marco and Sebastiano Ricci, Giovanni Antonio Pellegrini, and Antonio Bellucci.[1] The completion of Westminster Bridge was imminent, and its commissioners, among the most influential men of their day, included some of Canaletto's earlier patrons, such as the Dukes of Richmond and Bedford. It is not difficult to imagine that the subject would have appealed to the most prominent of view painters. Smith—by this date Consul Smith—probably supported Canaletto's move but does not seem to have made much effort to find work for him among those who had bought his Venice views.

As the English engraver, antiquary, and diarist George Vertue observed, when recording Canaletto's arrival in London at the end of May 1746, "he is much esteemed and no doubt but what Views and works He doth here, will give the same satisfaction—tho' many persons already have so many of his paintings."[2] By Vertue's account Canaletto, described as "a sober man turnd of 50," had already begun some views of the River Thames. The earliest of these was perhaps *London: seen through an Arch of Westminster Bridge* (C/L 412), which shows the centering of the arch still in place, and which was engraved by Samuel Wale for publication in 1747, with a dedication to Sir Hugh Smithson, also a commissioner of the bridge (for whose continuing association with Canaletto see cat. nos. 64 and 70).

NOTES

1. For the house decorations, see Croft-Murray, *Decorative Painting in England*, 1970, II, pp. 13–24, 163–66, 170–71, 179–80, 253–56, and 264–67, and for Amigoni's role in persuading Canaletto to go to England, *Vertue Note Books*, III, p. 132.
2. *Vertue Note Books*, III, pp. 130 and 132.

63. London: Westminster Bridge from the North on Lord Mayor's Day

Oil on canvas, 37¾ × 50¼ in. (95.8 × 127.5 cm)
Yale Center for British Art, New Haven; Paul Mellon
Collection
C/L 435

The subject is known from the engraving, inscribed *Canaleti Pinx. S. Wale delin. R. Parr sculp.*, and published early in 1747.[1] It is the procession of the Lord Mayor in the city barge to Westminster to be sworn in, a ceremony that took place each year on 29 October, the year in this case being 1746. The engraving supplies the names of the buildings and provides a lettered key to the barges which, beside that of the city, are those of the guilds: the Skinners, Goldsmiths, Fishmongers, Clothworkers, Vintners, Merchant Taylors, Mercers, and Drapers. As Mrs. Finberg noted, the Stationers' barge, omitted in the painting, was added in the engraving. Each of the flag-bedecked barges is rowed by twelve oarsmen. Three larger sailing ships fly the Union Jack, the plumes of trailing smoke denoting fired salutes. The river is awash with small pleasure craft. The Lord Mayor's barge, with eighteen oarsmen, lies more or less broadside in the foreground, and is perhaps positioned at a divergent angle in the interest of legibility. Against the horizon toward the left is Lambeth Palace, residence of the Archbishop of Canterbury. In the foreground (from right to left) are St. Margaret's, the parish church of Westminster, the twin towers and nave of Westminster Abbey, Westminster Hall, now the entrance to the Houses of Parliament, St. Stephen's Chapel and, behind the trees, St. John's Church, Smith Square.

The imaginary viewpoint is from the air at midstream. Canaletto shows the bridge complete, as the publisher of the print would no doubt have required, with the statues of the river gods Thames and Isis which, although intended, were never executed. In fact the centerings of certain of the arches were still in place when, in 1747, the fifth pier from the Westminster side began to settle, damaging the adjacent arches, so that the bridge was not formally opened until 1750. Westminster Bridge, designed by the Swiss engineer Charles Labelye, was the most important civic-building enterprise of the time, and—after the centuries-old London Bridge—only the second bridge in the city to cross the Thames. The river was of course the commercial heart of the nation. Until relatively recently it also afforded Londoners the pleasure of being on the water as well as a means of local transportation, as may be seen in the prints of Whistler and the paintings of Tissot.

As the drawing for the engraving was by Wale, Canaletto probably made only rough sketches, of which none survives that is directly related. The engraving may have enjoyed wide circulation and was the source of numerous variants by aspiring English topographical painters. While Canaletto

NOTE
1. Finberg, "Canaletto in England," 1920–21, p. 72, and for other views of the bridge, pp. 69–75. See also Allen, "Topography or Art," 1987, pp. 33–36.

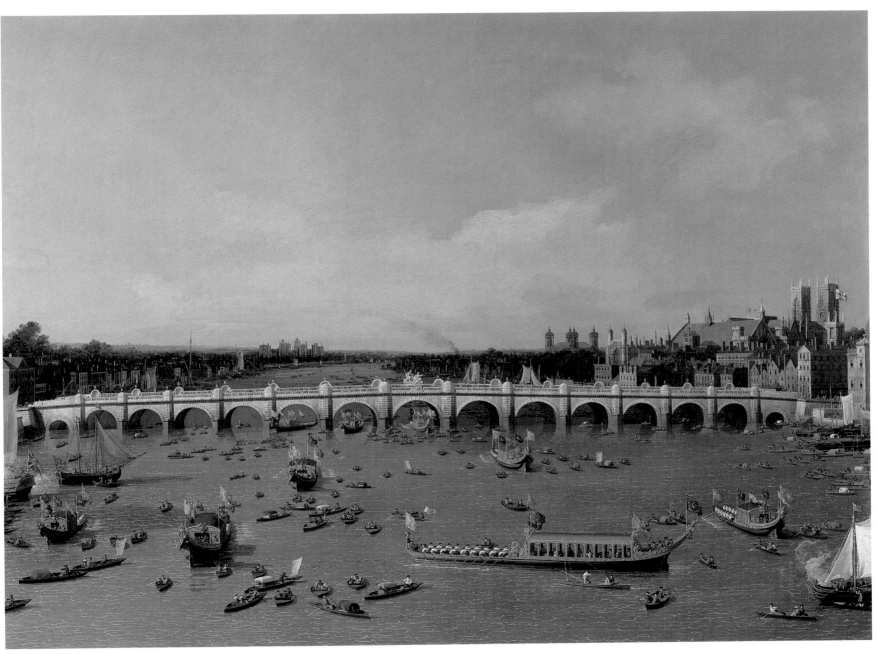

63.

himself did not paint this precise view again, Westminster Bridge was the most sought-after subject of his English years. There is a painting of the bridge (C/L 427), and also a drawing (cat. no. 111), showing five arches standing, a sight Canaletto never saw. One of a pair of views (C/L 426) sold to Prince Lobkowitz and taken to Prague shows five of the timber centers in place and the parapet incomplete, and may on that account be earlier than number 63. One of another pair (C/L 429) is in the Royal Collection and thus belonged to Consul Smith. The present picture was first recorded at public auction as recently as 1895.

64. Windsor Castle

Oil on canvas, 32½ × 53½ in. (82.6 × 135.9 cm)
His Grace the Duke of Northumberland
C/L 449

Windsor Castle, a residence of English sovereigns since William the Conqueror, may best be seen, as here, from the north. The State Apartments are at the left, and beyond the Norman Gateway, the Round Tower, with the Royal Standard flying, Henry III's Tower, and St. George's Chapel.[1] The wall and road in the left foreground have been replaced by the railway. In the meadows the townspeople are variously occupied with flute, spade, horse, fishing rod, and—upon the Thames—punt and pole. Windsor Bridge is in the distance at the right. The view, taken by Canaletto from a point now known as Romney Island, is opposite to that afforded by the windows of the Royal Library, and it is not greatly changed.

The painting bears a label set into its frame which reads:

> This picture was painted by Signor Canaletti
> who took the View from the window of the small
> Cottage at the end of the Enclosure next M.ʳ
> Crowle's Garden—& the Figures added by
> him at Percy Lodge. It was finished
> June the Eleventh 1747.

At Percy Lodge Sir Hugh Smithson, later first Duke of Northumberland and Canaletto's most loyal patron during the early part of his stay in England, had married in 1740 Lady Elizabeth Seymour, through whom he would receive the six Percy seats and claim to the ancient Percy title of Northumberland. *Windsor Castle* may have been painted as a gift to his father-in-law, the Earl of Hertford, or ordered by the earl on Sir Hugh's recommendation. Whatever the case, it belonged to him during his father-in-law's lifetime. The present Duke of Northumberland retains, among other com-

EXHIBITED
Venice 106

NOTE
1. J.G. Links, in *Canaletto*, exh. cat., 1982, pp. 76–77, no. 106.

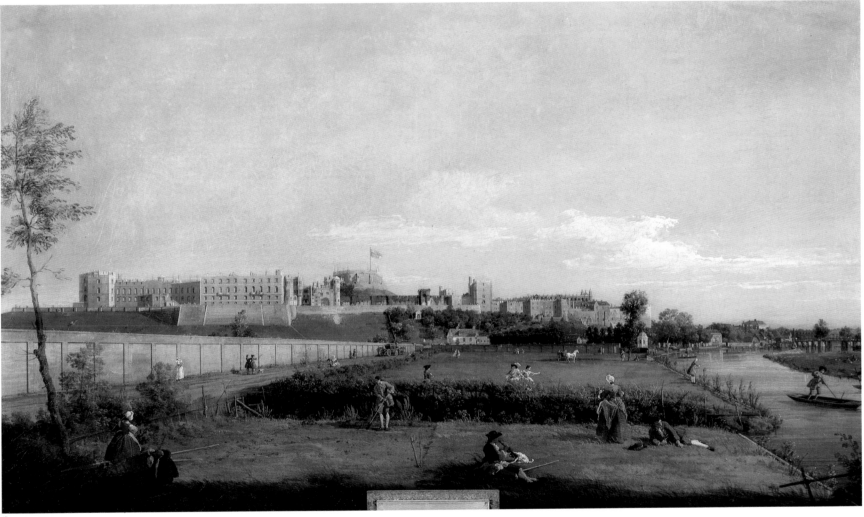

64.

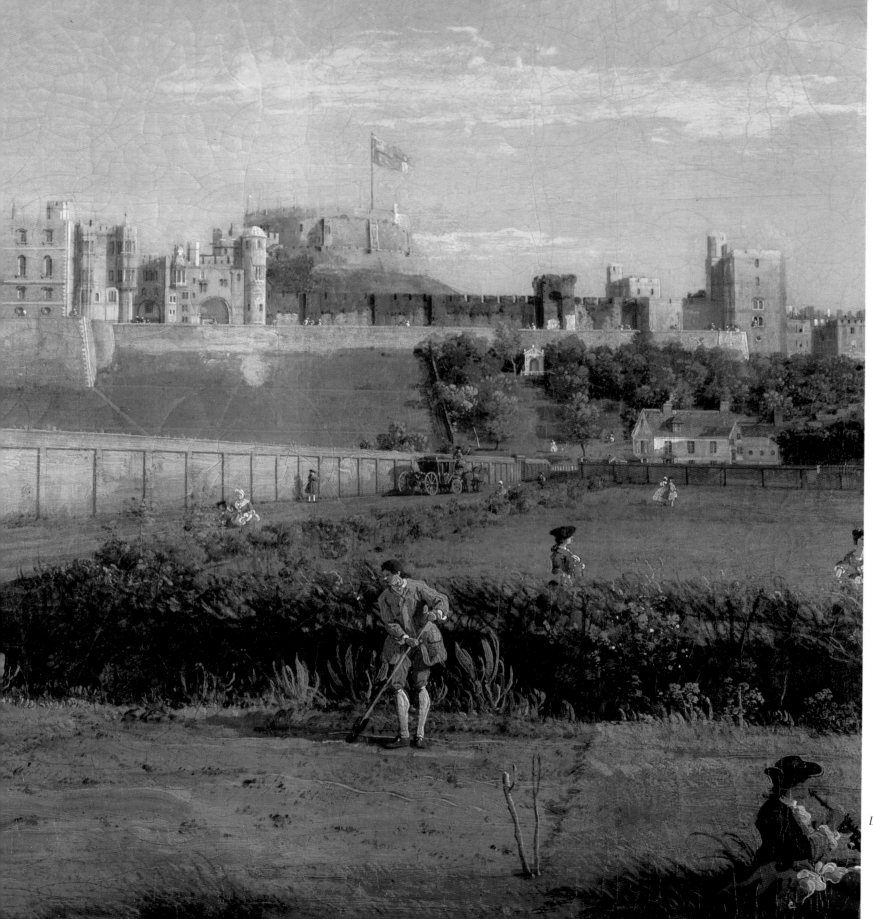

Detail of 64.

missions to Canaletto, views of three of the family properties: Syon (C/L 440), Alnwick Castle (C/L 408), and Northumberland House, London (cat. no. 70), all datable between the summer of 1749 and 1752/53.

Years before, Stefano Conti's agent Marchesini had stated that Canaletto always painted before the motif—an assertion that was manifestly incorrect. There being no reason to doubt the information provided by the label, *Windsor Castle* is actually the first recorded instance of his painting in situ (though the figures, as noted, are from a later moment). Six months, perhaps, had passed since he finished the painting representing the Lord Mayor's barge at Westminster (cat. no. 63), but the two canvases differ very greatly in feeling. This one, while a house portrait, conveys the late afternoon light and a sense of the lush landscape depicted that sets it apart from the topographical and reportorial exactitude of *Westminster Bridge*, and it is among the finest of the English views.

A Further Commission from the Duke of Richmond

The Duke of Richmond's old tutor, Thomas Hill, wrote to him on 20 May 1746, which must have been immediately after Canaletto's arrival in London. Hill had dined at the Duke of Montagu's (that is, in the house to the left of Richmond House in cat. nos. 65 and 66) with McSwiney who "got almost drunk." Hill went on to say that McSwiney had received from Canaletto a letter sent by "our old acquaintance the Consul of Venice" asking for an introduction to the Duke of Richmond. "I told him," continued Hill, "the best service I thought you could do him w^d be to let him draw a view of the river from y^r dining-room, which in my opinion would give him as much reputation as any of his Venetian prospects."[1] There is topographical evidence for dating the Richmond House paintings to the late summer of 1747, as well as their similarity in handling to the *Windsor Castle* picture.[2] It seems that the duke took a long time to respond to Hill's advice, or, and this is less likely, that Canaletto was too busy to accept the commission for what were to be the masterpieces of his English stay.

Sometime later, probably after returning from a brief visit to Venice in 1751, Canaletto painted a very wide view (C/L 439; see fig. 4) incorporating

NOTES
1. The letter is quoted by Finberg, "Canaletto in England," 1920–21, p. 27.
2. Hayes, *Burlington Magazine*, 1958, pp. 341–49.

much of the material from the two Richmond House paintings. For the new picture, Canaletto went back to the site, or rather to Loudoun House, just to the west and next door: any drawings he might have kept would not have been sufficient, as building operations had been undertaken meanwhile in connection with the widening of the thoroughfare from Westminster to Charing Cross. Changes in the cityscape are minutely recorded. Canaletto retained the later view of Whitehall, taking it back with him to Italy, and the story of its eventual sale appears in the entry for number 116.

65. London: Whitehall and the Privy Garden from Richmond House

Oil on canvas, 42 × 46 in. (106.7 × 116.8 cm)
The Trustees of the Goodwood Collections
C/L 438

NOTES

1. For the topography and history of Whitehall, see George S. Dugdale, *Whitehall through the Centuries* (London, 1950), particularly pp. 110–13, 115, and 117, and pls. 14, 15, 22, 23, 25, 28, 30, 41, 46, and 53. The illustrations are drawn from a collection of prints, drawings, and paintings of Whitehall assembled by R. J. Lister and belonging to the Treasury.
2. Francis Russell, in *The Treasure Houses of Britain*, exh. cat. (Washington, 1985), pp. 236–37, no. 157.
3. Hayes, *Burlington Magazine*, 1958, pp. 342–46, and figs. 10 and 13. The drawing now belongs to the British Museum.
4. Snowden, *London 200 Years Ago*, [1948], pp. 5, 7, and 27. Rocque was engaged as a surveyor, engraver, and map seller in premises near Hyde Park Corner for thirty years; his final revision of the London map, published in 1746, seems to have been in 1761.

The rather disorderly aspect of the view toward the north, taken from a window above the stable yard of the Duke of Richmond's house, encompasses in the foreground and near distance the site of the Royal Palace of Whitehall.[1] This enormous property, seized by Henry VIII from Cardinal Wolsey in 1529, had been the preferred residence of the Stuart monarchs. The palace and its precincts, which were larger than the Louvre, burned to the ground in 1698, leaving only Inigo Jones's Banqueting House, rising left of center beyond the lawn, and perhaps some part of the two-story brick building extending to the right in the direction of the river. A narrow thoroughfare, known simply as The Street and passing under the Tudor gate at the left, was widened in the 1720s to take in part of the old Privy Garden, and a structure between the gate and the Banqueting House was torn down to better accommodate the flow of traffic. After the fire, parcels of land were leased out: Lady Catherine Pelham remodeled the brick building, which had previously served as a cow house and a laundry; the Duke of Montagu's house, the back of which may be seen at the right, was built in 1733; and the Duke of Richmond's occupied part of what had been a royal bowling green. The Richmond name is preserved in that of the modern street, Richmond Terrace, which runs parallel to Downing Street and toward the Thames.

Beyond the Banqueting House and to the right are the spire of St. Martin-in-the-Fields, now fronting on Trafalgar Square, and one of the towers of Northumberland House, for which see number 70. Just visible to the left, near its present site, is Le Sueur's equestrian statue of Charles I, who was

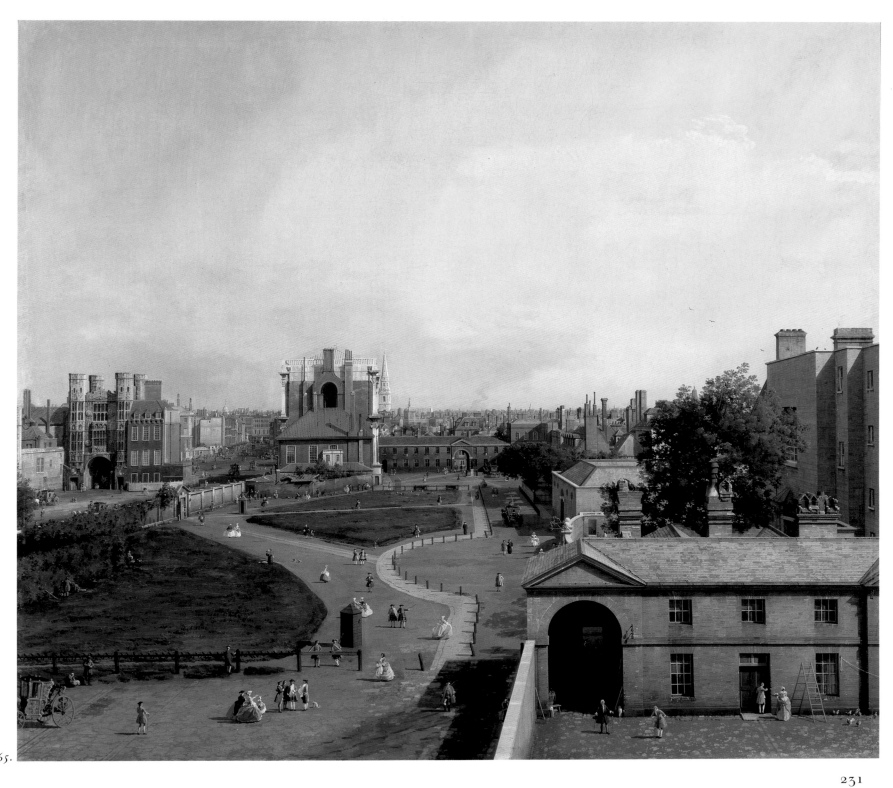

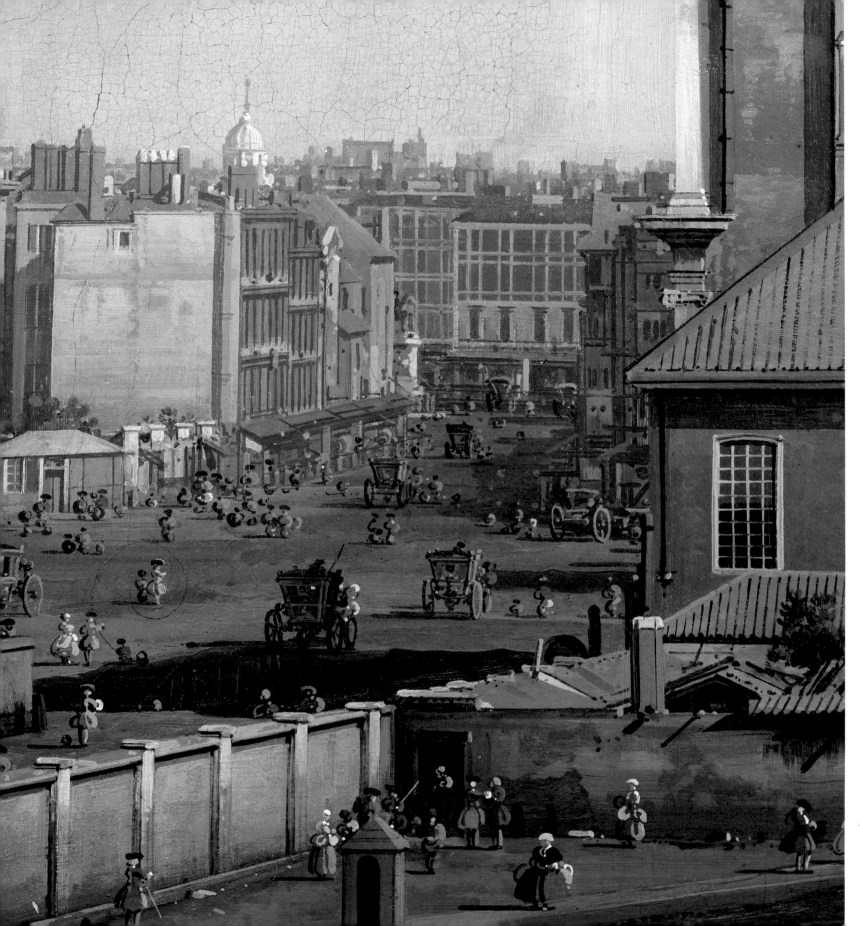

Detail of 65.

executed at Whitehall and was the Duke of Richmond's great-grandfather. Inside the stable yard, as Francis Russell has noted, is a figure with a cane who wears the riband of the Order of the Garter and must be Canaletto's patron; a servant in the Richmond livery color bows as he approaches.[2]

A drawing (C/L 754) encompassing much of what may be seen in this picture and its pendant shows, at the extreme left, evidence of demolition having to do with the laying out of Parliament Street, and the corner of a house which was to be pulled down in the autumn of 1747. On that account John Hayes has dated the drawing quite precisely to the summer or early autumn of that year.[3] This house, its enclosure, and even the tree are most precisely recorded in a map of London by John Rocque which was completed, and engraved by Parr, for publication in 1746.[4] The opportunity to study the view from a convenient vantage point above ground was in this case afforded Canaletto, whose ink and wash study is demonstrably accurate in detail, except perhaps in the farther distance. The spire of St. Martin-in-the-Fields and the tower of Northumberland House lie a little farther to the right than in the painting, and the profile of the city skyline is obscured in the drawing by the trees, but painting and drawing are so close in feeling that they cannot be separated by a significant interval of time. To judge from Rocque's map, and from Canaletto's own later view (C/L 439), which was taken at the window of an adjoining house, the buildings at the opposite end of the Privy Garden and the street are made to seem closer than in fact they were.

66. London: the Thames and the City of London from Richmond House

---

Oil on canvas, 42 × 46 in. (106.7 × 116.8 cm)
The Trustees of the Goodwood Collections
C/L 424

NOTE
1. Snowden, *London 200 Years Ago*, [1948], p. 27.

In the foreground is the terrace of Richmond House with, at the left, the house and terrace of the second Duke of Montagu. The water gate lies between and is reached by doors leading to a brick passageway. (These terraces would also have afforded a close and unobstructed view of Westminster Bridge to the south.) On the left bank of the river are the old buildings of the Savoy, fronting the water, Somerset House, with its tree-lined terrace and water stairs, The Temple (in the shade), St. Paul's Cathedral, and the spires of all of Wren's churches. On the right bank are tile-roofed sheds for housing timber and stone, and some workshops. The Lord Mayor's barge is one of the two large ones on the river. The ladies on Richmond House terrace are fashionably dressed—in brightly colored gowns worn over enormous panniers—so also the gentlemen, one of whom, carrying a stick and standing

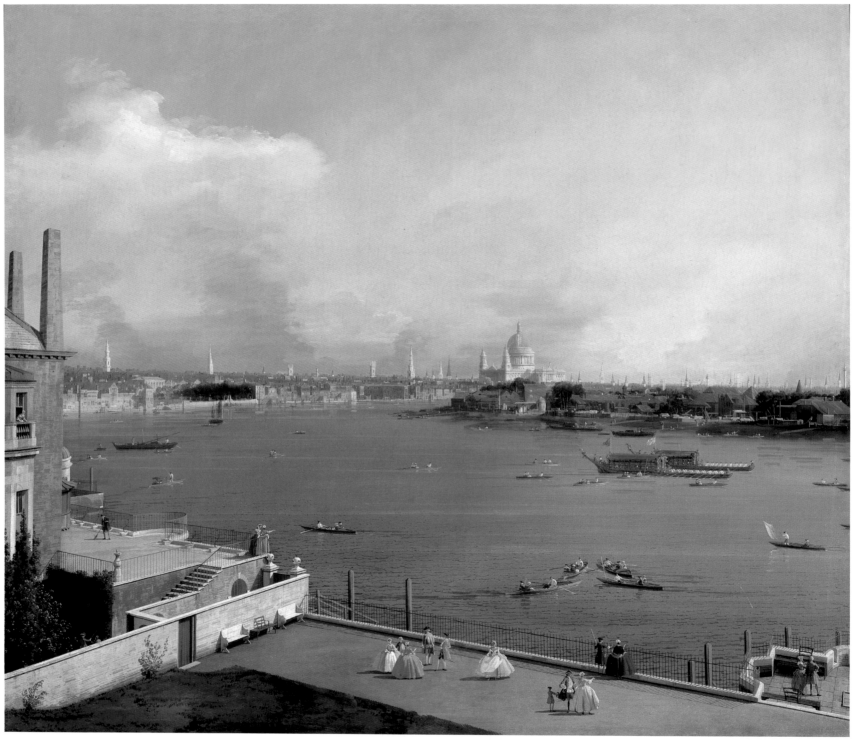

66.

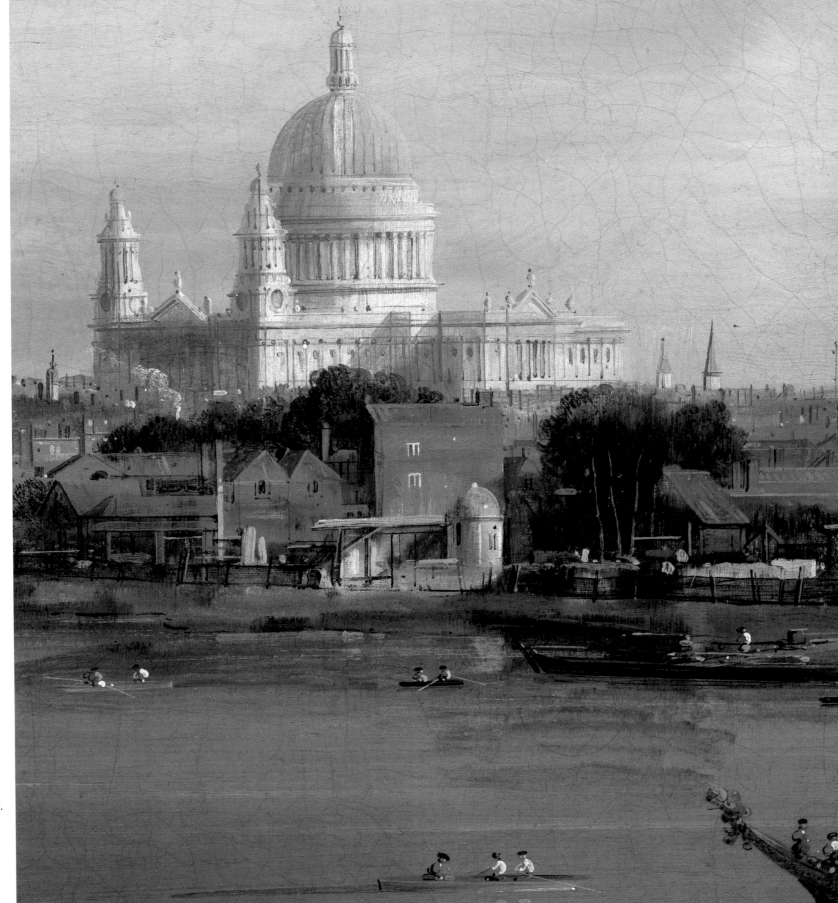

Detail of 66.

just at the center, must again be Charles Lennox, second Duke of Richmond, who died aged forty-nine in 1750. The picture suggests, as did Tom Hill's letter, the comfortably intimate terms of life among people of the same class in the eighteenth century. Often remarked upon is the delicate coloring and transparent, liquid handling of the pigments, the water flat, the landscape as if recently washed by rain.

The topography corresponds closely with that of two drawings, one already mentioned (C/L 754), and another (C/L 744) taking in more of the eastward view and the terrace, a garden wall, and that part of the house fronting closely on the river. The painting differs only in that the distant river banks and buildings have been brought closer, and the Thames is much less crowded with shipping (in this respect the drawing is reminiscent of certain of Canaletto's views of the Bacino di S. Marco). Rocque's map confirms the layout precisely and also shows the location of the old Privy Garden stairs (just south of the existing water gate) that had served the Royal Palace of Whitehall.[1] Richmond House was demolished in 1820, the Victorian city and the ministries of government engulfing all that remained except a small Tudor wine cellar that had served Wolsey and Henry VIII, and the Banqueting House with its splendid ceiling by Peter Paul Rubens.

67. London: Westminster Abbey, with a Procession of the Knights of the Order of the Bath

Oil on canvas, 40 × 40 in. (101.6 × 101.6 cm)
The Dean and Chapter of Westminster
C/L 432

The exterior of the abbey church of Westminster was in poor state of repair by the end of the seventeenth century, when Sir Christopher Wren was appointed to the surveyorship, and it was extensively refaced. Wren was succeeded by Nicholas Hawksmoor, during whose tenure and according to whose designs the west gable was constructed in 1734, and work on the "Gothick" towers undertaken in the following year; these may not have been completed until 1745.[1] The project is memorialized in the inscription beneath the gable, which cannot ever have been as legible as it is in Canaletto's picture: A:R:GEORGII II. VIII. A:D:MDCCXXXV. The commission was given to Canaletto by Joseph Wilcocks, Dean of Westminster and Bishop of Rochester from 1731 until 1756. It may be imagined that the dean had in mind a record of the ancient church as completed during his tenure, though a specific occasion is also recorded, namely the procession, following a ceremony of installation, of the Knights of the Order of the Bath, on 20 June 1749.[2]

The Duke of Montagu, Great Master of the Order, was ill (he died two weeks later on 5 July), so Lord de la Warr acted for him and is depicted—

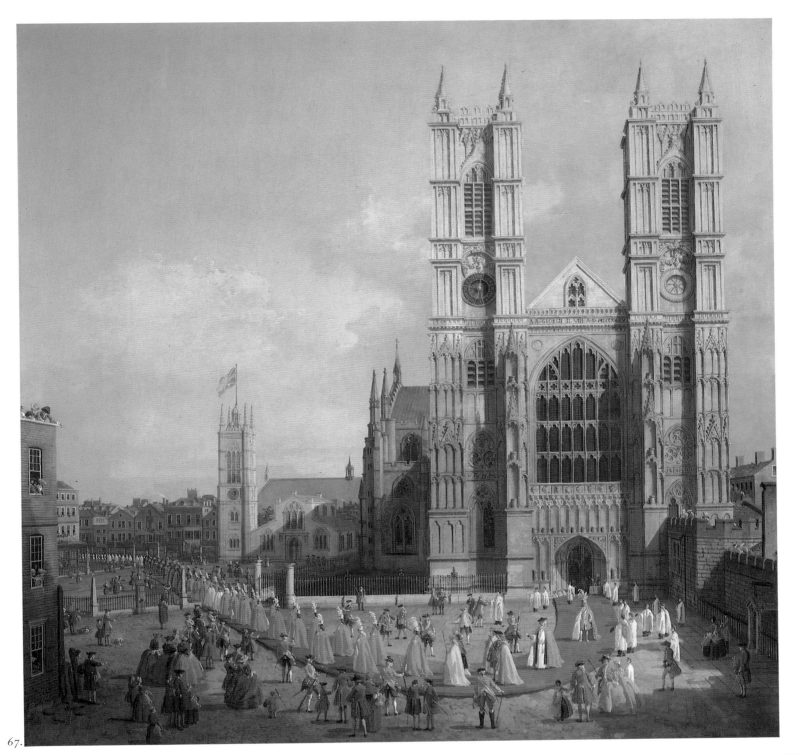

67.

EXHIBITED
Venice 103

NOTES

1. James Byam Shaw, in *Canaletto*, 1982, p. 75, no. 103; concerning the history of the abbey, see Kerry Downes, *Hawksmoor* (London, 1959), pp. 214–16 and 255–58; and *Royal Commission on Historical Monuments (England): An Inventory of the Historical Monuments in London*, I. *Westminster Abbey* (London, 1924), pp. 3–4, 17–18 and, for a photograph of the west front, pl. 3. The work of resurfacing the black and corroded exterior and the building of the west towers took nearly fifty years and was not completed until 1744–45, after Hawksmoor's death. See also Edward Wedlake Brayley, *The History and Antiquities of the Abbey Church of St. Peter, Westminster* (London, 1818–23), I, pp. 201–3, and II, pp. 4–6, where the transcription of the inscription is slightly at variance.
2. The precise event depicted was identified by Finberg, "Canaletto in England," 1920–21, pp. 35 and 68.

wearing the red mantle and white plumed hat of the order—in front of the west doorway, beneath the center of the facade. He is preceded by the dean, who has the red mantle over his clerical robes. The procession of knights makes its way through The Broad and King Street, which was shortly to be demolished in the course of building Parliament Street, passing in front of St. Margaret's church, the Union Jack flying from its tower. The roof of Westminster Hall is beyond. Soldiers, muskets in hand, line the walkway (their uniforms may recall those worn not long after by His Majesty's troops fighting in the American Revolution). Figures in white surplices gather outside the west doorway, their part in the ceremony completed, and one of them shakes the hand of a soberly dressed man among the spectators. In the immediate foreground onlookers crowd the windows and roof at the corner of a brick house, a detail reminiscent of Canaletto's Venetian views.

Canaletto received a limited number of major commissions while in England, and it is likely that this picture was painted shortly after the event took place. (The new exterior is rarely represented because it is relatively modern and long since blackened and illegible in detail.) The subject presented certain difficulties owing to the absence of local color in the architecture, the need to give due prominence to the great building, of which this canvas is in a sense a portrait, and the extreme solemnity and consequent lack of spontaneity of the occasion. The lighting, whether accurate or not, is delicate and beautifully observed, and the mannerism of handling the thick white pigment for details of costume is here very successful in its effect. The painting has hung in the Deanery at Westminster since it was completed.

68. Warwick Castle: the South Front

Oil on canvas, 29½ × 47⅜ in. (75 × 120.5 cm)
Thyssen-Bornemisza Foundation, Lugano
C/L 445

"This stupendous building is seated on a rock, to which it appears to be united rather by the hand of nature, than of art."[1] Warwick Castle from the south is indeed picturesque, and was thus described by one of the legions of visitors who have seen it from the approach to the bridge visible in this picture at the extreme right. Canaletto made five paintings and three drawings of the castle for Francis Greville, Lord Brooke, who was born in 1719 and received the title of Earl of Warwick in 1759.[2] Orphaned at the death of his father in 1727, he was brought up by Sir Hugh Smithson's mother-in-law with whose daughter, Elizabeth, he must have been on intimate terms. There can be little doubt as to the source of the introduction of patron to painter.

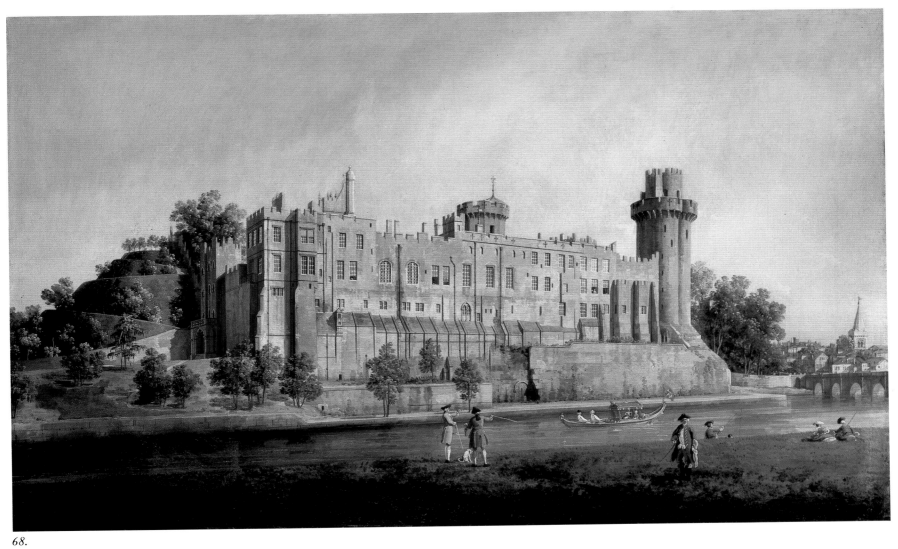

68.

The canvas representing *Windsor Castle* (cat. no. 64), which belonged to Smithson's father-in-law, was completed in June of 1747, and the view of Syon House (C/L 440) had, by Smithson's account, been started by 2 July 1749. Lord Brooke's first payments to Canaletto fall between these dates. Following Brooke's marriage in 1742, he planned extensive alterations to his castle and grounds at Warwick—of which, as David Buttery notes, he was very proud—eventually employing Lancelot Brown for the purpose. The first payment was not made to Brown until 26 December 1749.

Despite the many complicating factors outlined by Buttery, his evidence tends to show that the views of the south front, of which this is the largest and most important (in addition see C/L 443 and C/L 444, the paintings, and C/L 758, the drawing), are the ones carried out during Canaletto's first phase of work to Brooke's order. His account at Hoare's Bank, London, shows payments to the artist of £58 on 19 July 1748, and £31 10s (or 30 guineas) on 3 March 1749, and there is also a receipt of 28 July 1748 for the smaller sum of 10 guineas, written by Canaletto, the only one that exists other than those provided to Signor Conti nearly a quarter of a century before. While three of the south-front views show the castle as it was before the alterations, this canvas apparently records its planned appearance.

The castle, of great antiquity and on numerous occasions rebuilt, is seen across the River Avon, with Ethelfleda's Mount at the left, and the town of Warwick and bell tower of St. Nicholas's church at the right. The principal suite of rooms—the dining room, anteroom, drawing room, gilt room, and state bedchamber—are those with the larger windows on the main floor overlooking the Avon. The two related canvases are taken from a more distant viewpoint and show a pine at the top of the Mount, but otherwise no plantings or trees outside the castle wall at the left. A mill and weir lie at the base of Caesar's Tower, to the right, and there is a wall with a gate to the west. A house stands just to the north of the bridge on the approach to the castle entrance. In number 68 these have all been eliminated, which must have been Lord Brooke's wish. Plantings of well-grown trees have been added at the left while to the right along the river only retaining walls remain. The course of the Avon is unobstructed and upon it floats a small pleasure boat with a Venetian-style *felze* such as was envisaged by Brooke, who had taken a Grand Tour at an early age. In the event the mill was not demolished but rebuilt in Gothic style, and the weir was also for a time retained.

NOTES

1. William Smith, *A New and Complete History of the County of Warwick* (Birmingham, 1829), p. 36 and, for a description of the exterior and the principal rooms of the castle, pp. 39–42.

2. This entry and the following depend in great part on Buttery, *Burlington Magazine*, 1987, pp. 437–45, where the receipts were first published. The paintings and drawings referred to are cat. nos. 68, 69, 112, and 113, and C/L 443, 444, 446, and 758. The earliest account is that of Finberg, "Canaletto in England," 1920–21, pp. 67–68.

England: The Second Period

In the late summer of 1751 George Vertue reported that Canaletto had recently returned from an eight-month visit to Venice.[1] This can have been no later than July, when, on the thirtieth, the artist placed an announcement in the *Daily Advertiser*, inviting visitors to his lodgings in Silver Street, Golden Square, to see a new picture he had painted. Two years earlier, in 1749, Vertue had expressed the view that Canaletto's English work was inferior, proposing that the painter then established in London might be an impostor. This contemporary bias presages the by now long-established scholarly view that Canaletto reached his stride within ten or fifteen years, and that for the rest of his working life of more than thirty years the quality of his pictures very gradually declined. There can be no doubt that after initial success in England the demand for his work had fallen off, and he may have intended to remain in Venice had conditions there proven better. Neither can it be argued that the second period in England, which may have been interrupted by another trip to Venice, was especially fruitful, at least not in terms of the number of major commissions received. A later account, proposing to describe events in London, may have some bearing. It is that of the watercolorist Edward Dayes:

> The picture-dealing tribe carried their assurance so far, as to deny that Cannaletti was the person who painted his pictures at Venice, that is, on his arrival in London…they still persisted that the pieces now produced were not in the same style; an assertion which materially injured him for a time.… By this scheme they hoped to drive him from the country, and thereby to prevent him detecting the copies they had made from his works, which were in great repute.[2]

The influence of the art market is not of such recent date as we may think, and the nature of Canaletto's evidently private and uncommunicative temperament would have prevented him from being his own best advocate, but the quality of the work is not so much in function of its date as of the interest of the subject or the importance of the commission. After all, he is only one among many famous artists who failed to achieve more than a marginally comfortable living within his own lifetime.

NOTES

1. *Vertue Note Books*, III, p. 158, and see also p. 151. Finberg's account, "Canaletto in England," 1920–21, pp. 29–36, remains the standard source.
2. Edward Wedlake Brayley, *The Works of the Late Edward Dayes* (London, 1805), p. 322.

69. Warwick Castle: the East Front from the Courtyard

Oil on canvas, 29½ × 48 in. (75 × 122 cm)
Birmingham Museums and Art Gallery
C/L 447

The view is over the lawn within the court of Warwick Castle and encompasses (left to right) Guy's Tower, the Clock Tower and entrance gate, and Caesar's Tower, which is at the right in number 68.[1] Through the gate are the spire of the church of St. Nicholas and roofs and chimneys of the town, and the partly seen figures show that the pathway slopes steeply downward. The approach to the castle proper, at the extreme right, is graveled. Shortly after Canaletto painted and drew the east front from within, Lord Brooke and Lancelot Brown agreed on improvements to be made, and an oval lawn and carriageway were provided. Buttery proposes that the two young trees protected by fencing may have been planted on Brown's instruction. The figures are in general fashionably and colorfully dressed, and as several of them are studying the view, they may be tourist visitors. A finished drawing, differing slightly in detail, is number 113.

The pendant (C/L 446), nearly the same size and identically framed, shows the east front from the outside, and a comparable drawing is in the Robert Lehman Collection at the Metropolitan Museum (cat. no. 112). The payments to Canaletto for the second phase of work to Lord Brooke's commission were also drawn on his account at Hoare's Bank: 31 guineas on 24 March, and £50 on 27 July 1752. The additional Warwick views may therefore have been Canaletto's first work to be executed after his return from Venice.

Buttery argues, convincingly, that all of the paintings and drawings of Warwick Castle were at first owned by Lord Brooke and were installed in his London residence. One of the paintings of the south front (C/L 444) belonged for a time to the Peachey family, Georgiana Peachey having married in 1771 George Greville, who in 1773 succeeded his father as the second earl. The other four paintings remained in the family's possession, at Warwick Castle, until 1977.

NOTE

1. Buttery, *Burlington Magazine*, 1987, pp. 437–45.

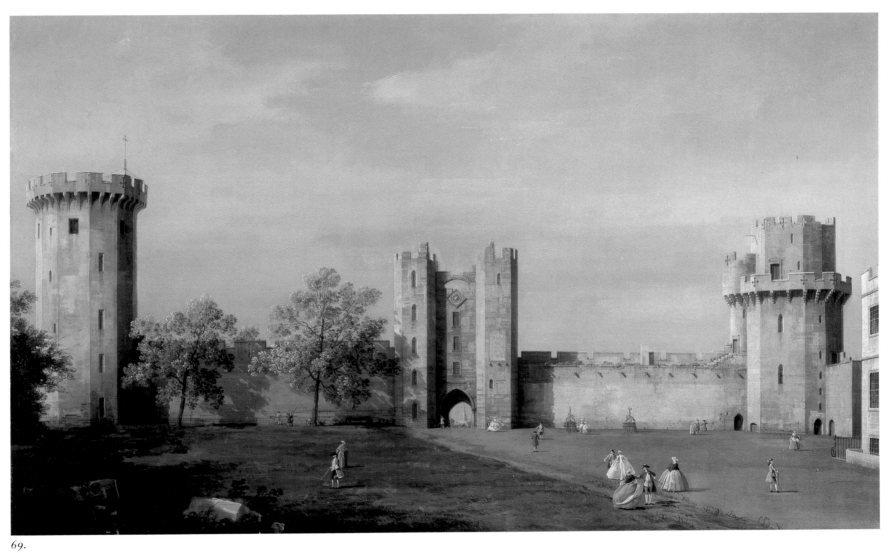

69.

70. London: Northumberland House

Oil on canvas, 47½ × 72 in. (120.7 × 182.9 cm)
His Grace the Duke of Northumberland
C/L 419

NOTE

1. Finberg, "Canaletto in England," 1920–21, pp. 40 and
59–60, who records, in addition to this painting and the
related drawing, nine other pictures including a view of
Northumberland House from the river. For the location of
the house, which was enormous and had a garden descending
to the Thames, see Rocque's map, in Snowden, *London
200 Years Ago*, [1948], p. 27.

In 1750 Sir Hugh Smithson, through his wife, had inherited the Percy fortune and the fabled Percy properties, and become the Earl of Northumberland. The Percy family mansion at Charing Cross, Northumberland House, was a magnificent Jacobean structure, built around a quadrangle and with a large garden abutting the site of the former palace of Whitehall.[1] One of the towers of the house is visible in number 65. The house was altered and the facade rebuilt in 1752. Canaletto must have painted it immediately thereafter, as a closely corresponding engraving—inscribed *Canaleti Pinxᵗ et Delinᵗ. T. Bowles Sculpᵗ.* and *In the Collection of the Earl of Northumberland.*—was published in 1753.

The new facade of the house, pale in coloring and with gilt weather vanes atop the corner towers, occupies nearly half the picture surface. Set off from the street by obelisks supporting lamps and posts to mark the wide footpath, it is flanked by much smaller buildings with shop fronts at street level and, at the right, by the bronze equestrian statue of Charles I upon its pedestal (in the approximate position it occupies today). The shops on the left have been identified from rate books and prove to be correctly represented by Canaletto: coffee and eating houses, a saddler, a trunk maker, and a hosier among them. The largest sign is that of the Golden Cross, a celebrated inn which was approached by the entrance below. A coach waits at the door, and another enters The Strand, at left center. The house stood at what is now Trafalgar Square and was demolished in 1873, making way for Northumberland Avenue. The lead lion, which looks here to be made of stone, was removed to Syon House, Middlesex, now the Duke of Northumberland's principal residence in the south.

The painting, with its remarkable picture of London life in Georgian times, was much copied, and there are versions seeming to show the hand of Canaletto in part. A drawing by Canaletto of this scene, now in Minneapolis, is number 114.

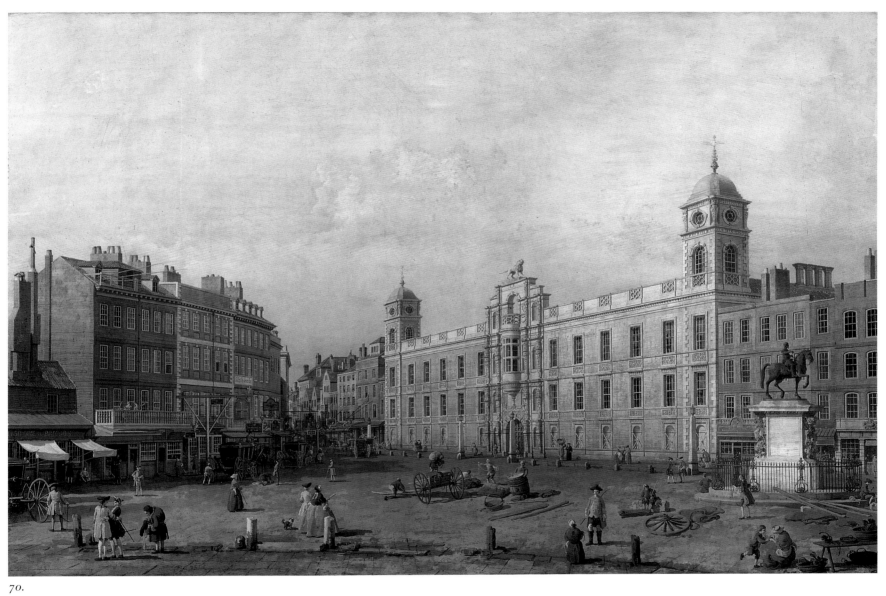

70.

71. London: Vauxhall Gardens, the Grand Walk

Oil on canvas, 19¾ × 29⅝ in. (50 × 75.3 cm)
Private Collection
C/L 431

EXHIBITED
Canada 107

NOTES

1. Two recent sources are T. J. Edelstein, *Vauxhall Gardens*, exh. cat., Yale Center for British Art (New Haven, 1983), with an essay by Brian Allen, "Vauxhall: The Landscape," pp. 17–24, and *Rococo: Art and Design in Hogarth's England*, exh. cat., Victoria and Albert Museum (London, 1984), pp. 75–98, nos. F1–F43, with an essay by David Coke, "Vauxhall Gardens," pp. 75–81. The first is mainly concerned with books and prints, the second with decorative arts and ephemera, both with extensive bibliographies.

2. See also Finberg, "Canaletto in England," 1920–21, pp. 65–66, and, for reproductions of three of the four prints after Canaletto, C/L, pl. 183, and Malcolm Warner et al., *The Image of London: Views by Travellers and Emigrés, 1550–1920*, exh. cat., Barbican Art Gallery (London, 1987), p. 131, no. 82 ill.

3. For an illustration of the print by Bowles after Wale, see *Rococo: Art and Design in Hogarth's England* (London, 1984), p. 90, no. F20 ill.

4. For illustrations, see *Rococo: Art and Design in Hogarth's England* (London, 1984), p. 87, no. F13 ill.; and Snowden, *London 200 Years Ago*, [1948], p. 29 ill.

246

A pleasure ground had long existed on the site, a short distance up and across river from Westminster, on the Surrey side, when Jonathan Tyers leased the property in 1728.[1] Much embellished, Vauxhall Gardens reopened to the public in 1732, and later became a model for similar gardens all over Europe, many of them even borrowing its name. Until 1750, when Westminster Bridge opened, the coach route was long and tedious, and visitors usually approached the gardens by boat, disembarking at Vauxhall Stairs to pass the late afternoon and evening hours walking about, listening to music, and dining alfresco in individual booths by the light of 1500 oil lamps. Roubiliac's statue of Handel was commissioned for the gardens, and many of the supper boxes were decorated with paintings by and from the workshop of Francis Hayman. Vauxhall had a long life and was patronized by Frederick, Prince of Wales (who was the ground landlord and attended the opening ridotto in June 1732), and George IV when Prince Regent; by Hogarth and Reynolds among artists; and by Dr. Johnson, Horace Walpole, and Oliver Goldsmith among men of letters. It closed in 1859. An auction sale was held, and what remained of the premises was demolished.

Canaletto painted the view afforded the visitor upon entering Vauxhall Gardens. The octagonal orchestra pavilion, built in 1735, is in the foreground at the right with, beyond, the organ house, erected two years later, and the Turkish Dining Tent, dating to the early 1740s. Supper boxes enclosing tables draped with cloths may be seen at the left, center, and far right, and atop the posts that separate them are a few of the many lamps. This part of the gardens was called The Grove, and was flanked by the Grand Walk, with the statue of Aurora in the distance. The season may perhaps be late spring when the shadows are long: here Canaletto invokes pictorial license, as the shadows should fall in the opposite direction. The atmosphere, tranquil and sedate, was reported on other occasions to have been quite intemperate.

An engraving after Canaletto of this subject, in reverse, was published by Robert Sayer and Henry Overton on 2 December 1751 as *A View of the Grand Walk &c in Vauxhall Gardens....Canaleti delin[t]. E. Rooker sculp.*[2] This was one of a set of four views of the gardens, the others—two engraved by J. S. Müller and one by Rooker—being the Grand South Walk, the Temple of Comus, and the Center Cross Walk. No drawings by Canaletto survive, but the images upon which the prints were based probably dated from the 1750 season. (In 1751 Canaletto was abroad, in Venice, until midsummer.) The buildings and decorations at Vauxhall grew more elaborate year by year. The

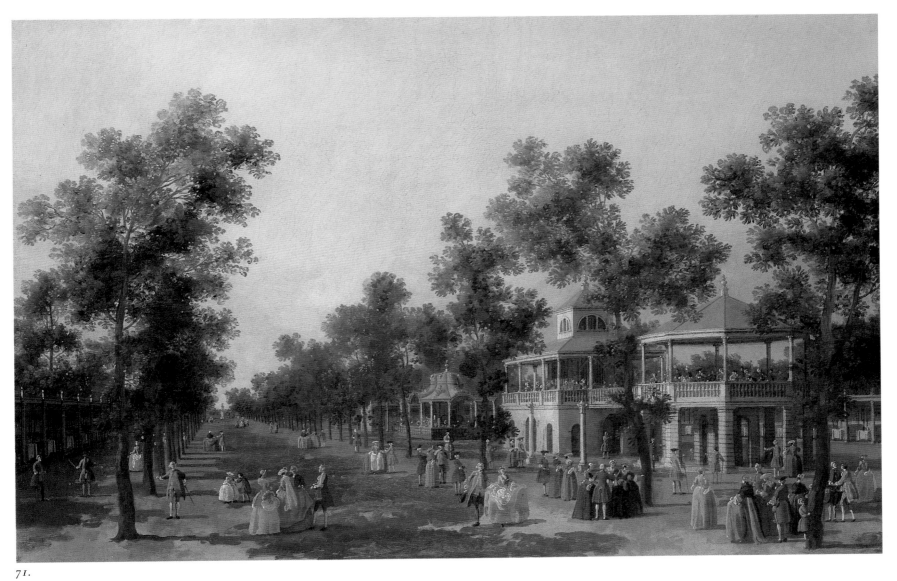

71.

Temple of Comus as seen in the engraving after Canaletto, for example, seems shortly thereafter to have been transformed by the addition of further embellishments into the Chinese Pavilions, as illustrated in a print by Bowles after Wale, which was also published in 1751.[3] As the purpose of such prints was promotional, out-of-date images would not have suited the purposes of either entrepreneur or publisher.

By comparison with the engraving of the Grand Walk, the present painting shows a less extensive view and there are many differences of detail. On account of the mannered handling of the faces and costumes, it must have come later, and perhaps the publication in 1751 of engravings of Vauxhall (and Ranelagh) after Canaletto brought some much-needed business to the artist's door in the following season. On the other hand, certain topographical details are difficult to account for: the orchestra pavilion and organ house appear as one much more elaborate structure in Maurer's etching of 1744 and Rocque's map of 1746.[4] It may be imagined that these buildings, with their pure and simple lines, had not looked as they do in this painting since prior to 1746, the year of Canaletto's arrival in London. As he was generally an accurate topographer, this would suggest that the commissioner of *Vauxhall Gardens* wanted a reminder of the earlier appearance of the pleasure garden, and that the painting was based on another image that we cannot now identify, or on a verbal description. Number 71 has a delicate, idyllic charm and is the only canvas by a major artist of this fashionable meeting place.

72. London: Ranelagh, interior of the Rotunda

Oil on canvas, 20⅛ × 29⅞ in. (51 × 76 cm)
Private Collection
C/L 421

Ranelagh, in the then village of Chelsea and within walking distance of St. James's, was opened in 1742 as a rival to Vauxhall Gardens, and the views here exhibited were painted as a pair.[1] The grounds were well appointed and provided with a canal, upon which a gondola carrying an orchestra rowed up and down, but the chief attraction was the Rotunda, built by William Jones and, as was often remarked, reminiscent of the Pantheon. The external diameter reportedly measured one hundred eighty-five feet, the internal, one hundred and fifty. The orchestra, originally installed at the center, was removed to one side, making room for the fireplace that warmed the encircling supper boxes, and this gave Ranelagh great advantage over Vauxhall on damp and chilly evenings. In all there were about a hundred boxes, each accommodating seven or eight people, and there was singing, as well as

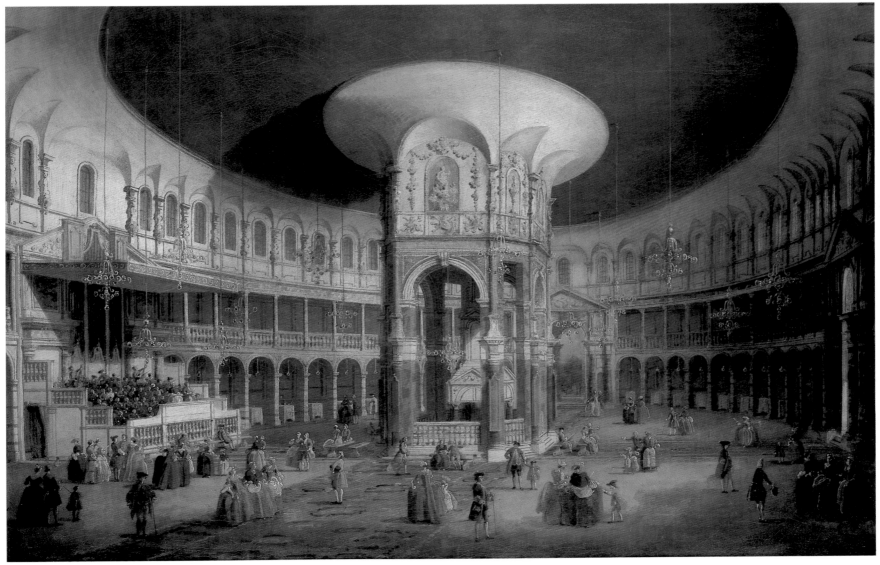

72.

EXHIBITED
Canada 106

NOTES
1. On Ranelagh, see Finberg, "Canaletto in England," 1920–21, pp. 43 and 60–62, who lists four prints, one of the interior and one of the exterior having certainly been published in 1751, and the variant of the present painting (C/L 420); and Levey, *The Eighteenth Century Italian Schools*, 1956, pp. 21–22, no. 1429
2. Hollis was also the owner of cat. no. 73.
3. Reproduced in C/L, pl. 181.
4. Reproduced in Corboz, *Canaletto*, 1985, II, p. 775, pl. s50.

orchestral and organ music, and occasionally dancing. The eight-year-old Mozart played his own compositions on the harpsichord and organ there in 1764. In this painting the orchestra numbers some thirty instrumentalists who seem to be playing. There are visitors walking or standing about listening to the music, but only one is seated in a box, and the balcony is still empty, suggesting that the hour is early. The interior is illuminated not by the many lamps and chandeliers, but by sunlight entering from the right; through the doorway on the opposite side the garden can be seen. The shadows assume soft, puffy shapes having little to do with nature, and the shape of the interior is slightly elongated, to permit a three-quarter view of the orchestra stand.

Canaletto painted another view of the interior of the Rotunda for Thomas Hollis (C/L 420), in 1754, which bears an inscription, now covered by the lining canvas, stating that it was done for the first and last time.[2] This was manifestly not the case. That picture, now in the National Gallery, London, is from the opposite viewpoint, with the orchestra on the right (see fig. 11). A print of the interior of Ranelagh Rotunda, differing in design and detail from both canvases, was published on the same date as the Vauxhall views, 2 December 1751. It is titled *An Inside View of the Rotundo in Ranelagh Gardens*, and was engraved by N. Parr after Canaletto.[3] As a companion piece—bearing the same date, issued by the same publisher, and also engraved by Parr after Canaletto—there was *A View of the Rotundo House, & Gardens, &c. at Ranelagh*.[4]

73. Old Walton Bridge

Oil on canvas, 19¼ × 30¼ in. (48.9 × 76.8 cm)
By Permission of the Governors of Dulwich
Picture Gallery
C/L 441

The bridge, some twenty-five miles upstream from Westminster, is seen from the north (Middlesex) bank of the Thames, looking southwest, and is presumably shown as it appeared in 1750, before the extension (seen in Canaletto's drawing, cat. no. 115) was built.[1] Its delicate, latticed superstructure appears to be curved and wider in the center, but old plans show it to have been straight and the bays of equal width throughout. Old Walton Bridge was paid for by Samuel Dicker, Member of Parliament, who lived in one of the houses among the trees on the opposite bank. An old label on the back gives the name of the original owner, Thomas Hollis, the English radical, known to have been a friend of Consul Joseph Smith. The inscription, which is covered by an old lining canvas, is transcribed as follows: *Fatto nel anno 1754. in Londra per la prima ed ultima volta con ogni maggior attentzione ad instanza del Signior Cavaliere Hollis padrone mio stimatiss°./Antonio Canal*

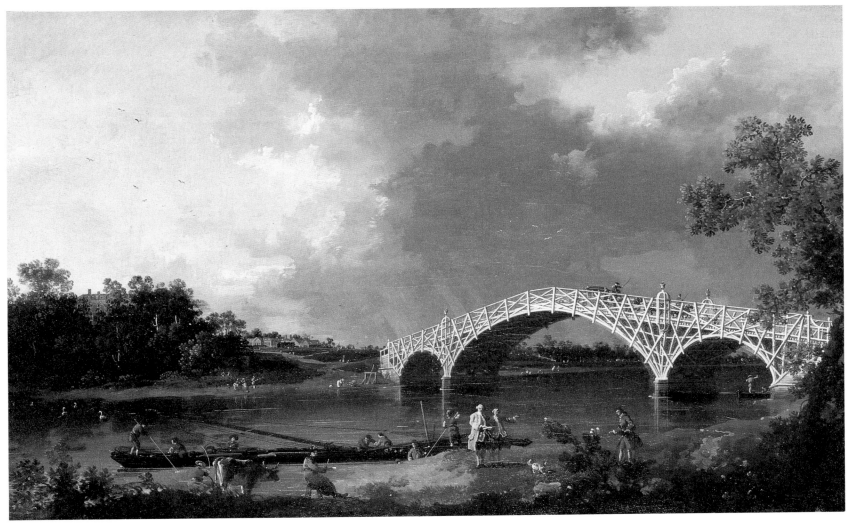

73.

251

EXHIBITED
Venice 108

NOTES

1. Peter Murray, *Dulwich Picture Gallery: A Catalogue* (London, 1980), p. 40, no. 600. For Hollis's commissions to Canaletto, Finberg remains the standard source, "Canaletto in England," 1920–21, pp. 41–44 and 66; see also J. G. Links, in *Collection for a King: Old Master Paintings from the Dulwich Picture Gallery*, exh. cat., National Gallery of Art, Washington, and Los Angeles County Museum of Art ([London?], 1985), pp. 44–46, no. 3; and Tessie Vecchi Doria, in *Canaletto*, 1982, no. 108, p. 78.

2. William T. Whitley, *Artists and Their Friends in England, 1700–1799* (London and Boston, 1928), I, pp. 118–19, quotes an old, privately printed catalogue of Hollis's pictures, in which number 73 is again recorded as having been painted in London in 1754. Portraits of the same figures and the dog are said to have been incorporated in Hollis's view of the Campidoglio (C/L 396) of 1755, for which see also Tessie Vecchi Doria, in *Canaletto*, 1982, no. 110, p. 79. Hollis and particularly his uncle, of the same name, were benefactors of Harvard University.

detto il Canaletto. Similar labels appear on five of the six pictures painted by Canaletto for Hollis who, according to a catalogue of his collection, appears in the foreground, with his friend Thomas Brand, to whom he bequeathed the painting, his servant Francisco Giovannini, and his dog Malta.[2] To the left is an artist at work, presumably Canaletto: he is seated on a low stool, pencil in hand, wearing a hat to shade his eyes from the sun and a long gown. A coach drawn by six horses crosses the wooden bridge, and the mast of the boat in the left foreground has been lowered, permitting the boatmen to pole their craft through the shallow water beneath.

Canaletto did not take his phrase "for the first and last time" very seriously, and it is far from certain that the words "painted in 1754" are correct. Some or all of Hollis's pictures, including this one, may well be of earlier date, and Canaletto painted the bridge a second time for Samuel Dicker (who received a similarly worded inscription) in 1755. From that painting he made a drawing, number 115, which was later engraved. None of Hollis's other pictures has the sensitivity and subtlety of this one, partly induced by the delicacy of the bridge (which had a short life of thirty years) and the changeable English weather. The inscriptions on the paintings of Hollis and Dicker and on Dicker's drawing are the only firm evidence of Canaletto's presence in England in 1754–55.

For the extent to which the painting may be capricious, see the catalogue entry for the drawing of the bridge.

74. London: Greenwich Hospital from the North Bank of the Thames

Oil on canvas, 27 × 41⅞ in. (68.5 × 106.5 cm)
National Maritime Museum, London
C/L 414

NOTE

1. R. K. Dickson, *Greenwich Palace: A History of What Is Now the Royal Naval College and the National Maritime Museum from Earliest Times to the Present Day* (Greenwich, 1948), pp. 13–35.

Some part of Greenwich Hospital, which houses the Royal Naval College and the National Maritime Museum, is built on the riverside site of the Palace of Placentia, birthplace of Henry VIII and Elizabeth I.[1] The oldest of the buildings now standing is the Queen's House, at the center, designed by Inigo Jones and completed in 1635 for Henrietta Maria, wife of Charles I (much of whose magnificent art collection was installed at Greenwich). After his execution the property was offered for sale by Parliament but, no buyers being found for a royal palace, it reverted to Charles II, during whose reign Lenôtre laid out the park, the King Charles building was erected to the west (part of the wing at the right), and the Royal Observatory took the place of an old castle on the hill. William and Mary founded the Royal Hospital in 1694

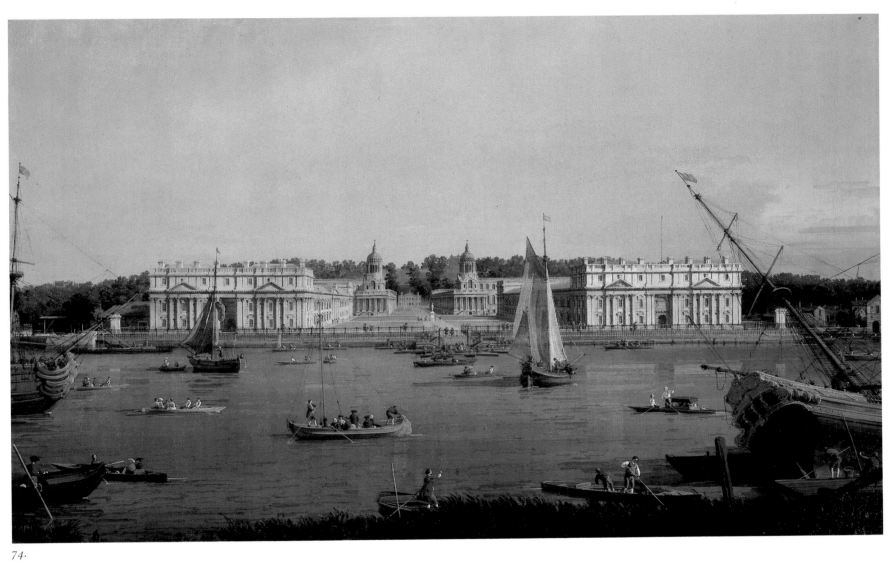

74.

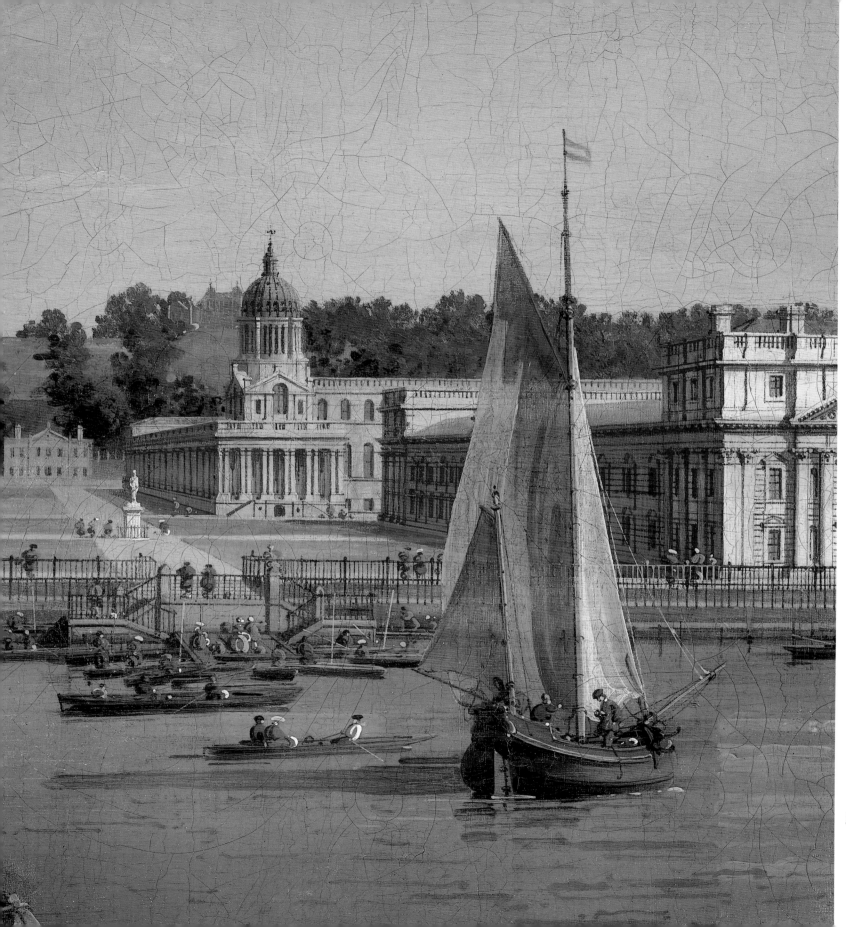

Detail of 74.

and—to designs of Wren, Hawksmoor, and their successors—it was largely completed in 1752.

The choice of subject for this canvas and a smaller and probably earlier version must have been inspired by the recent completion of Greenwich Hospital; they are among Canaletto's latest English views. The hospital is as seen from two viewpoints in a small park on the Isle of Dogs, now the site of the immense "Docklands" development. Wren's Greenwich Hospital, in its vast austerity and symmetry, is no more the subject than the shipping on the river, which always drew Canaletto's attention. He defined the limits of his composition with the prow of a barque and the careened stern of another sailing vessel, the rigging forming delicate, irregular webbed patterns against the water and the bright sky. Thames barges, rowboats, and pleasure boats ply between on the placid surface of the river.

Of the early history of this painting nothing is known. It was bought for the National Maritime Museum when on the London art market in 1939.

The Lovelace Capriccios

Canaletto is known to have received commissions for capriccios while he was in England, and a number of paintings of the kind that cannot be dated with confidence may well belong to the English years. There are many versions of some of these capriccios, and although there is no firm evidence, it is possible that in certain instances Canaletto may himself have been associated with their production. It seems unlikely that he presided over a studio of assistants in England, but he may have employed one or two in his later years there.

No other group of capriccios has the authenticity and interest of those known as the "Lovelace Canalettos," which were dispersed fifty years ago and are here reunited through the generosity of their various owners.[1] The fourth Earl of Lovelace, who consigned the six paintings to Sotheby's for sale in 1937, was descended from the third Lord King, who is said to have commissioned them. He, however, died in 1754, the date inscribed on number 77, and the commission may have been taken over by his brother, the fourth Lord King, who lived until 1767.

NOTE

1. Finberg, *Burlington Magazine*, 1938, pp. 69–70.

75. *Capriccio: River Landscape with a Ruin and Reminiscences of England*

Oil on canvas, 52 × 42 in. (132 × 106.7 cm)
National Gallery of Art, Washington;
Paul Mellon Collection
C/L 473

76. *Capriccio: River Landscape with a Column, a Ruined Roman Arch, and Reminiscences of England*

Oil on canvas, 52 × 41 in. (132 × 104.2 cm)
National Gallery of Art, Washington;
Paul Mellon Collection
C/L 474

The Kings lived at Ockham Place, Surrey, and both of these pictures suggest that Canaletto may have been asked to paint an English landscape with reminiscences of Italy, or vice versa.[1] Box Hill and Great Bookham, both near Ockham, are said to have provided the English elements, which may have been specifically suggested. There are no associated drawings of the English countryside, but many of the architectural motifs, Roman and perhaps also Paduan or Vicentine, appear in various of the highly finished, later *vedute ideate*: a Palladian villa and a bridge (C/L 782), a triumphal arch (C/L 808), the rough brickwork of another, and a freestanding column supporting a sculpture in the round (C/L 817), inventively combined—as here—in the interest of the picturesque. A number of these drawings are from Smith's collection, now at Windsor. Canaletto's renewed study of Roman monuments, resulting from Smith's commissions of the early forties, combined with his travels along the Brenta Canal and his visits to outlying areas

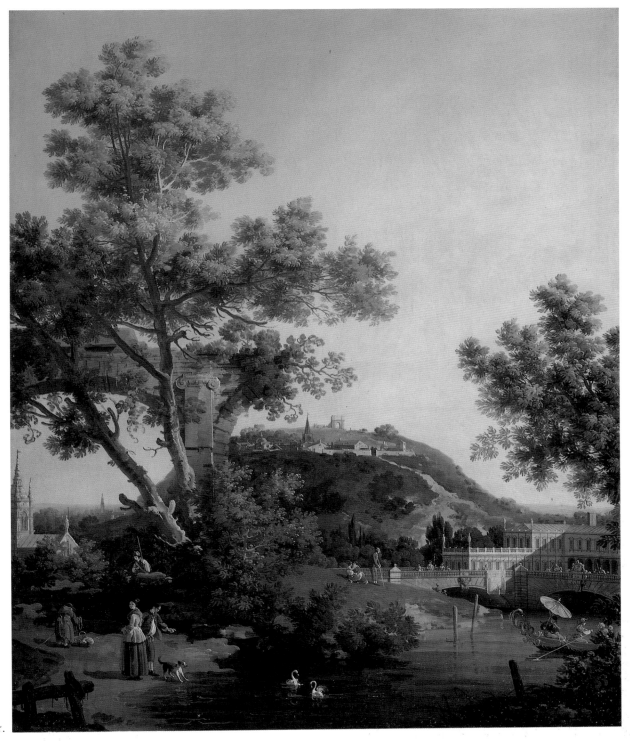

75.

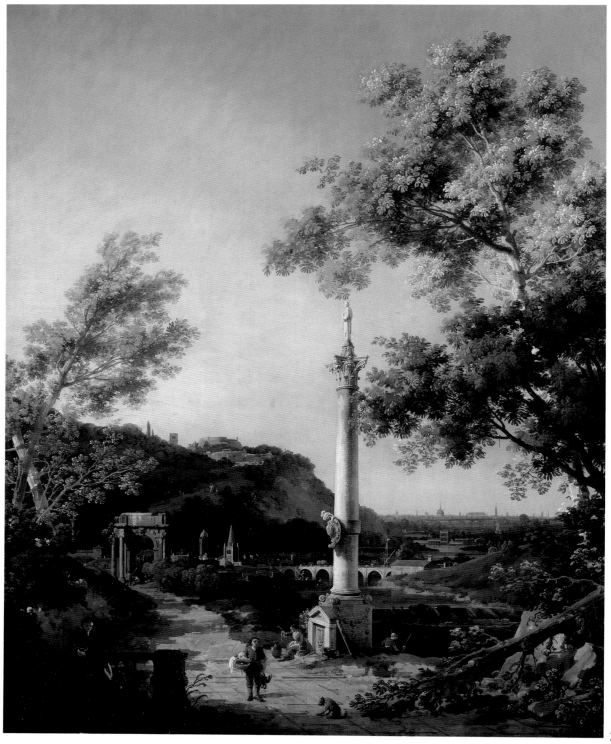

76.

of the Venetian lagoon, yielded material that continued to bear fruit while he was in England, and later again in Venice, until his death in 1768.

These are among the most exceptionally improbable, and successful, pictures of this type that Canaletto ever painted. The great English trees, at once decorative and closely observed, are combined with Italian architectural motifs varying dramatically as to period and style, and, in number 76, with a flat landscape of some complexity and brilliance. It comes as no surprise to find a Venetian lady shaded by a parasol afloat on the stream in an elaborately decorated pleasure boat. The paintings are among the many fine English Canalettos that formed part of Paul Mellon's collection.

NOTE

1. Fern Rusk Shapley, *Catalogue of the Italian Paintings*, National Gallery of Art (Washington, 1979), pp. 105–6, nos. 1909 and 1910.

77. Capriccio: a Sluice on a River, with a Reminiscence of Eton College Chapel

Oil on canvas, 32¼×45½ in. (81.9×115.6 cm)
Signed and dated (on the keystone of the arch):
A. C./1754
Private Collection
C/L 475

The small church or chapel on the left, abutted by a high stone wall, is in disrepair: weeds grow at the roof line, and a statue has fallen from one of the pinnacles. At an angle to this building and in front of a screen of shrubbery are a terrace with an arched opening beneath, a pool, a small weir, and a sluice gate in silhouette against the sky. The masts and in one case the sail of several small boats, their hulls hidden by the quay, lie in the near distance, and much farther away on the opposite bank of the river are a rotunda and other imaginary buildings. Canaletto used a straightedge to define the contours and courses of the stonework, which is smoothly and very precisely painted. By contrast the application of the priming with a coarse brush over most of the area of the sky must have been intended by the artist to give this particular and unusual effect. There is a related drawing (C/L 831), differing in many details and, exceptionally, reversing the composition.

Eton College Chapel is shown from the same angle in a painting (C/L 450) in the National Gallery, London, the details in both cases being far from the facts. It is generally assumed that a similarity to the chapel at Eton is intended, and if so Canaletto may have made a drawing of the chapel at the time he painted his picture of *Windsor Castle* (cat. no. 64) in 1747.

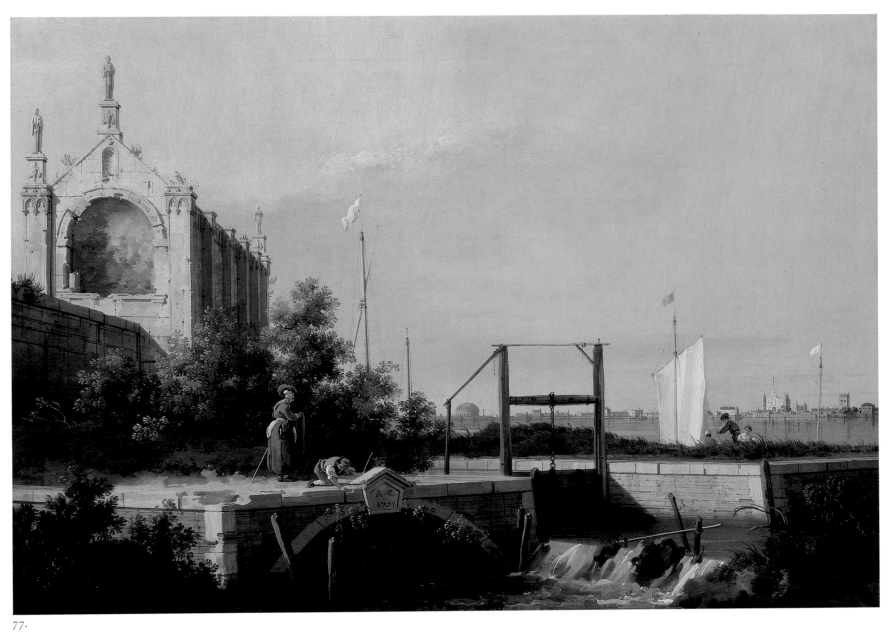

77·

78. The Island of S. Michele, with Venice in the Distance

Oil on canvas, 29½ × 48½ in. (75 × 123 cm)
Private Collection
C/L 367

NOTE

1. Pignatti, "'Sei Villaggi Campestri' dal Canaletto," 1969, pp. 23–28.

A small house stands just at the water's edge, and beside it is a walled enclosure opening onto the lagoon by way of a high wooden jetty. To the right, beyond the bank, the stone wall, and the roofs, is the campanile of the church of S. Michele, which stands on what is now the cemetery island. Venice can be seen in the distance, with the dome of S. Pietro di Castello at the extreme left, and the facade and bell tower of S. Francesco della Vigna. The picture takes its place comfortably among the imaginary views, though the buildings in Venice are more or less in their correct positions.

The scene must have appealed to Canaletto. Before leaving Venice he had made for Smith an ink drawing, now at Windsor (C/L 653), in which the skyline of Venice, the house, and the buildings beyond the wall, as well as the figures and boats, differ in various details. Another, more finished drawing with several washes (cat. no. 108) closely approximates the painting in its layout. Including these two drawings, at least six versions are known, one of them probably a copy by another hand.

After Canaletto's return to Venice, about 1755, three series of etchings after his drawings were published by Josef Wagner. Of six small prints in the set entitled *Sei Villaggi Campestri*, one, by Wagner himself, was based on the present image, and a second, by Fabio Berardi, on another composition represented in the Lovelace series (cat. no. 80).[1] Both are in reverse to the paintings and drawings described.

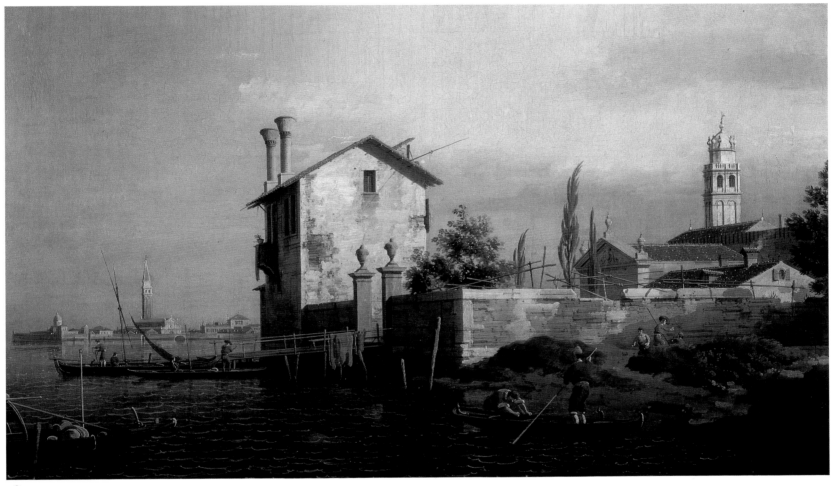

78.

79. Capriccio: Ruins with a Domed Church and the Colleoni Monument

Oil on canvas, 59¼ × 53⅛ in. (150.5 × 134.9 cm)
Private Collection
C/L 478

NOTE

1. Another composition was originally envisaged by Canaletto, as demonstrated by X-radiographs taken in the hope of shedding light on the numerous pentimenti and slight irregularities of surface. Beneath the church and fountain at the center is a much larger domed church resembling Sta. Maria della Salute, with a building or colonnade to the right and parallel to the picture plane. In the distance at the left there is a column, and behind the figure at the lower left an antique capital. It is difficult to imagine what motive would have occasioned so dramatic a change, particularly as X-radiographs of Canaletto's paintings rarely show significant discrepancies from the picture surface. On this point see Mucchi and Bertuzzi, *Nella profondità dei dipinti*, 1983, pp. 59–84 and 167–68, figs. 83–141.

This is one of the most unlikely of all of the painted capriccios in its combination, and compression, of unrelated motifs.[1] To the left, in the distance, is an antique arch not unlike the Arch of Titus, the subject of one of the five Roman paintings dated 1742, of which the *Arch of Constantine* (cat. no. 59) is another. In the background to the right, at the end of a paved street, is the Colosseum, and among the houses a freestanding Corinthian column carrying a statue, of the sort found in an etched view of Padua and in an imaginary drawing at Windsor (C/L 817), where it is likewise combined with a ruined masonry arch. The Colleoni equestrian bronze and its pedestal are accurately observed, from the direction opposite to that taken in the views of *SS. Giovanni e Paolo* (cat. nos. 5 and 10). The same bronze statue, facing left, and the antique arch also figure in an overdoor (C/L 476), dated 1744, which was one of the series commissioned by Smith and eventually sold to George III. Further, there is a painting in reverse to this one (C/L 477), much wider and with variations of detail, whose early history is unknown. In the present painting the precipitous recession from the foreground into the distance left and right increases the air of unreality. The figures—such as the boy in cap and apron carrying a wig—are exceptionally large and closely observed.

This painting and its companion, number 80, provide a rare chronological anchor for the later imaginary views: belonging as they do to a set of which one is dated 1754 (cat. no. 77), they are representative of the artist's work during his last years in England. Canaletto specialized in such dizzying combinations of buildings and other monuments—Venetian, Paduan, and Roman; he had been composing works of the kind for more than a decade and presumably continued to do so until the end of his life. Many are the difficulties encountered in dating (and in some cases attributing) the capriccios, and the Lovelace series is an important point of reference.

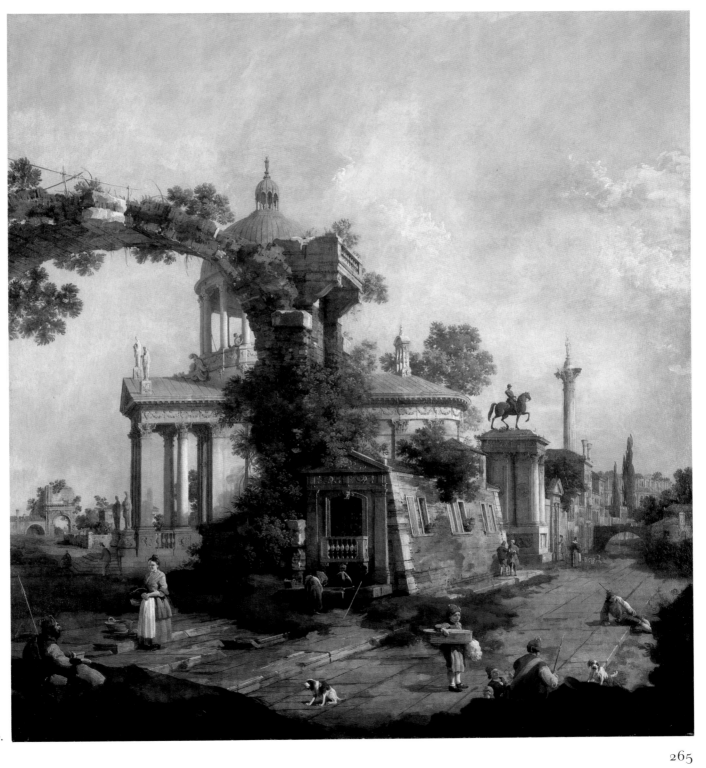

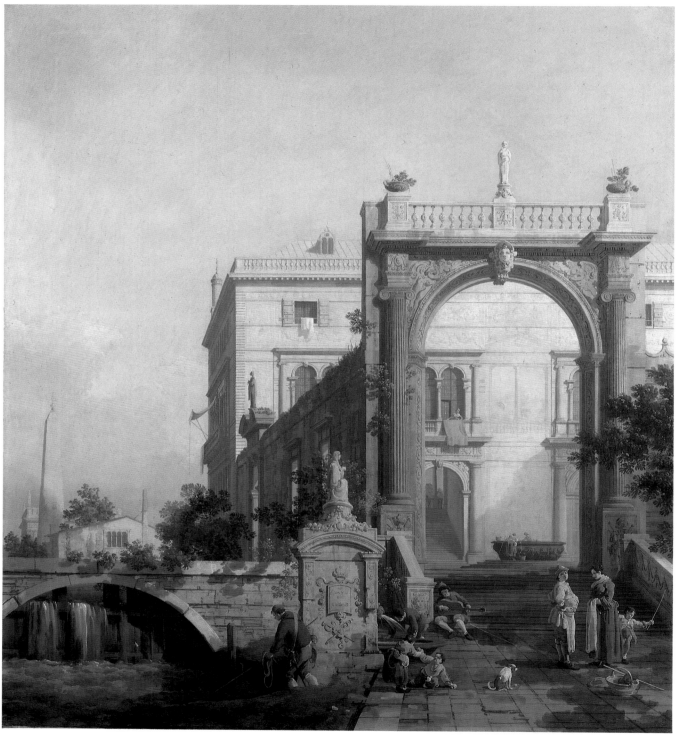

80.

80. Capriccio: with a Palace, a Bridge, and an Obelisk

Oil on canvas, 59¼ × 53⅛ in. (150.5 × 134.9 cm)
Private Collection
C/L 504

NOTE
1. Russell, *Burlington Magazine*, 1988, pp. 627–29.

The subject has long been known in two versions, the second of these (C/L 502) having no recorded early history. A third variant, recently published, was at Chesterfield House, London, before February 1752.[1] That painting is of unusual shape and has as a pendant a capriccio based on a drawing in the Royal Collection (cat. no. 107). Unless the Lovelace commission included pictures painted well before the dated *Sluice on a River*, number 77, it must be concluded that Canaletto reused at least one earlier composition. The arch and the palace figure in a related drawing (C/L 819) belonging to the Cleveland Museum of Art; there are differing opinions as to whether it dates from before or after the paintings.

The upright Italian capriccios (cat. nos. 79, 80) vary significantly in size from the upright views incorporating English landscapes (cat. nos. 75, 76), and it seems reasonable to picture the two pairs on the side walls of a room at Ockham Place, with numbers 77 and 78 at the ends, possibly as overdoors.

Venice: The Final Years

The first that is known of Canaletto after his departure from England, where he remained until 1755, as evinced by the date on the drawing of *Old Walton Bridge* (cat. no. 115), is his meeting in 1760 with John Crewe, described in the entry for the drawing of Piazza S. Marco (cat. no. 116). The few paintings that follow were executed after his return to Venice, most if not all of them in the early 1760s. The latest dated work is a drawing (cat. no. 127) of 1766, inscribed in Canaletto's hand with a note that it was made in his sixty-eighth year. The artist was not among the thirty-six founding members of the Accademia Veneziana di Pittura e Scultura, which was established in 1756, there being a bias in favor of figure painters, but he was eventually admitted, in September 1763. Canaletto died on 19 April 1768 and was buried in one of the communal tombs of the confraternity of the Santissimo Spirito at S. Lio, in the *contrada* of his birth.

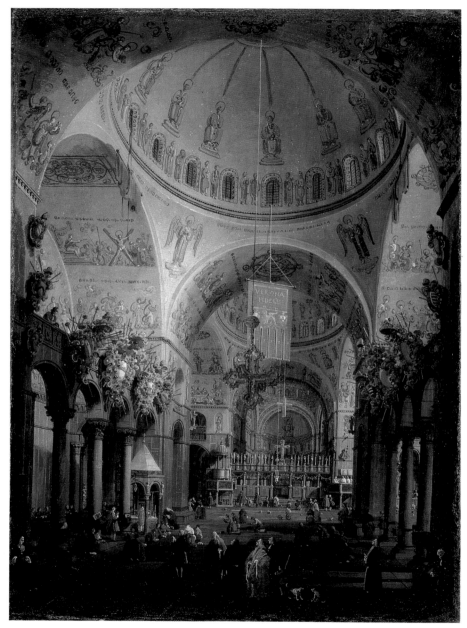

81.

81. S. Marco: the Interior

Oil on canvas, 17⅜ × 12⅜ in. (44.1 × 31.5 cm)
The Montreal Museum of Fine Arts's Collection;
Adaline Van Horne Bequest
C/L 79

EXHIBITED
Canada 116

The view of the interior of the eleventh-century basilica is eastward, from the Arco dell'Apocalisse toward the rood screen, which is festooned with garlands. Though no service is in progress at the high altar, the tall candles between the sculptures on the screen are lit, and there are a number of choristers in the ambo to the right. A priest officiates at the small altar or *capitello* beneath the nave arcade to the left, and a number of worshipers, some kneeling, attend. From a window in the Cupola della Pentecoste and in front of the Cupola dell'Ascensione hangs a banner inscribed VERONA FIDELIS. The practice of installing the coats of arms of the Doges in S. Marco had been disallowed in the early 1720s, but many of them may be seen here, and perhaps they were put up for certain feast days or on other occasions. The columns and the marble floor and revetment are largely undifferentiated, but the mosaic decoration, strongly lit from the south, is lovingly detailed: the Holy Spirit descending in tongues of flame toward the seated apostles around the Cupola della Pentecoste, for example, the angels in the pendentives below, and to the left, St. Andrew before the Proconsul and martyred upon the cross.

The picture has as pendant the *Scala dei Giganti* (C/L 81), or Giants' Staircase, in the courtyard of Palazzo Ducale. Nothing is known of the early history of these paintings. A smaller version of the interior of S. Marco (C/L 78), of differing proportions, was included among works sold to George III by Joseph Smith and is probably the consul's last commission to Canaletto. A rough sketch of the interior of S. Marco (cat. no. 124) has often been associated with these views. The paintings may be dated after Canaletto's return to Venice, about 1755, and before the sale of Smith's collection, about 1762.

A Commission from Sigismund Streit

Sigismund Streit (1687–1775) was born in Berlin and educated there at the secondary school Zum Grauen Kloster. Established in Venice from 1709, he made a considerable fortune as a merchant; he retired in 1750 and from 1754 lived primarily in Padua, where he died in 1775. A bachelor, he decided shortly after his retirement to provide his school with an endowment, and eventually he also presented his library and a small collection of paintings. The four Canalettos (cat. nos. 82, 83; and C/L 242, C/L 360), sent to

269

NOTES

1. Erich Schleier, in *Catalogue of Paintings: 13th–18th Century*, Picture Gallery Berlin, Staatliche Museen Preussischer Kulturbesitz (Berlin-Dahlem, 1978), pp. 85–88; Haskell, *Patrons and Painters*, 1980, pp. 315–16; and Erich Schleier, in *Canaletto*, 1982, pp. 79–87, nos. 111–14. Schleier's exhaustive and very fascinating account (1982) of Streit, his collection, and his commission to Canaletto is the source of the summary provided here.

2. In addition to C/L, pp. 641–46, see Miotti, "Tre disegni inediti del Canaletto," 1966, pp. 275–78. The drawings are now in Trieste.

Berlin in 1763, were extensively described by Streit in a list documenting his gifts to the Gymnasium zum Grauen Kloster.[1] Two of the series (cat. no. 82 and C/L 242, for which see fig. 8) are replete with personal associations, while the other two (cat. no. 83 and C/L 360) represent night festivals at Venice. The paintings, though undated, may now be assigned with some degree of certainty to the artist's later years in Venice.

Of the two not exhibited here, one represents the *Grand Canal: looking Southeast from the Campo Sta. Sofia to the Rialto Bridge* and the other the *Festival on the Eve of Sta. Marta*. In the Grand Canal view, at the left and on the far side of Campo Sta. Sofia, is Palazzo Foscari, where Streit lived and—in rooms overlooking the *campo*—had his place of business. A *burchiello* of the sort plying between Venice and Padua (the German merchant must often have used this form of transportation) is moored opposite, and beyond, on the *riva*, are several hostelries named by Streit, with the Fabbriche Nuove di Rialto beyond and, in the distance, a partial view of the Rialto Bridge.

The festival of Sta. Marta was celebrated primarily by the fishermen of the area around S. Niccolò dei Mendicoli, where the church and convent of Sta. Marta stood facing the lagoon beyond the westward end of the Giudecca Canal. Much of this entire quarter has long since been absorbed into the modern maritime station, with its warehouses and other facilities; it is an area that would have been familiar to a Venetian or long-time resident, but probably not to an occasional visitor.

Three sheets from the Corniani Algarotti album are preparatory to the two pictures described above: the reverse and obverse of one of them (C/L 596) afford a continuous view of the corner of Palazzo Sagredo, Campo Sta. Sofia, and the side and Grand Canal facades of Palazzo Foscari, while the others (C/L 617, 618) form a panorama of the buildings represented in the painting of the festival of Sta. Marta.[2]

82. Campo di Rialto

Oil on canvas, 46⅞ × 73¾ in. (119 × 186 cm)
Staatliche Museen Preussischer Kulturbesitz, Gemäldegalerie Berlin (loan of the Streit Foundation, Berlin)
C/L 282

By way of the gondola *traghetto* at Sta. Sofia, crossing the Grand Canal to the fish market opposite, Streit would have reached this *campo*, center of commerce and banking, in a few minutes time. The view is toward the west, so that the Rialto Bridge and the church of S. Giacomo (for which see cat. no. 7) lie behind the spectator. The Ruga degli Orefici (goldsmiths) and the Palazzo dei Dieci Savi are at the left, in shadow, with the campanile of S. Giovanni Elemosinario beyond, while the buildings at center and right are the Fabbriche Vecchie di Rialto. Vegetables, meat, and fowl are for sale

270

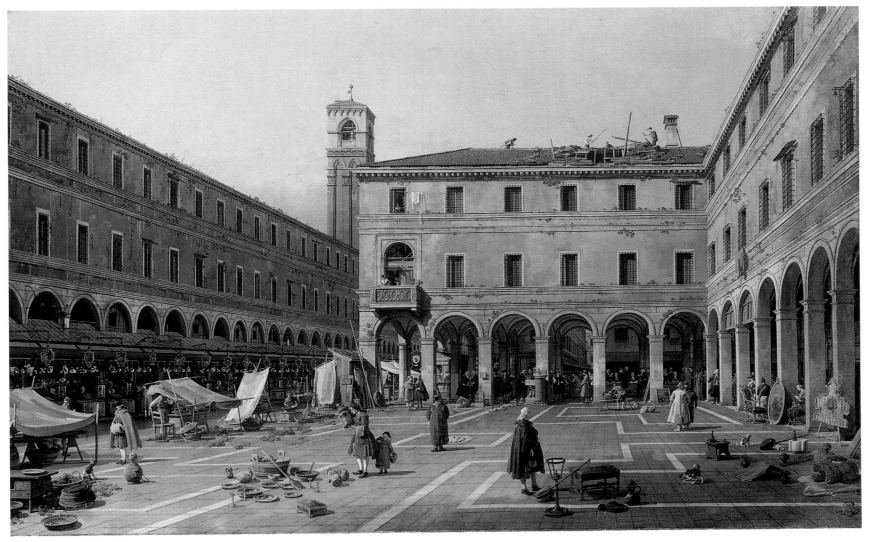

82.

271

EXHIBITED

Venice 112

NOTES

1. Rizzi, *Carlevarijs*, 1967, etching fig. 107.
2. Erich Schleier, in *Canaletto*, 1982, p. 85.

in the *campo*, as well as paintings, furniture, pottery, and other household goods. The vendors of objects in precious metals are more permanently established in stalls along the footpath bearing their name, and under the arcades to the west black-robed clerks transact the business of the state bank in the open air. Armenians in long coats and pointed hats and Jews in red caps people the square, and above, against the skyline, workmen repair and relay the red tile roof of the Fabbriche Vecchie.

The *campo* appears to be very much larger than it is; Carlevaris's print of the subject gives a more accurate impression.[1] As Erich Schleier points out, number 82 must have been painted in or after 1758, the earliest possible date for the pavement with its white meander pattern, which may still be seen there.[2] The entire series, it may be supposed, is datable to within four or five years of its dispatch to Streit's secondary school in Berlin.

83. *Night Festival at S. Pietro di Castello*

Oil on canvas, 46⅞ × 73⅝ in. (119 × 187 cm)
Staatliche Museen Preussischer Kulturbesitz, Gemälde-
galerie Berlin (loan of the Streit Foundation, Berlin)
C/L 359

One of four Venetian night festivals, the *festa* at S. Pietro took place each year on 28 June, the eve of the feast day of SS. Peter and Paul. The church and bell tower, backlit by moonlight, are seen from the far side of the Canale di S. Pietro, with, at the right, the plank footbridge leading to the island of Castello, which is at the northeastern corner of Venice, near the shipyards of the Arsenale. The building at the center, lit from within, was the residence of the Patriarch of Venice (the patriarchate was not transferred to S. Marco until the early nineteenth century), but was mistaken by Streit in his description of the picture for the canons' house.[1] In the *campo*, perhaps under the awnings, sweets were sold, and a puppet show is also in progress.

Moonlit views are extremely rare, in Canaletto's work, and in Venetian view painting in general. Among his near contemporaries, neither Carlevaris nor Francesco Guardi painted anything of the kind. It is possible that Streit, who must have chosen the subjects, was dissatisfied with Canaletto's night festival paintings: Schleier hypothesizes that the German merchant may on that account have commissioned from Gaspare Diziani's son, Antonio, a more extensive festival series of six canvases, painted shortly thereafter.[2]

Of the four views painted by Canaletto for Sigismund Streit, three (cat. nos. 82, 83, and C/L 360) were engraved by Giovanni Battista Brustoloni —two of these from drawings (one of which may be C/L 282[c]) by *Jo. Bap. Moretti et Filii*—and published by Lodovico Furlanetto, not earlier and possibly later than 1763, in the series *Prospectuum...Urbis Venetiarum*.[3]

EXHIBITED

Venice 113

NOTES

1. Erich Schleier, in *Canaletto*, 1982, p. 86.
2. Erich Schleier, in *Canaletto*, 1982, pp. 80–81.
3. Dario Succi, in *Da Carlevarijs ai Tiepolo*, 1983, pp. 83–86,
   and fig. 55, the print, in the same sense, after number 83. See
   also cat. nos. 122, 123.

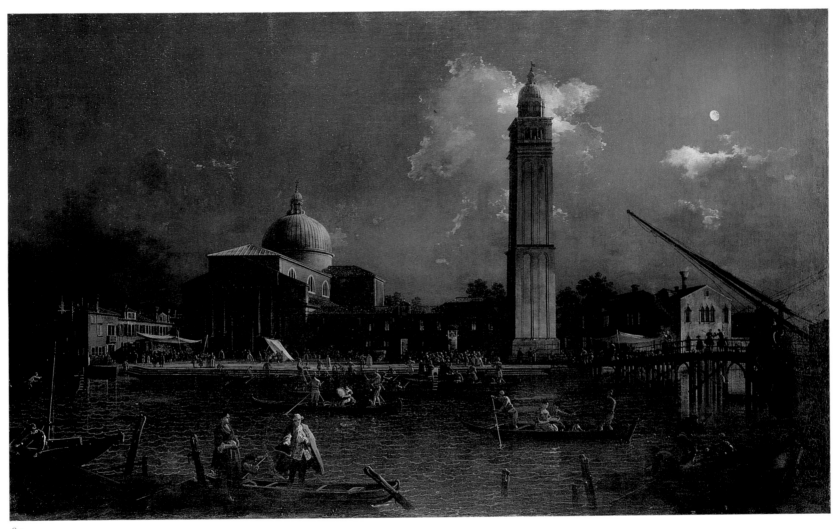

83.

273

84. Piazza S. Marco: looking South and West

Oil on canvas, 23 × 40⅝ in. (58.5 × 103.2 cm)
Los Angeles County Museum of Art; Gift of the
Ahmanson Foundation
C/L 54*

The view is from the Campo S. Basso (Piazzetta dei Leoncini), the area shown in number 55, to which the spectator would have had his back. The Torre dell'Orologio, or Clock Tower, in the right foreground, appears with its facade altered and a set-back top story added, work that was done about 1755. There is of course no point from which all of the elements of this composition could be seen simultaneously. The northward arch of S. Marco is shown open to its full height, although the top is in fact walled up. The foliage on the column in the left foreground might be intended as a reference to the capricious nature of the picture.

On removal of the relining canvas in 1971 the following inscription was found on the reverse: *Io Antonio Canal, detto il Canaletto, fecit. 1763* (I Antonio Canal, called Canaletto, made this. 1763). Canaletto had painted and drawn several of these "impossible" views before (there is one at the Wadsworth Atheneum, Hartford, C/L 54), but none of these is inscribed. In September 1763 he was elected to the Venetian Academy after having been passed over the previous January in favor of two artists now forgotten. There can be little doubt that this was because he was a view painter, a genre which did not find favor with the academicians.

The scale of the painting and the presence of the inscription, taken together with the fact that number 84 incorporates so many of the motifs for which over forty years the artist had shown a preference, suggest that he may have intended it for the Academy. If so, his fellow academicians perhaps indicated that a view painting would not be welcomed as a reception piece. The capriccio he finally gave the Academy, number 85, is dated 1765, and more than two hundred years were to pass before major examples of his work as a *vedutista* (cat. nos. 3, 4) could be seen in Venice.

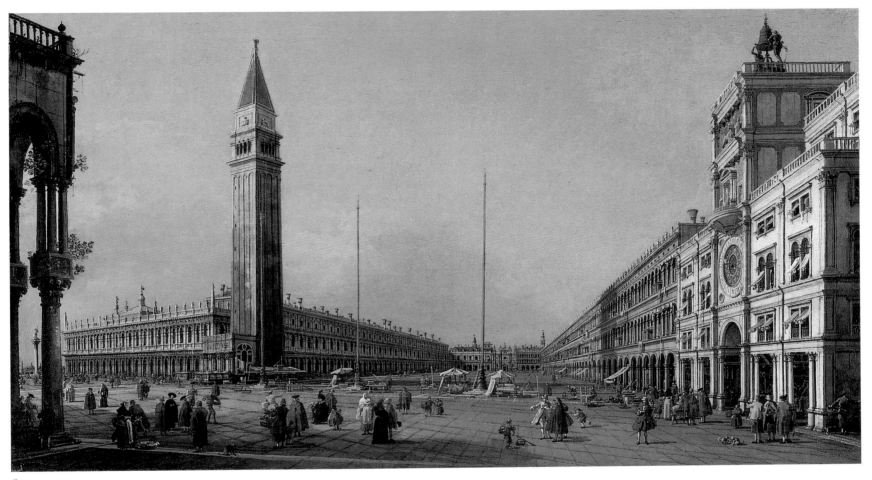

84.

85. Capriccio: a Colonnade Opening on to the Courtyard of a Palace

Oil on canvas, 51⅝ × 36⅝ in. (131 × 93 cm)
Signed and dated: ANTON . . . 1765
Gallerie dell'Accademia, Venice
C/L 509

EXHIBITED
Venice 116

NOTES
1. Sandra Moschini Marconi, in *Galleria dell'Accademia di Venezia: Opere d'arte dei secoli XVII, XVIII, XIX* (Rome, 1970), pp. 8–9, no. 13; and Giovanna Nepi Schiré, in *Canaletto*, 1982, pp. 87–88, no. 116.
2. Corboz, "Un capriccio non tanto capriccioso," in *Canaletto*, 1982, pp. 102–4; and Corboz, *Canaletto*, 1985, pp. 329, 387, and 433.

The signature is imperfectly preserved, but the date is reliable, the canvas having been presented by Canaletto, two years after his election as academician, to the Venetian Accademia di Pittura e Scultura.[1] There is a closely corresponding drawing (C/L 822), of whose early history nothing is known, and a sheet of rather slight sketches (C/L 626), one or more of which may in some way be connected with the design. The latter is inscribed by Canaletto *Per la cademia*.

To honor Canaletto, his capriccio was exhibited in Piazza S. Marco for the Festa della Sensa in 1777, and Zanetti referred to it in the second edition of *Della pittura veneziana* (1792). Engraved by Josef Wagner in 1779 as *Opera di Antonio Canal Pittor Accademico*, this painting must have enjoyed some celebrity during the artist's lifetime and in the years after his death, as Constable catalogues eight replicas, of which one or more may be autograph. There is no other painting by Canaletto in the Accademia and, until recently, it was the only work by the artist on public exhibition in Venice. Insofar as is known, and the question of replicas aside, number 85 is the latest painting from Canaletto's hand. Of the drawings exhibited, number 127 dates to the following year, and two others (cat. nos. 122, 123) belong to a series that may be from the same period.

André Corboz has remarked on the fluidity of the boundary between the real and the imaginary in Canaletto's art. For two hundred years or more number 85 has been regarded as a demonstration of perspective and a work of pure invention, but it may in fact be firmly anchored in Venetian topography.[2] Such a courtyard—with an exterior staircase and a wellhead at the center, paralleled by a portico supported on widely spaced columns—is to be found at Ca' d'Oro, on the Grand Canal, and if indeed Ca' d'Oro is the source, then Canaletto transformed a well-known Gothic palace into an apparently wildly capricious and unreal structure of baroque design. Only the (misplaced) Gothic portal remains. The other doorway, on the landing of the staircase, is after a design by Carlo Rainaldi for Palazzo Grillo in Rome—an architectural detail with which Canaletto would have been familiar through the medium of engraving. We do not know how the capriccio was received by his fellow academicians, nor the extent to which they may have appreciated a tissue of allusion that is perhaps an essential part of its fabric, yet beyond our full understanding.

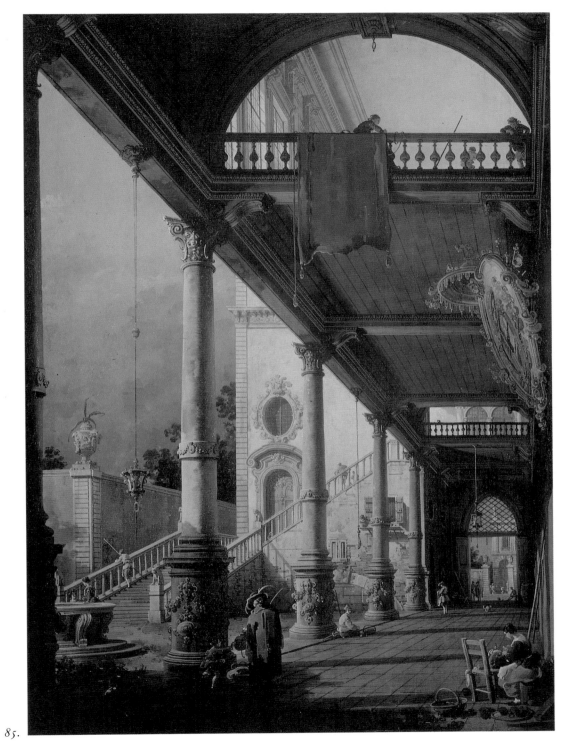

DRAWINGS

86. *Grand Canal: the Rialto Bridge from the North*

Pen and brown ink with red and black chalk, 5½ × 8 in. (14 × 20.2 cm)
The Ashmolean Museum, Oxford
C/L 593

EXHIBITED
Venice 3

NOTES

1. It has been suggested by Pignatti, *Canaletto: Selected Drawings*, 1970, no. 1r, that *lerberia* in the inscription is a misreading, for *Carbon*, but the word appears clearly in Canaletto's letter to Conti describing the painting, for which see the Appendix.
2. K. T. Parker, *Catalogue of the Collection of Drawings in the Ashmolean Museum* (Oxford, 1956), II, pp. 489–90, no. 975; and Bettagno, in *Canaletto*, 1982, pp. 35–36, no. 3.
3. Haskell, *Burlington Magazine*, 1956, p. 298.
4. For a facsimile reproduction of the figure studies, see Pignatti, *Canaletto: Selected Drawings*, 1970, no. 1v ill.

The inscription in Canaletto's hand reads: *Veduta del ponte di rialto infacza lerberia* (View of the Rialto Bridge opposite the vegetable market).[1] The drawing, probably a leaf from a sketchbook, is closely related to Stefano Conti's view of the same subject, number 8.[2] The word *Sole* is written at the point where the sun strikes the water in the painting. If number 86 was used by Canaletto as a preparatory drawing, as seems likely, the inscription suggests that he later gave it away. The drawing has been in the Ashmolean Museum since 1855 and, although it was always associated with the Conti picture, there was no certainty that it might not have been used for another of the same subject. The appearance of the companion drawing, number 87, which must have been used in connection with Conti's pendant view of the Grand Canal looking north, removes any doubts.

Alessandro Marchesini, in a letter to Conti, used the words "esso dipinge sopra il loco," which have been taken to mean that Canaletto painted on the site, as Marchesini must have intended.[3] It is possible that Marchesini felt justified in using the word "dipinge" after seeing this drawing, with its detailed presentation of the proposed composition. Number 86 could not have been drawn from any single viewpoint.

On the reverse of the sheet are some figure studies (C/L 833), reminiscent of Carlevaris and probably of an earlier date.[4]

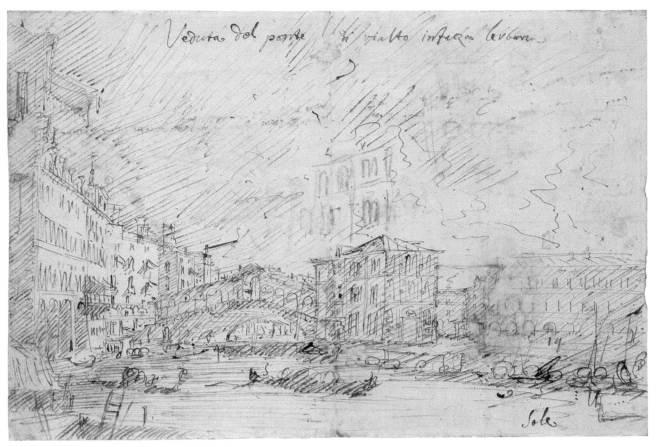

Veduta del ponte di rialto inverso levante

Sole

86.

281

87. Grand Canal: looking North from near the Rialto Bridge

Pen and brown ink, 6⅞ × 11¼ in. (17.5 × 28.5 cm)
Dr. Carlo M. Croce
C/L 592* (1989 ed.)

The drawing is inscribed, in Canaletto's hand, *Fondamenta*, above the approach to the Rialto Bridge. For the artist's description of the scene, see the entry for Conti's painting, number 9, where the scaffolding for the Palazzo Corner della Regina is also depicted. The presence of this scaffolding makes it certain that the drawing is associated with Conti's canvas of the same subject rather than with any of several other versions. The background buildings could not be seen at all from the purported viewpoint. In the drawing they are shown in correct proportion from the point which does bring them into view, whereas in the painting they are made to appear much closer.

The present drawing first appeared in the London salerooms in 1984. Nothing is known of its early history, though it may have belonged at one time to the owner of number 86. The two drawings differ significantly in size and would not have been conceived as a pair.

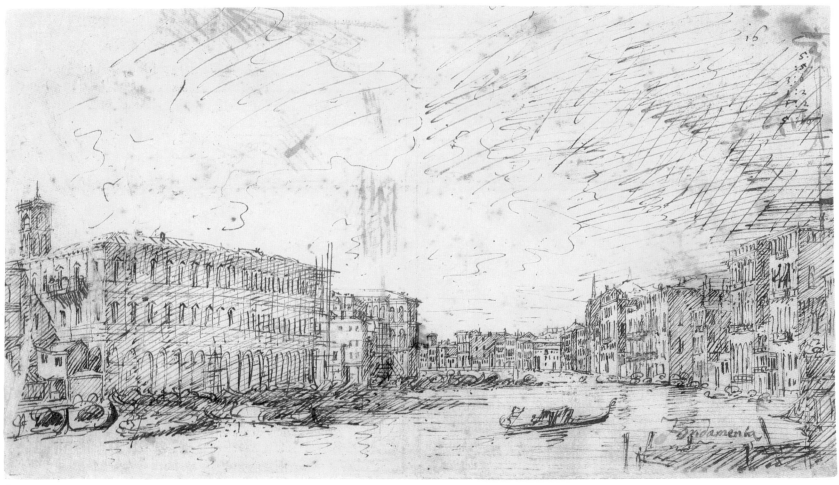

87.

88. The Piazzetta: looking North

Pen and brownish black ink over pencil, 9¼ × 7⅛ in.
(23.4 × 18 cm)
Her Majesty Queen Elizabeth II
C/L 548

NOTE

1. Parker, *Drawings of Canaletto*, 1948, p. 29, no. 2; and
   Pignatti, *Canaletto: Selected Drawings*, 1970, no. III. The
   other four drawings in this series are C/L 524, 530, 532,
   and 542.

For each of the six great paintings of Piazza S. Marco and the Piazzetta, which formed Canaletto's first commission from Joseph Smith, there is a drawing in pen and brown ink, of which this and number 89 are two.[1] They are not preliminary sketches, made on the ground, but more probably drawings for discussion between artist and patron as to the form the proposed paintings were to take, in this case the one with the same title, number 28 in the present exhibition.

The figures play an important part in the painting, but are only vaguely indicated in the drawing, and the Procurator and his attendant are not even suggested. In the painting the foreground was made more spacious to balance them. The viewpoint was moved slightly to the left so that more of the facade of S. Marco and less of the Biblioteca Marciana can be seen. The three flagstaffs, barely indicated at all in the drawing, play a prominent part in the painting. The distribution of the passages of deep shade that structure the composition have, however, been carried over from the compositional study to the finished work. Already, in the drawing, the artist made a number of departures from the facts in the cause of a better picture. The distance between the Library, on the left, and the column of St. Theodore, on the right, has been greatly widened. From the chosen viewpoint the Loggetta, at the base of the Campanile, partly obscures the Torre dell'Orologio so, for the background, Canaletto took a second viewpoint well to the right, from which the Clock Tower building can be seen in its entirety. Comparison of painting and drawing reveals much about Canaletto's method of working, but the site itself must be seen to make the comparison complete.

Drawing and painting have never before appeared together in the same exhibition.

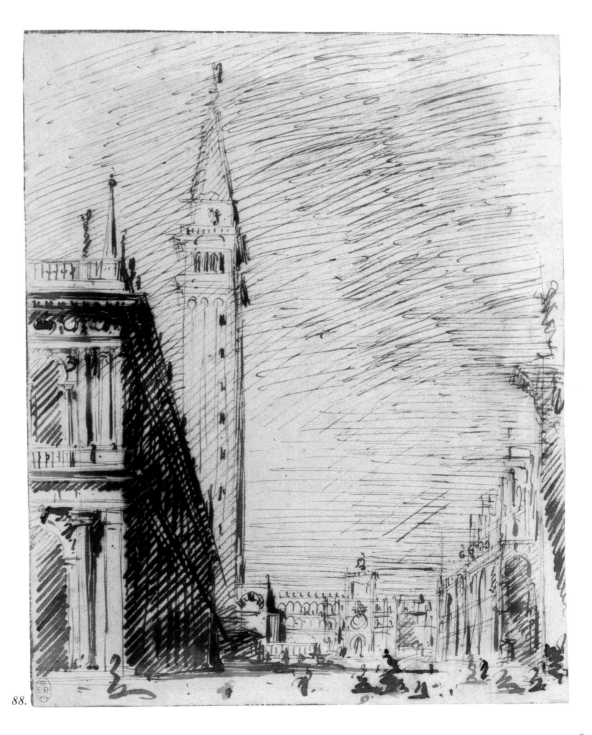

88.

89. Entrance to the Grand Canal: from the Piazzetta

Pen and brown ink over pencil, 9⅛ × 7⅛ in. (23.3 × 18.2 cm)
Her Majesty Queen Elizabeth II
C/L 580

EXHIBITED

London 49

NOTE

1. Parker, *Drawings of Canaletto*, 1948, p. 29, no. 3; Miller, in *Canaletto*, 1980, pp. 87–88, no. 49; and Miller, *Fifty Drawings by Canaletto*, 1985, no. 4.

As Charlotte Miller points out, the hatching is less dense in this drawing than in number 88, creating a less ominous atmosphere; unlike the other drawings in the series, there are no ruled lines in the architecture.[1] The position of the four elements of the scene—column, church, steps, and part of the Library—is quite arbitrary, there being no point from which they could be seen as portrayed. This also applies to the resulting canvas (cat. no. 29), in which the column was moved to a less dominant position in front of the Library, and the statue of St. Theodore was exchanged for the lion of St. Mark. One freely drawn figure appears here at the base of the column whereas in the painting the enlarged foreground is peopled with some of Canaletto's most detailed and vivid figures (see fig. 23).

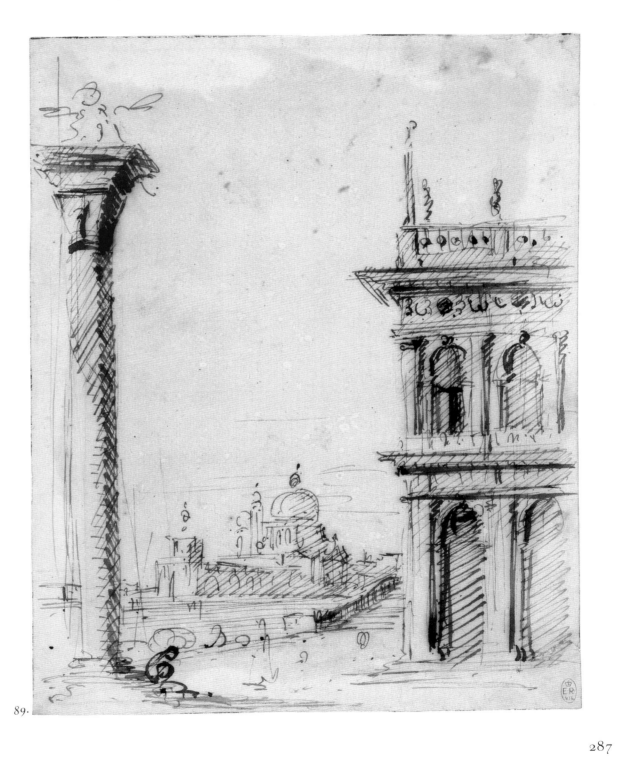

89.

90. *Grand Canal: the Rialto Bridge from the South*

Pen and brown ink over pencil, 5⅝ × 8 in. (14.2 × 20.3 cm)
The Metropolitan Museum of Art, New York;
Robert Lehman Collection, 1975
C/L 592

NOTE

1. George Knox, in *The Robert Lehman Collection: VI. Italian Eighteenth-Century Drawings* (New York and Princeton, 1987), pp. 20–22, no. 18, where both sides of the drawing are reproduced.

This drawing, one of two showing the bridge from the south (see also C/L 591), is taken from a point roughly opposite to that of number 86.[1] The slight misalignment from the horizontal and the open pen work suggest that it was made at the site. It may have been used for the copperplate at Holkham (cat. no. 21), though that painting shows more of the Riva del Vin to the left. One of the pictures at Woburn Abbey (C/L 225) has still more of the buildings along the *riva*, as does a finished drawing at Windsor (C/L 591). The small hut appears in the right foreground of both drawings, but in neither of the paintings.

On the other side of the sheet is a sketch of a pavilion (C/L 824 [I]), probably an imaginary subject, which was used in turn for a finished drawing (C/L 824 [II]) in a private collection in New York.

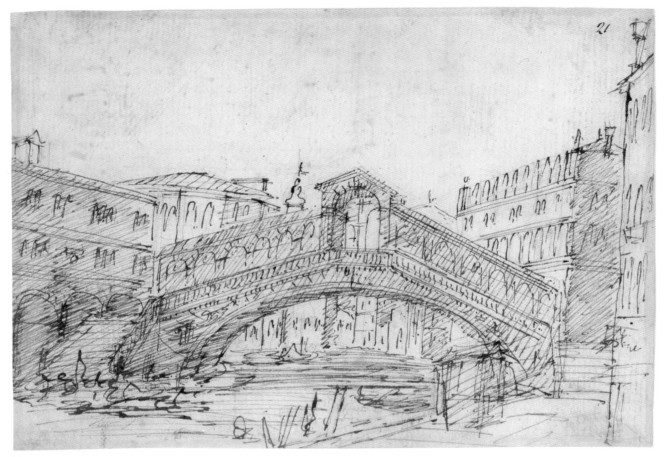

90.

91. *The Molo: looking West, with the old Fish Market*

Pen and brown ink, 7¼×10⅝ in. (18.6×27.3 cm)
Philadelphia Museum of Art; The John S. Phillips
Collection, acquired with the Edgar V. Seeler fund (by
exchange) and with funds contributed by Muriel and
Philip Berman
C/L 568

NOTES

1. The pencil inscription at the lower right is not by the artist, but was added at a considerably later date. In addition to C/L, see Pignatti, *Canaletto: Selected Drawings*, 1970, no. VI.
2. Information kindly supplied by Ann Percy of the Philadelphia Museum of Art.

The inscription in Canaletto's hand reads: *Veduta della pescharie* (View of the fish markets).[1] The fish markets to which Canaletto referred were later moved to the area close to the Rialto Bridge.

This drawing—ruled vertically in pencil—is from a sketchbook and may well be a preparatory study for Samuel Hill's painting, number 34. The sheet is comparable in size and style to a drawing of the Piazzetta (C/L 545), which is similarly inscribed by Canaletto and dated 1729, and it is reasonable to suppose that both are of the same moment. Number 91 appears to have been done from the ground, but for the painting Canaletto chose an assumed viewpoint that is higher and over the water, in order to show more of the buildings. Sketches such as this are extremely rare; those that exist seem to establish that Canaletto began with a sketch from the ground, raised his horizon for a more finished drawing (*Riva degli Schiavoni*, at Windsor, C/L 574, is an example), and raised it again for his painting, both the latter being done in the studio.

The present drawing, recently acquired by the Philadelphia Museum from the Pennsylvania Academy of the Fine Arts, belonged to the distinguished collection of European prints and drawings assembled during the third quarter of the nineteenth century by the Philadelphian John S. Phillips (1800–1876).[2]

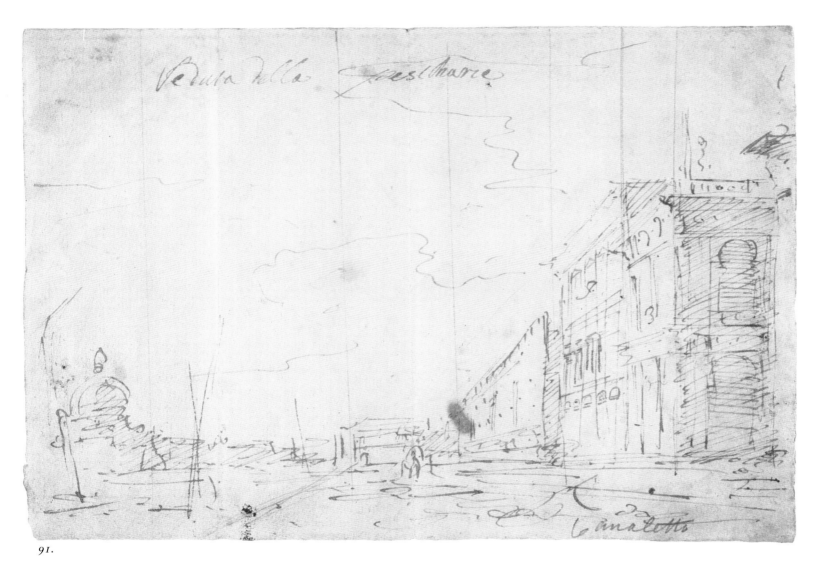

Veduta della Pescharia

Canaletto

91.

92. *The Bucintoro at the Molo*

Pen and brownish black ink, 8¼ × 12½ in. (21.1 × 31.8 cm)
Her Majesty Queen Elizabeth II
C/L 642

EXHIBITED
London 50; Venice 5

NOTES

1. Parker, *Drawings of Canaletto*, 1948, p. 30, no. 7; Miller, in *Canaletto*, 1980, pp. 89–90, no. 50; Miller, in *Canaletto*, 1982, p. 36, no. 5; and Miller, *Fifty Drawings by Canaletto*, 1983, no. 5.
2. Parker, *Drawings of Canaletto*, 1948, p. 30. The other drawings of the group are C/L 546, 565, and 577.

This sheet and number 93, *Riva degli Schiavoni: looking East*, are two of a group of six made by Canaletto either as finished drawings or for future use when painting similar subjects.[1] All except one entered Joseph Smith's collection; the sixth (C/L 573; see fig. 16), now at Darmstadt, is inscribed by Canaletto March 1729, giving an approximate date for the whole group which Parker described as "brilliantly free and atmospheric."[2]

Although the view could only have been observed from a boat, as Charlotte Miller notes, the horizontal ruled pencil line and the several verticals indicate that this drawing was worked up in the studio from rough sketches. A rather dilute brown ink was used, enabling the artist to draw quickly and smoothly with less angular effect than in the drawings of the Piazzetta (cat. nos. 88 and 89). Number 92 may well have been used for Smith's *Bucintoro Returning to the Molo on Ascension Day* (cat. no. 44). By the time that canvas was painted, however, Canaletto had completed several other versions.

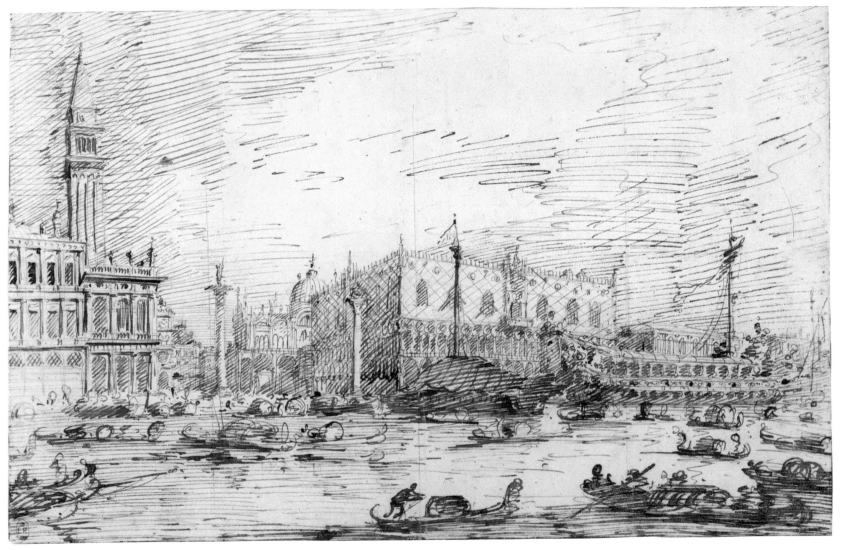

92.

93. Riva degli Schiavoni: looking East

Pen and brownish black ink over pencil, 7¾ × 12⅛ in.
(19.6 × 30.9 cm)
Her Majesty Queen Elizabeth II
C/L 574

EXHIBITED
Venice 9

NOTE
1. Parker, *Drawings of Canaletto*, 1948, p. 31, no. 10; and Miller, in *Canaletto*, 1982, p. 37, no. 9.

The view is the same as that of the dated drawing from the same group, now at Darmstadt (see cat. no. 92).[1] Smith certainly handled two or three paintings of the scene: catalogue number 33, possibly number 18, and almost certainly a third version (C/L 113), which was engraved by Visentini. However, he kept in his own collection no canvas representing this celebrated view, or its usual pendant looking in the opposite direction (see cat. no. 34). The many ruled lines in the drawing show, as in the case of number 92, that it would have been worked up in the studio, perhaps from sketches made from a boat.

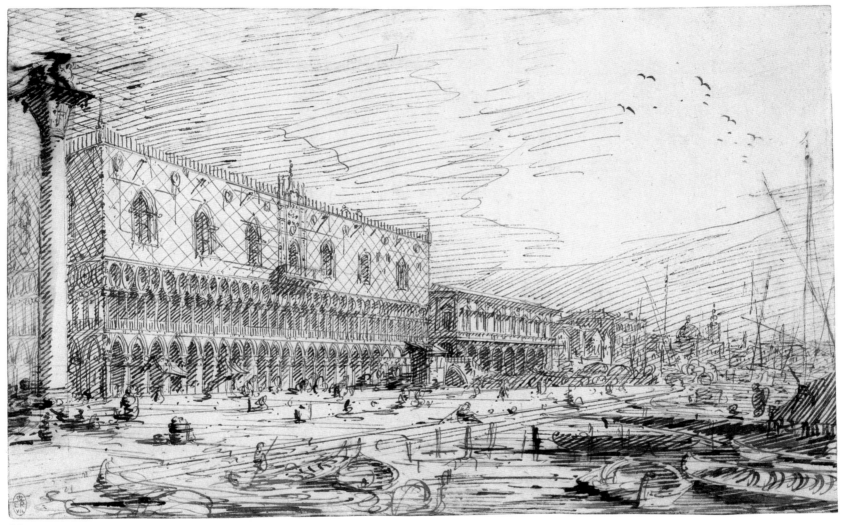

93.

94. Grand Canal: looking East, from near the Palazzo Corner

Pen and brown ink over pencil, 7⅜ × 10¾ in.
(18.9 × 27.3 cm)
Her Majesty Queen Elizabeth II
C/L 583

EXHIBITED
London 57

NOTE
1. Parker, *Drawings of Canaletto*, 1948, pp. 39–40, no. 53;
   Miller, in *Canaletto*, 1980, p. 94, no. 57; and Miller, *Fifty
   Drawings by Canaletto*, 1983, p. 37, no. 12.

The paper is identical in size and texture to that used for number 96, *S. Geremia and the Entrance to the Cannaregio*, which is inscribed on the reverse *16 Luglio 1734*, and the handling of the sky and the water is also similar.[1] Miller observes that the exceptionally low viewpoints and "some very spirited penwork" transform the present drawing into "a masterpiece of dramatic composition." Number 94 is based on a very free drawing (f. 3r) in the Accademia sketchbook, and that sketch must have been made from two different viewpoints, probably from a reclining position in the bottom of a boat. Both the sketch and this finished drawing are therefore topographically inexact, and Canaletto adds to his disregard of the facts by swinging the Dogana (left of center) well to the left of its true position. No known painting is closely related to the drawing, though the composition is to some degree reminiscent of number 31, a canvas presumed to be of significantly earlier date. The domes were drawn with the aid of a compass, and there is some ruling and pinpointing.

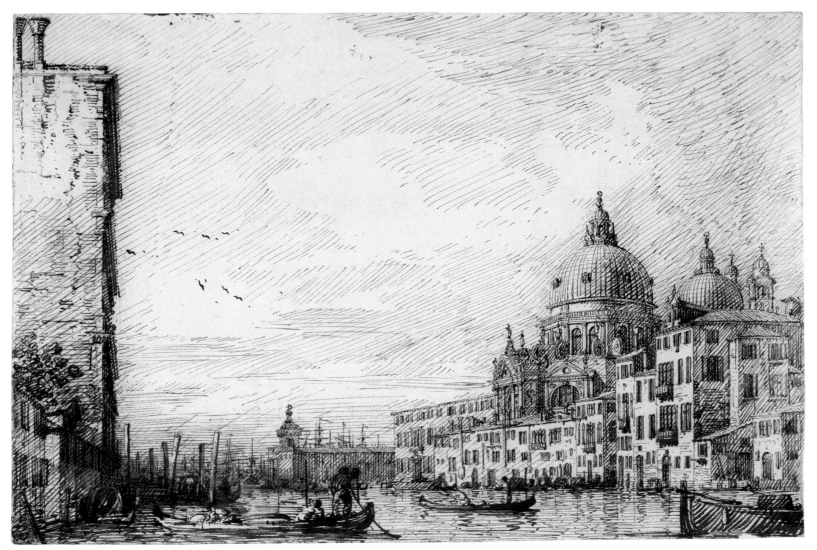

94.

95. Grand Canal: looking Northeast from the Palazzo Corner Spinelli to the Rialto Bridge

Pen and dark brown ink over pencil, 10⅝ × 14⅞ in.
(27 × 37.7 cm)
Her Majesty Queen Elizabeth II
C/L 590

EXHIBITED

Canada 37

NOTES

1. Parker, *Drawings of Canaletto*, 1948, p. 33, no. 21. The other finished drawings of the Grand Canal are C/L 584–86, 588, 591, 599, 600, and 602.
2. The drawings in the sketchbook are ff. 24v, 25r, 23v, 24r, and 22r, 21v, 23r, and 22v, in that order. In addition to C/L, see Pignatti, *Il quaderno*, 1958, particularly p. 39, where the sheets are illustrated in sequence.

This drawing and numbers 94 and 96 are among eleven highly finished views of the Grand Canal belonging to the Royal Collection.[1] Nothing comparable to them is known outside Smith's own collection, and it can hardly be coincidence that, with one exception (cat. no. 94), they all show subjects of paintings which had passed through his hands. They are not copies of these paintings, as were Visentini's engravings, but works of art in their own right which Smith perhaps wished to own as mementos of pictures he had parted with. The related canvas in this case is at Woburn Abbey (C/L 209), one of the group of twenty-four which Smith is now known to have sold to the fourth Duke of Bedford. The composition looks back to the early Grand Canal view at Dresden (cat. no. 6).

Eight of the preparatory studies in the Accademia sketchbook must have been used by Canaletto for number 95 and for the painting.[2] In the present drawing there is some ruling, in both pencil and ink, and some pinpointing.

298

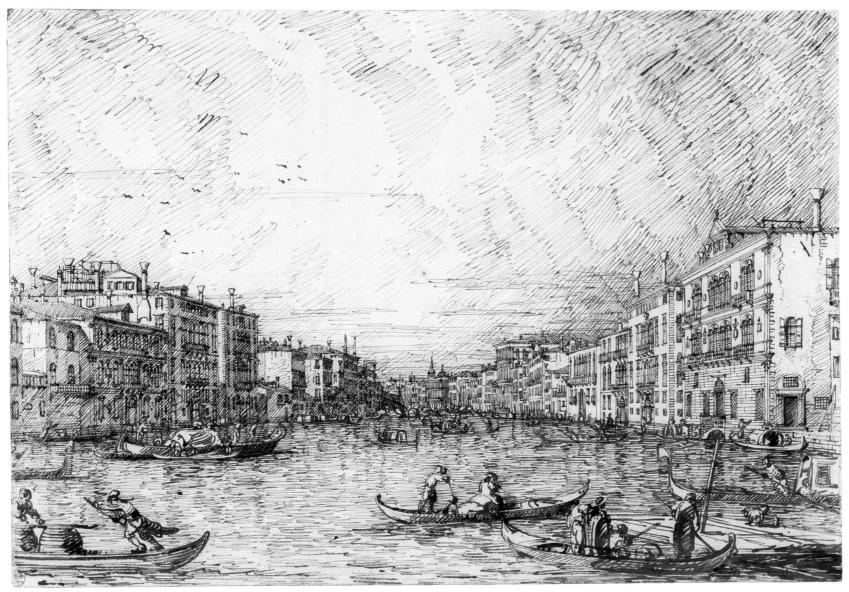

95.

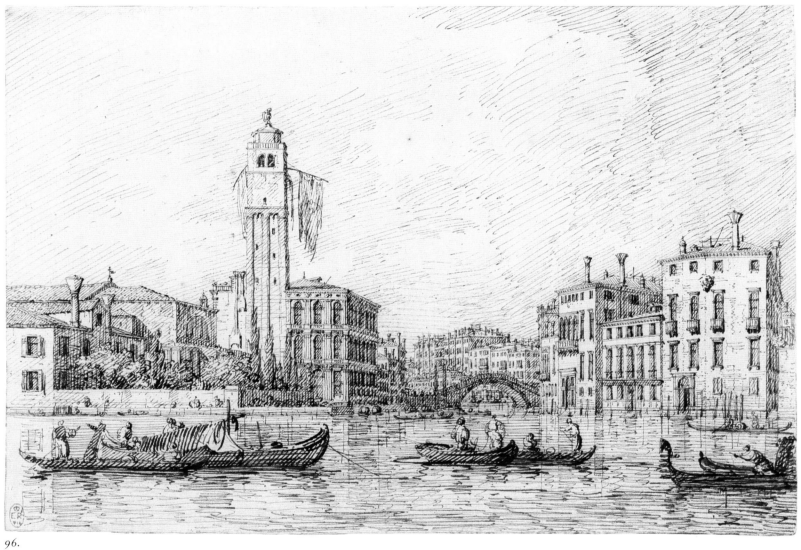

96.

300

96. Grand Canal: S. Geremia and the Entrance to the Cannaregio

Pen and brownish black ink over pencil, 7⅜ × 10⅝ in. (18.8 × 27 cm)
Her Majesty Queen Elizabeth II
C/L 598

EXHIBITED
London 56

NOTE
1. Parker, *Drawings of Canaletto*, 1948, p. 36, no. 37; Miller, in *Canaletto*, 1980, p. 92, no. 56; and Miller, *Fifty Drawings by Canaletto*, 1983, p. 37, no. 11.

On the reverse of this drawing is an inscription by Canaletto, *16 Luglio 1734*; although known to exist from an old note on the mount, the date was only recently revealed during restoration.[1] Number 96 provides the only example of a drawing of the Grand Canal of which Joseph Smith also retained a painting. The drawings are otherwise of subjects which had been sold as paintings to the Duke of Bedford or the original owner of the Harvey series. The painting of the entrance to the Cannaregio (C/L 251) was later altered by Canaletto to include a statue and a balustrade on the quay at center left, which were installed in 1742, and Visentini's engraving after the painting was similarly altered. As would be expected, neither of these elements appears in the present view.

Miller notes that, compared with other Grand Canal drawings, "the handling is less forceful, the pen is rather finer and the overall result less substantial and less lively." The pen work is even and contrasts of light and shade are largely absent; there is some pinpointing and ruling in both pen and ink. The sheet illustrates the point that Canaletto cannot always be relied upon for consistency of style and quality.

97. The Molo: looking West, with the Fonteghetto della Farina

Pen and brownish black ink over pencil, 7½ × 10¾ in. (19 × 27.2 cm)
Her Majesty Queen Elizabeth II
C/L 569

98. The Molo: looking West, with the Fonteghetto della Farina

Pen and brownish gray ink with gray wash, over pencil, 7⅜ × 10⅝ in. (18.8 × 26.9 cm)
Her Majesty Queen Elizabeth II
C/L 570

The west end of the Molo is one of the few areas of central Venice to have changed drastically since the eighteenth century. The old Granaries, of which a small part is seen on the right, have been replaced by gardens. The Fonteghetto della Farina (from which the wheat supply was controlled) later became the Accademia and now houses the Port Authority. Beyond is the former Palazzo Vallaresso, now the Hotel Monaco, and left of center the tower, long since demolished, which gave its name to the old Palazzo Venier dalle Torreselle.

The drawings are very similar in design and show Canaletto in one case working with his usual medium of pen and brown ink and in the other adding gray wash.[1] There were several such pairs in Smith's collection, all of about the same date, the late 1730s. The buildings at center and right in

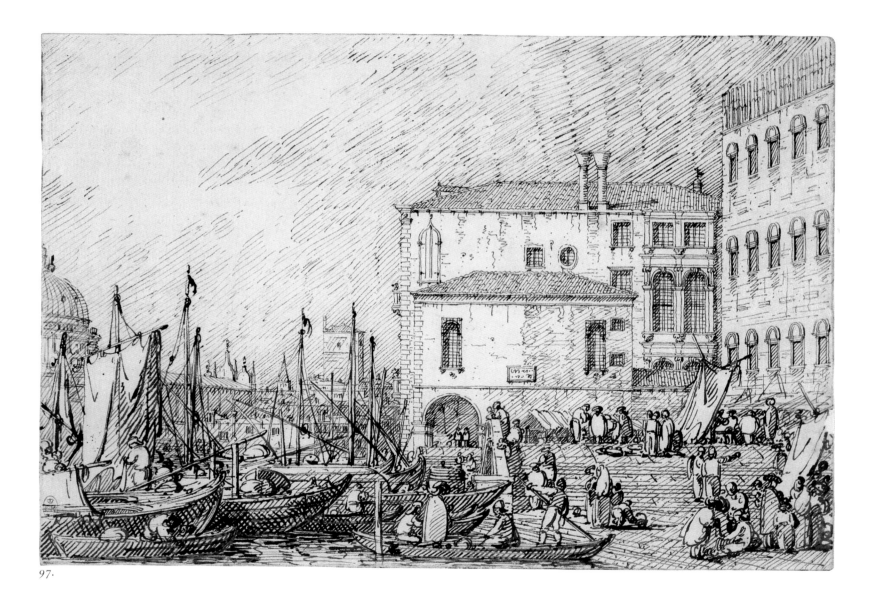

97.

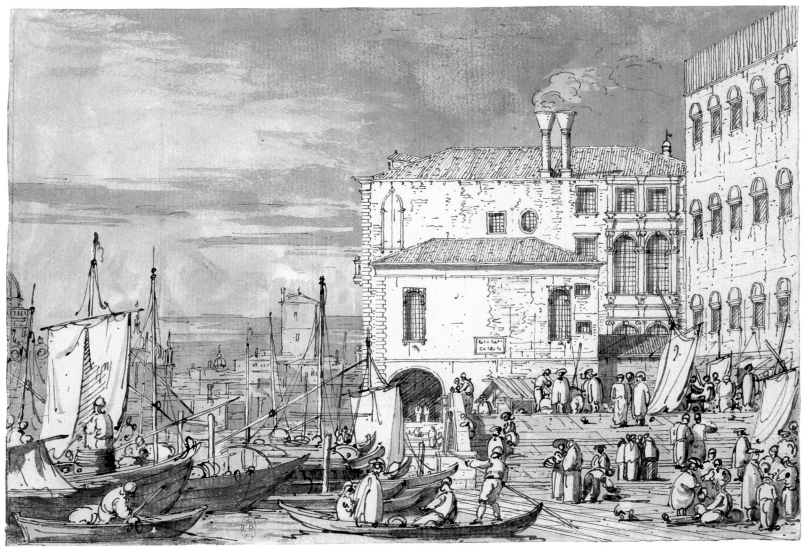

98.

EXHIBITED

Canada 35 (no. 98); London 62 and 63; Venice 12 and 13

NOTE

1. Parker, *Drawings of Canaletto*, 1948, pp. 38–39, nos. 48 and
   49; Pignatti, *Canaletto: Selected Drawings*, 1970, no. XXII
   (no. 98); Miller, in *Canaletto*, 1980, pp. 97–98, nos. 62 and
   63; Miller, in *Canaletto*, 1982, p. 38, nos. 12 and 13; and
   Miller, *Fifty Drawings by Canaletto*, 1983, pp. 15 and 38,
   no. 17 (no. 98).

numbers 97 and 98 correspond closely in detail, but in the wash drawing the churches and palaces on the far side of the canal have been shifted toward the left and much simplified. The same is true of the rigging of the boats. There is some ruling and pinpointing in each of the drawings.

Charlotte Miller suggests that Canaletto's adoption of wash may have been due to curiosity and to the urge to expand his repertoire, but that a more pressing motive was probably the need to save time. The latter argument is not entirely convincing. It is generally agreed that these early wash drawings are less successful than their pen and ink counterparts. As Miller points out, Canaletto's mastery of the new medium improved, but the wash always remained subsidiary to pen and ink and was therefore rarely the expressive medium it was for some of his contemporaries.

99. S. Marco: the Crossing and North Transept

Pen and brownish black ink over pencil, 10¾ × 7⅜ in.
(27.2 × 18.8 cm)
Her Majesty Queen Elizabeth II
C/L 556

EXHIBITED

London 60

NOTES

1. Parker, *Drawings of Canaletto*, 1948, p. 34, no. 30; Pignatti,
   Canaletto: Selected Drawings, 1970, no. LV; Miller, in
   Canaletto, 1980, p. 97, no. 60; and Miller, *Fifty Drawings
   by Canaletto*, 1983, p. 37, no. 15.
2. A preparatory drawing and an engraving of the reliquary
   were made by Visentini, presumably in commemoration of,
   and directly after, its transfer to S. Marco. The annual
   ceremony of veneration is described in the inscription. For
   the print, see Succi, in *Canaletto & Visentini*, 1986, p. 216,
   no. 1, ill.

The subject is that of the painting, number 37, though there are certain differences: the figures here are shown full-length and are more strongly lit from the west, the ambos are without hangings, and the arch of the crossing frames the composition at both sides.[1] Pignatti proposed a date after 1755 for the drawing, but this has not been generally accepted, and numbers 37 and 99 are regarded as belonging to the 1730s. In Miller's view the highly sophisticated handling of the pen suggests that this sheet is the later of the two works. Once thought to be night scenes, both more likely show the interior of the basilica by day.

Some significance must attach to the reliquary sarcophagus displayed, under a canopy and flanked by lighted candles, in the north transept (see also C/L 559 and cat. no. 127). The reliquary is the object of specific devotions in another drawing (C/L 557) closely related to this one and, as Miller observes, it resembles the one containing the relics of a Venetian Doge, the Blessed Pietro Orseolo, which was brought in state to S. Marco on 7 January 1732. The reliquary, housed in the Treasury of the basilica, was displayed for public veneration on 14 January each year.[2]

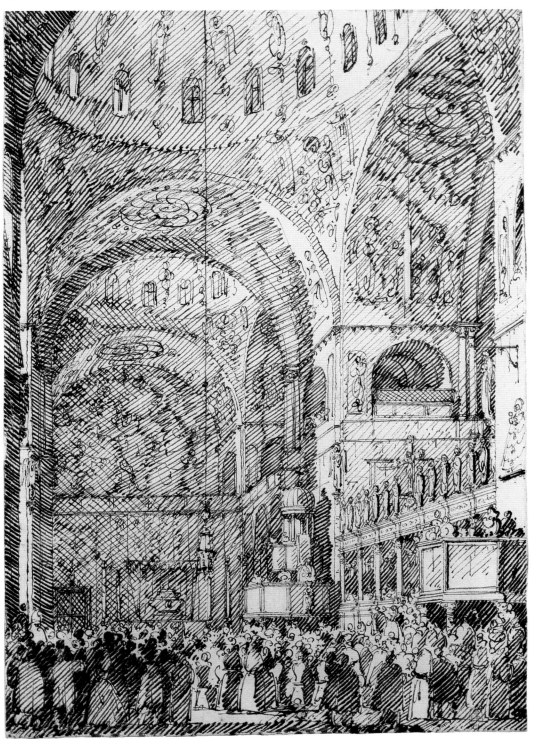

99.

100. Piazza S. Marco: looking South

Pen and dark brown ink over pencil, $7\frac{1}{8} \times 14\frac{7}{8}$ in.
(18.3 × 37.7 cm)
Her Majesty Queen Elizabeth II
C/L 537

EXHIBITED
London 67

NOTE
1. Parker, *Drawings of Canaletto*, 1948, pp. 41–42, no. 62;
Miller, in *Canaletto*, 1980, p. 101, no. 67; and Miller, *Fifty Drawings by Canaletto*, 1983, pp. 16 and 38, no. 21.

Together with two other drawings in the Royal Collection (C/L 538 and 547) and half a dozen paintings, this is one of a group sometimes called "impossible" views.[1] Such images go further than the plausible, wide-angle compositions for which the artist would have had to move his eyes, or his viewpoint. Sometimes adduced as evidence of Canaletto's use of the camera obscura or *camera ottica*, they are more likely to be the result of the artist's imaginative rearrangement of the relationships of well-known buildings one to another. Canaletto may occasionally have employed optical instruments, but they would not have been of service in such a case.

Parker found these views "interesting but not very pleasing," whereas Miller reasonably suggests that both Smith and Canaletto would have regarded, for example, the two (not three) elongated flagpoles which tower over S. Marco as a "highly ingenious optical joke." Some will find an element of considerable wit, and it should be remembered that Canaletto's last painting of Piazza S. Marco (cat. no. 84, signed and dated 1763) is composed on similar lines. Nor was Canaletto the first to indulge in such capriciousness: Carlevaris made distorted images as early as 1703, and plate 1 of Lovisa's *Gran Teatro* of 1720 must have provided the model for another impossible view, the drawing of the Piazzetta toward the west (C/L 547).

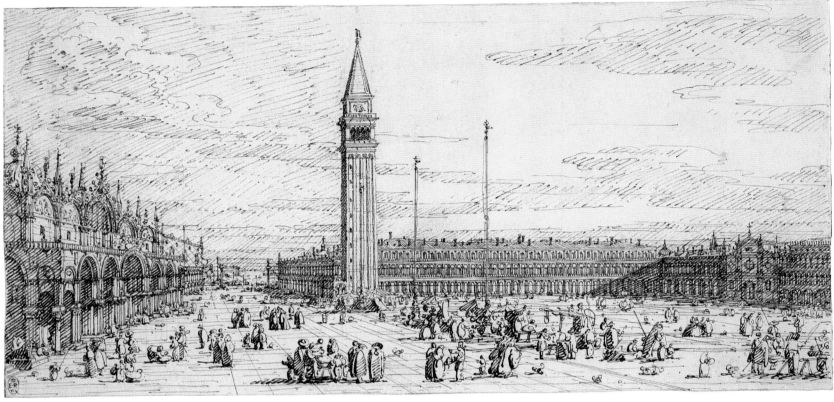

100.

307

101. Venice from the Punta della Mota

Pen, brown ink, and gray wash, over traces of pencil
6⅛ × 13⅝ in. (15.6 × 34.6 cm)
Her Majesty Queen Elizabeth II
C/L 522

EXHIBITED
Canada 80; London 68; Venice 29

NOTE
1. Parker, *Drawings of Canaletto*, 1948, pp. 42–44, no. 66;
Pignatti, *Canaletto: Selected Drawings*, 1970, no. XXIII;
Miller, in *Canaletto*, 1980, p. 101, no. 68; Miller, in *Canaletto*,
1982, p. 42, no. 29; and Miller, *Fifty Drawings by Canaletto*,
1983, p. 38, no. 22.

This panoramic view and number 102 are two of four drawings made near the Mota di S. Antonio, in Canaletto's day the most easterly point in Venice proper.[1] The boat to the Lido stops nearby at the entrance to the public gardens, and visitors to the Biennale will have seen the center of the city from roughly the same angle. The Euganean Hills are at the extreme left in the distance; the domes on the island of the Giudecca are those of the Redentore and the Zitelle; the church and bell tower of S. Giorgio may be seen through the rigging of the ship with, to the right, the facades of the Granai and Palazzo Ducale in strong light, the Campanile and domes of S. Marco, the dome of S. Zaccaria, and the bell tower of S. Giorgio dei Greci. Many of the distant buildings have been widened in proportion to their height, and the Mint and Library have been replaced on the Molo by an arcaded building resembling the Procuratie Nuove. For the water, the pen work and wash are applied horizontally, and all of the gondolas and smaller boats lie parallel to the picture plane, increasing the effect of breadth. Of the views represented in the panoramic drawings only this one is largely unchanged.

Toward the north from the Mota di S. Antonio is the Castello district with the island and church of S. Pietro, one of the oldest quarters of Venice, but little visited, as it is now a largely modern residential area. Canaletto devoted a second panoramic drawing (C/L 523) to this subject.

The four drawings are in complete contrast to the work Canaletto had been doing previously, and probably mark a moment in the early 1740s when, for the first time, the demand for his view paintings had fallen off. Miller draws attention to the fact that the artist realized the full potential of the wash medium for the first time in these sheets; never again, she adds, did Canaletto use wash so expressively or with such sensitivity. The sites would have been known to Smith, who owned the drawings, but not to occasional visitors to the city. The subjects were never repeated, though there are paintings and drawings of the *bacino* taken from a point closer in on the Riva degli Schiavoni.

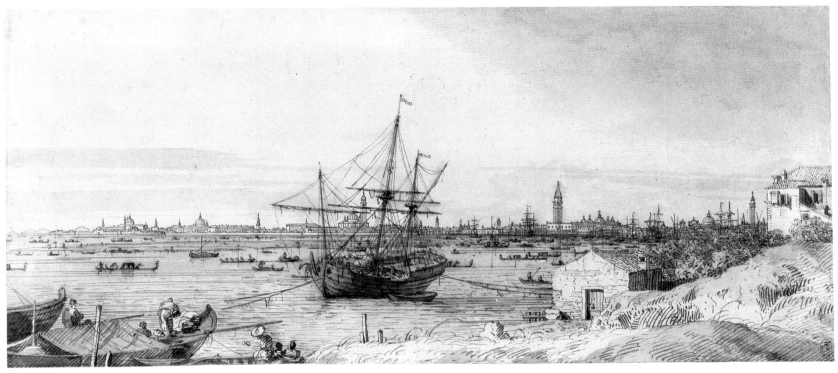

101.

102. *Islands of the Certosa and Sta. Elena*

Pen, brown ink, and gray wash, over pencil, 6⅛ × 13⅞ in.
(15.5 × 35.2 cm)
Her Majesty Queen Elizabeth II
C/L 650

EXHIBITED
London 71; Venice 30

NOTES
1. Parker, *Drawings of Canaletto*, 1948, p. 44, no. 67; Pignatti,
   Canaletto: Selected Drawings, 1970, no. XXV; Miller, in
   Canaletto, 1980, p. 103, no. 71; Miller, in *Canaletto*, 1982,
   p. 42, no. 30; and Miller, *Fifty Drawings by Canaletto*,
   1983, p. 38, no. 25. This is one of two cases in which
   W. G. Constable's title has been changed.
2. See Succi, in *Canaletto & Visentini*, 1987, pp. 169–73 and
   260–61, nos. 43, 43 bis, 47, and 47 bis, ill. Pignatti first drew
   attention to this connection.

The third and fourth drawings in the group made near the Mota di S. Antonio represent Sta. Elena.[1] In the one not exhibited (C/L 649) the buildings on the island are in profile and, beyond, trees along the westward bank of the Lido separate the water from the sky. Here Sta. Elena is shown on the right, with a distant view of the Lido at the center and, to the left, the island and church of the Certosa. Sta. Elena and the adjoining Olivetan monastery appear much as they do in a small etching by Visentini, one of a series of vignettes first published by Pasquali early in 1739 as illustrations to a new edition of Francesco Guiccardini's *Istoria d'Italia*.[2] The Isola della Certosa was also among Visentini's subjects, though as seen from a very different viewpoint. Smith played a major role in this publication, which would doubtless have been known to Canaletto.

The church of Sta. Elena is little changed, but the monastery and other buildings are gone and the island has been joined to Venice proper, modern buildings engulfing the little that remains of an earlier time. The church and convent of the Certosa were suppressed and finally demolished in the nineteenth century. Elsewhere, at S. Francesco del Deserto and S. Lazzaro degli Armeni, for example, churches and conventual cloisters still stand amid orchards and gardens, and life on the islands of the lagoon is perhaps much as it has always been.

The present drawing is perhaps the most remarkable of the four, in that the buildings serve primarily to emphasize the broad, largely undifferentiated expanses of shallow and deeper water and sky. There are few boats, few figures, and—for the architecture—a minimum of detail. All four sheets are creased at the center and seem to be double pages from the same sketchbook. In three of the four, the exception being the other view of Sta. Elena (C/L 649), there is some ruling in pen or pencil. The presence of ruled lines, taken together with the precision and finish of every detail, would suggest that they were not made on the ground but in the studio, as close to nature as they are.

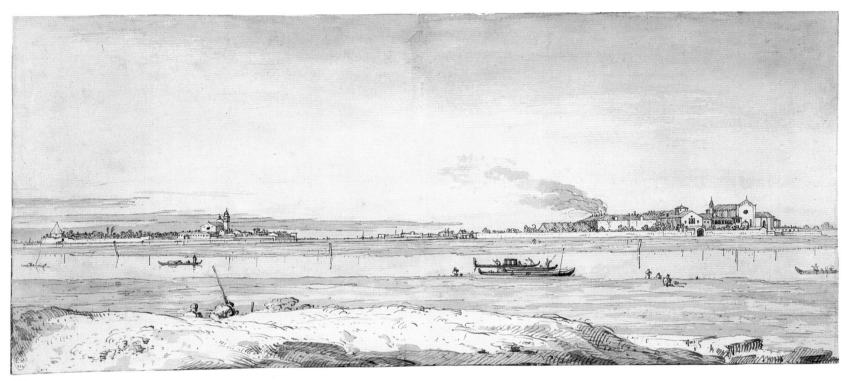

102.

103. Roofs and Houses near the Lagoon

Pen and brown ink over red chalk, 7⅜ × 8¾ in.
(18.7 × 22.2 cm)
Fogg Art Museum, Harvard University, Cambridge,
Massachusetts; Bequest of Charles A. Loeser
C/L 665

EXHIBITED
Canada 102

NOTES
1. Bromberg, *Canaletto's Etchings*, 1974, p. 37, no. 1 ill.;
   for this drawing see Agnes Mongan and Paul J. Sachs,
   Drawings in the Fogg Museum of Art (Cambridge, Mass.,
   1940), p. 158, no. 311; and Pignatti, *Canaletto: Selected
   Drawings*, 1970, no. XXXIX.
2. Corboz, *Canaletto*, 1985, p. 350. For the print see Bromberg,
   Canaletto's Etchings, 1974, pp. 94–97, no. 12.

Canaletto introduced antique columns into what seems otherwise to be among studies made "prese da i Luoghi."[1] At the right, above the roofs of the houses and distant buildings bordering the water along the horizon, he has written *più largho*, indicating that he wanted an effect of greater breadth. There is a very slight sketch in ink on the reverse, and the sheet, seemingly torn from a sketchbook, has been mended.

André Corboz has pointed out that the roofs at the right, when reversed, and the house with the four chimney pots are closely related to motifs at the center of the etching *Imaginary View of Venice*, which is dated by Canaletto in the undivided plate 1741.[2] The roofs shelter boatyards in the etching; the house has become a villa, and toward the left there is a ruin with an antique column.

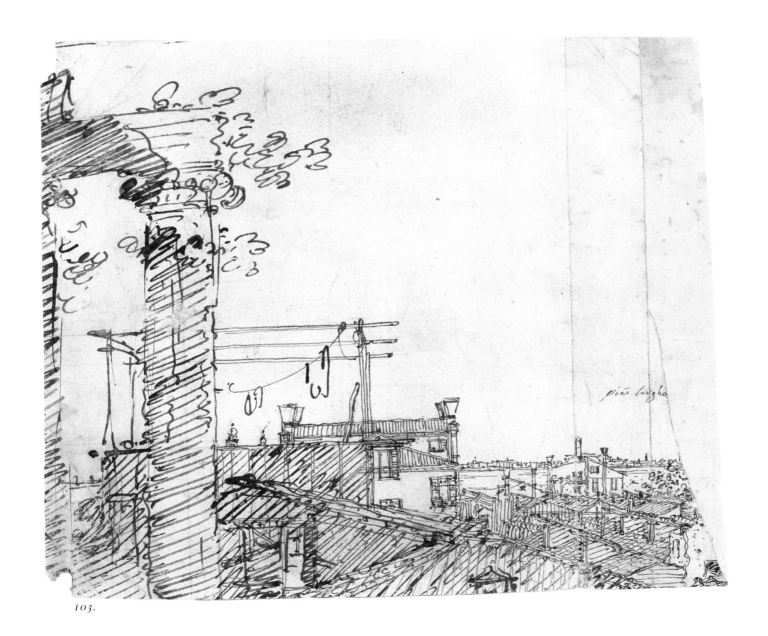

103.

più lungho

104. Panoramic View of Houses and Gardens by a River, perhaps at Padua

a. Pen and brown ink over red chalk, 5⅝ × 15¼ in. (14.2 × 38.7 cm)
The Pierpont Morgan Library, New York
C/L 695(a)

b. Pen and brown ink over red chalk, 5⅝ × 15⅜ in. (14.2 × 39.2 cm)
Fogg Art Museum, Harvard University, Cambridge, Massachusetts; Bequest of Charles A. Loeser
C/L 695(b)

EXHIBITED

Canada 90 and 91

NOTES

1. Agnes Mongan, "Notes on Canaletto Drawings in the Fogg Art Museum," *Old Master Drawings* 13 (1938), pp. 34–36; Agnes Mongan and Paul J. Sachs, *Drawings in the Fogg Museum of Art* (Cambridge, Mass., 1940), pp. 154–56, no. 307; and Jacob Bean and Felice Stampfle, *Drawings from New York Collections: III. The Eighteenth Century in Italy*, exh. cat. (New York, 1971), pp. 67–68, no. 156.
2. Bromberg, *Canaletto's Etchings*, 1974, p. 9, and see also pp. 78–81, no. 9.
3. Reproduced in C/L on pl. 231.
4. Bromberg, *Canaletto's Etchings*, 1974, p. 81.

From all appearances these two sheets represent Canaletto's first study, perhaps made on the ground, of a composition which would provide material for a painting, number 58 (see the entry on that work), an etching, two finished drawings from Smith's collection, now at Windsor (C/L 696 and 697), and a small, later picture.[1] Bromberg identifies the campanile as that of Dolo on the Brenta.[2] The drawing, she points out, provides the only known instance of a sketch in reverse serving as a preliminary study for a print. (Numbers 103 and 105 are other examples of drawings relating to etchings in which the compositions are reversed.) In all of the images depending from this one, the near bank of the river, figures, and trees have been added in the foreground.

Along the top of the Morgan Library sheet there are free sketches in red chalk of the roofs of two of the houses and of the waterwheel; the more complete study in chalk, below, was reaffirmed or corrected in ink. Some color and lighting notations in Canaletto's hand are *B* for *bianco* (white), *R* for *rosso* (red), and *sciaro tutto* for a shaded area. The Fogg sheet is inscribed in Canaletto's hand at the left margin, near the campanile, *cornise piu alta* (cornice higher), but the campanile in the etching is not the same. On the reverse of number 104b there is another, very slight sketch, together with Canaletto's name and the date 1742 (twice, once canceled).[3] The authenticity of these inscriptions has been questioned.[4]

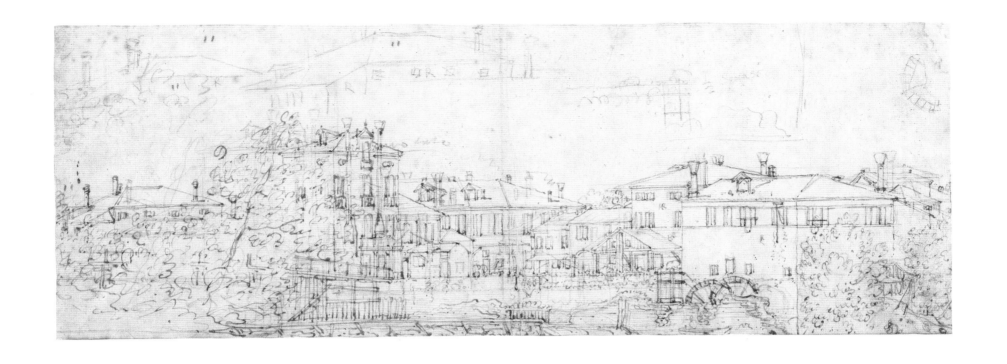

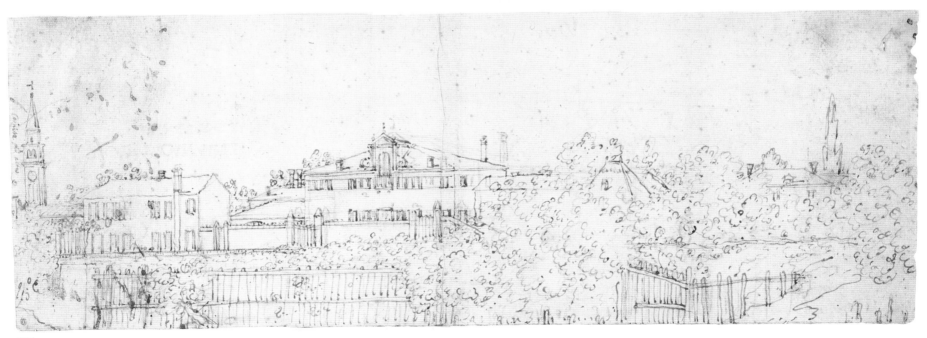

105. Padua: Houses

Pen, brownish black ink, and gray wash, over pencil,
7⅜ × 6⅜ in. (18.6 × 16.1 cm)
Staatliche Museen Preussischer Kulturbesitz,
Kupferstichkabinett, Berlin
C/L 691

EXHIBITED
Venice 21

NOTES
1. The addition to the sheet measures 4 × 15.8 cm. See Pignatti,
   Canaletto: Selected Drawings, 1970, nos. XXXII and XXXI;
   Bettagno, in *Canaletto*, 1982, pp. 40–41, no. 21, and p. 45,
   no. 42; and Dreyer, *Vedute*, 1985, pp. 34–35, no. 38.
2. See C/L, pls. 230–31, for examples.
3. For the Corniani Algarotti album, see C/L, pp. 641–46, and
   Miotti, "Tre disegni inediti del Canaletto," 1966, pp. 275–78,
   and for Ricci, Levey, *Later Italian Pictures*, 1964, p. 94, no. 593,
   and pl. 110.
4. See Bromberg, *Canaletto's Etchings*, 1974, pp. 134–37,
   no. 24, and also C/L 469 and C/L 692.

Canaletto added a piece of paper at the bottom edge of the sheet, ruling it in ink, and signing it boldly *Io Zuane Antonio da Canal, deto il Canaleto / lò dissegnià è / fatto* (I Zuane Antonio da Canal, called il Canaleto designed and made it).[1] Such an inscription is rare but not unique in the artist's work of the later years.[2] The pencil notation at the lower left corner, *Vista in Padoua esata*, indicates that the subject, a view in Padua, is observed rather than imagined; this is open to question and the note, in any case, is probably not in Canaletto's hand. The drawing is ruled vertically in pencil, and at first, judging from a slight underlying sketch, the roof lines for the houses at the left and right were intended to be higher.

This is Canaletto's most felicitous variation on a theme that evolved in the course of restatement in more than one medium. An ink drawing (C/L 691*) from a dismembered sketchbook—the so-called Corniani Algarotti album —seems to represent the artist's first idea for the composition, and may have been inspired by a work of Marco Ricci.[3] Among the small paintings by Ricci in tempera on leather that belonged to Joseph Smith and are likely to have been known to Canaletto is *The Courtyard of a Country House*, whose essential elements are a terrace, approached by an outside stair, shaded by a vine, and with an arch beneath. Canaletto's sketch incorporates most of these elements, and a wellhead in the foreground, though he omits the vine, and the tree that closes Ricci's composition at the left, and introduces instead a house in the near distance beyond the terrace. The various motifs, much elaborated, recur in an etching entitled *The Terrace*, in which a house with a Venetian-style roof terrace appears at the left; this composition is cropped at the bottom, so that only the top of the arch and part of the staircase may be seen.[4] The present, highly finished drawing is by contrast an upright, and the composition is in reverse to the etching. The terrace and the buildings beyond are more broadly described, but the foreground courtyard and its contents are elaborated in detail. The staircase, of wood, descends to the doorway of the house on the left, not to the ground. Effects of light differing from those in the print are skillfully suggested with wash. On balance the drawing is probably the later of the two, and the presence in both of an obelisk suggests that the view is to some degree capricious.

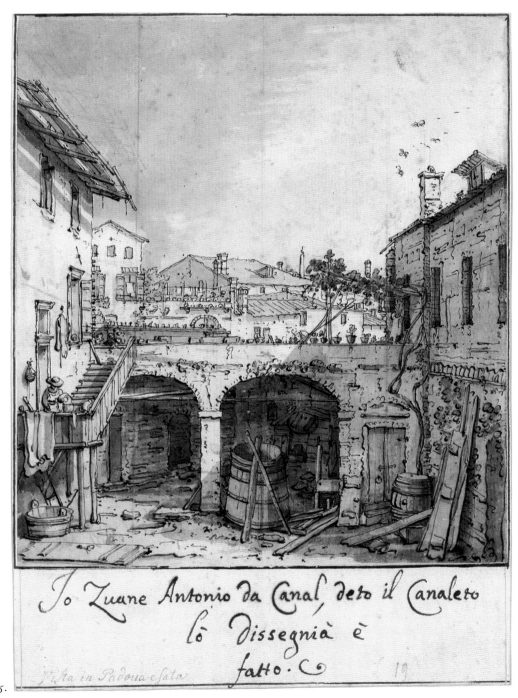

Io Zuane Antonio da Canal, deto il Canaleto
lò Dissegnià è
fatto.

106. Padua: the Brenta Canal and the Porta Portello

Pen, brown ink, and gray wash, 7¼ × 10⅜ in.
(18.5 × 26.5 cm)
The Metropolitan Museum of Art, New York;
Robert Lehman Collection, 1975
C/L 676 note

NOTES

1. George Knox, in *The Robert Lehman Collection: VI. Italian Eighteenth-Century Drawings* (New York and Princeton, 1987), p. 24, no. 20.
2. Frits Lugt, *Les Marques de collections de dessins & d'estampes* (Amsterdam, 1921; reprint, The Hague, 1956), p. 335; and *Catalogue raisonné... le Cabinet de feu M' Mariette...* (Paris, 1775), p. 46, no. 274. The Metropolitan Museum copy of the Mariette sale catalogue is annotated RB, and the drawing was in the Randon de Boisset sale, Paris, 27 February–25 March 1777, no. 299, sold, according to an annotated copy at the Frick Art Reference Library, to "Belizare." The other part of lot 274 (for which see C/L 276 note, and, in the 1989 ed., C/L 603**) was sold at Christie's, London, on 13 December 1984 as no. 75, consigned by the descendants of Lord Islington. It is inscribed *Giesuiti in Venezia* below the pen borderline, and it measures 31.2 × 25.8 cm.
3. Quoted in George A. Simonson, "Antonio Canale (Canaletto) and His Painting in the Metropolitan Museum," *Art in America* 2 (1914), p. 367.
4. Kozakiewicz, *Bernardo Bellotto*, 1972, II, p. 28, fig. 34, and p. 30, no. 34.

The painting representing Porta Portello, number 57, and a finished ink and wash drawing in the Albertina, Vienna (C/L 676), focus on the masonry wall extending from the gate into the foreground, and the grassy bank beyond; there are a few minor variations of detail between the two. By contrast, a study in brown ink owned by Smith, which is in the Royal Collection (C/L 675), and this highly finished sheet share an imagined viewpoint high above the middle of the canal.[1] The bridge in the Royal Collection and Lehman drawings is supported on piers at three points rather than two; in the Windsor drawing, but not in this one or the other variants of the composition, the span closest to the bridge is a drawbridge, and only in the Windsor drawing is a hut at the opposite end omitted.

W. G. Constable noted that Pierre-Jean Mariette (1694–1774), the famous French collector and connoisseur, owned a drawing of the subject. In fact this was number 106, which bears his mark (Lugt 1852) at the lower right, and was included in the 1775–76 sale as part of lot 274, sold to Randon de Boisset: "Autre vue en travers du Port de Padoue, ornée de bateaux & figures fort intéressantes, d'une plume fine & légere, lavée d'encre de la Chine." (Another view across the Gate of Padua, ornamented with very interesting boats & figures, in a fine & delicate pen, washed with China ink.)[2]

In a letter of 12 January 1768 to his friend the Venetian architect Temanza, Mariette recorded his admiration of this particular drawing, and of Canaletto as a view painter: "M. Canale est excellent dans son genre. J'ai de lui quelques dessins qu'il a fait dans sa ferveur, entre autres une vue de Padoue, qui est un excellent morceau. Si je trouvais quelque autre dessin de lui, du même temps et de la même force, j'en ferais volontiers l'acquisition."[3]

Bellotto also made a drawing of this subject, which is now at Darmstadt.[4]

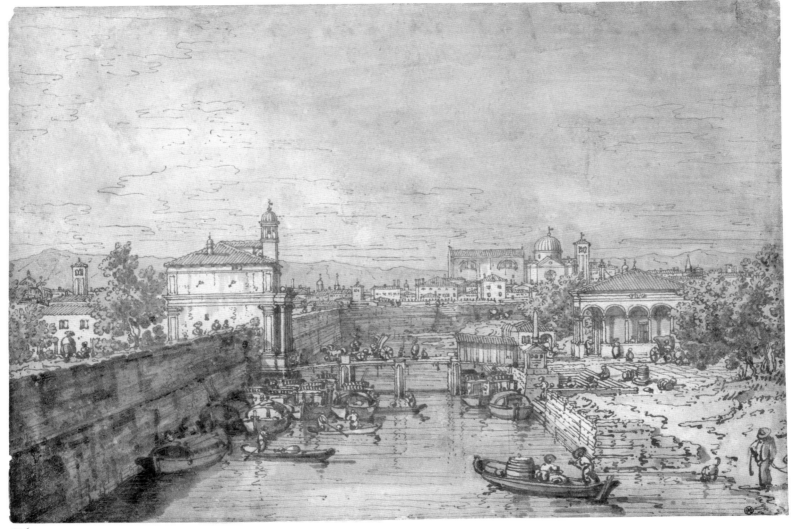

106.

319

107. A Farm on the Outskirts of Padua

Pen, brownish black ink, and gray wash, over pencil,
12⅜ × 15¾ in. (31.4 × 39.9 cm)
Her Majesty Queen Elizabeth II
C/L 694

EXHIBITED
Canada 89; London 93

NOTES

1. Parker, *Drawings of Canaletto*, 1948, p. 46–47, no. 84;
   Miller, in *Canaletto*, 1980, p. 118, no. 93; and Miller, *Fifty
   Drawings by Canaletto*, 1983, p. 39, no. 47.
2. Corboz, *Canaletto*, 1985, pp. 125, 127, and fig. 138.
3. Russell, *Burlington Magazine*, 1988, pp. 627–29 and fig. 61.
4. Corboz, *Canaletto*, 1985, pp. 31, 127, and 136 n. 80; and
   Kozakiewicz, *Bernardo Bellotto*, 1972, II, pp. 189–90,
   nos. 245 and 246 and pls. 245 and 246. For the watermill at
   the lower right, see Bromberg, *Canaletto's Etchings*, 1974,
   where the *Imaginary View of Padua* is illustrated on p. 89.

The drawing is one of many resulting from Canaletto's trip to the mainland in the early 1740s, a journey undertaken with his nephew Bernardo Bellotto.[1] Parker considered it "particularly sensitive and masterly in execution," and unconnected with any painting, etching, or other drawing. Miller, on the other hand, found the dark washes rather heavy and arbitrary. While Parker was inclined to identify it as a view after nature, Corboz points out that the landmarks of Padua, in the background, have been rearranged, and that the so-called farmhouse resembles a villa near Vicenza.[2]

Canaletto himself must have had some regard for this highly finished sheet, since he took it (or perhaps a preliminary sketch for it) to England with him, and used it for one of the capriccios (C/L 514* [1989 ed.]) he painted for Chesterfield House in London.[3] For Lord Chesterfield's painting, though, Canaletto converted the modest farmhouse into a small palace. Bellotto must have sketched the same building while on the mainland: as Corboz also notes, he used it in two of his capriccios, combining it in one case with a building which also appears among Canaletto's etchings.[4] The arches of the loggia are incised with the point of dividers, and there is some ruling in pencil defining the vertical contours of the buildings.

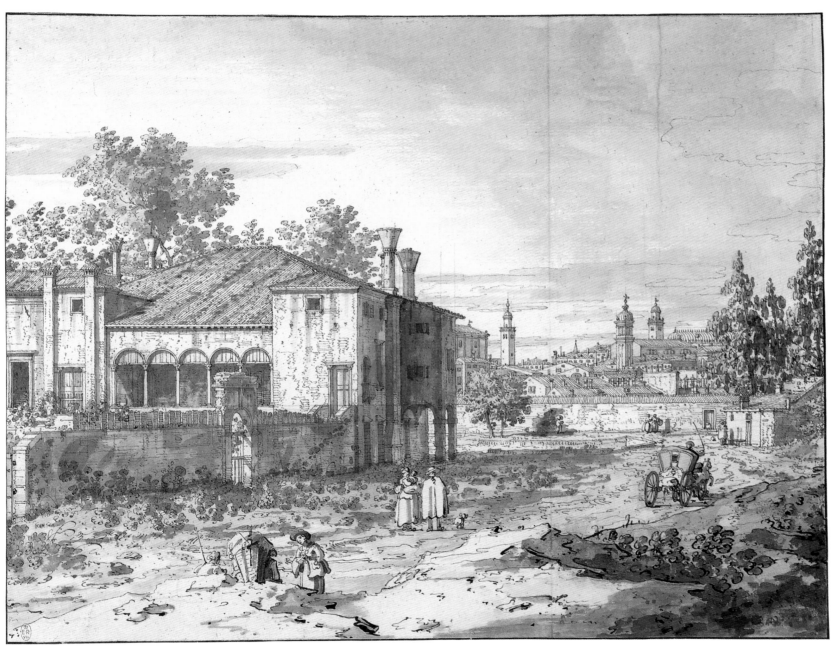

107.

108. The Island of S. Michele, with Venice in the Distance

Pen, brown ink, and gray wash, over pencil, $7\frac{7}{8} \times 11$ in.
(20 × 27.9 cm)
The Ashmolean Museum, Oxford
C/L 654

EXHIBITED

Canada 100; Venice 62

NOTE

1. K. T. Parker, *Catalogue of the Collection of Drawings in the Ashmolean Museum* (Oxford, 1956), II, p. 492, no. 980; and Bettagno, in *Canaletto*, 1982, p. 50, no. 62. See also Pignatti, "'Sei Villaggi Campestri' dal Canaletto," 1969, pp. 23–24, 26, no. 4, and fig. 25.

This sheet is closer to the composition of the painting from the Lovelace series, number 78, than is the ink drawing incorporating the same motifs that belonged to Smith and is in the Royal Collection (C/L 653).[1] Details common to number 108 and the Lovelace picture are the deep overhang of the cottage roof, the arrangement of the gables and roofs within the walled enclosure, their juxtaposition with the campanile of the church of S. Michele, and the profile of the skyline of Venice against the distant horizon. In both, Canaletto repositioned the bell tower of S. Francesco della Vigna and omitted that of S. Pietro di Castello. Wagner's much later engraving, in reverse to the present drawing, is dependent upon it. The gently swaying cypress is a constant element of a much-imitated design.

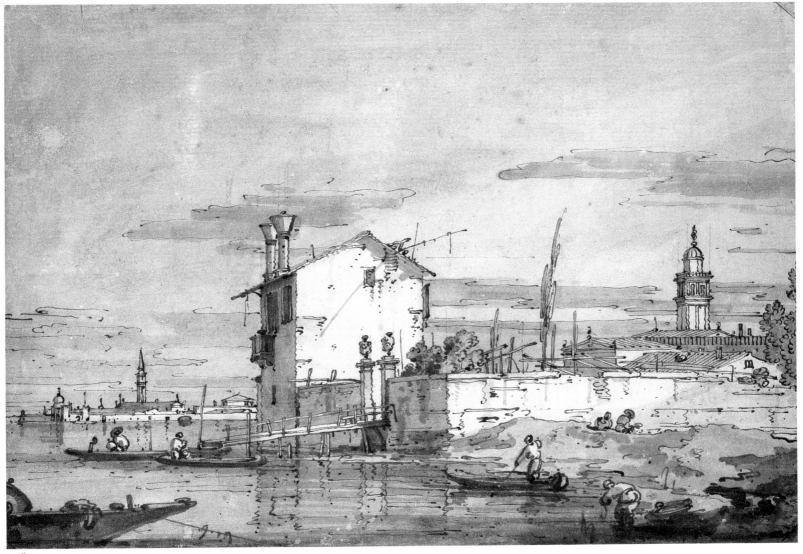

108.

109. Capriccio: with Reminiscences of the Ponte delle Navi and Verona

Pen, brown ink, and gray wash, over pencil, 9 × 14⅞ in.
(25.1 × 37.9 cm)
Her Majesty Queen Elizabeth II
C/L 792

NOTES

1. Parker, *Drawings of Canaletto*, 1948, p. 54, no. 120, and
   Corboz, *Canaletto*, 1985, pp. 114–16, and 139 nn. 215 and 217,
   who explores the relationship with Bellotto and questions the
   attribution of this drawing to Canaletto. For the related
   views by Bellotto, see Kozakiewicz, *Bernardo Bellotto*, 1972, I,
   pp. 44–45, and II, p. 80, nos. 101–3, and pls. 101–3.
   Kozakiewicz does not mention number 109. The title has been
   changed, as Parker's reference to Chioggia, taken up by
   W. G. Constable, cannot be substantiated.
2. Miller's view is expressed in an appendix to the forthcoming
   reprint of Parker, *Drawings of Canaletto*.

The buildings along the riverbank, and to a lesser extent the bridge, correspond with the left half of each of three views (a drawing and two paintings) by Bernardo Bellotto, of Verona and the Ponte delle Navi as seen from the north.[1] Canaletto transformed the scene by eliminating two of its most important and readily identifiable elements—a ramp leading downward from the bridge into the foreground, and a tall, crenellated tower adjoining the guardhouse at the right—and in the distance he substituted an open body of water resembling the lagoon for the banks of the Adige. A difficulty arises in that there is no other reason to believe that Canaletto ever worked in Verona. Number 109 may constitute the only evidence that he did, or he may have based this quasi-capriccio on a topographically accurate drawing or painting made by Bellotto in Verona and brought back to Venice. This would presumably have been in the years just prior to Canaletto's departure for England in 1746.

Miller draws attention to the almost black wash, which in her view produces a dead effect, and Parker pointed out that at the lower left the ink seems to have run, which is unusual in the work of so technically proficient an artist as Canaletto.[2] There is some freehand ruling, and pinpointing, and the arches of the bridge are incised with the point of the dividers.

Moreover, this is one of three drawings (see also C/L 780 and C/L 827, the right-hand third) which were included in an album of Visentini drawings when Smith's collection was bought by George III. Skilled though it is in execution, number 109 must be regarded with some doubt.

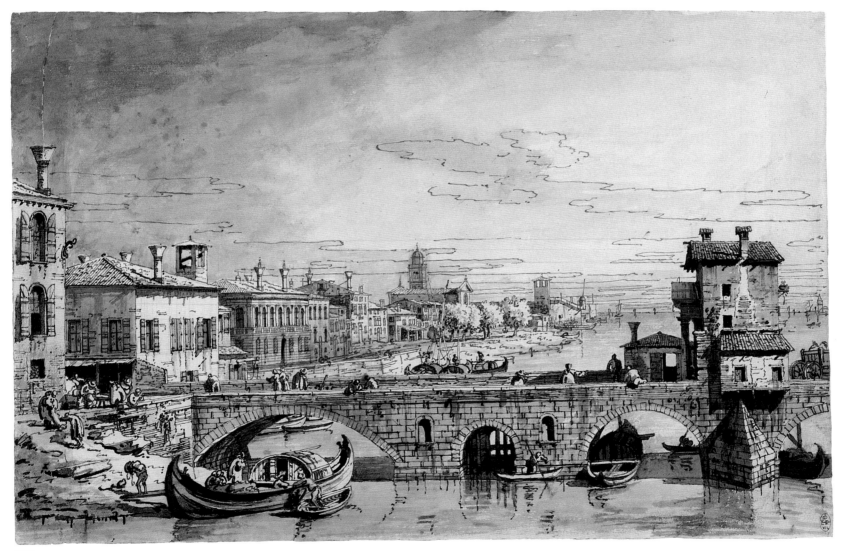

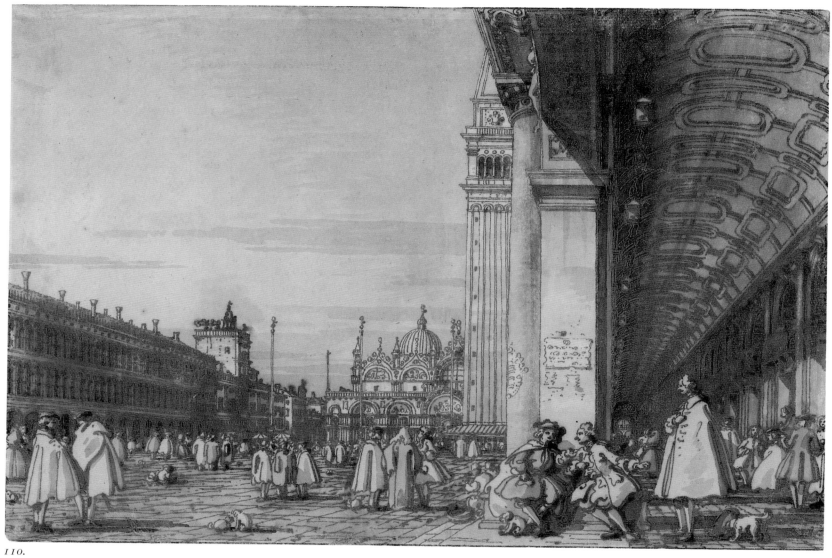

110.

110. Piazza S. Marco: looking East from the Southwest Corner

Pen and brown ink with brown and gray wash,
9 × 13⅛ in. (22.8 × 33.3 cm)
The Metropolitan Museum of Art, New York;
Robert Lehman Collection, 1975
C/L 526

NOTES

1. George Knox, in *The Robert Lehman Collection: VI. Italian Eighteenth-Century Drawings* (New York and Princeton, 1987), pp. 25–26, no. 21.
2. For the painting, see Levey, *The Eighteenth Century Italian Schools*, 1956, pp. 23–24, no. 2516; and for the drawing (C/L 525), Parker, *Drawings of Canaletto*, 1948, p. 40, no. 57. See also C/L 841 and 842. A third drawing, not fully catalogued in C/L, was in the Reveley collection: Felice Stampfle and Cara D. Denison, *Drawings from the Collection of Lore and Rudolf Heinemann*, exh. cat. (New York, 1973), p. 32, no. 29.

To the right is the colonnade of the Procuratie Nuove with, in the foreground and middle distance, ladies and gentlemen gathered near Florian's Café.[1] This half of the sheet is closely related to a painting in the National Gallery, London (C/L 20, fig. 5), in which the gentleman standing at the right holds a cup and saucer, and to another drawing (C/L 525), also horizontal, that belonged to Smith and is in the Royal Collection.[2] There are minor differences between the two drawings and between them and the painting, but number 110—highly finished and elaborately washed—compares favorably with Smith's and is slightly closer to the National Gallery picture.

The painting certainly dates from after Canaletto's return to Venice from England. Neither drawing shows the 1755 addition to the Torre dell'Orologio, and this suggests that both were done before he left for England in 1746.

111. London: the Thames, looking towards Westminster from near York Watergate

Pen and brown ink with gray wash, 15¼ × 28¼ in.
(38.8 × 71.8 cm)
Yale Center for British Art, New Haven;
Paul Mellon Collection
C/L 747

NOTES

1. John Baskett and Dudley Snelgrove, *English Drawings and Watercolors, 1550–1850, in the Collection of Mr. and Mrs. Paul Mellon*, exh. cat. (New York, 1972), p. 13, no. 15.
2. Clovis Whitfield, *Views from the Grand Tour*, exh. cat., Colnaghi (New York, 1983), pp. 22–23, no. 7.
3. R. J. B. Walker, *Old Westminster Bridge* (London, 1979).

At the near right is York Watergate (still in its original position, though the Embankment now runs between it and the river) and just beyond, the wooden water tower (a familiar landmark in London prints and drawings, long demolished).[1] Up river, center, is Westminster Abbey. Westminster Bridge, in the distance at the left, is in course of construction, with five arches extending from the Westminster side, still with their centerings. A painting (C/L 427) reproduces the subject almost exactly.[2]

The drawing and painting present a puzzle. When Canaletto arrived in London in May 1746 the bridge was almost finished, and he painted it accurately for Prince Lobkowitz (C/L 426) and correctly, except for a minor detail, in catalogue number 63. If in this drawing he intended to show it as it had been when begun, in 1739, he made a grave error because the middle arch was the first to be built and by the time the Westminster side was reached in 1744 there were eight, not five, arches. Canaletto may have cop-

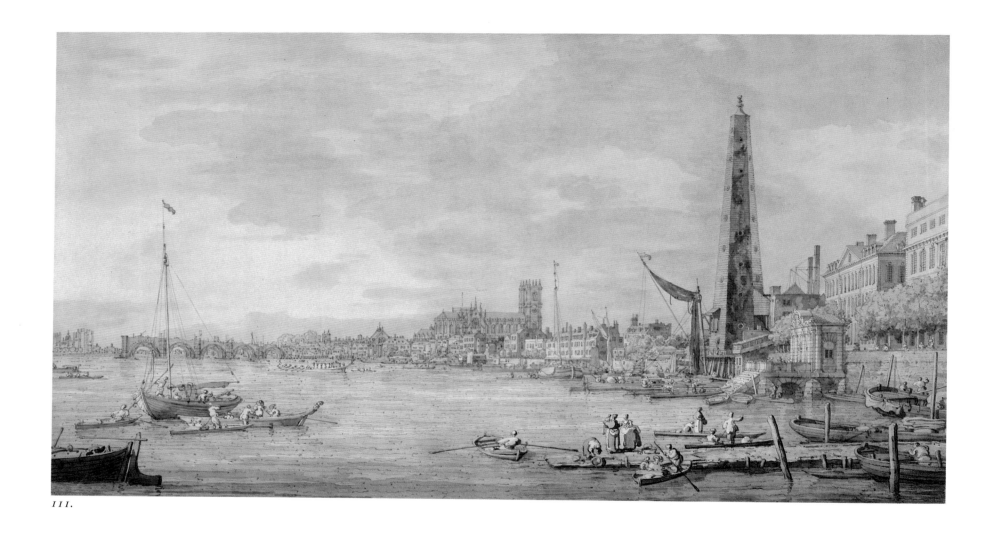

III.

ied an inaccurate drawing or relied on misinformation. The problem is not made easier by the existence of a painting by Samuel Scott which also shows the incomplete bridge in a form it never took. Progress in building the bridge is now beyond dispute, having been fully documented by R. J. B. Walker in a recent book on the subject, and no satisfactory explanation can be offered of the fanciful features of this otherwise realistic drawing.[3]

112. Warwick Castle: the East Front from the Outer Court

Pen and brown ink with gray wash, 12½ × 22⅛ in. (31.6 × 56.2 cm)
The Metropolitan Museum of Art, New York; Robert Lehman Collection, 1975
C/L 759

113. Warwick Castle: the East Front from the Courtyard

Pen and brown ink with gray wash, 12½ × 22½ in. (31.7 × 57.1 cm)
The J. Paul Getty Museum, Malibu
C/L 760

NOTES

1. The essential account is that of Buttery, *Burlington Magazine*, 1987, pp. 437–45. For the Lehman drawing, see also George Knox, in *The Robert Lehman Collection: VI. Italian Eighteenth-Century Drawings* (New York and Princeton, 1987), pp. 22–23, no. 19, who notes that the verso of the drawing is inscribed, in a later hand, *Ingresso del Castello de Lord Brooke a Warwick*.
2. "Acquisitions/1986," *J. Paul Getty Museum Journal* 15 (1987), p. 209, no. 96, recording an inscription on the reverse, *Warwick Castle Canalletti*.

Lord Brooke's commission to Canaletto to paint the east front of Warwick Castle is described in the entry for number 69.

The castle is approached through the gateway beneath the Clock Tower in number 112; the viewpoint is from the outer court (which was destroyed toward the end of the eighteenth century) with, at the right, a tollhouse, a gate, and houses of the town.[1] The courtyard, from which the same gate is seen, is much as it appears in the second drawing (cat. no. 113), and the entrance to the castle itself is on the right.[2] Both are lit from the left, suggesting that one drawing may have been made in the early morning and the other in the late afternoon.

The two sheets were seemingly intended as a pair, and both bear the collector's mark of Paul Sandby, an English topographical artist who made four aquatints of Warwick Castle, which he dedicated to the second Earl of Warwick, together with a number of watercolors. An 1809 inventory of the castle lists twelve drawings by Sandby hanging in the Little Study, and the second earl may perhaps have given him this pair of Canalettos in part payment. The two drawings, sold at Christie's in 1812, after Sandby's death, found their way back to Lady Eva Dugdale—a member of the Brooke (Warwick) family—who in turn sold them in 1920, and they were finally separated in 1935, when the Fauchier-Magnan collection was broken up. Canaletto's third drawing of the castle (C/L 758) belonged to yet another member of the family but was returned in 1907, and, together with four of Canaletto's paintings, it hung at Warwick until all were dispersed.

Canaletto's drawn and painted views of the east front are associated by Buttery with payments made in March and July of 1752. The drawings may

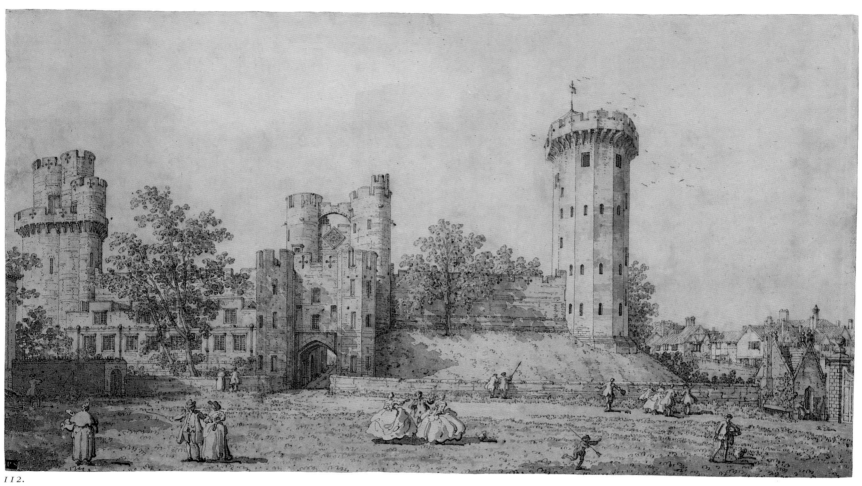

112.

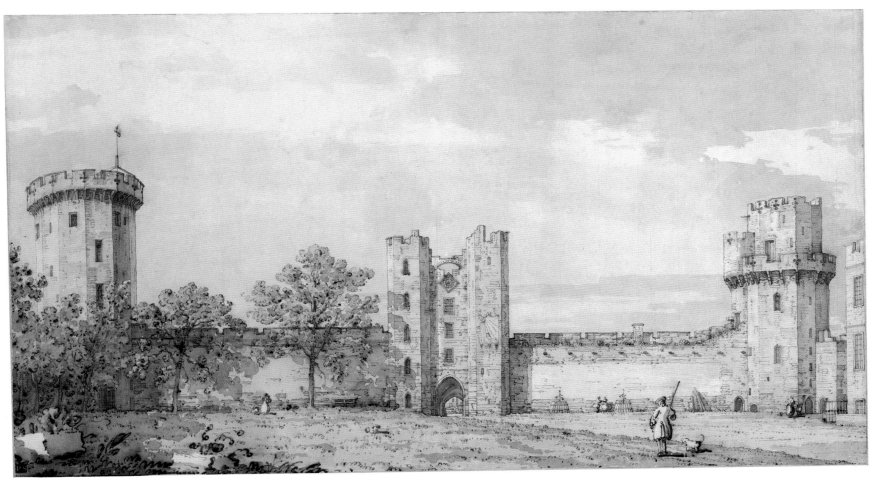

113.

be the earlier of the two pairs, and the basis for the paintings, though there is a slight topographical difference between the two views taken from within the courtyard. Several trees standing in front of Guy's Tower, to the left, and a door giving access to the tower, as seen in the drawing, are replaced in the painting by an uninterrupted stretch of lawn and a lancet window at the tower's base. There are a few more figures in the paintings, and more of the lawn is seen, increasing the effect of breadth.

114. London: Northumberland House

Pen and brown ink with brownish wash, 11⅜ × 16¾ in. (29 × 42.5 cm)
The Minneapolis Institute of Arts; The John De Laittre Fund, 1923
C/L 740

EXHIBITED
Canada 114

NOTE
1. Henry Reveley, *Notices Illustrative of the Drawings and Sketches of Some of the Most Distinguished Masters* (London, 1820), p. 249, as "a View of Northumberland House and Charing Cross, in pen and Indian-ink." Reveley mentions also his drawing of St. Mark's Place (for which see cat. no. 110, n. 2) and, belonging to Mr. Peachey (with possible reference to whose family see cat. no. 69), "a large drawing of Westminster Bridge, when building, with many figures, which is capital." This could be the drawing exhibited here as number 111.

For a description of the house and its owners, see the entry for number 70. The view is roughly eastward, with the Strand at left center, Northumberland House at right center, and the equestrian statue of Charles I in the foreground to the right. The paving and posts in the foreground of the painting and the posts marking the footpath in front of the house are here omitted. The figures differ in many details, and in the drawing more can be seen of the buildings at the far right.

Number 114 is not a preparatory study for the Duke of Northumberland's picture, which is from a slightly different viewpoint, but is instead an independent, finished drawing. An engraving published by Robert Sayer in 1753 is closer to the painting; it is inscribed *Canaleti Pinx' et Delin'. T. Bowles Sculp'*, presupposing the existence of another autograph sheet whose whereabouts is unknown.

The duke commissioned a number of paintings from Canaletto and may have ordered this drawing as well. George Reveley (1699–1766), younger brother of the duke's mother, Philadelphia, is a possible candidate as recipient, given the fact that number 113 is known to have been owned by his great-grandson Hugh Reveley (1812–1889) in 1876.[1]

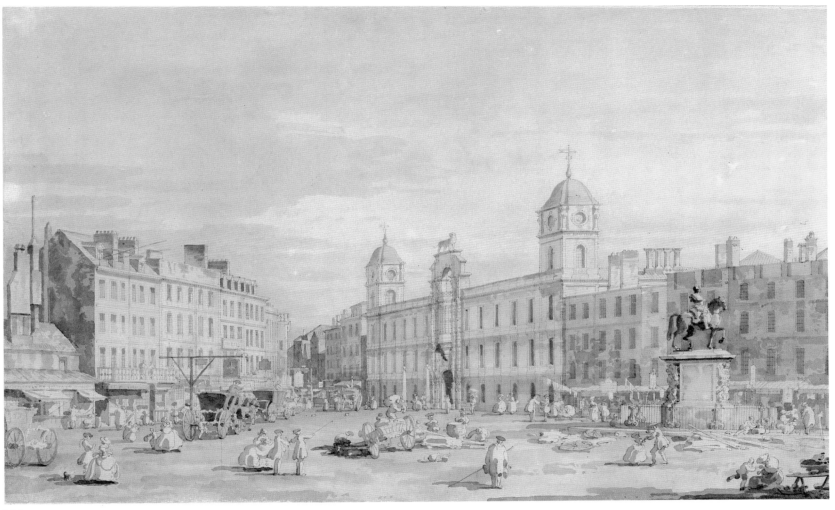

114.

115. Old Walton Bridge

Pen and brown ink with gray wash, 11⅜ × 26¾ in.
(29 × 68 cm)
Yale Center for British Art, New Haven;
Paul Mellon Collection
C/L 755

NOTE

1. John Baskett and Dudley Snelgrove, *English Drawings and Watercolors, 1550–1850, in the Collection of Mr. and Mrs. Paul Mellon*, exh. cat. (New York, 1972), p. 13, no. 16; and Corboz, *Canaletto*, 1985, p. 74.

The drawing is signed and dated in Canaletto's formal hand: *Disegnato da me Antonio Canal detto il Canaleto appresso il mio Quadro Dippinto in Londra 1755 / Per il Signore Caualiere dickers*. [Drawn by me Antonio Canal called Canaleto after my Picture Painted in London 1755 / For Signore Cavaliere Dickers.][1]

A painting of Old Walton Bridge is number 73. In the distance, left, of that picture, in front of the houses, can be seen the remains of another bridge, built in 1662 across flooded ground to give access to the ford and ferry in use before the bridge across the Thames River was constructed in 1750. In the present drawing, and in the painting referred to by Canaletto in his inscription (C/L 442, also now at Yale), there is a stone extension leading from the wooden bridge to the old bridge. This does not appear in the Dulwich picture (cat. no. 73), nor do the stone abutments shown in the Yale versions.

The wooden bridge was paid for by Samuel Dicker, M.P., whose house can be seen in the background, and who also commissioned the painting at Yale; the back of the lining canvas bears an inscription, no doubt transcribed from one on the original canvas, which is in much the same terms as that on Hollis's picture (cat. no. 73), but substituting the date 1755 for 1754. The dates on the Yale painting and drawing are the latest evidence of Canaletto's presence in England and provide the last that is known of him until 1760.

Number 115 may have been used for an engraving published by J. Jarvis, and dedicated to Dicker, which identifies the houses seen. Sheep are substituted for the dogs in the foreground.

There is no reason to doubt the date of 1755 on Dicker's painting as the year in which it was executed, or that the painting and the present drawing show the facts as they were. Dicker would hardly have wished otherwise, regardless of the artistic effect. It is generally assumed that the Hollis picture was also painted in the year in which it was inscribed, 1754, that it showed the bridge as it was then, and that the stone extension was a later addition. It is unsafe, however, to make any of these assumptions. There is no record of any extension having been made to the bridge after it had been built, and unless it could carry traffic across flooded ground it would hardly have served its purpose. On the other hand, there is every reason to suppose that more than one of Hollis's pictures had been painted well before the date put on them when he bought them. The Dulwich (Hollis) painting of the bridge may not show the facts as they were at any time: there is a strong possibility

115.

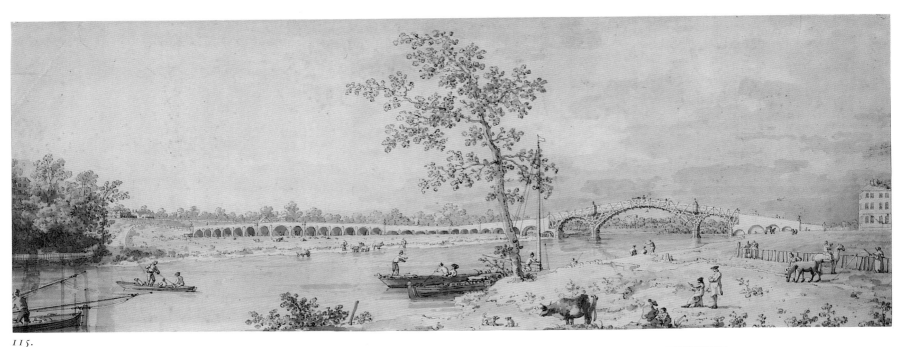

Disegnato da me Antonio Canal detto il Canaleto appresso il Mio Quadro Dippinto in Londra. 1755
Per il Signore Cavaliere diKent.

that it is in the nature of a capriccio, omitting the features Canaletto found inartistic, and altering the true shape of Old Walton Bridge. It may have been painted for Canaletto's own pleasure at any time after the bridge was opened in 1750 and kept by him until, in 1754, a buyer for it appeared, and the figures were added to his requirements.

116. Piazza S. Marco: looking East

Pen and brown ink, 15 × 9¾ in. (38.1 × 24.8 cm)
The Lord O'Neill
C/L 528

Piazza S. Marco is seen from the southwest corner, framed by the arch through which the visitor passes to reach the part of the city within the loop of the Grand Canal. To the right is the Procuratie Nuove with, in the distance, S. Marco, the Campanile, and a glimpse of Palazzo Ducale. There are a number of booths at the base of the Campanile, and an awning supported on tent poles extends the length of the Piazza. The drawing was reportedly seen in the making by John Crewe, later the first Lord Crewe, who was traveling with his tutor, the Reverend John Hinchliffe, and was in Venice in 1760. Hinchliffe's grandson, Edward Hinchliffe, recounted the following story of the two travelers in Venice:

> [They] chanced to see a little man making a sketch of the Campanile in St. Mark's Place: Hinchliffe took the liberty—not an offensive one abroad, as I myself can testify—to look at what he was doing. Straightway he discovered a master-hand and hazarded the artist's name 'Canaletti'. The man looked up and replied *'mi conosce'*. Thereupon a conversation ensued, and Canaletti, pleased to find so enthusiastic a judge of drawing, invited Hinchliffe to his studio, who waited upon him there the following day, and inspected his paintings and drawings. The visit terminated most agreeably to the traveller. Having requested Canaletti to allow him to purchase the painting about to be made from the sketch he had seen the artist take, Canaletti not only agreed to this, but, in addition, presented him with the sketch itself, as a complimentary gift: and a very valuable one my grandfather esteemed it, and so did his eldest son, at whose death it became the property of the present Lord Crewe, by purchase, and is now at Crewe Hall.[1]

(Relevant not to the present drawing but in connection with the painting of *Whitehall and the Privy Garden* [C/L 439, fig. 4] is an addition to the story told in 1856 by Hinchliffe's grandson. Canaletto, he reports, also showed Hinchliffe and Crewe the Whitehall picture, which he told them he had refused to sell while in England, wishing to keep it as a memento of his visit

EXHIBITED
Canada 125

NOTE
1. Edward Hinchliffe, *Barthomley* (London, 1856), p. 53; and Links, *Canaletto and His Patrons*, 1977, p. 84.

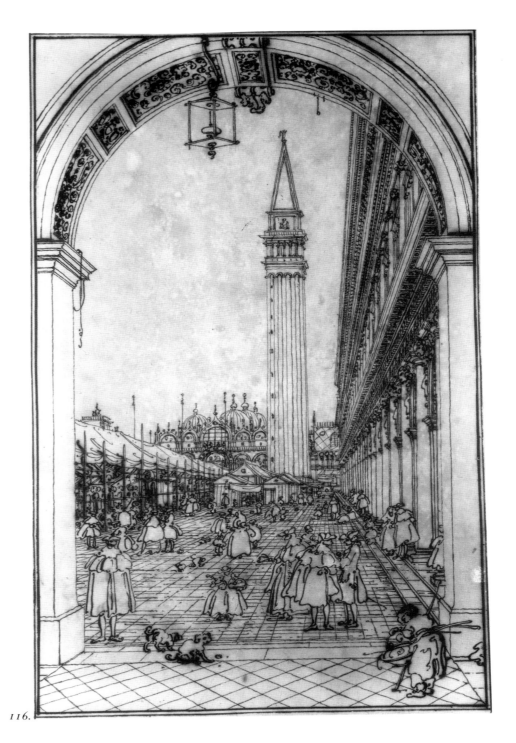

116.

to that country. Canaletto allowed himself to be persuaded to sell the painting to John Crewe. It now belongs to the Duke of Buccleuch.)

Although written almost a century after the event, there is no reason to doubt the substance of Hinchliffe's grandson's report. The details, however, present difficulties. "The painting about to be made from the sketch" can be identified (C/L 19); it belonged to the Hinchliffe family until 1836. Number 116 long remained with the Crewes and must have been part of the 1760 purchase, although it is clearly not a sketch but a studio product. Possibly Hinchliffe referred to it as a sketch because it is in outline only, but this would not explain what became of the sketch Canaletto was seen making in the Piazza. It is of course just possible that Canaletto took drawings of the kind into Piazza S. Marco with him in the hope of a sale such as occurred in this case.

117. Riva degli Schiavoni: looking East

Pen and brown ink and gray wash, 14 × 9½ in.
(35.6 × 24.1 cm)
Private Collection

On the reverse of the old mount of this unpublished drawing is the mark (Lugt 1420) of the English collector John Barnard (died 1784): *JB. N.º 792*.[1] Barnard is known to have owned two other drawings by Canaletto—*Capriccio: with Reminiscences of Richmond House* (C/L 786a), bearing the consecutive number, 793, and *Piazza S. Marco: looking West* (C/L 531), numbered 1086.[2]

Canaletto made many paintings and drawings of the Riva degli Schiavoni looking toward the east, but only one is closely comparable to number 117. It is a small, upright canvas (C/L 116) and has as a pendant a view from the Campo S. Basso (C/L 41) which shows the Torre dell'Orologio after the remodeling of 1755. For this reason, as well as on grounds of style, the present drawing must be a late work. The foreground column is in such steep perspective that only part of the figure of St. Theodore is visible, a detail differing from the comparable painting. The brickwork of the *bacino* facade of Palazzo Ducale is indicated only by a grid of intersecting diagonals, the white of the paper increasing the effect of bright sunlight.

NOTES

1. Frits Lugt, *Les Marques de collections de dessins & d'estampes* (Amsterdam, 1921; reprint, The Hague, 1956), pp. 255–57, who, however, does not mention any drawings by Canaletto.
2. The capriccio (C/L 786a) excludes Westminster Bridge, and in other details is not entirely realistic; a variant of C/L 786, it incorporates the terrace and river facade of Richmond House, rather than Old Montagu House, as may be seen by comparison with C/L 744.

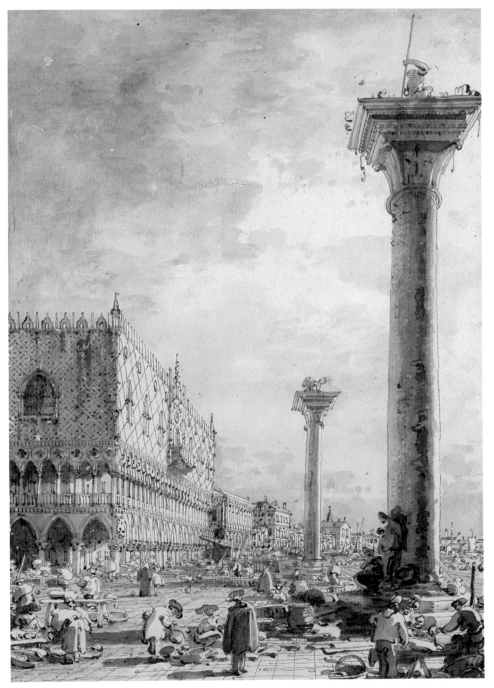

117.

118. Capriccio: Terrace and Loggia of a Palace on the Lagoon

Pen, black ink, and gray wash, over pencil, 14¼ × 20⅞ in. (36.3 × 53.1 cm)
Her Majesty Queen Elizabeth II
C/L 821

EXHIBITED
London 96; Venice 63

NOTES
1. C/L, p. 167.
2. Parker, *Drawings of Canaletto*, 1948, pp. 57–58, no. 141; Pignatti, *Canaletto: Selected Drawings*, 1970, no. LXIII; Miller, in *Canaletto*, 1980, p. 120, no. 96; Miller, in *Canaletto*, 1982, pp. 50–51, no. 63; and Miller, *Fifty Drawings by Canaletto*, 1983, p. 39, no. 50.
3. Corboz, *Canaletto*, 1985, p. 299.

On the angle of the loggia is a cartouche carrying a chevron, the coat of arms of the Canal family, sometimes used by Canaletto as a signature.[1]

"Grandly conceived and superbly executed," writes Charlotte Miller, "this imposing composition is one of the finest of all Canaletto's drawings, proof that late in his career he could produce work of the highest calibre."[2] Parker describes the drawing as a perspective tour de force, noting that in this it resembles the artist's Academy submission, of 1765 (cat. no. 85). Presumably, and despite Pignatti's view to the contrary, it dates from before 1762, and it is probably the last drawing by Canaletto acquired by Consul Smith before he sold his collection to George III.

Number 118 incorporates the placid waters of the lagoon, with mud flats and fishermen, many boats, suggestively and loosely drawn, and an elaborately fanciful view of the Dogana with the church of Sta. Maria della Salute. The colonnade of the loggia, as Corboz remarks, is reminiscent of that of the Procuratie Nuove, and the flights of stairs recall the Scala dei Giganti in the courtyard of Palazzo Ducale.[3] There are traces of a preliminary drawing in pencil throughout, and numerous pentimenti (unusual for Canaletto), over ruling, and pinpointing, indicative of a carefully cogitated design. This brilliant sheet is a marvelous finale to the selection of drawings graciously lent to the exhibition by Her Majesty Queen Elizabeth II.

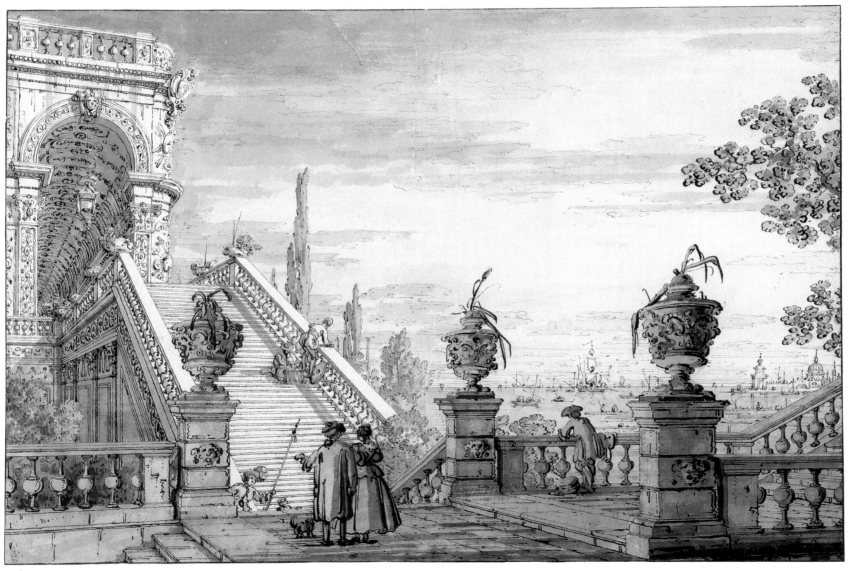

118.

119. Capriccio, with a Roman Triumphal Arch and Ruins

Pen, brown ink, and gray wash, over traces of pencil,
15 × 21¼ in. (38.1 × 54 cm)
The Metropolitan Museum of Art, New York;
Harris Brisbane Dick Fund, 1946
C/L 807

EXHIBITED

Canada 98

NOTES

1. Corboz, "Sur la prétendue objectivité de Canaletto," 1974,
   pp. 211 and 217 n. 30; and Corboz, *Canaletto*, 1985,
   pp. 116–17, and 139 n. 219.
2. See also C/L 848 (I and II).
3. Corboz. *Canaletto*, 1985, p. 117, fig. 123; and for Piranesi's
   prints of Pola, Alessandro Bettagno, ed., *Piranesi*, exh. cat.,
   Fondazione Giorgio Cini, Venice (Vicenza, 1978), figs. 118–21.

The triumphal arch is that at Pula (Pola), a port and archaeological site on the Istrian peninsula in modern Yugoslavia, which for centuries lay within Venetian territory.[1] Canaletto, it may be assumed, never visited the Adriatic coast. A finished drawing (C/L 848*) incorporating the amphitheater at Pola is after a Piranesi etching, published in 1748 in *Antichità Romane fuori di Roma*, of which Consul Smith possessed a copy.[2] Canaletto shows the amphitheater amid hills and ruined arches, with, in the foreground, a small harbor resembling the one on the Molo in Venice. For the present sheet the source is less certain. In another of Piranesi's etchings the arch at Pola is seen at roughly the same angle, but it is in a very much ruined state, without sculptural detail, and without the fractured stone of the second column from the left as seen here. Corboz draws attention to the fact that Canaletto's arch is the more archaeologically correct.[3]

Among the figures is an artist or amateur, seated, and sketching the ancient monument. The triumphal arch is surrounded by antique columns, other ruined arches, a church tower that may be reminiscent of England, and, at the right, the mast of a boat and a distant view of the lagoon. This drawing, large and highly finished, is double and triple washed over fine pen work, accomplished in every detail.

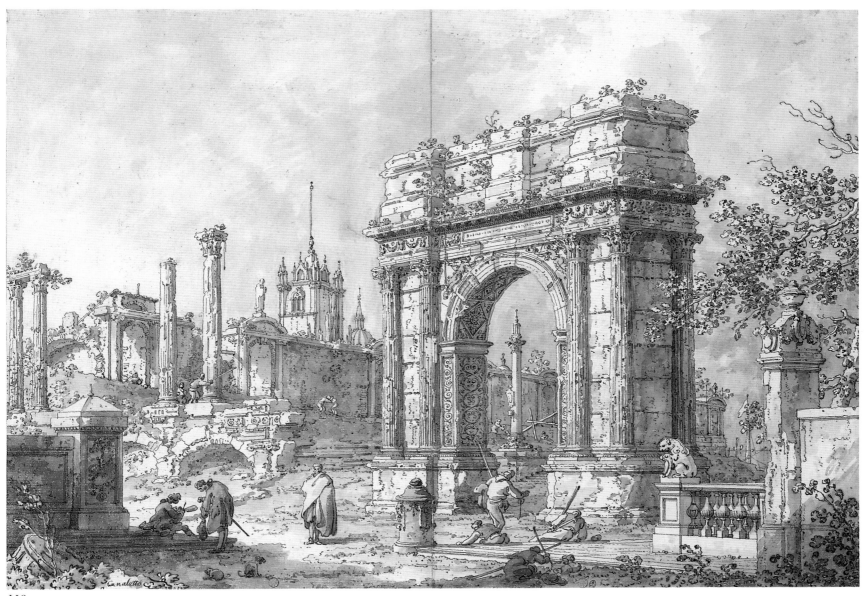

119.

343

120. A Cottage in Front of a Flight of Steps

Pen, brown ink, and gray wash, over pencil, heightened with white, 9⅞ × 13⅞ in. (25.2 × 35.3 cm)
Staatliche Museen Preussischer Kulturbesitz, Kupferstichkabinett, Berlin
C/L 699

NOTE

1. Pignatti, *Canaletto: Selected Drawings*, 1970, no. LXII; and Dreyer, *Vedute*, 1985, p. 34, no. 36.

Over the door of the outbuilding at the left is a chevron with an oval cartouche.[1] Canaletto used this reference to the family arms as a signature on a number of drawings, four etchings, and two paintings. It would be unusual if these ramshackle buildings—capriciously combined with a flight of stairs—were entirely imaginary, and perhaps they recall something seen on the mainland. Unpruned shrubs pattern the skyline, vines cascade over wooden planters, and the fencing, cask, and timbers belong in a country farm-yard. The modest components belie an inventive imaginary design and the most skillful handling. Canaletto rarely used white heightening, as here, and the drawing is thus associable with drawings preparatory to Brustoloni's etchings of the *Feste Ducali*, for which see catalogue numbers 122 and 123.

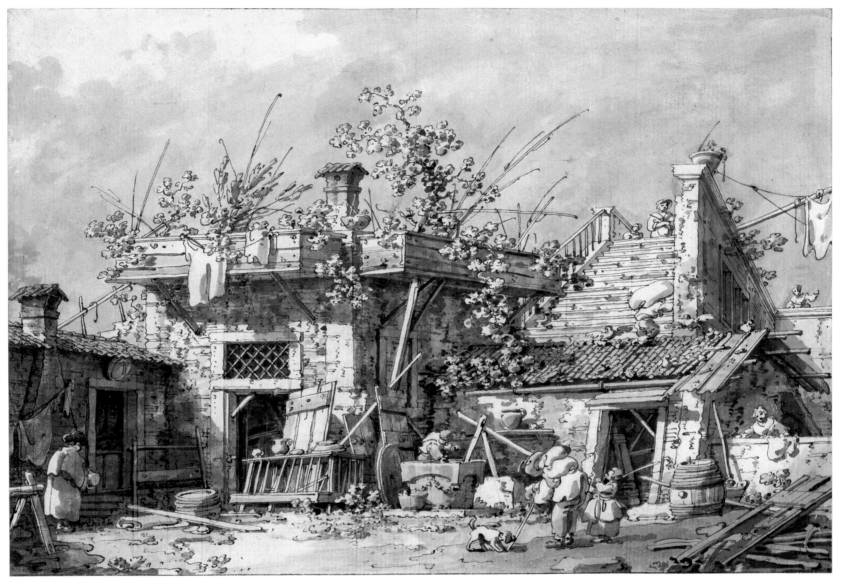

120.

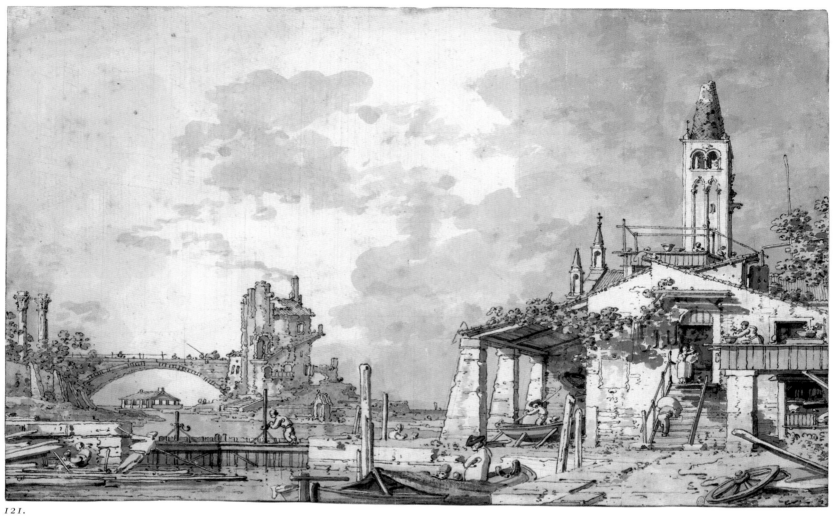

121.

121. Capriccio: House, Church, Tower, and Bridge by a Lagoon

Pen, brown ink, and gray wash, over traces of pencil,
10¼ × 16¼ in. (25.9 × 41.3 cm)
The Metropolitan Museum of Art, New York;
Rogers Fund, 1943
C/L 797

NOTES

1. Jacob Bean and Felice Stampfle, *Drawings from New York Collections*: III. *The Eighteenth Century in Italy*, exh. cat. (New York, 1971), p. 67, no. 155.
2. Succi, in *Da Carlevarijs ai Tiepolo*, 1983, pp. 75–77, nos. 44–47, ill.
3. Josephine L. Allen, "Capriccio by Canaletto," *Metropolitan Museum of Art Bulletin*, n.s. 4, no. 5 (1946), p. 125 ill.

This drawing is the most successful of a series of variations on a theme. The material—boat shed, antique columns, bridge, and ruined tower—is not only familiar, but specifically reminiscent of earlier lagoon and mainland views.[1] The campanile, similar to the one at Dolo on the Brenta, is here combined with other typically Venetian motifs. The bell tower, house, and columns appear in two paintings (C/L 485) whose compositions are in reverse to the present sheet, and in a print by Fabio Berardi, in the same sense as the drawing, but differing from it and from the paintings in certain details. Berardi's print belongs to an untitled series, published by Wagner, and dating after Canaletto's return from England.[2]

An unrelated architectural sketch, in pencil, is barely visible at the upper left, and, on the verso, there is a faint drawing (C/L 608) in graphite of buildings along a Venetian canal.[3] The latter has been identified as Rio S. Barnaba.

Le Feste Ducali

Of a series of ten drawings by Canaletto representing ceremonies and festivals in which the Doge took part (C/L 630–39), two are here exhibited.[1] The drawings were found in a bookseller's in Venice by Sir Robert Colt Hoare between 1787 and 1789, when the well-known dealer Giovanni Maria Sasso reported to Sir Abraham Hume that they were as fine as any paintings. The entire series descended in the Hoare family, remaining at Stourhead in Wiltshire until dispersed at public auction in 1883.

Canaletto's drawings were preparatory to a set of engravings—twelve in all—by Giovanni Battista Brustoloni, each of which is inscribed *Antonius Canal pinxit* and *Jo. Bap. Brustolon inc.*[2] There are, however, a number of instances where *pinxit* was used on an engraving for which no painting is likely to have existed. Confusion has arisen from the fact that Francesco Guardi made paintings of all twelve subjects (Musée du Louvre, of which four are deposited elsewhere), but no painting has been found of any one of them which is generally accepted as by Canaletto, and it must be concluded that at least ten of the engravings were made from Canaletto's drawings or from copies of them reversed for the engraver.[3]

NOTES

1. Nine of the ten drawings were exhibited in Venice in 1982, for which see Bettagno, in *Canaletto*, 1982, pp. 51–52, nos. 64–72.
2. Succi, in *Da Carlevarijs ai Tiepolo*, 1983, pp. 87–93, nos. 59–66, summarizes the current state of knowledge as to the date of publication of Brustoloni's prints, which combine etching and engraving.
3. Arnauld Brejon de Lavergnée and Dominique Thiébaut, eds., *Catalogue sommaire illustré des peintures du musée du Louvre*: II. *Italie, Espagne, Allemagne, Grande-Bretagne et divers* (Paris, 1981), pp. 185–86, nos. 319–25 and 20009; and Morassi, *Guardi*, [1973], pp. 175–81, and 354–57, nos. 243–54, and figs. 268–84.

Eight of the prints were announced (though none were as yet printed) by the publisher, Furlanetto, in March 1766. Four months later, in July, Furlanetto secured permission to extend the series to twelve images in all. The precise date of publication of the full set is, however, unknown. The sheet depicting the Giovedi Grasso festival (cat. no. 122) bears the arms of Doge Alvise Mocenigo IV, who was elected in 1763. It seems improbable that the coat of arms is a later addition: there had been an election in 1762 (Doge Marco Foscarini's tenure was brief), but prior to that none since 1752, when Canaletto would have been in England. Given what we know of the artist, it is unlikely that he would have portrayed the Doge presented to the people in the basilica (C/L 630) and the subsequent procession through Piazza S. Marco (C/L 631) if he had not seen these events in many years. There is no record of the eleventh and twelfth finished drawings by Canaletto, and perhaps he never completed them: the order for the *Feste Ducali* must have been his last major commission.

122. *The Doge Attends the Giovedi Grasso Festival in the Piazzetta*

Pen, brown ink, and gray wash, over pencil, heightened with white, 15 × 21¾ in. (38.1 × 55.2 cm)
Private Collection
C/L 636

EXHIBITED

Venice 70

NOTES

1. Links, *Canaletto*, 1982, pp. 9–11.
2. Bettagno, in *Canaletto*, 1982, p. 52, no. 70. The drawing corresponds with Brustoloni's print number 7.

The Giovedi Grasso festival was for centuries celebrated by the Venetians on the last Thursday before the beginning of Lent. The Doge, beneath a furled awning at the center of the arcade facing the Piazzetta, is here surrounded by the populace, standing in the foreground, and seated in temporary boxes and grandstands erected for the occasion. The men balancing on poles, and on each other's shoulders, to form a human pyramid are performing a Venetian acrobatic stunt called the Labors of Hercules. The ropes hanging at either side of the temporary pavilion, which is decorated with statues and trophies of arms and garlanded with flowers, are in preparation for the Volo del Turco, in which a suitably costumed man or boy descends from the top of the Campanile to present flowers and poetic compositions to the Doge. The entertainments of the day concluded with a display of fireworks set off from the pavilion in the Piazzetta.

The composition is exceptionally felicitous and incorporates a number of Venetian landmarks: a corner of the basilica, Palazzo Ducale, the onion-shaped bell tower of S. Giorgio, the column and statue of St. Theodore, and the Library, Loggetta, and Campanile. Among hundreds of figures, many

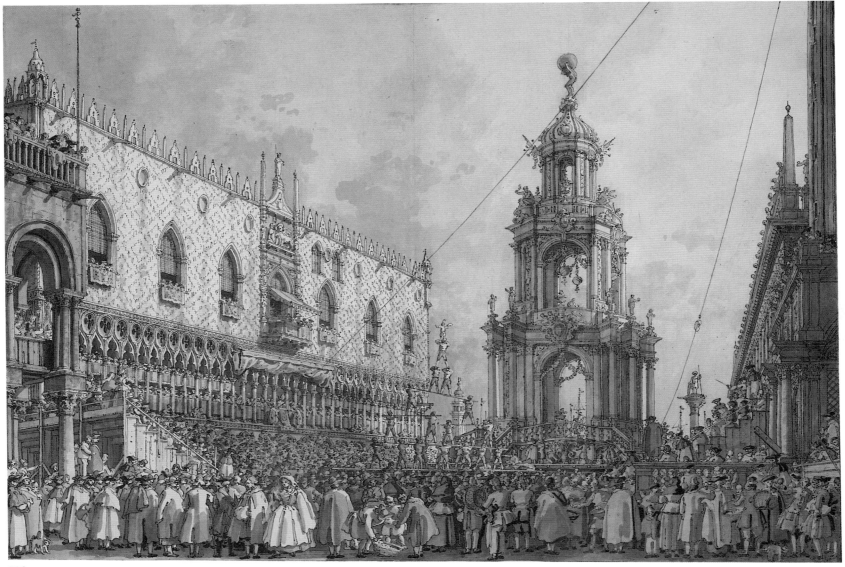

122.

masked, those in the foreground are shown in full length and tellingly described. The political decline of the Serenissima did not bear contemplation and, as Links points out, the Venetians took care that their visitors (a characteristic group is at the far right) should as often as possible be treated to an atmosphere of irrepressible gaiety and to the Carnival festivities upon which, increasingly, their livelihood and well-being depended.[1]

Brustoloni's print is supplied with a lengthy descriptive title, in the early editions in Latin: *Die Jovis postrema Bacchanaliorum Serenissimus Princeps e ducali Palatio conspicit populares ludos, perantiquae victoriae monumenta.*[2]

123. The Annual Visit of the Doge to Sta. Maria della Salute

Pen, brown ink, and gray wash, over pencil, heightened with white, 15 × 21¾ in. (38.1 × 55.2 cm)
Private Collection
C/L 637

EXHIBITED
Venice 71

NOTES
1. C/L, p. 152.
2. Bettagno, in *Canaletto*, 1982, p. 52, no. 71. The present sheet corresponds to number 8 of Brustoloni's prints, and the two drawings here exhibited thus relate to the series announced by Furlanetto in March 1766.

The annual visit of the Doge to Longhena's church of Sta. Maria della Salute —built as a thank offering following the deliverance of the city from the plague of 1630, and completed in 1687—took place each year on 21 November, the feast day of the Purification of the Virgin. A temporary bridge, here seen at the right, was built across the Grand Canal for the occasion. (A bridge of the kind is still built each year, across the Giudecca Canal, for the feast of the Redeemer.) The Doge, just in front of the umbrella, ascends the steps of the church in procession, having disembarked from the lavishly decorated *peota* standing at the water's edge. The *Feste Ducali* are, as W. G. Constable noted, "as elaborate as any drawings Canaletto ever made.... At the same time they are largely the result of an extremely dexterous use of a series of calligraphic gestures, set within skilfully contrived designs."[1]

The descriptive inscription accompanying Brustoloni's print reads as follows: *Annua votiva profectio Serenissimi Principis, comitante Senatu, ad aedem Deiparae Virginis de Salute, ob cives a pestilentia servatos.*[2]

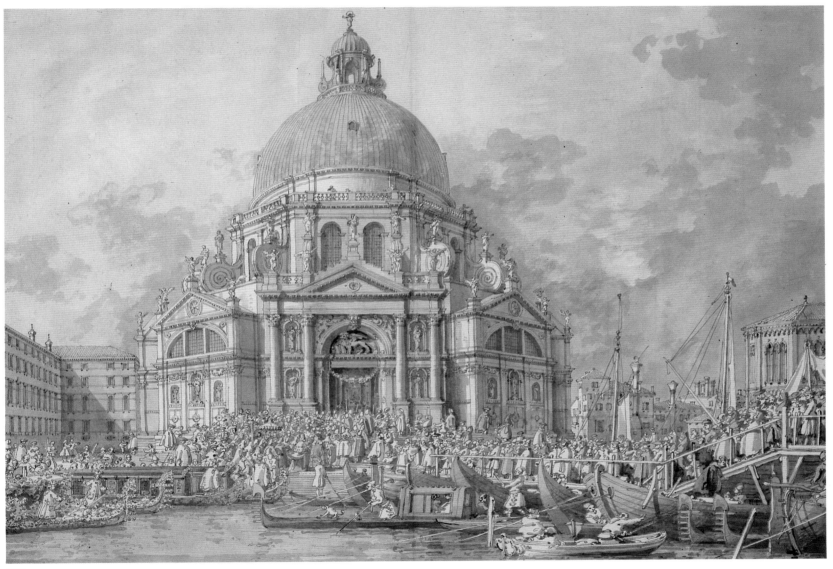

123.

124. S. Marco: the Crossing and Choir

Pen and brown ink over pencil, 11 × 7½ in. (28 × 19 cm)
The Metropolitan Museum of Art, New York;
Robert Lehman Collection, 1975
C/L 561

NOTES

1. George Knox, in *The Robert Lehman Collection*: VI. *Italian Eighteenth-Century Drawings* (New York and Princeton, 1987), p. 26, no. 22. For an earlier painting and two drawings of the crossing and north transept, see cat. nos. 37 and 99, and C/L 557; and for later drawings of comparable subjects, cat. no. 126, C/L 559, and C/L 560.
2. Alice Binion, "Three Drawings by Canaletto," *Master Drawings* 18, no. 4 (1980), p. 375, and pl. 47B, publishes this drawing and two others by Canaletto at Leipzig for the first time.
3. C/L, pp. 641–46, and Miotti, "Tre disegni inediti del Canaletto," 1966, pp. 275–78. Binion does not describe the paper nor mention an inscription on the Leipzig sheet.

Insofar as is known, Canaletto's drawings of interiors are all of the basilica of S. Marco.[1] This rough sketch, in ink over more extensive notation in graphite, is similar to a sheet in the Museum der Bildenden Künste, Leipzig, which shows the crossing and apse from a more distant viewpoint and from a slightly different angle.[2] The two drawings were probably made on the ground, and within a short interval of time, though it should perhaps be noted that the ambo in the Lehman drawing is draped, while the three ambos in the Leipzig sheet are not. The two drawings are generally thought to be late works and are perhaps associable with one or another of two paintings showing the crossing and apse from the west end (C/L 78, in the Royal Collection and thus datable before 1762, and cat. no. 81), or with the finished drawing representing *The Doge Presented to the People in S. Marco* (C/L 630), which is preparatory to the first of Brustoloni's prints of the *Feste Ducali*, published no earlier than 1766.

Number 124 belonged to the so-called Corniani Algarotti album (Francesco Algarotti's daughter married a member of the Corniani family), of which thirty-five leaves, varying in size but done on the same finely ribbed paper, are known.[3] Each is described on the verso, in the hand of the same former owner or dealer, as a rare original sketch by Canaletto. The drawings are now widely dispersed; sixteen of them—including this one—belonged to Italico Brass, and sixteen others to Dr. Alfredo Viggiano, both of Venice.

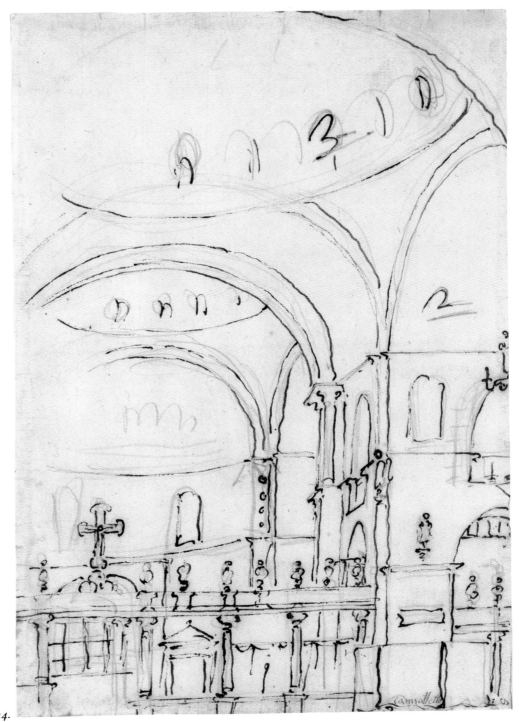

124.

125. Campo S. Basso: Houses on the North Side

Pen and brown ink over black chalk, with some red chalk,
17 × 11½ in. (43.3 × 29.5 cm)
Staatliche Museen Preussischer Kulturbesitz,
Kupferstichkabinett, Berlin
C/L 540

EXHIBITED
Canada 92; Venice 56

NOTES
1. Pignatti, *Canaletto: Selected Drawings*, 1970, no. XIV; Bettagno, in *Canaletto*, 1982, p. 48, no. 56; and Dreyer, *Vedute*, 1985, p. 33, no. 34, and fig. 32 (the verso).
2. Likewise inscribed *uolta*; the sale catalogue refers to "figures on the reverse."
3. For a view of Campo S. Basso from the opposite direction, see cat. no. 55.

This drawing of two houses with shops fronting on the *campo* is copiously inscribed in Canaletto's hand.[1] At the top, beneath the number 59, is the artist's description of the subject: *prima parte dela uista dela piaza di S. Basso uerso S. Gimignian. / che uà unita con il folio 58. e uolta.* (first part of the view of the Piazza di S. Basso toward S. Geminiano, which goes together with folio 58). *Volta* is an advice to the viewer to turn the page and is found on a number of drawings which are from dismembered sketchbooks. There are other notes, as to the business of the several shops, and directions, such as *più basso*, or lower. On the reverse of this unusually large sheet is another detailed drawing, of parts of the Torre dell'Orologio, and reference is made in the inscription to the adjoining sheet (C/L 541, sold in 1921, whereabouts unknown), which shows all of the buildings along the north side from the church of S. Basso to the Clock Tower and a little beyond.[2]

More than a dozen of these numbered sheets are known (cat. no. 126 is another), some figure drawings but mostly architectural studies. Although no number is repeated, the sheets must come from more than one sketchbook. Dates as early as about 1730, by comparison with the sketchbook in the Accademia, and after 1755, by association with the drawing of Campo Sta. Sofia from the Corniani Algarotti album (C/L 596), have been suggested. There is a clue, as the missing sheet and the verso of this one show the top story of the Torre dell'Orologio without the addition that was made about 1755 (it can be seen at the right of cat. no. 84). Given Canaletto's interest in, and accuracy concerning, such matters, it is unlikely that the two drawings are later than 1755. Their diagrammatic nature, however, renders the dating uncertain.[3]

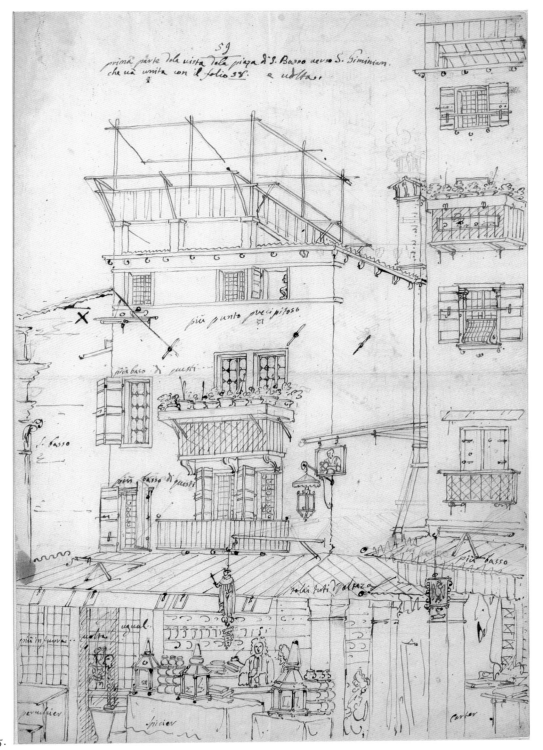

59

prima parte dela vista dela piaza d'S. Basso verso S. Siminian.
che va unita con il folio 58. e volta.

più punto precipitoso

X

più baso di questi

S. Basso

più baso di questi

più baso

più in nuova

ugual.

125.

126. Studies of Men, Standing

Pen and brown ink over black chalk, 11¾ × 6½ in.
(29.8 × 16.4 cm)
The Metropolitan Museum of Art, New York; Purchase,
Joseph Pulitzer Bequest, 1939
C/L 840

NOTE

1. Jacob Bean and Felice Stampfle, *Drawings from New York Collections*: III. *The Eighteenth Century in Italy*, exh. cat. (New York, 1971), p. 70, no. 162.

On one side of the sheet is a study of a man in a tricorn hat and cape, together with further drawings of his head—the profile, in ink, and a three-quarter view, in chalk. On the reverse is a man wearing a cap and an apron, smoking a pipe. Both sides are inscribed *40/uolta*.[1] Number 126 appears to have come from the same sketchbook as a sheet inscribed *11/uolta* in the Courtauld Institute, London (C/L 839), which similarly shows, on recto and verso, two men standing. Those men were used in a painting of *S. Giacomo di Rialto* (C/L 298) whose date, however, is also uncertain. Very few of Canaletto's figure studies have survived, particularly as compared with the number of those by Carlevaris. The pen work of number 126 is supple and accomplished.

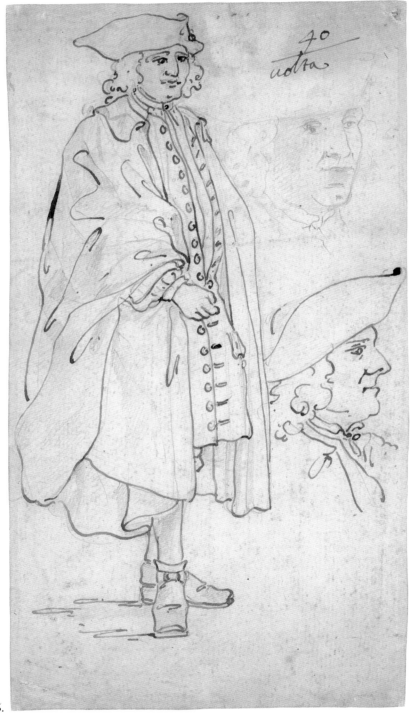

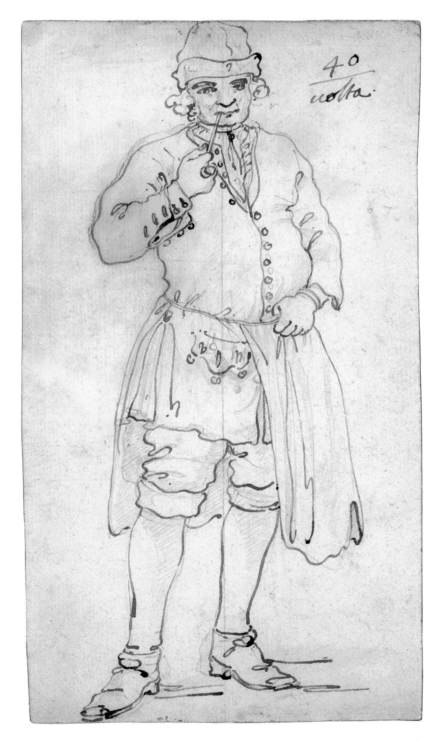

126.

127. S. Marco: the Crossing and North Transept, with Musicians Singing

Pen and brown ink and gray wash, 14 × 10⅝ in.
(35.5 × 27.1 cm)
Hamburger Kunsthalle
C/L 558

EXHIBITED
Canada 126; Venice 75

NOTE
1. Pignatti, *Canaletto: Selected Drawings*, 1970, no. LXV; Alice
Binion, "Some New Drawings by Canaletto," *Master Drawings* 14, no. 4 (1976), pp. 390–92; and Bettagno, in *Canaletto*, 1982, p. 53, no. 75.

The drawing is inscribed below in Canaletto's formal hand: *Io Zuane Antonio da Canal, Hò fatto il presente disegnio, delle Musici che Canta nella Chiesa Ducal di S. Marco in Venezia in ettá de- / Anni 68 Cenzza Ochiali, Lanno 1766.* (I Zuane Antonio da Canal, Have made the present drawing, of the Musicians who Sing in the Ducal Church of S. Marco in Venice at the age of / 68 Years Without Spectacles, The year 1766.)[1] The drawing and Canaletto's description of it leave little more to be said. This is the last dated work from his hand. Canaletto died at about seven in the evening on 19 April 1768 after a five-day illness.

There are diagrammatic line drawings in ink for the pulpit (C/L 560) and for the architectural and sculptural components (C/L 559). In a third sheet, now at Weimar (C/L 558* [1989 ed.]), Canaletto prepared an elaborate ruled study in pencil of the lower half of the composition, sketching a number of figures, and reaffirming those in the foreground in ink. The cloaked figure in profile at the right of the finished drawing appears also in the Weimar sheet but at the left and in reverse. Complex and fugitive effects of light are conveyed by the delicate gray washes.

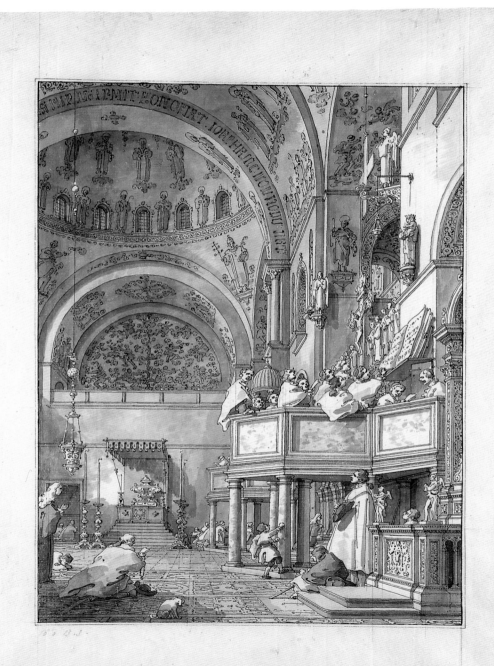

Io Zuane Antonio da Canal, Hò fatto il presente disegnio delli Musici che Canta nella Chiesa Ducal di S. Marco in Venezia in'età de Anni 68 Cenzza Ochiali, L'anno 1766.

127.

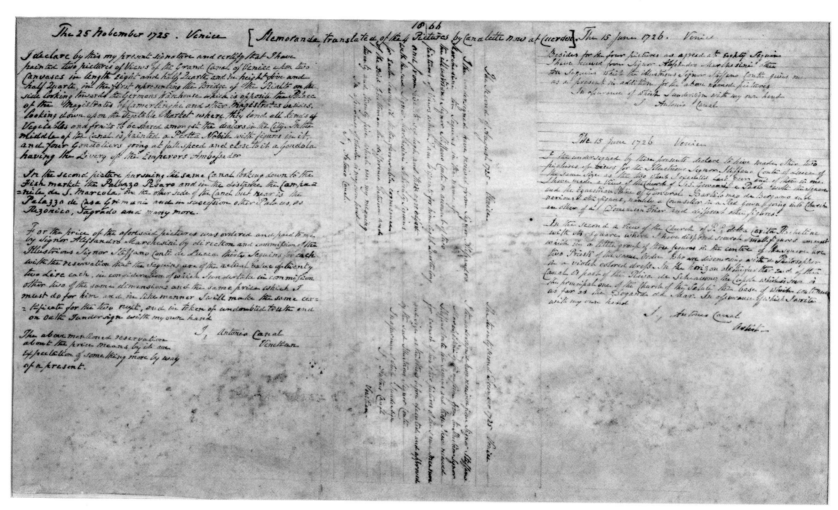

The 25 November 1725. Venice   [Memoranda translated of the 4 Pictures by Canalette now at Cuerdon]   The 15 June 1726. Venice

I declare by this my present signature and certify that I have painted two pictures of Views of the Grand Canal of Venice upon two canvases in length eight and half Quarte and in height five and half Quarte, in the first representing the Bridge of the Rialto on the side looking towards the Germans Warehouse which is opposite the Place of the Magistrates of Camerlinghi and other Magistrates besides, looking down upon the Vegetable Market where they land all kinds of Vegetables and fruits to be shared amongst the dealers in the City. In the middle of the canal is painted a Pietta Nobile with figures in it, and four Gondoliers going at full speed and close to it a Gondola having the Livery of the Emperors Ambassador

In the second picture pursuing the same canal looking down to the Fish market the Palazzo Pisaro and in the distance the Camera = niello de S. Marcola on the other side of the Canal but near is the Palazzo de Casa Grimani and in succession other Palaces, as Flozonico, Tagrado and many more.

For the price of the aforesaid pictures was ordered and paid to me by Signor Alessandro Marchesini by direction and commission of the Illustrious Signor Steffano conti de Lucca thirty Sequins for each with the reservation that the Sequins are of the actual value of twenty two Lire each, in consideration of which Sum I declare in commission other two of the same dimensions and the same price which I must do for him and in like manner I will make the same cer = tificate for the two right, and in token of undoubted truth and on oath I undersign with my own hand

The above mentioned reservation about the price means by it an expectation of something more by way of a present.

I, Antonio Canal
Venetian.

The 15 June 1726   Venice

Besides for the four pictures as agreed at eighty Sequins I have received from Signor Alessandro Marchesini three Sequins which the illustrious Signor Steffano Conti gives me as a present in addition for the above named pictures

In assurance of which I undersign with my own hand

I, Antonio Canal

1866

Appendix

Five documents in Canaletto's hand have remained with the four paintings (cat. nos. 8–11) commissioned of the artist by Stefano Conti of Lucca: three are receipts of payment, and the others are descriptions of each of the two pairs of views. The transcriptions are those contained in a sixth document, dated 1866 and made at Cuerdon, when the pictures were in the possession of the descendants of Robert Townley Parker.

The second of August 1725—Venice

*I the undersigned have received from Signor Alessandro Marchesini ten Se-
quins in the name of the illustrious Signor Steffano Conti on account of two
pictures of Views which I am to execute for him eight Quarte long and from five
to six high and these agreed for with the said Signor Marchesini at twenty
Sequins for each leaving it to the favourable cognisance of the said Gentleman
the difference between and twenty and twenty five which was my meaning*

In assurance of which is my own hand

I, Antonio Canal.

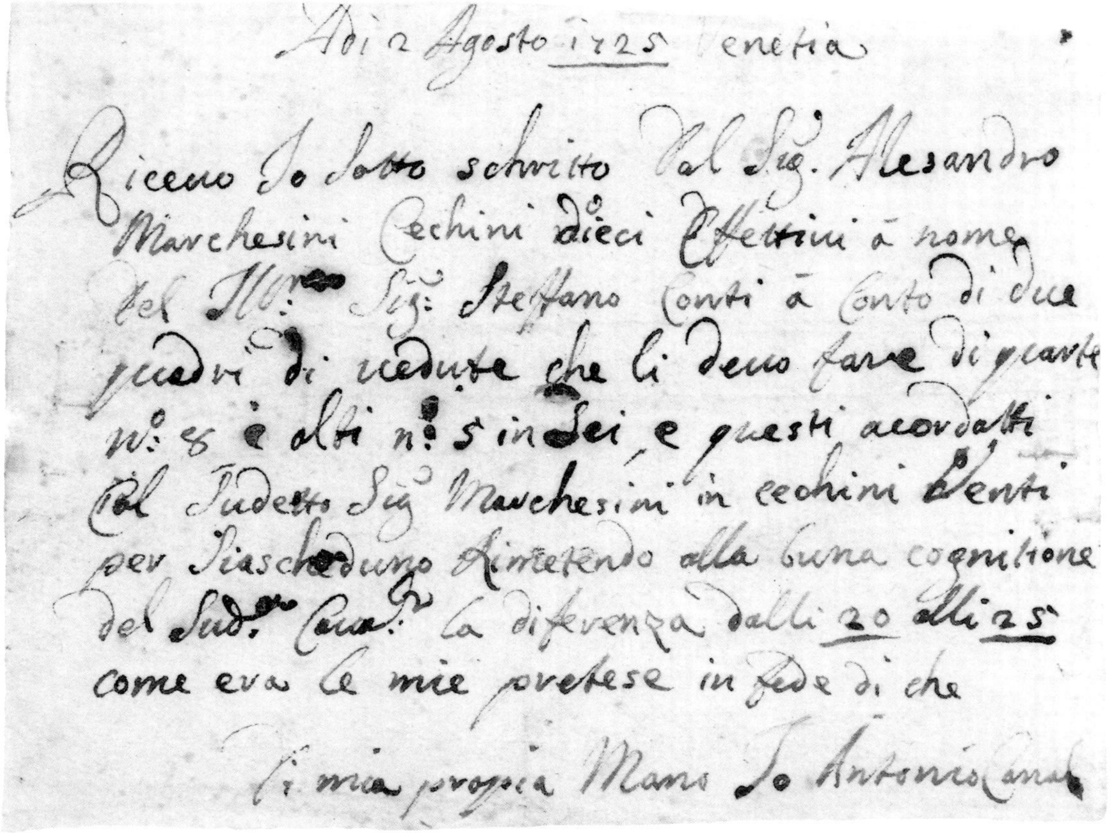

Adi 2 Agosto 1725 Venetia

Ricevo Io sotto scritto dal Sig: Alesandro
Marchesini Cechini dieci Effettivi à nome
del Ill:mo Sig: Steffano Conti à conto di due
quadri di vedute che li devo fare di parte
N:o 8 è altri n:o 5 in Sei, e questi acordatti
col sudetto Sig: Marchesini in cechini Venti
per Siascheduno Rimetendo alla buna cognitione
del Sud:o Cav: La diferenza dalli 20 alli 25
come era le mie pretese in fede di che

Di mia propria Mano Io Antonio Canal

363

The 25 November 1725. Venice

I declare by this my present signature and certify that I have painted two pictures of Views of the Grand Canal of Venice upon two Canvases in length eight and half Quarte and in height five and half Quarte, in the first representing the Bridge of the Rialto on the side looking towards the Germans Warehouse which is opposite the Palace of the Magistrates of Camerlinghi and other Magistrates besides, looking down upon the Vegetable Market where they land all kinds of Vegetables and fruits to be shared amongst the dealers in the City. In the middle of the Canal is painted a Peotta Nobile with figures in it, and four Gondoliers going at full speed and close to it a Gondola having the Livery of the Emperors Ambassador

In the second picture pursuing the same Canal looking down to the Fish market the Palazzo Pesaro and in the distance the Campanile de S. Marcola, on the other side of the Canal but near is the Palazzo de Casa Grimani and in succession other Palaces, as Rezonico, Sagrado and many more.

For the price of the aforesaid pictures was ordered and paid to me by Signor Alessandro Marchesini by direction and commission of the Illustrious Signor Steffano Conti de Lucca thirty Sequins for each with the reservation that the Sequins are of the actual value of twenty two Lire each, in consideration of which I undertake in commision other two of the same dimensions and the same price which I must do for him and in like manner I will make the same certificate for the two next, and in token of undoubted truth and on oath I under sign with my own hand

I, Antonio Canal
Venetian

The above mentioned reservation about the price means by it an expectation of something more by way of a present.

Adi 25 Nouenbre 1725 Venetia

Dichiaro con La presente mia Sottoscritta e atesto auer dipinto
due quadri di uedute di Venetia del Canal Grande sopra
due telle di Lungezza quante otto e Meza et per altezza
quante cinque e Meza. Nella prima il Ponte di rialto
dalla parte che guarda uerso il Fontico de Todeschi, che
resta dimpeto la Fabrica de Magistrati de Camerlengi; et
altri piu Magistratti con altre fabriche uicine che si adimanda
dell'erbaria, doue sbarca ogni sorte derbazi e frutami per dispensare
alle arti per la Città Nella Metta del Canale è dipinto una
Peotta nobile con figure entro con quatro gondolievi che ua scorendo,
et pocco uicina una gondola à liurea del Ambassiator del Imperator.

Nel secondo quadro continuando L'istesso Canale che si adimanda le
Fabriche fino le peschevie; il Palazzo Pesaro e nel fondi il campanile
di S. Marcola, dall'altra parte del Canalle, che uicino il Palazzo di Cà
Grimani e continua altri Pallazi ciouè Reronico e Sagredo e molti altri.

Per il prezzo delli due Sudetti quadri mi fù ordinatti e pagatti dal Sig:
Alessandro Marchesini per ordine e comissione del Ill.mo Sig: Steffano Conti
di Lucca in Cechini trenta per cadauno con la riserua, et se li cechini
presentemente Valle lire uentidue L'uno, per ciò tengo in comissione
per altri due della stessa misura et L'istesso prezzo che deuo
farli, e tanto farò L'istesso Atestatto per li due altri Suseguenti,
e per Segno di autentica uerità fe Giuramento di mia Mano
Mi Sotto Schriuo

La sudd.a riserua circa il pretio signifisa che ne pretende   Io Antonio Canal
qualche cosa di piu di regalo   Venetiano

The twenty second December 1725 Venice

I the undersigned have received from Signor Steffano [read Alessandro] Marchesini by Commission from the Illustrious Signor Steffano Conti ten Sequins and these I have received for earnest of two other pictures of the same measure and size as the others before executed and approved by the said Illustrious Signor Conti.

In assurance of which I undersign
I, Antonio Canal
Venetian.

The 15 June 1726. Venice

Besides for the four pictures as agreed at eighty Sequins I have received from Signor Alessandro Marchesini other ten Sequins which the illustrious Signor Steffano Conti gives me as a present in addition for the above named pictures
In assurance of which I undersign with my own hand
I Antonio Canal

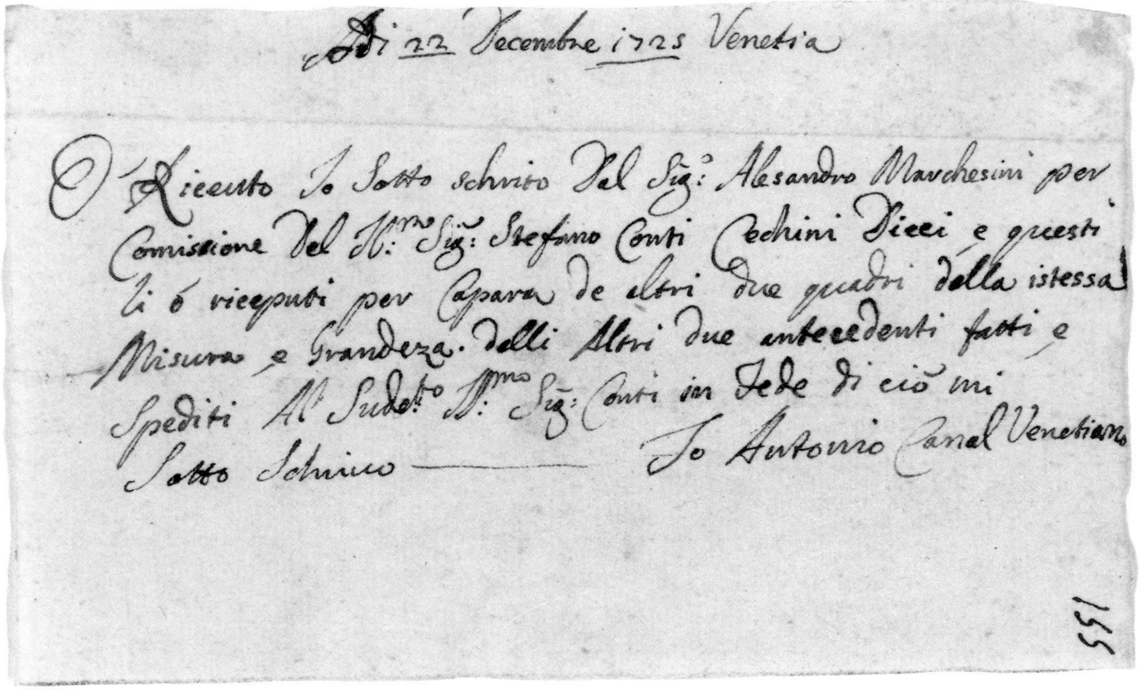

Adi 22 Decembre 1725 Venetia

O Ricevuto Io Sotto schrivo Dal Sig:r Alesandro Marchesini per
Comisione Del Ill:mo Sig:r Stefano Conti Cechini Dieci e questi
li ò ricevuti per Caparra de altri due quadri della istessa
Misura e Grandezza Delli Altri due antecedenti fatti e
Spediti Al Sudetto Ill:mo Sig:r Conti in fede di ciò mi
Sotto Schrivo ————————   Io Antonio Canal Venetiano

551

Di 15 Giugno 1726 Venetia
I

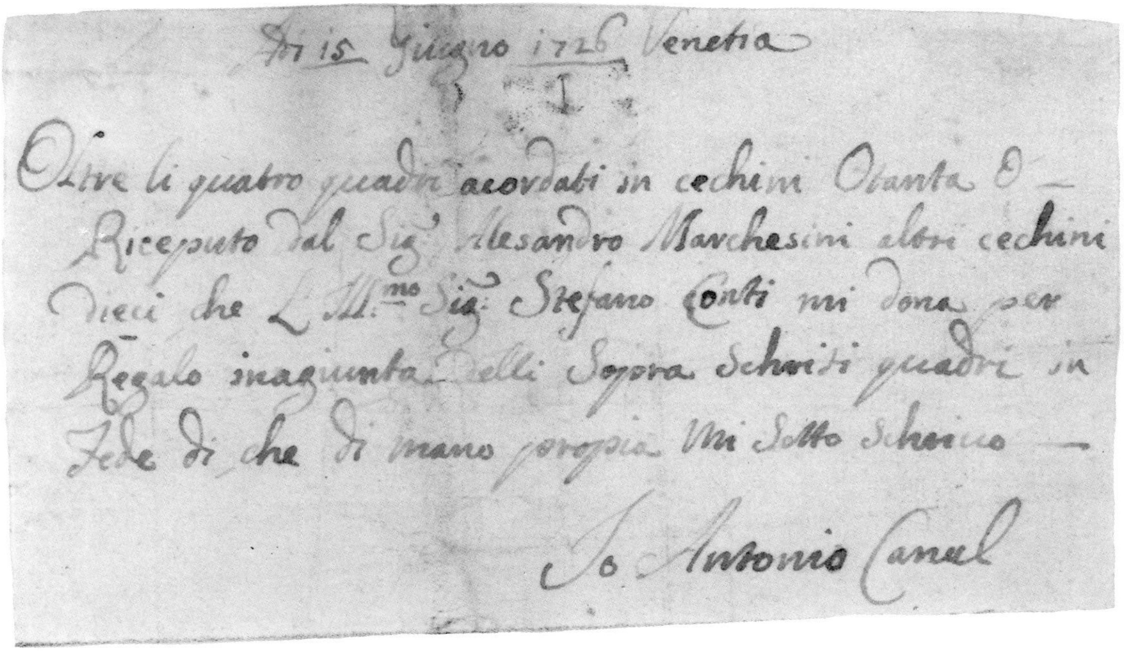

Oltre li quatro quadri acordati in cechini Otanta O—
Ricevuto Dal Sig:r Alesandro Marchesini altri cechini
Dieci che L Ill:mo Sig:r Stefano Conti mi dona per
Regalo inaquinta Delli Sopra schriti quadri in
fede di che di mano propria Mi Sotto Schrivo ——

Io Antonio Canal

367

The 15 June 1726   Venice

I the undersigned by these presents declare to have made other two pictures of views for the Illustrious Signor Steffano Conti of Lucca of the same size as the two which I executed last year and of these in one I have made a View of the Church of S.S. Giovanni e Paolo with the Square and the Equestrian Statue of General Bartolomeo da Bergamo and various other figures, namely a Counsellor in a Red Gown going into Church an other of a Domenican Friar and different other figures.

In the second a View of the Church of P.P. della Carita Rochetini with its Square where I have disposed several small figures amongst which in a little group of three figures in the centre of the Square are two Priests of the same Order who are discoursing with a Philosopher in a violet colored dress. In the horizon at the further end of this Canal is part of the Riva de Schiavoni, the Cupola which is seen is the principal one of the Church of the Salute the base of which continues as far as the Dogana da Mar. In assurance of which I write with my own hand

I, Antonio Canal
Artist—

Di 15 Giugno 1726 Venetia

Dichiaro con la presente Io sotoscrito auer fatto altri due quadri di uedute à Ill.mo Sig. Stefano Conti di Lucca, della stessa grandezza dell'altri due, che feci l'anno antecedente e queste ò fatto in uno la Veduta della Chiesa di S.to Giouani e Paolo con il campo, e la statua à Cualo del General Bortolam.o da Bergamo et altre figure uarie cioè un Conselier in uesta rossa, che in atto d'andar in chiesa, altro Fratte della religion Dominicana con altre figurine diuerse —————————————————

Nel Secondo la Veduta della Chiesa de P.P. della Carità Rochetini con la sua Piazza doue ò ripartido Molte figurine tra le quali in un grupeto di tre figurine nel mezo del campo ui sono due padri della medema Religione, che discove con un saccio in uesta pauonazza. Nel orizonte in fondi al canal ui e parte della Riua de Schiauoni. La Cupola che si uede souna la Principale della chiesa della Sallute che continua la sua fondamenta sino alla Doana da Mar in fede di che scrissi di Mano propria.

Io Antonio Canal Pitor.

Selected Bibliography

Allen, Brian. "Topography or Art: Canaletto and London in the Mid-Eighteenth Century." In *The Image of London: Views by Travellers and Emigrés 1550–1920*, pp. 29–48. Exh. cat. by Malcolm Warner. Barbican Art Gallery. London, 1987.

Arisi, Ferdinando. *Gian Paolo Panini e i fasti della Roma del '700*. 2d ed. Rome, 1986.

Ashby, Thomas, and W. G. Constable. "Canaletto and Bellotto in Rome—I and II." *Burlington Magazine* 46 (May and June 1925), pp. 207–14 and 288–99.

Barcham, William L. *The Imaginary View Scenes of Antonio Canaletto*. Ph.D. diss., New York University, 1974. New York and London: Garland, 1977.

————. "Canaletto and a Commission from Consul Smith." *Art Bulletin* 59 (September 1977), pp. 383–93.

Bettagno, Alessandro. "In margine a una Mostra." *Notizie da Palazzo Albani* 12, nos. 1–2 (1983), pp. 222–28.

Brandi, Cesare. *Canaletto*. Milan, 1960.

Briganti, Giuliano. *Gaspar van Wittel e l'origine della veduta settecentesca*. Rome, 1966.

————. *The View Painters of Europe*. Translated by Pamela Waley. London, 1970.

Bromberg, Ruth. *Canaletto's Etchings*. London and New York, 1974.

Brosses, Charles de. *Lettres d'Italie du Président de Brosses*, I. Edited by Frédéric d'Agay. Paris, 1986.

Buttery, David. "Canaletto at Warwick." *Burlington Magazine* 129 (July 1987), pp. 437–45.

Canaletto. Exh. cat. by Oliver Millar (paintings) and Charlotte Miller (drawings). The Queen's Gallery, Buckingham Palace. London, 1980.

Canaletto: Disegni, dipinti, incisioni. Exh. cat. by Alessandro Bettagno et al. Fondazione Giorgio Cini, Venice. Vicenza, 1982.

Canaletto e Guardi. Exh. cat. by K. T. Parker and J. Byam Shaw. Fondazione Giorgio Cini. Venice, 1962.

Canaletto & Visentini: Venezia & Londra. Exh. cat. by Dario Succi et al. Ca' Pesaro. Venice, 1986.

Chaloner, W. H. "The Egertons in Italy and the Netherlands, 1729–1734, with Two Unpublished Letters from Joseph Smith, Sometime H. M. Consul at Venice." *Bulletin of the John Rylands Library* (Manchester), 32 (March 1950), pp. 157–70.

Constable, W. G. "Some Unpublished Canalettos." *Burlington Magazine* 42 (June 1923), pp. 278–88.

————. "An Allegorical Painting by Canaletto and Others" (letter). *Burlington Magazine* 96 (May 1954), p. 154.

————. *Canaletto*. 2 vols. 1962. 2d ed., rev. by J. G. Links. Oxford, 1976. 3d ed., with supplement by J.G. Links. Oxford, 1989. (Abbreviated reference throughout is C/L; unless otherwise specified, references are to 2d ed.)

————. *Canaletto*. Exh. cat. Art Gallery of Toronto, National Gallery of Canada, Ottawa, and Montreal Museum of Fine Arts, 1964–65.

Conti, Antonio. *Prose, e poesie*, II. Venice, 1756.

Corboz, André. "Sur la prétendu objectivité de Canaletto." *Arte Veneta* 28 (1974), pp. 205–18.

————. *Canaletto: Una Venezia immaginaria*. Catalogue compiled by Anna Tortorelo. 2 vols. Milan, 1985.

Croft-Murray, Edward. *Decorative Painting in England, 1537–1837*. II. *The Eighteenth and Early Nineteenth Centuries*. London, 1970.

Da Carlevarijs ai Tiepolo: Incisori veneti e friulani del Settecento. Exh. cat. by Dario Succi et al. Musei Provinciali, Palazzo Attems, Gorizia, and Museo Correr, Venice, 1983.

Donzelli, Carlo. *I pittori veneti del Settecento*. Florence, 1957.

Dreyer, Peter. *Vedute: Architektonisches Capriccio und Landschaft in der venezianischen Graphik des 18. Jahrhunderts*. Exh. cat. Kupferstichkabinett, Staatliche Museen Preussischer Kulturbesitz. Berlin, 1985.

Finberg, Hilda F. "Canaletto in England." *Walpole Society* 9 (1920–21), pp. 21–76.

————. "Joseph Baudin, Imitator of Canaletto." *Burlington Magazine* 60 (April 1932), pp. 204–7.

————. "The Lovelace Capriccios." *Burlington Magazine* 72 (February 1938), pp. 69–70.

Fogolari, Gino. "L'Accademia Veneziana di Pittura e Scoltura del Settecento." *L'Arte* 16 (1913), pp. 241–72, 364–94.

Hadeln, Detlev von. *Drawings of Antonio Canal, Called Canaletto*. Translated by Campbell Dodgson. London, 1929.

Haskell, Francis. "Stefano Conti, Patron of Canaletto and Others." *Burlington Magazine* 98 (September 1956), pp. 296–300.

————. *Patrons and Painters*. Rev. ed. New Haven and London, 1980.

Hayes, John. "Parliament Street and Canaletto's Views of Whitehall." *Burlington Magazine* 100 (October 1958), pp. 341–49.

Kozakiewicz, Stefan. *Bernardo Bellotto*. Translated by Mary Whittall. 2 vols. London and Greenwich, Conn., 1972.

Levey, Michael. "Canaletto's Regatta Paintings." *Burlington Magazine* 95 (November 1953), pp. 365–66.

————. *The Eighteenth Century Italian Schools*. National Gallery Catalogues. London, 1956.

————. "The Eighteenth-Century Italian Paintings Exhibition at Paris: Some Corrections and Suggestions." *Burlington Magazine* 103 (April 1961), pp. 139–43.

————. *Canaletto: Paintings in the Collection of Her Majesty the Queen*. London, 1964.

————. *The Later Italian Pictures in the Collection of Her Majesty the Queen*. London, 1964.

————. *The Seventeenth and Eighteenth Century Schools*. National Gallery Catalogues. London, 1971.

Links, J. G. "A Missing Canaletto Found." *Burlington Magazine* 109 (July 1967), pp. 405–9.

————. *Views of Venice by Canaletto, Engraved by Antonio Visentini*. New York: Dover, 1971.

————. *Canaletto and His Patrons*. London and New York, 1977.

————. *Canaletto*. Ithaca, N.Y., 1982.

Longhi, Roberto. *Viatico per cinque secoli di pittura veneziana*. 1946. Reprinted in *Opere complete di Roberto Longhi*, X, pp. 5–63. Florence, 1978.

Lorenzetti, Giulio. *Venezia e il suo estuario*. Venice, [1926]. English translation, *Venice and Its Lagoon*. Rome, [1961].

Mariette, Pierre-Jean. *Abécédario*, I. Edited by Ph. de Chennevières and A. de Montaiglon. Paris, 1851–53.

Mazza, Barbara. "Le vicenda dei 'Tombeaux des Princes': Matrici, storia e fortuna della serie Swiny tra Bologna e Venezia." *Saggi e memorie di storia dell'arte* (Fondazione Giorgio Cini, Venice) 10 (1976), pp. 79–102, 141–51.

Miller, Charlotte. *Fifty Drawings by Canaletto from the Royal Library, Windsor Castle*. London and New York, 1983.

Miotti, Tito. "Tre disegni inediti del Canaletto." *Arte Veneta* 20 (1966), pp. 275–78.

Morassi, Antonio. "Problems of Chronology and Perspective in the Work of Canaletto." *Burlington Magazine* 97 (November 1955), pp. 349–53.

————. *Michele Marieschi (1710–1743)*. Exh. cat. Galleria Lorenzelli. Bergamo, 1966.

————. "Saggio su Giambattista Cimaroli, collaboratore del Canaletto." *Arte Veneta* 26 (1972) pp. 167–76.

————. *Guardi*. Venice, [1973].

Moschini, Vittorio. *Canaletto*. Milan, 1954.

Moureau, Adrien. *Antonio Canal, dit le Canaletto*. Les Artistes Célèbres. Paris, 1894.

Mucchi, Ludovico, and Alberto Bertuzzi. *Nella profondità dei dipinti: La radiografia nell' indagine pittorica*. Milan, 1983.

Norwich, John Julius. *A History of Venice*. 2 vols. London, 1977–81. Reprinted in one vol., New York, 1982, 1985.

Orlandi, Pellegrino Antonio, edited and expanded by Pietro Guarienti. *Abecedario pittorico*. Venice, 1753.

Pallucchini, Anna. *Canaletto*. Milan, 1958.

Pallucchini, Rodolfo. *La pittura veneziana del Settecento*. Venice and Rome, 1960.

————. "Per gli esordi del Canaletto." *Arte Veneta* 27 (1973), pp. 155–88.

Parker, K. T. *The Drawings of Antonio Canaletto in the Collection of His Majesty the King at Windsor Castle*. Oxford and London, 1948. New ed., rev. by Charlotte Miller, forthcoming.

Pignatti, Terisio. *Il quaderno di disegni del Canaletto alle Gallerie di Venezia*. Venice, 1958.

————. "'Sei Villaggi Campestri' dal Canaletto." *Bollettino dei Musei Civici Veneziani* 14, no. 3 (1969) pp. 23–28.

————. *Canaletto: Selected Drawings*. Translated by Stella Rudolph. University Park, Pa., and London, 1970.

Puppi, Lionello, with introduction by Giuseppe Berto. *L'opera completa di Canaletto*. Milan, 1968; reprinted 1981. English translation, with introduction by David Bindman, published as *The Complete Works of Canaletto*. New York, 1968.

Rizzi, Aldo. *Luca Carlevarijs*. Venice, 1967.

Ruskin, John. *Modern Painters*, I. 1843. Reprinted in *The Works of John Ruskin*, III. Library Edition, ed. E. T. Cook and Alexander Wedderburn. London, 1903.

Russell, Francis. "The Pictures of John, Fourth Duke of Bedford." *Apollo* 127 (June 1988) pp. 401–6.

————. "Canaletto and Joli at Chesterfield House." *Burlington Magazine* 130 (August 1988) pp. 627–30.

Snowden, W. Crawford. *London 200 Years Ago*. Introduction by E. G. R. Taylor. London, [1948].

Succi, Dario. *Venezia nella felicità illuminata delle acqueforti di Antonio Visentini*. Treviso, 1984.

Toledano, Ralph. *Michele Marieschi: L'opera completa*. Milan, 1988.

Vedute italiane del '700 in collezioni private italiane. Exh. cat. Museo Diocesano d'Arte Sacra, Sant' Apollonia. Venice, 1987.

Vertue, George. *Vertue Note Books*, III. In *Walpole Society* 22 (1933–34). Also *Vertue Note Books*, V. In *Walpole Society* 26 (1937–38).

Vivian, Frances. *Il Console Smith: mercante e collezionista*. Vicenza, 1971.

Wallen, Burr. *The William A. Gumberts Collection of Canaletto's Etchings*. Exh. cat. Santa Barbara Museum of Art. Santa Barbara, 1979.

Watson, F. J. B. *Canaletto*. London and New York, 1949.

————. *Eighteenth-Century Venice*. Exh. cat. Whitechapel Art Gallery, London, and the Museum and Art Gallery, Birmingham, 1951.

————. "G. B. Cimaroli: A Collaborator with Canaletto." *Burlington Magazine* 95 (June 1953), pp. 205–7.

————. "An Allegorical Painting by Canaletto, Piazzetta, and Cimaroli." *Burlington Magazine* 95 (November 1953), pp. 362–65.

————. "A Note on Joseph Baudin's Copies after Canaletto." *Burlington Magazine* 97 (November 1955), pp. 353–54.

————. "Joseph Baudin Again." *Burlington Magazine* 109 (July 1967), pp. 410–13.

————. "Canal, Giovanni Antonio." In *Dizionario biografico degli italiani*, XVII, pp. 647–51. Rome, 1974.

Zampetti, Pietro. *I vedutisti veneziani del Settecento*. Exh. cat. Palazzo Ducale. Venice, 1967.

Zanetti, Anton Maria, [the Younger]. *Della pittura veneziana e delle opere pubbliche de' veneziani maestri*. Venice, 1771.

Index

CREDITS

All paintings in the Royal Collection and all drawings from the Royal Library, Windsor Castle, are Copyright Reserved to Her Majesty Queen Elizabeth II.

Photographs have been supplied by the lenders. Following are additional credits:
Jörg P. Anders 82, 83, 105, 120, 125, and fig. 8; Joseph H. Bailey fig. 2; Osvaldo Böhm 3, 4; Richard Caspole 63, 111, 115; Carlo Catenazzi 8, 9, 10, 11; Philip A. Charles 50, 58, 122, 123; Geoffrey Clements 31; A. C. Cooper Ltd. 12, 14, 15, 28, 29, 37, 39, 40, 41, 42, 43, 44, 45, 46, 47, 53, 59, 60, 61, 64, 65, 66, 67, 68, 69, 70; Prudence Cuming Associates Ltd. 71, 72; Reale Fotografia Giacomelli 85; Jeremy Marks 73; Brian Merrett 81; Richmond and Rigg Photography 23; Royle Publications Ltd. fig. 4; Sächsische Landesbibliothek 5, 6, 7; Speltdoorn et Fils 16, 17, 24, 25; Rodney Todd-White & Son 33, 34.

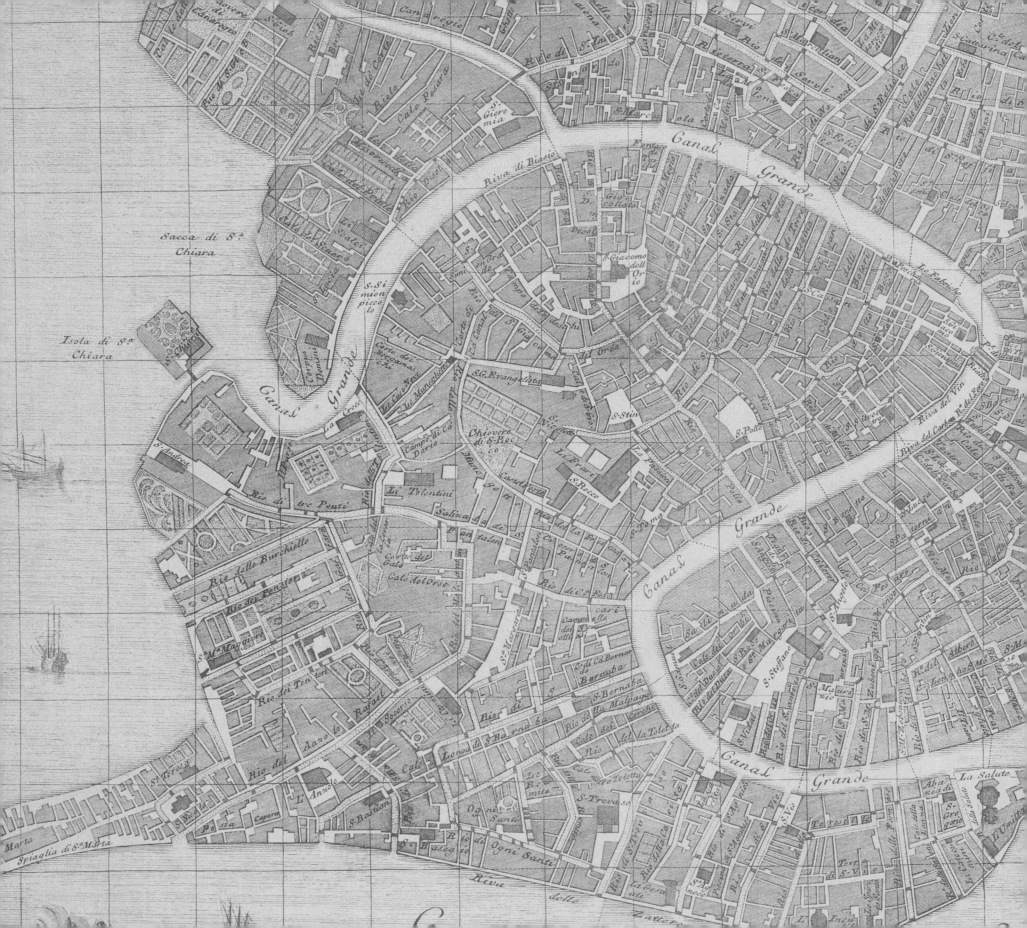